North Pole Legacy

North Pole Legacy

THE SEARCH FOR THE ARCTIC OFFSPRING OF ROBERT PEARY AND MATTHEW HENSON

S. Allen Counter, DMSc, PhD

Foreword by Deirdre Stam

Skyhorse Publishing

Skyhorse Publishing books may be purchased in bulk at special discounts for sales promotion, corporate gifts, fund-raising, or educational purposes. Special editions can also be created to specifications. For details, contact the Special Sales Department, Skyhorse Publishing, 307 West 36th Street, 11th Floor, New York, NY 10018 or info@skyhorsepublishing.com.

Skyhorse® and Skyhorse Publishing® are registered trademarks of Skyhorse Publishing, Inc.®, a Delaware corporation.

Visit our website at www.skyhorsepublishing.com.

10 9 8 7 6 5 4 3 2 1

Library of Congress Cataloging-in-Publication Data is available on file.

Cover design by Tom Lau

Cover photo credit: Background photograph of the *Robert Peary Sledge Party Posing with Flags at the North Pole*; Peary and Henson photos courtesy of the Library of Congress

Print ISBN: 978-1-5107-2637-6

Ebook ISBN: 978-1-5107-2638-3

Printed in the United States of America.

Remembered by What I Have Done

Up and away, like a dew of the morning
That soars from the earth to its home in the sun;
So let me steal away, gently and lovingly
Only remembered by what I have done.

My name, and my place, and my tomb all forgotten,
The brief race of time well and patiently run
So let me pass away, peacefully, silently,
Only remembered by what I have done.

Gladly away from this trail would I hasten,
Up to the crown that for me has been won.
Unthought of by man in rewards or in praises—
Only remembered by what I have done.

Not myself, but the truth, that in life I have spoken;
Not myself, but the seed that in life I have sown
Shall pass on to ages—all about me forgotten,
Save the truth I have spoken, the things I have done.

Sincerely yours
Matthew Alexander Henson

Poem found in Matthew Henson's diary, Matthew A. Henson
Collection, Morgan State University, Baltimore.

CONTENTS

FOREWORD TO THE 2018 EDITION
BY DEIRDRE STAMM

By the 1980s, when S. Allen Counter began to take an interest in the contact of Arctic explorer Robert Peary and his assistant Matthew Henson with the Greenland Inuit, it may have seemed to most readers that the story of the North Pole conquest was largely played out. The old debate of who got to the magic spot first seemed to have stalled with supporters of Peary and Frederick Cook at loggerheads. New insights into the exploration of the polar region were slow in coming, despite the partisan and non-partisan efforts of astronomers, physicists, mathematicians, historians, latter-day explorers, and nautical experts to find the definitive answer to the Peary-Cook debates over who got there first, or indeed whether either made it at all. There were outposts of research such as the Peary-MacMillan Arctic Museum and Arctic Studies Center at Bowdoin College, of course, where curators diligently combed through hard evidence of all kinds to piece together a detailed and objective narrative of Peary's years in the Arctic. By then, however, public attention to exploration was focused elsewhere, such as continental Antarctica, outer space, and more mundane but promising regions of scientific research. The human element was certainly considered by researchers in Peary/Henson studies, but more through the lens of the hard rather than soft sciences. There were some exceptions. There had been published anthropological observations of the Inuit culture, most notably by explorer Vilhjalmur Stefansson. And interest in Henson largely invoked contemporary racial issues by the 1980s. But in general, public interest in exploration seemed to have turned elsewhere.

Neurophysiologist and social historian Counter introduced a unique blend of methodologies to the understanding of the Peary/Henson experience in the far North with his book *North Pole Legacy: Black, White and Eskimo* (1991). Acting as participant observer and ultimately as actor in the lives of the explorers' Inuit progeny, Counter overcame many physical and administrative barriers to develop personal relationships with the indigenous descendants of Peary and Henson, to elicit community memories of their forebears, and ultimately to bring about meetings in the US of the explorers' US and Inuit descendants. Sharing African-American ancestry with Henson, Counter was particularly interested in the life experiences of Henson and his Inuit descendants, and of the possible role of racial prejudice in their lives.

Counter brought storytelling skills to the presentation of his findings, resulting in his highly readable and enlightening book. In doing so, he provided new evidence about the personal interactions of Peary's parties with the Greenland Inuit. Social issues of race, sex, class, motivation, exploitation, and loyalty are addressed indirectly as Counter tells the personal stories of a few dozen Inuit whose lives were intimately affected by their shifting familial relationships to Peary and to Henson.

Those looking for evidence of racial prejudice in Peary's northern ventures can certainly find it, but compared with many contemporaries, he tended to respect ability and practicality when he saw it. While in the North, he lived on intimate terms with those identified as racially "different," albeit within constraints of western notions of class and rank. Peary's long-standing relationship to Henson, an African-American considered of lesser social status, provides one example, of such close dependence and physical proximity. Peary's relationship to the Greenland Inuit (or "Eskimos" in his time) constitute another example. The race question for Henson was more complex. He seemed to have been entirely comfortable with the Inuit, who recognized that his coloration was similar to theirs, and for this and other reasons welcomed him with particular warmth. In fact he is described as living at least as often in Inuit households as with fellow expedition members.

From his Arctic experience and from its literature, Peary developed an appreciation of Inuit men as able hunters, providers, and responsible heads of households. He took full advantage of their skills, rewarding their work with the kinds of remuneration that generated long-term cooperation and loyalty. Peary also appreciated and exploited the skills of Inuit women in turning arctic resources into forms that could be eaten, worn, and enjoyed. He wrote admiringly of their skills: "Household duties are as carefully practiced (allowing for differences in materials) as in any domestic circle." (Robert E. Peary, *Nearest the Pole*, New York, Doubleday, Page & Company, 1907, p. 380.) Inuit women performed their duties while nurturing children in conditions that may strike us today as impossibly uncomfortable, inconvenient, and even hazardous. Although it has made many modern readers uncomfortable to acknowledge this fact, indigenous women were also valued by many Northern adventurers for the companionship and sexual comforts that they could provide to men far from home and lonely for female contact.

Peary himself developed a sexual relationship with a very young, already married woman named Ahlikahsingwah, who bore him two boys. The first, Anaukaq, died young, and the second, Kali, born in 1906, lived well into old age. Henson too maintained a seemingly stable relationship with an Inuit woman named Akatingwah who in 1906 bore Henson one child, also named Anaukaq. He, like Kali, lived into old age. According to Counter, the husbands of these women, who were brothers, in effect adopted the explorers' children. Both Kali and (Henson's son) Anaukaq were alive at the time of Counter's visit and figure prominently in his story.

Henson's generally-accepted liaison with his Inuit consort yielded many practical advantages, which would otherwise have been unavailable to him, leading to facility in the Eskimo language, superior native-style clothing, well-honed skills in dog driving, and knowledge of food acquisition and preparation. The entire expedition, in effect, benefited from Henson's close liaison with his close Inuit companions.

Henson clearly indicates his approval of Eskimo marital arrangements in recollections of a courtship conversation with his second wife Lucy Ross, whom he married in 1908. The exchange might strike the modern reader as a kind of test of Lucy's acceptance of Henson's unconventional domestic history.

Asked if he thought that Inuit women are pretty by Lucy Ross's mother, Henson addressed his response to Lucy:

> Yes, the Eskimo women are pretty . . . At least, the Eskimo men who marry them think so." [Mrs. Ross continued,] "You mean they really marry . . . I thought they were—were immoral and very dirty. . ." [Henson directed his answer to Lucy.] "Eskimos marry. . . but like innocent children, without laws and church, for they have neither. . . [but] sometimes I think they are more moral than we are, for they're honest and never lie. They marry to raise families, and a man is always happy when his wife presents him with a child, even if it isn't his." (Bradley Robinson, *Dark Companion*, Robert M. McBride & Company, New York, NY, p. 180-181.)

In more modern times, some have criticized Peary, and to a lesser degree Henson, for the "abandonment" of children born of these intimate relationships with Inuit women. While the behavior of both Peary and Henson in this matter could be seen as reflective of their time and circumstances, the story is complicated by the fact that neither man grew up with a father and neither had firsthand experience of paternal responsibility and nurturing. A further complicating factor is that Henson never had the resources to help his Inuit son, had he wanted to.

The philosophical and moral questions raised by the story of the Inuit children of Peary and Henson are legion and confounding, especially from a position of hindsight. While Counter touches by implication on delicate matters of race, sex, class, motivation, exploitation, and loyalty, he largely avoids speculation and judgment. His is a factual telling of the story of the Peary and Henson Inuit family experiences over many decades subsequent to the departure of the explorers in 1909. The account culminates with the affecting description of the Inuit families' emotion-filled meetings in 1987 in the US with some of their American cousins.

NORTH POLE LEGACY

CHAPTER ONE

✳ ✳ ✳

Anaukaq, Son of Mahri-Pahluk

The old Polar Eskimo, bent slightly at the waist, steps briskly across the pack ice toward his team of sled dogs. Curled up like giant woolen balls, partially covered by a recent blizzard, the wolflike beasts come to life in response to his calls, *"Kim-milk! Kim-milk!* [Dog! Dog!]." They shake the crusted snow from their thick coats and yawn with soft howls as Anaukaq greets each of them by name and pats its head. Sensing that they are about to be hitched up for a trip, the dogs wag their tails and begin whining excitedly, for a Polar Eskimo dog would much rather be running than sleeping.

With graceful, measured movements, Anaukaq untangles the traces that tether each dog to stakes driven deep in the hard snow— traces now made of durable nylon rather than of the more perishable sealskin used in his youth. The dogs prance about and snap at one another playfully as he connects them, one by one, to the front of an eight-foot wooden sled with tall rear upstanders. He beckons me to a thick deerskin seat at the rear of the sled and we're off, rushing down the hillside toward the frozen bay with Anaukaq cracking his whip above the dogs' ears.

As we head out of the settlement, Anaukaq's eighteen-year-old grandson Nukka runs from his house and jumps on the sled, whip in hand. The family has assigned him to chaperon his grandfather over

3

the dangerous mounds of broken ice scattered across the bay—
subtly, of course, so as not to hurt the old hunter's feelings.

The eight dogs pull us much faster than I had thought possible.
"*Wock, wock, wock, wock,*" the old man yells, directing the dogs to the
left. "*Ahchook, ahchook, ahchook*" and, like the turning wheels of a car,
the dogs and sled move to the right. Anaukaq looks back at me and
laughs as he detects my admiration. Dogsled driving is considered a
Polar Eskimo's most valuable skill, and Anaukaq is exceptionally
good at it.

No doubt this skill was learned, yet perhaps he was born with a
talent for it. For if he is who he says he is, his father was reputed to be
among the greatest dogsled drivers in the world. Anaukaq has told
me that he is the son of Matthew Alexander Henson, one of the first
two Americans to reach the North Pole. This claim has been corroborated by other Polar Eskimo elders, who still refer to Henson as
"Mahri-Pahluk," meaning "Matthew the Kind One," a name given
him by their forebears nearly a century ago. More telling still, Anaukaq has a much darker complexion than the other Eskimos and very
curly black hair—a trait rarely found among his people. Matthew
Henson, too, was *kulnocktooko* [dark skinned]. He was, in fact, the
only black known to have visited this Arctic region before Anaukaq
was born.

*   *   *

After about a half hour's ride, we reach our destination: the offshore
seal traps set by Anaukaq's son Avataq, who is some hundred miles
away hunting walrus. Anaukaq chops a hole in the ice around a rope,
which is tied to a stake. Once the rope is free, he tugs several times to
see whether there is a seal attached. "No luck," he says. "We'll come
back tomorrow." Anaukaq seems to take great delight in this chore.
As an old retired hunter who now for the most part is confined to his
village, he would feel useless if he did not have some food-gathering
responsibilities, so his five sons permit him to travel up and down
the bay, accompanied by his grandchildren, to examine their traps.

Returning to the warmth of his son Ajako's home, a boxlike wood-
en structure that the Eskimos still call an "igloo," we pull off our

snowshoes and prepare to enter the main room of the house in our socks. Anaukaq leans over and with a pocket knife cuts off a sliver of walrus heart hanging just inside the door. *"Mahmaktoe* [Tasty]", he says, looking at me with an inviting smile. He cuts a second sliver and hands it to me. I reluctantly put the raw, bloody meat in my mouth saying to myself, "It's okay. It's only cardiac muscle," but thinking all along that it tastes simply like dull, uncooked meat. *"Mahmaktoe,"* I say, without conviction.

As we enter the central room, Anaukaq's daughter-in-law Puto is scraping the fat from a polar bear skin so that it can be properly stretched to make pants for her son Nukka, who has just killed his first *nanook* [polar bear]. The sweet aroma of polar bear meat in Puto's stew on the stove permeates the house. As a gesture of good will and respect for her father-in-law, Puto pulls a small piece of fat from the polar bear skin and hands it to him.

"Thank you," Anaukaq says. "Mmmm, very tasty!" The old-timers love this delicacy. "For you, here," he says, offering me a slice.

"No, thanks, my friend." I point to the kitchen. "I will wait for the *nanook* that is being cooked out there." I will only eat cooked polar meat because of the high risk of trichinosis from eating it raw. As the Polar Eskimos themselves are aware, trichinosis has been a major health problem within their community for many years, primarily as a result of their consumption of raw polar bear and bearded seal.

Anaukaq laughs politely. "Okay, but it's very tasty."

Eventually the stew is ready, and Anaukaq's granddaughter Malina serves me a portion with some hot tea. The polar bear meat has been boiled thoroughly without any spices, because none grow in this desolate part of the world and so they are hard to come by. Nevertheless, it is quite flavorful.

"Mmm, *mahmaktoe,"* I say, to the delight of everyone present. Each nods with pleasure.

As we sit and eat, Puto resumes scraping the polar bear skin with her *ulu,* a small, flat, half-moon shaped utility knife that Eskimo women use for everything from flensing seals to slicing foods. After a while I sense that Anaukaq is watching me closely. I look up, and our eyes meet. He smiles, a little embarrassed that I caught him staring.

He reaches over and rubs my head, then his own hair, and laughs. "Curly! We have the same curly hair. We are the same people, black people."

"Yes, that's right," I agree, as everyone in the room breaks into laughter.

"You must be my relative," he says.

"Well, in spirit, perhaps, but not by family line." He seems a bit disappointed. It is not the first time he has said this to me. He finds it difficult to believe that we are not related, because he has never seen another black person outside of his own family. Can he really be who he says he is? I believe him, but I wonder.

I have come to Moriussaq, this tiny Eskimo village some one thousand miles above the Arctic Circle, because of my special interest in Matthew Henson. For many years he has been my hero, and I have struggled to gain him the recognition he deserved but never received during his lifetime. Henson was among the most successful Arctic explorers of all time, yet he remains relatively unknown in his own country. The reason for this paradox is as clear as American history, and it all comes down to a single world: *race*. Because Henson was black, his achievements were overshadowed by those of his white companion, Comdr. Robert Edwin Peary.

On April 6, 1909, Henson, Peary, and four Polar Eskimos reached a point that the two Americans determined to be the North Pole. During their previous eighteen years together in the Arctic, Henson and Peary had risked life and limb together in over ten thousand miles of exploration. They had made several other attempts at the Pole, coming closer each time but never attaining their goal. They had discovered meteorites, new fauna, and previously unknown geographical features, such as the fact that Greenland is an island rather than a continent that extended to the North Pole. Throughout, Henson had been an invaluable asset to Peary—as dogsled driver, mechanic, navigator, translator, and friend. So it was only fitting, and only fair, that they reached the top of Earth together and "nailed the Stars and Stripes to the Pole."

Once their goal was achieved, Henson and Peary left Greenland for the United States, never to return. But both left behind a legend and a legacy. Anaukaq is part of that legacy.

Anaukaq tells me that since his childhood, he has heard many wonderful stories about the great Mahri-Pahluk. Having no memory of his father, he has only these stories to go by, but the stories have made him very proud. Matthew Henson, he says, was the most popular outsider ever to visit his land. Polar Eskimo legends and songs tell of how masterfully Mahri-Pahluk could drive a dogsled, hunt a walrus, and skin a seal. They also tell of his long trek north across the great sea ice, with Ootah, Seegloo, Egingwah, Ooqueah, and Peary, to the strange place they call the North Pole. The Eskimos, it is said, would never have traveled so far from their land were it not for Mahri-Pahluk's presence and persuasion. Henson knew most of the 218 members of the tribe and spoke their difficult language fluently. Peary was known to the Eskimos as the commander of the expeditions, the one who could provide them with pay in the form of valuable goods. But Henson was known as the man who made the expeditions work. Even the great Ootah said that while the other outsiders were like children in the ways of the Eskimo, Mahri-Pahluk was a natural in their world. He was one of them.

CHAPTER TWO

✳ ✳ ✳

"You must be a Henson"

My trip to Moriussaq had its origins in a conversation that took place some years earlier in Stockholm, Sweden. I was a visiting professor at the Karolinska Nobel Institute at the time, and my colleague Dr. Erik Borg invited me to dinner. Over the years Erik, his wife, Birgitta, and their children had become my adopted Swedish family, and I had often dined at their home in the suburb of Bromma.

On this particular occasion we were joined by Erik's old schoolmate Peter Jacobson and his family. Peter had recently returned from Greenland and was keen on telling us about his trip. After dinner, when the conversation turned to Arctic exploration, I mentioned that a black American had made significant contributions to that field. To my surprise, both the Jacobsons and the Borgs knew about Matthew Henson. The Swedes, like other Scandinavians, are fond of Arctic lore and history. They grow up on stories of explorers such as Roald Amundsen and Peter Freuchen, much as American children do on tales of Daniel Boone and Davy Crockett.

Peter told us of rumors that there were some dark-skinned Eskimos in Greenland who might be the descendants of Henson, as well as others of particularly light complexion who might be the offspring of Commander Peary. The possibility of "white" Eskimos was not surprising, since it was well known that many Danish men stationed

8

in Greenland over the years had fathered children with Eskimo women. But the notion of "black" Eskimos intrigued me. I made a mental note to investigate this matter later.

During the next few years I read everything I could about Henson and Peary, hoping to uncover some evidence that would confirm or disprove the rumors Peter Jacobson had heard. I learned a great deal about the history of polar exploration, the controversy surrounding the conquest of the Pole, and the unique relationship between Henson and Peary, but I found no mention of Amer-Eskimo offspring in Henson's and Peary's own writings, and nothing elsewhere that went beyond rumor or innuendo. In the end I became convinced that the key to this mystery could not be found in any library or archive. If Henson and Peary had in fact left behind children in the Arctic, surely the Eskimos themselves would know. Perhaps only they would know. I decided I would have to ask them.

* * *

The most difficult thing about visiting polar Greenland is getting there. Commercial transportation is limited to southern Greenland, where most of the inhabitants of this sparsely populated island live. Only American and Danish military planes serving the American air base at Thule are permitted in the northern part of the country. Built in 1955 on land traditionally occupied by a large group of Eskimos, who were forced to move, Dundas Air Force Base was established as part of an early-warning system and frontline defense against Soviet air attacks.

Permission for nonmilitary personnel to travel in the area is rarely granted, except for approved scientific studies and exploration. I therefore decided to apply to the Danish government for permission to conduct "a scientific study of ear disease in Eskimos and to interview some of the Polar Eskimos who were familiar with early American explorations in the area." My proposed audiological study was serious. As a neurophysiologist, I had read extensively about the ear problems of Eskimos. Of particular interest to me were studies showing that Eskimos from Canada and lower Greenland suffered an unusually high degree of sensorineural ("nerve") hearing loss. Sensorineural hearing impairment is irreversible and generally results from aging, ototoxic compounds, genetic factors, viruses, or noise trauma. Since no one had ever conducted a systematic hearing study of the Polar Eskimos, who are considered tribally and culturally different from Canadian Eskimos, such an undertaking seemed worthwhile. This way, even if my search for the descendants of Henson and Peary proved fruitless, I would have something to show for my efforts.

In the spring of 1986, at the end of a long trail of formal letters, long-distance phone calls, and lengthy applications, the Danish authorities granted my request. Several weeks later the First Space Wing of the U.S. Air Force gave me special permission to fly to Dundas Air Force Base on one of their C-141 transports. After arriving in Thule, I was forced to delay my journey to the Eskimo settlements because of high winds along the mountainous seacoast. Eventually, however, I boarded a helicopter that carried me to remote Moriussaq.

As the helicopter hovered over the edge of the tiny village, about a dozen young Eskimos ran out of their houses to greet me. The pilot set the aircraft down between two large orange oil drums that marked the landing zone and turned off the rotating blades. The young villagers rushed toward us, eager to collect any mail or supplies we might have brought and to get a look at their visitor. Unpacking my gear with the aid of the Eskimos, I asked if Tobius was among them.

"Yes," responded the short, round-faced man standing next to me, smiling. "I am here. Welcome to my village."

I had been directed to this settlement of about twenty families by a Polar Eskimo hunter named Panigpak Oaorana, who worked for the Danish ministry at Thule. Panigpak, who spoke only a little English, referred me to Tobius, who had previously worked at the base but now lived in Moriussaq. I asked Tobius if there was a family of dark-skinned Eskimos living in Moriussaq who were the descendants of Matthew Henson.

"Yes, there is such a family. Mahri-Pahluk's family lives there, and over there, and over there," he said, pointing to three different "igloos" in the distance.

"Will you take me over to meet them?" I asked.

"Yes, I take you." We headed off in the direction of the houses. "How do you know of this family?" Tobius asked.

"From your friend Panigpak, at the base," I replied.

"Oh, I see. They will be happy to see you."

"Why? Are they expecting me?"

"Oh, no," Tobius said, and then fell silent.

"Or is it because I am black?" I asked.

"I think so," he said with a mischievous grin. "No black person has ever come here before."

As we walked toward the settlement lugging my equipment and heavy backpack, I learned that Tobius had no formal training in English but had picked up the language over the years through his work at the air base. He was disappointed, he told me, that the base was now off-limits to most Polar Eskimos, though he agreed with the government's efforts to preserve traditional Inuit culture by minimizing outside influences, including alcoholic beverages. I questioned Tobius more about the dark-skinned Eskimo family.

"The old father lives there, just over there, in that igloo," he said, pointing to a small wooden structure covered with faded blue paint that lay just ahead of us.

"Let us visit the 'old father' first," I suggested.

We gave wide berth to the big dogs tethered to stakes along the way and zigzagged around their large droppings, which seemed to be strewn everywhere. Many of the fierce-looking canines howled or yelped at our approach. When we finally reached the cottage, built in the style of a New England "saltbox," Tobius climbed the steps and knocked loudly on the door. We could hear noises inside, and the voice of a man saying in Eskimo what must have been, "I'm coming." Soon a dark-complexioned, elderly man with curly hair, high cheekbones, and Eskimo eyes appeared in the doorway. He was wearing a gray flannel shirt with its collar exposed under a bulky white sweater, gray wool trousers, and sealskin boots. Tobius, a big, full-toothed grin on his face, said something to the man in Eskimo and then turned to me. I smiled, extended my hand, and said (in the rehearsed Eskimo that I had learned from Panigpak), "*Hi-nay* [Hello], I am Allen Counter, from the United States." The old man turned to Tobius, who translated. With a pleasant smile and soft laugh, the old man turned back and carefully examined my face.

"I am looking for the family of *Myee-Paluk*—Matthew Henson," I continued.

Tobius quickly corrected me, *"Mah-ri Pah-luk."*

I tried again, this time to the satisfaction of both men, *"Mahri-Pahluk."*

"Hi-nay," the old man said, cheerfully grasping my hand. "I am Anaukaq, son of Mahri-Pahluk."

"Son of Mahri-Pahluk?" I said incredulously, turning to Tobius. Could this be true? Offspring, yes, but could it be possible that this man is the *son* of Matthew Henson? His dark hair, smooth skin, and muscular frame did not appear to be those of a man old enough to be Henson's son. Henson had left Greenland for the last time in September 1909. Any Eskimo child of his would therefore have to be at least seventy-seven years old, yet this man looked to be in his sixties, at most. Perhaps he is a grandson, I thought, and Tobius erred in his translation. After all, Henson and Peary had been in the area since 1891, sometimes up to four years at a stint, so they certainly could have fathered children who begat other children. But Tobius made it clear that there had been no mistranslation.

"Yes, he is the son of Mahri-Pahluk," he said. "All of us up here know that."

I studied Anaukaq's face in detail. Everything about the appearance of the man said that I was looking at a descendant of Matthew Henson. Even his laugh and gestures were curious, somehow different from those of Panigpak and Tobius. Then again, I thought, maybe I was seeing what I wanted to see.

He tried to communicate something to me in his native tongue. I turned to Tobius. "What did he say?"

"He says you must be a Henson, and you have come to find him," Tobius said with an inquisitive smile on his face. I could see in Anaukaq's expression that he was elated by the thought and anticipated an affirmative response.

"Unfortunately, I am not a member of the Henson family," I said and then added, "but I have come here as a friend, looking for any Polar Eskimo descendants of Mahri-Pahluk."

Tobius translated. "I am Anaukaq, son of Mahri-Pahluk," the old man proudly reiterated. "I am pleased that you have traveled to Moriussaq to see me."

* * *

We spent the next few days getting acquainted. Using his cane, Anaukaq walked me about the village, introducing me to his relatives and neighbors. One day, as we sat drinking some spiced tea that I had brought along, we talked at length about Anaukaq's early life. What he knew of his father he had learned from his mother and the older Eskimos who had known Mahri-Pahluk. To their knowledge, he was the only child Henson fathered in the Arctic. Anaukaq said that he was born on Peary's *omiak* [ship] in 1906. He then went on to tell me numerous stories about his life, particularly his childhood. As I listened, I became increasingly convinced that this vigorous, eighty-year-old "black" Eskimo was in fact the son of Matthew Alexander Henson. And I had found him—alive and well. I felt good inside.

In subsequent conversations, over the next couple of weeks, Anaukaq talked with me more and more personally, as if I were the long-lost relative he had hoped for. "You are the first *kulnocktooko* to visit my home," he said. "I never thought anyone who looked like me would ever come to visit. I am very happy you came." From time to time he would ask, "Are you sure you are not a Henson?" then laugh warmly. "You look very much like you could be one of my relatives." He would then rub the hair on my head and say, "Very good," after which he would touch his own hair. "The same. Your hair is the same as mine." It became a kind of ritual between us, and each time we both would laugh. I noticed that he always clapped his hands when he laughed, as I have seen so many black Americans do.

"I have often wondered whether the curious urge to search for Matthew Henson's descendants way up here might not be based on some unknown biological kinship to Henson's family," I told Anaukaq. "But I don't think we're related."

Yet even if I were not his relative, what about other relatives? Anaukaq wanted to know. "Did Mahri-Pahluk have any children over there? Do I have any brothers and sisters in America?"

"I do not know," I replied, "but to my knowledge your father had no children by his American wife, Lucy Ross Henson, whom he married after your birth."

"Is that true?" He chuckled. "You mean my father had no American wife when he was with my mother?"

"No, not until after you were born."

He laughed again. "Peary had two wives, one Eskimo and one in his own land. I thought maybe Mahri-Pahluk had two wives also."

"No, he married Lucy in 1908, the year he and Peary left the United States for their last attempt to reach the Pole. They had no children then or later." I could not be certain about other children from other relationships, of course, but I said I would be happy to initiate a search for possible relatives when I returned to the United States. Anaukaq wanted to know more about Lucy Henson, but information about her is so sparse I could only tell him a little about her background. At times he looked so disappointed at my lack of information that I had to reassure him I would do my best to track down his American relatives.

"All my life I have wanted so much to see my father or someone from his family," Anaukaq told me. "When I was young, I would talk with my friends about traveling to the land of my father to visit him, but I had no way to get there. Then one day I realized he must be dead, and I dreamed of seeing his birthplace and burial place." He paused, then continued. "My children too have wondered about their relatives over there. Even if I never meet them, I would like to have my children see their American relatives." The poignancy of his expression was occasionally relieved by an awkward laugh, as if he were a little embarrassed about sharing such deep personal feelings with so new an acquaintance. When he was much younger, he said, he had often wondered why his father had never come back to visit him or sent for him to visit his distant homeland.

I explained to Anaukaq that even if his father had wanted to return to the Arctic, it would have been very difficult for him to do so. I described the obstacles that anyone of that era, and especially an African American, would have faced in trying to make such a journey. Even if Henson had wished to join one of the later expeditions led by his old friend Comdr. Donald B. MacMillan, it is doubtful he could have spared the time or the money. Having secured a minor post with the U.S. Customs Service in New York, he would have risked losing his job by taking an extended leave of absence. As it was, he and his wife both had to work full time in order to make ends meet.

"Akatingwah, my mother, held a special place in my heart," Anaukaq said, after I had finished. "She was a feisty, tough, independent woman and a good mother." She died when Anaukaq was a teenager, but his memories of her remained vivid. He told me, as did some of the older Eskimo women in the area, that Mahri-Pahluk loved Akatingwah but realized that she had been "given" by her family—in the Eskimo way of marriage—to an Inuit man named Kitdlaq. So his mother was technically "married" when she first lived with Matthew Henson in 1902. Her husband was a hunter who traveled regularly by dogsled across the ice between Ellesmere Island in Canada and northwest Greenland. He also worked as a hunter and in other capacities for Peary's expeditional teams. It was not uncommon then for married Eskimo women to cohabit with men other than their husbands for short periods, though this custom was usually confined to those within the community and was misunderstood by outsiders. What seems to have been unique about Henson's relationship to Akatingwah is that the Polar Eskimos believed him to be a tribal relative and accepted him as such.

Several of the older Eskimo women in Moriussaq later told me that when Akatingwah gave birth to a dark-skinned baby with never-before-seen curly hair, everyone in the village knew at once that it was Mahri-Pahluk's child. Like Anaukaq, they also expressed the belief that Matthew would have taken his "Eskimo wife" to his homeland if she had not already been given in marriage to another man.

Anaukaq himself seemed to have thought little about how different his life might have been if that had actually happened. As it was, he felt fortunate that his Eskimo stepfather had adopted him and reared him. Even after Akatingwah died, Kitdlaq had continued to be a "kind father" to him. Anaukaq loved and admired his stepfather, who taught him how to be a good father and a *peeneeahktoe wah* [great hunter], skilled in the ways of the Eskimo people.

CHAPTER THREE

✻ ✻ ✻

The Amer-Eskimo Hensons

"I was married to Aviaq for fifty-four wonderful years, and we had seven children. My wife died in 1975. She is buried over there." Anaukaq pointed to a small graveyard just beyond the settlement. "I miss my wife dearly. I have been very lonely since her departure."

Like most modern-day Eskimos, Aviaq is buried in a plot marked by a white Christian cross rather than in a traditional Eskimo surface-stone grave. In the past, Polar Eskimos buried their dead by covering the entire body and a few cherished possessions with stones. Men were typically buried fully clothed in their animal-skin garments alongside their sled and lead dog, strangled and tied to the sled for travel in the afterlife. Women were also clad in traditional sealskin attire and were buried with an oil lamp and *ulu* at their side. It is said that before the arrival of Christian missionaries at the turn of the century, a dead woman's youngest infant would be strangled and placed in the grave out of fear of possible disease and because an unnursed infant was a burden to a wandering band of Arctic hunter-gatherers.

Since Aviaq's death, Anaukaq's sons and grandchildren help to look after him, stopping by his house whenever they can to make sure that he is all right.

"It is still not the same as having a wife for company," he told me.

"She used to go on hunting trips with me, and some years we traveled by dogsled hundreds of miles up and down the coast."

On more than a few occasions, Anaukaq remembered, he and his wife had come close to death while out on the ice.

"I shall never forget the time Aviaq and I were out on a hunting trip, many days north of here, and I left her and the children behind at the igloo while I headed out to hunt seals. I located several seal breathing holes and a few seals on the ice, basking in the sun. As I crawled across the ice behind a white cloth screen, stalking the animals, I decided to climb up on a large hummock of ice to get a good aim. I never noticed that the ice was slowly shifting. After a few minutes, the ice hill cracked under my weight, and I went tumbling into a gaping crevasse, about two-men high. When I didn't return to the igloo, Aviaq became worried. She left the younger children in the care of the older ones and set out looking for me. I heard her calling my name and I yelled back 'Aviaq, my wife! Aviaq, my wife! Here!' She found me and helped me out of the crevasse. I was so happy with my Aviaq. She saved my life."

Some of the women of Moriussaq commented that Anaukaq and Aviaq had a model relationship. In fact, Aviaq had confided to several of her friends that she and Anaukaq had had only one fight in all their years of marriage. One old woman, Kayqeehuk, reminisced about her first meeting with Anaukaq:

"When I was a young girl of about fifteen, living with my parents near Savissivik, some people visited our settlement and stopped to speak to my father. There was a young boy, also about fifteen, with them named Anaukaq, who looked unlike any Inuit I had ever seen. He was very dark with the most beautiful curly hair. I wanted to touch his hair. I had never seen anything like it. I thought he was such a handsome man, the handsomest man I had ever seen. I and several of the other girls in my settlement wanted to marry this boy. Years later, we were a bit jealous when we learned that he had chosen Aviaq as his wife."

* * *

Matthew Henson was sixty-two years old and residing in New York City when, unknown to him, his first grandson was born on December 3, 1928, in polar Greenland. Anaukaq, then about twenty-two, and Aviaq, about seventeen, named their first son after Anaukaq's beloved stepfather, Kitdlaq. This, Anaukaq said, was his greatest tribute to the man who had accepted him as his own blood-kin and had been a wonderful father to him.

Anaukaq took great pride in teaching his firstborn son to become a *peeneeahktoe wah*. Like most Eskimo men, he wanted his son to learn to be a good provider for his family and his village and to earn the respect of his peers. Early on Kitdlaq proved to be a quick learner and a skillful hunter. Like his father before him, he killed his first polar bear at the age of thirteen. By the time he was sixteen, he was a master kayaker and had developed an excellent reputation as a walrus hunter. He would approach the walrus prey by kayak and thrust his harpoon into the lung area from a few meters away. The injured walrus would then dive deep, carrying the harpoon tip and attached rope with it. A ballooned sealskin float attached to the other end of the rope prevented the walrus from diving too deep and served to mark its location. After a prolonged struggle, Kitdlaq and his companions would kill the walrus with their harpoons or guns. One large walrus could feed a family and their vital sled dogs for many weeks.

Then tragedy struck. Hunting alone, Kitdlaq one day approached a large bull walrus that appeared to be sleeping on an ice floe. Creeping up on the animal in the silent kayak, he got within a few meters before he raised his harpoon and prepared to hurl it into the animal's body. Just as he let go of the harpoon, the animal was aroused by another walrus, and it turned its head toward Kitdlaq. The harpoon missed its mark and only grazed the beast's neck.

The bull quickly slid from the ice floe into the water, where walruses can move with incredible speed. Kitdlaq tried to flee as fast as he could, but the wounded walrus overtook him and struck his kayak savagely with its head and tusks. The mighty blow split the kayak in half, sending Kitdlaq flying into the frigid water, head first. Some say that the walrus then struck Kitdlaq with its pointed tusks, killing him instantly. Others believe that he simply froze to death in the icy water. In any case, Kitdlaq, the first grandson of Matthew Henson, died a terrible death when he was sixteen years old.

The loss of their first child devastated Anaukaq and Aviaq. Not since his stepfather, the first Kitdlaq, died had Anaukaq felt such pain and sadness. According to Polar Eskimo tradition, a death should not be openly mourned for more than a few days. But the deceased's name is not to be uttered again in the settlement for an indefinite period. During this time everyone in the community bearing the name of the deceased must give up his or her name until a new child is born in the settlement. The child is then given the name of the deceased, at which point all others may resume using their original names. Anaukaq told me that he had mourned his son's death for years and still had not gotten over it fully.

In the weeks that followed, I met most of the other members of the Amer-Eskimo Henson clan: sons, grandsons, and great-grandchildren. We talked at length about the family heritage, and they made it clear that they felt very special to be the progeny of Matthew Henson, about whom they knew much more than I had anticipated. Like Anaukaq, many expressed a desire to visit the United States and meet their American relatives. Like Anaukaq, too, they found it difficult to believe that I was not myself a Henson. They questioned me incessantly: Would their relatives look like me? Were they all *kulnocktooko*? What did Mahri-Pahluk's wife look like?

For the moment, I had too few answers.

* * *

Bam! Bam! Bam!

A loud, frantic noise at the door of my little wooden hut awakened me from a sound sleep around 2 A.M. I poked my head out of my sleeping bag and tried to orient my senses. "Allen! Allen! Come, Allen! Avataq! *Ahvuk!* Avataq! *Ahvuk!*" the voice at the door was shouting excitedly. Dogs behind the hut were barking wildly and growling at each other. I could hear a gruff voice yelling at them, as if trying to bring them under control. The door flew open and the freezing air rushed into my already cold room, causing me to shiver as if I had been splashed by icy water. In the doorway stood Nukka, Anaukaq's grandson. He hurriedly beckoned me to come outside with him. "Allen, Avataq. *Ahvuk.*" As I rushed to put on my boots and down parka (I had been sleeping fully clothed because of the room's cold temperature), I realized that Nukka was calling the name of Avataq, Anaukaq's oldest son. But the other word, *ahvuk*, I did not understand.

At first I thought that perhaps Avataq had taken ill or been hurt, and they wanted my help. Then, as Nukka and I dashed off toward Anaukaq's house, I began to worry that something had happened to Anaukaq. Just behind the house, I could see the silhouette of a broad-shouldered, stocky man trying to untangle his sled dogs. Moving closer, I saw that he was dressed in a thick, thigh-length leather parka with a fur-lined hood to protect his head and face. His knee-length trousers were made entirely of polar bear fur and his boots were traditional high-top sealskin *kamiks*.

It was Avataq. He had just returned from a hunting trip and was working by the light of a kerosene lantern, tethering his dogs and preparing to remove his quarry from the sled. He turned to me and smiled. "*Ahvuk*," he said proudly, pointing to his sled. I walked over to the sled and removed the deerskin cover to reveal three large walrus heads with long ivory tusks, as well as slabs of bloody meat stacked two feet high, filling the entire eight-foot sled. To the Polar Eskimos, who prize the walrus particularly, it was an impressive harvest.

"Avataq, *peeneeahktoe wah*, huh?" said Nukka admiringly.

Avataq stored most of the *ahvuk* meat in a small wooden shed, similar to a chicken coop, just behind his house—a natural, year-round refrigerator. Other slabs were placed on racks some four feet above the ground, high enough to be beyond the reach of the dogs.

Born in 1933, the second child of Anaukaq and Aviaq, Avataq is about five feet four inches tall, with a stocky build, dark complexion, and straight black hair. His big, warm smile is a bit comical because of a missing front tooth. With his high cheekbones, Eskimo eyes, and straight hair he reminds one of a Southeast Asian, perhaps a Javanese. As a child, Avataq briefly attended a Danish missionary school, where he learned to speak some Danish and do simple arithmetic. Yet in most respects he has remained faithful to the traditional Eskimo way of life. Registered with the Greenlandic authorities as a full-time hunter, he earns his livelihood by hunting narwhal, seal, and rabbits in the summer, and walrus, polar bear, and seal in the spring and winter. He is, in fact, the most celebrated hunter in the area, renown for his courage and expert techniques. Walrus hunts are his specialty, but he is equally adept at hunting seals and polar bears.

Avataq and his wife, Minaq, have five children: three girls, Malina, Louisa, and Cecilia; and two boys, Jakub and Magssanguaq. Though he is only ten years old, Magssanguaq, the youngest, is already an accomplished hunter in his own right. During my stay I saw him return from the hunting grounds with four large seals and numerous birds.

* * *

Our vigil on the rock-strewn, desolate mountainside had been long and uneventful. Rising up from the shoreline of Wolstenholm Sound to the craggy peak where we sat, the terrain reminded me of a moonscape or the surface of some unknown, lifeless planet. Not far from me, a man wearing polar bear pants and an anorak sat atop a large rock, peering through binoculars out over the distant waters. Suddenly the quiet was broken by the roar of a huge iceberg thundering down a nearby glacier and hitting the water with the force of a bomb. The sentry did not stir. He had been there many times before, and he knew that when nature spoke, all a man could do was listen. He was searching the bay for schools of *kahlayleewah* [narwhal]. He must not lose his concentration. The vigil could go on for hours, even days. One must be patient.

Below us, just above the shoreline, sat a fifteen-foot kayak made from a light wooden frame and covered with off-white tarpaulin material. A few decades ago this kayak would have been constructed from whale and walrus bones and covered with stitched sealskin. In the center of the kayak was an opening, just large enough to accommodate the slightly built Eskimo. At the stem was a neatly coiled nylon rope connected to the removable tip of a seven-foot wooden harpoon, which lay parallel to the line of the craft within reach of the pilot. Attached to the other end of the rope and placed behind the hunter's seat was a large, balloonlike sealskin float that looked like a stuffed seal with feet when fully inflated. To the left of the seat, a high-caliber rifle sat on the flat part of the stem, balanced precariously and pointing forward. Lying perpendicular to the long axis of the boat, just behind the seat, was the kayaker's distinctive double paddle. Although even the slightest swaying motion of the boat can cause a hunter to lose his rifle and gear, the expert Eskimo kayakers can travel long distances at impressive speeds with remarkable balance and stability.

There were only three tents on the mountainside, including my own. The sentry, and the leader of our expedition, was Ussarkaq, Anaukaq's third son. Like his brother Avataq, the fifty-year-old Ussarkaq is a full-time hunter, best known for his skill as a hunter of narwhals and for his ability to handle a kayak. In fact, he is the kayak-racing champion among the Polar Eskimos, often competing with young men in their teens, twenties, and thirties. A respected leader within his family, he is also well known for his sense of humor.

"Do you want to become a great narwhal hunter?" he asked me, seemingly serious. "Then take off that red parka. You'll scare off the narwhals." I looked at him incredulously, having no intention of taking off my parka for any reason. But Ussarkaq just laughed. "Come over to the tent for some tea, and we will teach you some funny Eskimo words."

He called down to his eighteen-year-old son, Massauna-Matthew. Ussarkaq had been on watch for three hours; it was time for his son to relieve him. Massauna-Matthew, named for Matthew Henson, emerged from the tent. He is much darker in complexion than the other Eskimo Hensons and has spirally curled hair. Anaukaq says that he is "my favorite grandson because he and I have the curliest hair in the family."

Ussarkaq gave Massauna the binoculars and returned with me to the tent for some hot tea that his son had prepared. After drinking a cup, he rubbed his eyes, now aching from the long watch, and promptly dozed off. But not for long.

"*Kahlayleewah! Kahlayleewah!*" shouted Massauna-Matthew, running down the mountainside to the sea. Ussarkaq sprang from his deerskin mat, rushed out of the tent, and headed down the slope to his kayak. There he met Massauna, who was pointing in the direction of four large narwhals in the center of the bay, breaching the surface like dolphins. Ussarkaq and Massauna quickly but carefully lifted the kayak and carried it to the water's edge. Ussarkaq slipped into the tightly fitting seat and pulled a rubber sealer over the remaining open space surrounding his body. Massauna then gave the stern of the kayak a shove, and Ussarkaq pushed off with his paddle.

Once in the water, Ussarkaq paddled rapidly with the classic, rotating movements of the Eskimo kayaker. He moved with grace and speed through the bay, gliding toward the narwhals. The kayak moved through the water so quietly that it slipped up on the school of narwhal before they could detect it. Ussarkaq tried to head the single-tusked mammals off before they could reach the mouth of the bay. The hunter and kayak became smaller and smaller in the distance, soon visible only through the binoculars. When he reached the narwhals, they appeared confused as they scattered about the kayak, their blowholes spouting water and air all around him.

Ussarkaq selected a large male that had breached right in front of his kayak. His harpoon found its mark in the animal's head, causing it to thrash about wildly before submerging. The attached rope lying on the kayak uncoiled in seconds as the animal dove deep into the water, trying to free itself. The sealskin buoy flew off the kayak into the bay when all the rope had run out. The buoy disappeared beneath the surface, then reappeared, traveling away from the kayak at high speed. This was a good sign and meant that the harpoon tip was fixed securely in the narwhal's flesh. Ussarkaq paddled frantically after the moving float. When it changed direction, he changed direction. After about forty-five minutes of chasing the buoy, Ussarkaq was exhausted. His strokes became slower and more labored, but he could not stop to rest. Finally, the buoy, too, began to move more slowly, and Ussarkaq moved in on it. He picked up his rifle and steadied his aim in the direction of the buoy, waiting for the narwhal to surface for air. Moments later the big, gray-black mammal broke the water's surface, its spouting blowhole marking the spot. Ussarkaq fired two rounds. The water all around the thrashing animal turned bright red. Then the movement stopped. Ussarkaq quickly paddled to the narwhal and plunged a metal pipe down its throat.

Placing his mouth around the open end of the pipe, he blew air into the animal's lungs and stomach, bloating it so that he could keep it afloat and tow it more easily behind his kayak.

The half-ton narwhal would feed Ussarkaq's family for more than a month. Ussarkaq and his wife, Simigaq, have seven children—four boys and three girls—ranging in age from seven to twenty-four. The girls are named Arnakitsoq, Aviaq, and Eqilana. The boys are Massauna-Matthew, Thomas, Avatak, and Peter. The family lives in Siorapaluk, the northernmost settlement of Greenland.

* * *

Anaukaq's fourth son, Ajako, is a part-time hunter who lives near his father in Moriussaq. Forty-eight years old, about five feet seven inches tall, with dark curly hair and deep brown skin, Ajako is considered very handsome by the villagers. The manager of the local government-run general store, he serves as a sort of unofficial mayor of the settlement. His store, which also functions as a post office, bank, and transport service, is restocked once each year when a Danish ship laden with food and dry goods comes to Moriussaq during the summer thaw.

Ajako and his wife, Puto, have five children: three girls, Nadiketchia, Sabina, and Aviaq; and two boys, Jens and Nukka. Like good parents everywhere, Ajako and Puto try to provide as much as possible for their children and take great pride in their children's achievements. One day, for instance, I found them out on the frozen bay, commemorating Nukka's first polar bear kill by preparing the skin so that it could be made into trousers for their son.

Dressed in his own polar bear pants, deerskin parka, and sealskin mittens trimmed with polar bear fur, Ajako chopped a hole about three feet in diameter in the ice using a spearlike metal tool. Puto stood beside him, dressed in native sealskin boots and an imported gray down-filled jumpsuit that she had purchased through the local trade cooperative. Ajako dunked the huge skin in the icehole, moving it up and down in the frigid water, much as one washes a shirt by hand in a tub. After a few minutes of washing, he took the pelt out of the water and spread it over the snow. He and Puto then threw some snow on top of the bearskin, after which they began stomping and dancing on it with their boots. They repeated the process several times until they were satisfied. Ajako then beat the skin repeatedly with a stick to remove the residual water, snow, and ice. *"Daymah!* [It is finished.]" He threw the limp skin over his shoulder, and we headed for home.

* * *

Vittus, Anaukaq's fifth son, lives a life much different from his older brothers. Trained as a machinist by the Danes, he works on various kinds of equipment now making its way into the Eskimo settlements. Forty years old, he is physically well built and about five feet nine inches tall, making him the tallest of Anaukaq's five sons. "I am a black man," he is fond of boasting, though in fact he looks more "pure Eskimo" or Asian than any other member of his immediate family. He is said to take after his mother more than his siblings, in temperament as well as physical appearance. He is very soft-spoken but at the same time friendly and outgoing. Vittus and his wife, Cecilie, have five children: three boys, David, Avatak, and Anaukaq; and two girls, Lila and Aviaq.

When Anaukaq's sixth and youngest son was born, he and his wife decided to name their new baby after the son they had loved and lost and the stepfather Anaukaq had so revered. Young Kitdlaq was raised in much the same way as the other children in the family, yet in some ways he was given special treatment. Ever conscious of the fate of their eldest child, Anaukaq and Aviaq were more protective of their youngest. He was not permitted to hunt alone, as the other boys were at his age. He was forbidden by his father to use a kayak until far beyond the age when most Eskimo boys learn to do so, and even then he was required to have a companion at all times.

Kitdlaq succeeded in becoming a good hunter, but he also excelled in the Danish missionary school. Anaukaq and Aviaq moved the family from Savissivik to Moriussaq when Kitdlaq was ten so that he and the other children could get some schooling. Now thirty-eight, Kitdlaq is a part-time hunter and a teacher in the small elementary and junior high school in the Eskimo village of Qaanaaq. Kitdlaq is about five feet six inches tall; he is dark-complexioned and could easily pass for a black American. He and his wife, Kista, have three young daughters: Tina, Avortungiaq, and one-year-old Aviaq.

"When we were growing up, we were a typical Eskimo hunter family," Kitdlaq told me one day as he worked on his kayak. "We, all five sons, traveled from place to place with our parents in search of the good hunting grounds. We all slept together in one igloo. We ate together and sang together. We also played together as friends, and we learned hunting skills from each other and our father. My big brothers really took care of me. They treated me kind of special because I was the baby of the group. But they also taught me to be strong and to provide for myself.

"When I was a child, some of the other children who wanted to be mean would occasionally taunt me by saying that my skin was dark and dirty. They would say, 'Go wash your face.' At first this hurt me very much. But my big brothers would tell me not to worry about the teasing. They would support me and tell me to be proud of my *kulnocktooko* heritage. My father too would say that we should be proud to be the descendants of Mahri-Pahluk.

"As I grew older, I thought a lot about my grandfather. My family used to say that we must have relatives in America, but they never did anything about it. We couldn't. Anaukaq, my father, used to say that he wanted more than anything to travel to Mahri-Pahluk's homeland and meet his American relatives. He thought that he must have relatives in America, maybe some half brothers and half sisters. He would say to us children, 'If I don't live to meet Mahri-Pahluk's American relatives, I want you to travel there one day to meet them.' I always hoped we could fulfill his dream as a family, especially before my mother died."

Between the birth of Vittus and Kitdlaq, Anaukaq and Aviaq had a baby girl whom they named Akatingwah. She died at age six of unknown causes. Each brother told me of his profound sense of loss at the death of his only sister.

* * *

Anaukaq enjoyed introducing me to the members of his family and instructing me in the ways of his people. But most of all, he enjoyed talking about the old days. As he reminisced, he mentioned another relative whom he referred to as "Cousin Kali." He told me that Kali—pronounced "Karree" by many of the Eskimos—was the son of Robert Peary and his best childhood friend.

Taken aback, I asked Anaukaq if he was certain that Kali was Peary's son.

"Oh, yes," he said seriously, "Kali is the son of Peeuree and an Eskimo woman named Ahlikahsingwah." He stretched out each syllable so that I would better understand the pronunciation.

"Most Americans do not know that Peeuree fathered children in Greenland," I said.

Anaukaq chuckled. "Yes, Peeuree had two wives, a Peeuree wife in America and Ahlikahsingwah up here." He laughed again and clapped his hands.

"Did Peeuree have other children with Ahlikahsingwah?" I asked.

"Oh, yes," he replied. "He had another son with Ahlikahsingwah named Anaukaq, like me."

"Older or younger?"

"Older. Oh, maybe five or six years older. But he is dead now."

Anaukaq said that Kali was also born aboard Peary's ship, the *Roosevelt*, in 1906. In fact, Anaukaq and Kali were born within days of each other. Yet the reason they called each other "cousin" had less to do with the circumstances of their birth than with the fact that their mothers married two Eskimo brothers, Kitdlaq and Peeahwahto. Both men, he said, worked for Peary as hunters. Kitdlaq later adopted Mahri-Pahluk's son, Anaukaq, while Peeahwahto adopted Kali and his older brother, also named Anaukaq. After Peary and Henson left Greenland for good in 1909, Kitdlaq and Peeahwahto took their wives and children to the island of Qeqertarsaaq, now Herbert Island, where they lived between hunting trips for about fifteen years.

Young Anaukaq and Kali became the best of friends. They played together as children and hunted together as young men. According to Anaukaq, Kali was "a great seal hunter, and like a brother to me." Although they had not spent any time together since becoming adults, they still referred to each other affectionately.

Anaukaq said that Kali still lived on Qeqertarsaaq, about forty miles north of his settlement. When I expressed an interest in visiting him, Anaukaq implored me to do so, in part because Kali would be able to provide additional information about the North Pole legacy of Robert Peary and Matthew Henson.

"You will like my cousin Kali," he said. "Give him my best regards."

CHAPTER FOUR

* * *

Cousin Kali

Approached from the southeast, Qeqertarsaaq looks much like an ancient castle rising from the sea—an isolated, snowcapped mountain surrounded by barren white plains. Located some twenty-five miles off the coast of northwest Greenland, it is a well-known hunting ground for walrus and seals, just as it was when Robert Peary camped there in the late 1800s. Today it has few human inhabitants. The only settlement, if such it can be called, consists of a few scattered dwellings. It was there that I found the man Anaukaq called "Cousin Kali," son of "Peeuree."

As I neared my destination, I saw a young man of about twenty years old bending over a freshly killed seal, methodically slicing it to pieces. Using a large hunter's knife, he made a small incision just under the mouth and then cut the skin vertically in a single line from chin to tail flipper. He next peeled away the animal's skin in one piece, much as one would remove a diver's wet suit. He walked a few paces to a platform made of old timber and placed the valuable pelt on a wooden rack, well beyond the reach of his dogs, tethered a few yards away. The pelt would be stretched later and made into boots, gloves, or possibly a woman's hooded jacket or *amaut*.

Returning to the skinless animal, the hunter began to flense its fleshy pink blubber, tossing some of the scraps to the dogs. The dogs caught the chunks in the air and gulped them down. He made sure that each dog got a piece, then stored the rest of the blubber on the rack. Another vertical incision, this one deep into the seal's throat and down to the tail, spilled its innards over both sides of the carcass. He carefully removed the liver, stomach, intestines and other organs. The intestines would be dried and used for tubing or, perhaps, for a shirt. The undesirable innards would be fed to the dogs, the rest would be eaten by the hunter and his family.

The young man then quartered the animal, saving every piece of flesh for food. Nothing was lost. With blood covering his hands and a few spots on his face, he turned and smiled at me as he passed on his way to store the meat. It was the first time he had acknowledged my presence. He had a round face with perfectly even white teeth. His skin was pale and only his eyes and high cheekbones suggested that he was Eskimo. His smile was difficult to interpret, at once friendly and cautious, warm yet reserved. Still, I smiled back and then moved on.

Entering the tiny settlement, I spotted a rather fit-looking, slightly graying "white" man with animated eyes, standing in the entrance of a small wooden house. He was wearing a tan pile-and-wool turtleneck sweater, heavy dark trousers, and sealskin boots. Wanting to know who the visitors were, he came out of his house to meet me, smiling cheerfully, and graciously greeted my translator Navarana Qavigaq-Harper, the great niece of Ootah. He was lighter in complexion than the other Eskimos I had met but similar in stature. His eyes were more Asiatic than Anaukaq's, and his gray-black hair much thinner.

Before I left the United States, I had carefully studied photographs of all the men who accompanied Commander Peary on his various Arctic expeditions. Right away, I could see a striking resemblance between "Cousin Kali" and Robert Peary. Still, I could not be certain that the man who now stood before me was Peary's son, since other white explorers in the region had reportedly fathered children with Eskimo women. By comparison, verification of Anaukaq's identity had been much simpler because Matthew Henson was the only black explorer to visit northern Greenland in the early 1900s.

Like Anaukaq, Kali assumed that I must be a Henson. Why else would the first black American he had ever seen have come so far to meet him? I explained to Kali that I was not myself a Henson but had come to the region in search of the progeny of Matthew Henson and Robert Peary.

"I am Kali Peeuree," he said.

"Are you the son of Robert Peary, the explorer who came to this area many years ago to reach the North Pole?" I asked.

"Yes, I am the son of Peeuree, the friend of Mahri-Pahluk," he responded, with a smile and obvious pride. "You know, it was Mahri-Pahluk who took my father to the North Pole," he said. "My father could not have reached the pole without Mahri-Pahluk."

Kali invited me into his igloo, where we sat down and talked over some tea I had brought along. "Don't you have anything stronger?" he asked with a mischievous grin.

"No, only tea and coffee," I said.

Kali laughed. "How are you going to tolerate the cold up here without some good whiskey to keep you warm?"

I told him I shared his sentiments, but that the Danish government prohibited the transport or use of unauthorized alcoholic beverages in the area.

Again he laughed. "What do they know? Every man needs a good drink once in a while."

Kali said that he was eighty years old. He did not know the exact date of his birth but knew that he was born in the late summer of 1906. I tried to get him to talk about his father but he seemed somewhat reluctant. He preferred to talk about other matters.

"How is my cousin Anaukaq?" he asked.

"He is very well, and he sends you his regards," I replied.

"I have not seen him in many years, but I have thought of him often," Kali said. "I heard some years ago that he was very ill. Then later I learned that he had overcome this illness."

"Well, when I visited him, he was in good health and eating well," I said. "In fact, a few days ago, he and I ate *ahvuk* together."

"You have eaten *ahvuk*?" Kali asked with apparent amazement. "Did you like it?"

"Yes," I said. "It was tasty."

"That is wonderful. You should have brought me some. Did Ana-ukaq hunt this *ahvuk*?" he said, smiling as if he were teasing me.

"No, his son Avataq killed the *ahvuk*, but I am sure that Anaukaq is still a great hunter, just as you are. Both of you could still hunt the *ahvuk* if you so desired." This evoked a proud laugh. I had evidently said the right thing to flatter the old hunter.

"Oh, maybe," he said. "I try to shoot a seal now and then if I pass one on the ice, but I leave the hunting to my son, Talilanguaq, and my grandson Ole. They are both *peeneeahktoe wah*."

"Where do you come from?" Kali inquired.

"The United States. Boston," I said.

"How far away from Qeqertarsaaq is that?" he asked.

"Several thousand miles away. Here, I'll show you." I drew a rough map of Greenland and the United States on my interview notepad. "You are here, and Boston is here," I said, pointing to marks on the map.

"Mmmm, seems very far away. Is that where Mahri-Pahluk's family lives?" Kali asked.

"I'm afraid I don't know. But I would think they might live in Maryland, about here on the map," I said, pointing. "That is where Mahri-Pahluk was born."

"What about Peeuree. Where was he from?" Kali asked.

"He was born in Pennsylvania, about here on the map, but he grew up in Maine—here, north of Boston."

"Is his family still there?" he asked.

"I honestly don't know where his family lives, but I can try to find out when I return to the United States," I said.

Kali said nothing. He just stared at the map for a while, expressionless.

In subsequent conversations, Kali opened up to me and talked about his own family. Kali and his wife, Eqariusaq, had five children—two boys and three daughters. Like Anaukaq, Kali had suffered the loss of his first son. Peter (his Christianized name) had died some years earlier from a gunshot wound which the authorities ruled to be self-inflicted. Some family members and other local Eskimos suspected that Peter had been the victim of foul play following an alcohol-related argument with a close acquaintance. Whatever the truth of the matter, it was clear that his death remained a source of profound grief. "It hurts when I speak of him," Kali said.

Everyone I spoke with had nothing but praise for Peter, who is survived by his wife and three children. He was, by all accounts, handsome, charming, bright, and a natural leader. He was also a skilled hunter. As a young man he traveled throughout northwest Greenland with Ussarkaq Henson, Anaukaq's third son, who eventually became his best friend. Peter and Ussarkaq hunted together and even courted their respective wives together. According to Ussarkaq, they often discussed their common dream of one day visiting America to search for their relatives, but Peter died before they could make any concrete plans.

After Peter's death, Kali's second son, Talilanguaq, assumed responsibility for supplying the family with most of its food. Now forty-five years old, Talilanguaq bears a remarkable resemblance to photographs of young Robert Peary. He is reputed to be one of the best all-round hunters in the region, just as his father had been in his younger days. On occasion he has also worked as a guide for the European adventurers who regularly visit the area. Hoping to secure some niche in history or simply to live out their fantasies, these would-be explorers hire highly skilled Eskimo dogsled drivers such as Talilanguaq to take them to the North Pole. The Eskimos joke about their employers, many of whom treat the journey as if it were a long taxi ride. Others end up traveling part of the distance by plane. Nevertheless, Talilanguaq himself seemed proud to have followed in his grandfather's footsteps. I later learned that both his brother Peter and Avataq Henson had journeyed to the Pole at some point in their lives.

Talilanguaq's son Ole, who is nineteen years old, also works as a hunter, having chosen to follow the traditional Eskimo way of life rather than attend school and take a job with the Danes. It was Ole I had seen carving the seal when I first reached the settlement. Talilanguaq has one other son, Ossmus, and three daughters, Paulina, Tukumaq, and Om'ayekeycho.

Talilanguaq's eldest sister, also named Paulina, is a teacher in the village of Qaanaaq and a well-known figure in local Greenlandic politics. She is the mother of three sons, one of whom recently committed suicide. Another son, named Sip'soo, has worked around the American air base at Thule and speaks some English. Now in his thirties, he changed his name to Robert Peary II a few years back, ostensibly in defiance of taunts at school about his racial mixture.

Kali's other daughters, Marta and Mikissuk, are the wives of hunters and also live in Qaanaaq. Marta bore no children of her own but has adopted three Inuit orphans, while Mikissuk has five children.

Although Kali clearly preferred to focus on the present, the longer we talked, the more he reminisced about the past. He retained especially fond memories of Anaukaq. "Cousin Anaukaq is one of the greatest men I have known," he said. "Perhaps there has been no greater hunter in our country. Until he injured his eye in a hunting accident some years back, he was the best hunter around."

"We were the best of friends in our youth," he continued. "We always felt that we belonged to the same family because our Eskimo fathers, Kitdlaq and Peeahwahto, were brothers, and we lived together as one family for most of our youth. As young boys, we always called each other's father 'uncle,' and we called each other 'cousin.'"

Kali reiterated what Anaukaq had told me about Ahlikahsingwah's relationship with Robert Peary. He said that his mother was already married to Peeahwahto when she first became involved with Peary in 1896, and that she worked as Peary's personal maid or "laundress." At the same time, Peary hired Peeahwahto as a hunter for his expedition, supplying him with a rifle and sending him away from the camp for extended periods. Peeahwahto and the other Eskimos were apparently aware that Peary was having sexual relations with Ahlikahsingwah. No one knows how Peeahwahto felt about this relationship, but many of the other Eskimos resented it.

In 1900 Ahlikahsingwah gave birth to Peary's first son, whom she named Anaukaq. Peary called the child "Sammy." Little Anaukaq Peary later developed the nickname "Hammy" among the Eskimos, many of whom have difficulty pronouncing the "s" sound. According to Kali, his brother Hammy died at the age of twenty-seven after developing "a hole in his stomach," most likely a perforated ulcer.

In 1903 Ahlikahsingwah gave birth to a daughter name Ahveahkotoo, who is believed to have been fathered by Peeahwahto. She, too, died many years ago.

Peeahwahto adopted Anaukaq-Hammy and Kali Peary and raised them as his own sons. He took them everywhere, especially on his long hunting trips across the great ice to the northern parts of Ellesmere Island, where game was abundant. He taught both boys to hunt and provide for themselves. If he had any ill feelings because they were fathered by another man, Peeahwahto never evinced this to Hammy or Kali. Peeahwahto died when Kali was about twelve years old. Ahlikahsingwah remarried, this time an Eskimo named Ulloriaq. At first Kali got along well with his new stepfather, but as time went on their relationship deteriorated, and, eventually, at age sixteen, Kali left home.

Kali's feelings about his real father, Robert Peary, were complicated. "I don't have much feeling for him," he told me. "But I have nothing against him. Peeuree did nothing for me when I was growing up. He did not help me or my mother in any way. It was my mother who meant everything to me. She raised me and looked after me like a good mother. Some of the Eskimo people used to call her a cheap woman because of her relationship with Peeuree. This kind of talk caused her great pain and sadness. I never thought anything was wrong with her. I loved my mother. But I was ashamed of the name-calling she had to endure after Peeuree abandoned us. The other children often teased me for being part *kadoona* (white-skinned). This used to hurt me. [But] my mother was very protective of me."

Not surprisingly, Kali never identified with the Danes or other white Europeans with whom he occasionally came in contact. Like Anaukaq, he thought of himself exclusively as an Eskimo. When our discussion turned to the conquest of the North Pole, a subject in which he professed little interest, Kali made it clear that his own hero in that saga was neither Peary nor Henson, but Ootah. "Without Ootah and the other Eskimos," he said, "they never would have made it to the North Pole."

Kali's regard for Ootah is shared by most Polar Eskimos, including the Hensons. Renown for his dogsled driving and hunting skills as well as for his bravery, Ootah was thirty-one years old when he accompanied Peary and Henson on the 1906 polar expedition that fell short of its goal by some 120 miles. Witnessing the dejection of the Americans, he promised that if they ever made another attempt, they could count on his participation. True to his word, he was there to greet Peary's ship when it returned to Etah two years later.

By all accounts Ootah was on particularly friendly terms with Matthew Henson, whom he seems to have genuinely liked and admired. Together the two men prepared for the final assault on the Pole, hunting game and setting up the advance camp that would serve as the launching point. Once the expedition was underway, Ootah joined Henson in breaking the trail. Even when some of the other Eskimos turned back out of fear of the "ice devil," Ootah stayed on.

Henson later reported that on April 3, 1909, three days before they reached the Pole, he was pushing his sled across a lane of moving ice when the ice slipped from beneath his feet, plunging him and his sled into the frigid water. Struggling frantically to pull himself out, but unable to grip the ice with his gloved hand, he had just about given up hope when Ootah grabbed him by the neck of his parka, pulled him to safety with one hand, and with the other hoisted the dogsled out of the water. He had saved Henson's life as well as the sled carrying the expedition's vital navigational and scientific equipment.

As a tribute to Ootah's contributions to Arctic exploration, the northernmost point of land in the world, an island just off the coast of northern Greenland, was recently named in his honor.

Yet if Kali thought of himself first and foremost as an Eskimo, he was still curious about his American relatives. He knew that he had had an older half sister whom the Eskimos called *Ahnighito* (Snowbaby). The daughter of Robert Peary and his wife, Josephine, who accompanied her husband on one of his early expeditions, she was believed to be the first white child born in the Arctic. But she had been taken back to the United States long before Kali was born. Kali later learned that some of the American Peary family had visited the Cape York region of Greenland in 1932 to dedicate a monument to their father. According to some of the Eskimos who went to meet them, Ahnighito was among those present. Kali hoped that I could tell him more about the American Pearys, but unfortunately I knew little about them. I did tell him, however, of Anaukaq's interest in meeting his American relatives and of my plans to assist him in achieving that goal.

"When we were young men," Kali remembered, "Anaukaq and I talked about going over there to find our fathers, but it was never possible for us to go. If cousin Anaukaq goes over there to visit his relatives and see Mahri-Pahluk's grave, I would like to join him. I would like to meet my father's other family."

I gave him my word that I would search for his American relatives as well and would see whether I could arrange for him to meet them.

I stayed with Kali and his family for several weeks. During that time I became convinced that he was indeed "the second son of Ahli-kahsingwah and Peeuree." In part I was persuaded by a physical resemblance to Robert Peary and in part, by his own testimony and that of other older Eskimos in the area. But most of all, it was the way he talked more than the words he spoke that erased any lingering doubts: the sorrow that filled his eyes when he described his mother's relationship with "Peeuree"; his insistence that he was not a *kahdonah* but an Eskimo; the longing he expressed to see his father's grave and meet Peary's "other" American family. Intuition may be an unreliable guide, but if this man was not the son of Robert Peary, it was clear that he had spent his entire lifetime believing he was.

* * *

Before leaving Qeqertarsaaq, I tested Kali's hearing as part of my audiological study. Like Anaukaq and other hunters I had examined, he too had a degenerative nerve-hearing loss caused by the repeated use of high-powered rifles. Otherwise, he was in excellent health.

"Perhaps we could get the Greenlandic government to provide you with a hearing aid," I suggested.

"Oh, I hear what I want to hear," he joked. " I would rather have them give me a good bottle of whiskey."

Kali was not a heavy drinker, but he enjoyed a glass of spirits now and then. Active and spry for his age, he was continually joking and telling stories. As I had with Anaukaq, I felt that with Kali I had made a new friend.

CHAPTER FIVE

✳ ✳ ✳

"Hallelujah!" / "Not interested"

Determined to keep my promise to Anaukaq and Kali, I began my search for their American relatives as soon as I returned to the United States. I started by working my way through the telephone directories of New York City, Matthew Henson's home for more than fifty years, and Charles County, Maryland, his birthplace. My efforts produced no leads, however, until several newspapers printed the story of my journey north.

"Hallelujah! God bless you, son, for finding our relatives," shouted Olive Henson Fulton, rushing forward to embrace me. "We never knew Uncle Matt had any children."

By now she was squeezing me with excitement. She gave me a big kiss on the cheek, and as she stood back to look at me I could see the tears streaming down her cheeks. "I can't believe it," she said again and again. "Uncle Matt has children in the Arctic."

Olive is a brown-skinned woman of sixty years with a round face, wavy white hair, and a warm, sincere demeanor. About five feet four inches tall and full-figured, she is the image of everyone's favorite aunt. After reading about my discovery of Anaukaq and Kali in the *Boston Globe*, she had called my Harvard office and excitedly told me that her grandfather, David Henson, was Matthew Henson's brother, and she, Matthew's great-niece. She also said that she had photographs of her grandfather and her Uncle Matt, which she would be happy to show me. We arranged to meet at her home in the Roxbury community of Boston.

Concerned about my ability to locate her house as well as for my safety in her neighborhood, Olive had come out to the corner to meet me. I spotted her from a distance, waving her arms above her head. She then led me to her first-floor apartment in a modest two-family house situated at the edge of a train track. We sat down in a small, quaintly furnished living room, surrounded by shelves of books that extended from floor to ceiling.

After some small talk to get better acquainted, we began to review the history of the American Henson clan. We talked at length—at times laughing together, at times choking with emotion—and the more we talked the more convinced I became that I had indeed found a consanguineous relative of Matthew Henson. Olive showed me photographs of several family members, including her grandfather, David Henson, who bore a clear resemblance to Matthew at the same age. She explained that her grandfather had migrated to Boston from Maryland around the turn of the century. There he had married and raised five children, one of whom was her father, George.

As a young girl, Olive had traveled with her family to New York on many occasions to visit with her great-uncle Matt. During these visits he would talk with his curious little niece about his trip to the North Pole, showing her photos, maps, and artifacts from the Arctic.

"I felt so proud when I saw Uncle Matt," she recalled. "He was always impeccably dressed and dignified, and he spoke so humbly of his achievements. Uncle Matt had a love for children, although he had no children with his wife Lucy. He would always give me a big hug, sit me on his knee, and tell stories about his life with the Eskimos in Greenland.

"I remember that one time I couldn't wait to return to my school in Boston to tell the other children about my great-uncle who had gone to the North Pole with Admiral Robert Peary. But when I told my classmates and teachers, no one believed me. In fact, one teacher scolded me and called me a liar in front of the class and sent me home from school. This crushed me. When my father came home I told him what had happened. He held me in his arms and said, 'Don't worry, dear. We know the truth. In our hearts, we can keep the truth even if they don't want to know it.' This memory has stuck with me throughout my life and made me determined to share with everyone the stories that Uncle Matt told me."

A clerk at a nearby Veterans Administration hospital, Olive had volunteered some of her off-duty time to work with youngsters from inner-city neighborhoods. Hoping to instill in them a sense of cultural pride, she taught them about their African-American heritage and the contributions made by black Americans in all walks of life. She taught them about Martin Luther King, Jr., about Malcolm X, and, of course, about her own great-uncle, Matthew Henson.

Now, with my discovery of the existence of Anaukaq, a new chapter had been added to her great-uncle's story. When I showed her photographs of Anaukaq and his family, Olive's eyes welled with tears. "My goodness, Anaukaq looks just like Uncle Matt. Incredible!" she said. "I can still see him in some of the grandchildren and great-grandchildren as well. Are they okay? Do they have enough food and clothes and things?"

"Well, they do not have many material things," I replied, "but they are fine. They all have jobs as hunters to provide food for their families, and some have jobs with the Danish government."

"Can I do anything for them?" she asked. "I don't have much but I could send them something, you know, to help them if they need it."

I told her I didn't think that would be necessary, but that I would be returning to Greenland in a few months and would tell Anaukaq about her. I knew Anaukaq would be thrilled to know that I had found his cousin Olive.

"Is there any way I can go up there with you?" she asked. "I don't mind the rough travel if you get me there."

"That may be possible in the future," I told her. "But first I would love to bring Anaukaq and Kali here. Both have told me that their lifelong dream has been to visit America to meet their relatives and see their fathers' graves."

"Then please bring them," Olive said. "They can stay right here with me. I can host a big family reunion with all of our relatives. They all want to meet our Eskimo relatives. There are about thirty-five of us here, and others you might find in other parts of the country. They can all come to Boston. We can invite the Peary family, too. I'll cook some good American soul food for them: fried chicken, ham, sweet potatoes, cornbread, black-eyed peas, homemade ice cream—everything."

I laughed. "Did you know that they eat most of their food raw?"

Olive paused, then said, "Well, I'll prepare something raw on the side. But *everybody* likes soul food."

As we bade each other an emotional farewell, Olive began searching among her things for a gift to send Anaukaq. After considering several articles, she settled on a beautiful multicolored wool blanket that she had recently knitted.

"Please tell Anaukaq that his cousin Olive wants him to have this," she said.

We also selected several family photographs for Anaukaq—one of Olive, one of her grandfather David, one of her father, and a few of other members of the American Henson clan. I knew that Anaukaq would love all these presents. I could imagine his reaction and could even hear his infectious laughter ringing out over the tiny village of Moriussaq.

*   *   *

I had no idea which Peary family members were alive or where they lived, although I knew that Peary and his wife, Josephine, had had several children. Marie Ahnighito Peary, their eldest child, had gained early notoriety as the first white person born in northwest Greenland. The story of her birth in 1894 was later recounted in a popular book entitled *Snowbaby*, written by her mother. A second child, Francine, had died in infancy. Their third child, Robert E. Peary, Jr., was born in 1903.

My search for Admiral Peary's descendants began at his alma mater, Bowdoin College in Brunswick, Maine. Bowdoin is the home of the Peary-MacMillan Arctic Museum, which I had visited previously to collect photographs of Peary, Henson, and other members of their expeditionary teams. It was there that I learned that Marie Peary had married Edward Stafford and had two sons, Edward P. Stafford, Jr., and Peary Stafford.

I decided to try to track down the Staffords, but, as it turned out, they contacted me first.

"Are you Dr. Allen Counter?" the caller asked, identifying himself as "a member of the Peary-Stafford family."

"Yes, I am," I replied. "I'm so glad you called. I have been trying to locate some of the American Pearys." There was silence at the other end of the line. "Well, what do you think about the news of Kali?" I continued excitedly.

"I have read articles about your work in the Arctic and your statements about the so-called offspring of Robert Peary," he said in a cold, flat voice.

I assured the caller that I had indeed "found a man and his family in Greenland who say they are the descendants of Admiral Robert E. Peary."

"Why are you doing this?" he asked accusingly.

"I beg your pardon?" I said.

"Why are you doing this?" he repeated. "Why are you bringing this out?"

I explained that I simply wanted to share with members of the Peary and Henson families the fact that I had found two families in northwest Greenland who had convinced me they are the descendants of Robert Peary in one case and of Matthew Henson in the other.

"I thought that perhaps you might like to make contact with them," I said somewhat uncomfortably. "Have I upset your family by revealing information about Kali? I mean, if I have, I have certainly not done so intentionally."

"Our family just wondered what your motives are for making this thing public," he responded. "We are not pleased with all of this."

I reassured him that I meant no disrespect or harm to the family. When he indicated his desire to end the conversation, I asked him whether he thought that there were people in the American Peary family who might be willing to meet Kali, and if so, would he give me their names.

"Not interested," he said.

Hoping to elicit some sign of compassion, I offered to send some photographs of Kali and his family and asked whether someone might be willing at least to write to them. "They are a very lovely family," I said.

The caller then told me that one member of the Peary-Stafford family had been designated as "our representative" to handle all public information on Robert Peary and his memorabilia. "I'll give you his telephone number. You should call him," he said. He gave me the number and said good-bye. Before he could hang up, I quickly asked him if we could discuss the matter again. I emphasized that it had been Kali's lifelong dream to meet his American relatives.

"I don't know," he said, politely but coolly. "I will call you if I think we should talk."

I never heard from him again.

My first contact with the Peary family left me shaken and depressed. Amid all the excitement of my discovery, I had never considered the possibility that the Pearys might not welcome the news I was bringing them. Upon reflection, however, I came to realize that the Pearys' mistrust was understandable, if not fully excusable. There was, to begin with, the issue of "legitimacy." The Pearys were probably embarrassed by the fact that the admiral had fathered a child out of wedlock, perhaps believing that it tarnished his image and compromised his achievements. In addition, they might have suspected financial motives. Both Kali and Anaukaq were, technically speaking, Americans. Both were born on an American ship, the USS *Roosevelt*, to American fathers undertaking a mission in the service of their country. Robert E. Peary held the rank of commander in the U.S. Navy at the time, while Matthew Henson was officially listed as Peary's "valet," which was, in most cases, the highest naval rank then attainable by a black. Maybe, I thought, the Pearys suspected that Kali intended to lay claim to a share of the family inheritance or seek some other form of recompense. Although I couldn't be certain that such fears underlay their rejection of Kali, I knew that neither Kali nor I had ever considered asking the Pearys for anything but a warm and friendly welcome. I just needed to convince the Peary family that this was the case.

The Peary-Stafford family's designated "representative" was no less cold and guarded than the first person I had spoken with. I introduced myself, this time mentioning my work at Harvard in an effort to convey credibility. I told him I was calling at the suggestion of one of his relatives. He seemed to have been expecting to hear from me. He began by raising the same question I had encountered before: "Why are you bringing this out before the public now?"

I repeated my story to him.

He told me that his family already knew about Peary's Eskimo offspring and that his "Uncle Bob," the explorer's son, had met one of his relatives on a trip to Greenland in the 1920s. I told him that I found this rather odd because Kali had said that he'd never met any of his American relatives.

"Maybe," I suggested, "your uncle met Kali's brother Anaukaq who, the Eskimos say, was also Peary's son."

"Don't believe everything the Eskimos tell you," he responded brusquely.

I was surprised to learn that the American Pearys already knew something about the admiral's Amer-Eskimo progeny. But I was equally intrigued to learn that Robert Peary, Jr., was still alive. My quick calculations told me that he must be around eighty-three years old. The family representative confirmed this and informed me that Robert Jr. was currently living in Augusta, Maine.

Wouldn't it be great, I thought to myself, if Kali and Robert Jr., half brothers who had been separated throughout their lives, were at last brought together? I shared the thought of a brother-to-brother meeting with the family representative.

"I will speak to him about it," he promised, adding that he personally believed "such a meeting is out of the question. We're not interested."

I decided to press the issue. "Why is your family so opposed to meeting this kindly old man who does not have many years left and who simply wants to meet some of his American relatives? Why are you and your family reacting this way?"

"Dr. Counter, you don't understand," the family representative said. "Let me share a story with you." He proceeded to tell me a long story about a film on the North Pole discovery that had appeared on

American television some years ago, featuring Rod Steiger as Robert Peary and Richard Chamberlain as Frederick Cook. (He never mentioned Matthew Henson or who played his role.) "When we saw that Richard Chamberlain was playing the role of Cook, we knew the film was going to do our grandfather in," he said. The film had "totally distorted my grandfather's image and discredited his name," he continued, leaving his family "greatly disturbed." He then drew an analogy between the film and my own efforts to bring Kali and Anaukaq to the United States. While he understood that "these Eskimos would welcome a free ticket to America," he also believed that the publicity attending their return would tarnish the Peary family image.

When he finished his story, I told him in a conciliatory tone that I was sorry the television show had been so negative in its portrayal of his grandfather's achievements. "I am in no way trying to discredit that legacy," I assured him, "but to validate it. And I appeal to you and your family not to view me or Kali in the same light as this movie. I would simply like for you to see Kali as a human being who has a genuine desire to meet his American relatives before he dies. He has said that to me."

Apparently unmoved by my words, the family representative reaffirmed that the Peary-Staffords had no interest in meeting with Kali and his family. He again reminded me of the still-extant "supporters of Peary's adversary Frederick Cook, who liked this kind of information and who would use it as ammunition against Peary's credibility as the discoverer of the North Pole."

I made further appeals, but to no avail. No matter what I said, I could not break the link in his mind between my own motives and the machinations of those who sought to discredit Admiral Peary. Frustrated as I was, I became even more unsettled when the suggestion was made that Kali might not actually be Robert Peary's son, but rather the son of some other member of his expeditionary team. I was convinced that if the Pearys would only agree to meet the man, to see his face and listen to his story, any doubts they might have about his paternity would quickly be erased. Additional evidence could be found in the testimony of those older Eskimos who knew about the relationship between Peary and Ahlikahsingwah.

"Well," the family representative groaned, "we can't be sure of this or just what all went on up there."

"If you have such strong doubts about the validity of Kali Peary's claims, sir, we can easily settle this question beyond a shadow of a doubt with a relatively simple new blood test called a DNA fragmentation analysis—that is, if Kali and his half brother would agree to such a test."

"No," he answered. "Such a test would be demeaning for both men."

The family representative then fell back on another argument, claiming that Peary had been forced by local custom to engage in sexual relations with the indigenous women, including Ahlikahsingwah. "That was a condition of Peary's association with the Eskimo villagers who served his expeditionary interest. He had to have sex with the women before he could gain their confidence."

This contention was based on a long-standing myth about polar Eskimo culture, the notion that men routinely offered their wives to outsiders. This was not the case. Within the Eskimo community, men and women alike exchanged spouses with one another for reasons of fertility and, in some cases, pleasure. But non-Eskimo men who engaged in sex with Eskimo women usually exchanged Western material goods for favors. At times the women's husbands also derived some material benefit from such relationships, such as a gun or a hatchet or cooking utensils. Existing records of such liaisons further suggest that the women who consorted with outsiders, and especially with Westerners, were often criticized for their behavior by other members of the community.

Robert Peary's relationship with Kali's mother, Ahlikahsingwah, seems to have fit this pattern. Peary had known Ahlikahsingwah since she was a child and may have developed an intimate relationship with her when she was a teenager. Peary employed his mistress as his laundress and bodyservant and hired her husband, Peeahwahto, as a hunter, supplying him with a rifle. According to Kali, his mother subsequently fell into disrepute within the Eskimo community because of her relationship with Peary.

As my conversation with the Peary family representative came to a close, I asked him to find out whether any of his relatives felt differently from him about meeting Kali. I was especially interested in talking with Robert Peary, Jr., although I was also concerned about the emotional impact such a discussion might have on him. The spokesperson said he would pass along my request and even agreed to send me the names of some family members so that I could contact them myself. I suspected that his willingness to provide such information reflected his certainty that all the Pearys shared his views.

In the weeks that followed, I spoke with many more members of the Henson family, all of whom seemed delighted to learn of their Amer-Eskimo relatives. Like Cousin Olive, they wanted to send gifts to Greenland and to help in any way they could to bring about a reunion in the United States.

Meanwhile, I called various members of the Peary family and told them of my plans for another visit to northern Greenland. I wanted to know if I could take Kali some word or letter or anything that would indicate that his American relatives were now aware of him and that they cared about him. Some of those I contacted refused to discuss the matter, while others made it clear that they were not interested in communicating with Kali.

During the same period, I received a discouraging letter from someone claiming to be related to a member of one of Peary's early expeditionary teams. Hostile in tone, the letter stated baldly that I was off the mark in my efforts to "exalt" Henson and to "question" Peary. The writer accused me of using "bastardy" as a way of discrediting Peary.

A short time later, a letter from one of the Peary family members similarly charged me with exalting Henson at the expense of Peary. This second letter arrived soon after I gave a lecture at the Woods Hole Oceanographic Institution and Marine Biological Laboratories for scientists and local citizens. After the lecture, I was interviewed on a local radio program about the significance of Matthew Henson's contribution to Peary's Arctic successes. My comments had apparently been reported to the Peary-Staffords. The same letter once again tried to explain away Peary's sexual relations with Eskimos as cultural rituals in which he had reluctantly engaged in order to advance his nobler mission.

Despite such criticism, I still hoped to persuade the Pearys that they were wrong about me and, more important, wrong in refusing to get in touch with Kali. After learning that Robert Peary, Jr., had a son who lived with him in Augusta, Maine, I decided that I would broach the subject of a reunion with him. When I reached Robert Peary III by telephone, I found him pleasant and soft-spoken. He expressed the now familiar concern about the effects of media reports of Kali on his grandfather's image and reminded me that the designated Peary-Stafford representative spoke for him, too. Yet unlike the family representative, he seemed willing to consider my point of view and showed some sensitivity to what I was trying to do. Nevertheless, he was still opposed to any further publicity about the "so-called" Peary Eskimo offspring and unwilling to arrange a meeting between Kali and his father.

As I prepared to set out again for the Arctic, I wrestled with the question of what I would tell Kali. I knew that telling him the truth would hurt him deeply. Yet I could not conceive of lying to him either. I could certainly leave out parts of the story in good conscience. He did not need to know, for instance, that some of the Pearys had apparently known about him for years but had never seen any reason to contact him or even to acknowledge his existence. But I would have to tell him that I had spoken with some of his American relatives and that they had expressed no interest in meeting him, at least not in public. I would try to explain why they reacted as they did, and I would continue to hold out hope that they might eventually change their minds. Finally, if I could arrange for the Amer-Eskimo Hensons to visit the United States, I would give him the opportunity to accompany them so that he could at least visit the grave of his father. Beyond that, there was little that I could offer Kali other than the knowledge I had gained through my own research into the lives of Robert E. Peary and Matthew A. Henson, the fathers that he and his "cousin" Anaukaq had never known.

CHAPTER SIX

✳ ✳ ✳

Black and White Partners

Matthew Henson was born on August 8, 1866,[1] in Charles County, Maryland, the son of freeborn sharecroppers who worked on a large farm near what is today the town of Nanjemoy. When he was about four years old, his parents moved the family some thirty miles north to Washington, D.C., where jobs for blacks as servants and technical workers were available. Within a few years, however, both of his parents died, and Matthew and several of his siblings were taken in by an uncle who also resided in Washington.

In 1879, at the age of thirteen, Henson left school and went to Baltimore, hoping to land a job on one of the many ships leaving port. Throughout his young life he had been fascinated by stories of life at sea and had marveled at the men who worked the steamboats on the Potomac. He later told a biographer that he was fortunate enough to meet an elderly sea captain in Baltimore who was looking for a cabin boy to assist him. Given the job, Henson set out on voyages that would take him around the world in the years that followed. Bright, eager to learn, hardworking, and exceptionally strong for his age, he became "an able-bodied seaman" and sailed to such exotic venues as China, Japan, North Africa, and the Black Sea. During his years at sea he continued his education, studying geography, mathematics, history, the classics, and the Bible under the captain's tutelage. He also displayed a knack for learning foreign languages, a talent that would serve him well throughout his life.

When the captain of the ship died in 1884, Henson, now eighteen years old, gave up seafaring for a time and returned to the United States. During the next two years he traveled up and down the eastern seaboard, taking on whatever odd jobs might be available to a young black man in need of work.

In 1886, Henson returned to Washington, D.C., and moved in with his sister Eliza and her family at 3003 West P Street in the northwest section of the city. Soon thereafter he found a job as a clerk at F. W. Stinemetz & Sons, an exclusive capital furrier. Charged with responsibility for storing furs, recording sales, and keeping an accurate inventory of goods in the warehouse, Henson quickly earned the trust and respect of his employers.

Yet while he continued to work diligently at his job, he was in fact biding his time. Already a seasoned world traveler, he longed to resume the adventurous life he had known. All that was needed was the right opportunity.

The man who would afford Matthew Henson that opportunity had led a far different life. Born on May 6, 1856, in Cresson, Pennsylvania, Robert Edwin Peary was the only child of Mary Webster Wiley and Charles Nutter Peary. Following his father's death in 1858, Peary and his mother had moved back to the family's home state of Maine. It was there that Robert Peary was raised and educated.

A bright and physically active child, Peary performed superbly in school and soon developed a reputation as a dedicated achiever. His academic successes eventually earned him a scholarship to Bowdoin College in Brunswick, Maine, where he majored in civil engineering and also participated in a variety of sports and social organizations. He graduated from Bowdoin second in his class, with a Phi Beta Kappa key, in 1877.

No matter how much he accomplished, however, Peary always seemed to aspire to more. From an early age he had made it clear that he intended to make his mother proud of him. He wanted to achieve great things. He wanted the world to know his name.

Grand as his ambitions were, Peary's professional career began modestly enough. After graduating from Bowdoin he moved to

Washington, D.C., to work for the U.S. Coast and Geodetic Survey Office. In the next two years he came to be regarded as one of that agency's best draftsmen, enabling him to become an officer with the rank of lieutenant in the U.S. Navy Corps of Civil Engineers. Both of these jobs gave him access to the resources of the government's civil engineering offices and the opportunity to travel widely.

It is difficult to say just when Peary developed an interest in Arctic exploration. Some believe that it was a long-standing interest that can be traced back to a childhood fascination with the adventurous accounts of the Arctic explorer Elisha Kent Kane. Others contend that it was Baron Nordenskjold's book on Greenland that initially aroused Peary's curiosity about the far north. In any case, the first clear expression of Peary's interest in the Arctic occurred in 1886, when he requested and received a six-month leave of absence from the U.S. Navy to reconnoiter the Greenland ice cap east of Disco Bay.

That summer Peary sailed to an area of Greenland some two hundred miles north of the Arctic Circle to determine the feasibility of reaching the North Pole by an overland route. Braving constant danger and surviving a series of narrow escapes, Peary and a Danish assistant made the first recorded journey to the interior ice cap of lower Arctic Greenland, reaching a record altitude of 7,525 feet above sea level on July 15, 1886.

Upon returning to Washington, Peary formally presented his findings, which included excellent maps of the Greenlandic interior. Praised by scientists and laypeople alike, these reports gave him his first taste of popular recognition. Invitations to lecture poured in and he was soon elected to the American Society for the Advancement of Science.

Although the success of the Greenland expedition reinforced Peary's belief that he could reach the North Pole, his naval obligations forced him to postpone his quest indefinitely. During the next two years he worked on several inland waterways projects, performing admirably in each instance. Then, in 1888, he was assigned to an ambitious new government-sponsored project in Nicaragua. The project involved a study of the feasibility of cutting a shipping canal through lower Nicaragua that would connect the Atlantic and Pacific oceans. Mindful of the strategic and commercial significance of the venture, Peary regarded the assignment as another opportunity to win the renown he so eagerly sought.

In preparation for his departure, Peary took a collection of valuable furs he had acquired in Greenland to Stinemetz & Sons for storage. It was not the first time he had visited the firm. On several previous occasions he had brought other Arctic furs, which he eventually planned to sell. Each time, in addition to meeting with the proprietors, he had encountered a young black man who seemed to share his passion for exploration. Intelligent, articulate, forthright, and courteous, Matthew Henson had made a strong impression on Lieutenant Peary. The two men had exchanged travel stories and perhaps talked of future journeys. Now, as Peary readied himself for his new mission, he decided to offer Henson a job as his "personal assistant" in Nicaragua. Henson accepted.

Before hiring Henson, Peary had had little contact with black Americans. Like most European Americans of his time, he seems to have accepted common shibboleths about the "natural superiority" of the white race, views that found backing in much of the "scientific" literature of the period. Yet the state where he grew up had few African-American residents and no tradition of legalized racial slavery. Peary's own understanding of the biological basis of racial difference is reflected in several of his writings. For example, in 1885 he wrote, "If colonization is to be a success in Polar regions, let white men take with them native wives, then from that union may spring a race combining the hardiness of the mothers with the intelligence and energy of the fathers."[2] Another writing refers to "the mixed race in South Greenland, which, in spite of the fostering care of the Danish Government, is still like most half-breed human products, inferior to the original stock."[3]

Some of Peary's other writings, however, suggest that he believed that members of all races were human beings first and foremost. His upbringing had taught him to be charitable to his less-fortunate, though "inferior," brethren. In a culture steeped in racism, Peary's racial attitudes might thus be described as sympathetic, even "liberal," if not truly enlightened.

Whatever Peary may have thought about blacks in general, it is clear that he developed a sincere respect for Matthew Henson. During the year the two men worked together in the steamy jungles of Nicaragua, Henson's multiple skills as a mechanic, carpenter, and navigator proved invaluable. Peary later lauded his assistant for his "intelligence, faithfulness, and better than average pluck and endurance"[4]—qualities usually attributed at the time exclusively to white males. Henson reciprocated by praising Lieutenant Peary's fairness, noting that "it was with the instinct of my race that I recognized in him the qualities that made me willing to engage myself in his service."[5]

Although Peary and Henson went their separate ways after returning to the United States, their shared experience in Nicaragua forged a bond between them that would not be easily broken. In the context of the time, their relationship was as close to a friendship as one could imagine between a white boss and a black assistant. They also complemented each other. In Henson, Peary had found an experienced, multitalented aide willing to travel anywhere in support of his ventures. In Peary, Henson had found a well-disposed white sponsor, without whom he had no hope of satisfying his own thirst for travel. Of more immediate and practical importance to Henson, Peary also represented a potential source of continued employment. It was with this in mind that Henson wrote to the lieutenant soon after arriving back in Washington.

> *West Washington D.C.*
> *Aug 1st 1888*
> *Mr. R.E. Peary*
>
> *Dear Sir*
>   *I write you these few lines hoping that they may find you enjoying the best of health and that you are having a good time. I arrived in Washington all safe last Saturday at 11/30.*
>   *Mr Peary please let me know when you are going back to Nicaragua, for I will be pleased to go with you again. I have not had any work yet. I now come to a close hoping to hear from you soon.*
>
> *M.A. Henson*
> *#3003 P Street. Georgetown D.C.*[6]

Still unable to find work, Henson wrote Peary a second letter some months later.

Dear Sir

I write you a few lines to let you know that all is well at this present time. As I had written to you before I am not doing any work yet and if you want me to go back with you when you go back to Nicaragua I will be pleased to go with you indeed sir. And if you want me I would like to know as soon as I can. And I would like to stay for a year or more or as long as you stay, if I pleased you with my work when I was with you before.

And I hope to hear from you soon.

From a friend,
Matthew Henson

When he did not hear anything from Peary, Henson returned to his old job at Stinemetz. Then, in early 1889, Peary wrote to ask if Henson would be interested in working as a "messenger" at the League Island Navy Yard in Philadelphia, where Peary had recently been reassigned. Though it was not the opportunity Henson had hoped for, he quickly accepted. What he did not yet know was that Peary had already begun making plans for his first polar expedition and intended to take Henson along.

Peary moved to Philadelphia soon after his marriage in 1889 to Josephine Diebitsch, the daughter of a prominent Washington professor. Henson followed in the spring of 1890, taking up residence at 1524 Burton Street in the heart of the city's black community.

Philadelphia was widely regarded at the time as one of the better American cities for blacks. For much of the nineteenth century it had boasted the largest freeborn black population in the United States. Until they were displaced through the organized efforts of Irish and German immigrants, blacks dominated many of the city's trades, including carpentry, masonry, and blacksmithing. As a result, many black Philadelphians had achieved a level of economic prosperity and social respectability uncommon, if not altogether unknown, among African Americans elsewhere.

Yet as young Matthew Henson discovered, gaining entry into the city's black community was not easy. Despite his wide-ranging experience and respectable position as an employee at the navy yard, he was still considered an outsider. He had little in the way of formal education and did not belong to any of the trade organizations that served as the main source of employment for many black men.

Hoping to gain acceptance and get ahead, Henson joined a local church and began attending Sunday outings in the influential Juniper Street area of the black community. It was on one such occasion in late September 1890 that he met Eva Helen Flint, a twenty-two-year-old sales assistant in a local store. Henson was charmed by the attractive Eva, and she by him. He began to frequent the store where she worked, bringing her small gifts to show his affection. From time to time, he would see her strolling through the park on Sunday evenings with the other young African-American Philadelphia ladies. Eva was a fabulous dresser whose passion for fine clothes complemented Henson's own dapper style. The two seemed made for each other. After a month of secret meetings, Eva invited Matthew home to meet her family.

The Flints were a large, educated, and conservative family that had moved to Philadelphia from Washington, D.C., to work in the thriving trades. Although inclined to be skeptical of a young man pursuing the hand of any of the Flint women, they were thoroughly charmed by the twenty-three-year-old Henson. The men, especially, were captivated by his tales of travel and adventure. In addition, his position at the navy yard was considered auspicious, since government jobs often carried pensions that could guarantee a family a modicum of economic security for a lifetime.

Matthew and Eva courted for several months, seeing each other as often as possible after work and on Sundays. By now, they were very much in love and seriously considering marriage. But Henson wanted to wait until he had saved enough money to purchase a home, ideally in the Juniper Street community. He also worried about his ability to support Eva's love of material things. Perhaps most important, his desire to settle down with Eva conflicted with his lust for adventure, and he knew that it would be difficult to reconcile these two impulses. Eva, on the other hand, was convinced she had found the right man and was eager to get away from the rigid control of her parents and brothers at home.

The issue of marriage was still unresolved when Robert Peary summoned Henson to his office in late February 1891. Peary had just received a letter from the navy granting him a long-sought leave of absence for the purpose of exploring northwest Greenland. He asked

Henson to come along as his personal assistant. Flattered by the invitation, Henson immediately accepted. This was, after all, the opportunity Henson had been waiting for, a chance not only to resume his travels but to distinguish himself and his race in the process. Perhaps no less than Peary, Henson sought recognition, although in Henson's case the goal was not so much fame as social acceptance. He had always admired the educated, successful blacks of Washington and Philadelphia but never felt their equal. Now, given the opportunity to go where no one, black or white, had ever gone before, he could surpass them in achievement. At the same time, he could disprove once and for all the widely held theory that black-skinned people could not survive in the Arctic, thus providing further proof of racial equality.

Acceptance of Peary's offer did present certain problems, however. In the first place, Henson could not obtain a leave of absence from his own position at the navy yard. If he gave up his job, there was no guarantee that he would get it back upon his return. In addition, he would have to give up his regular, fifteen-dollar weekly wage in exchange for an annual salary of fifty dollars. This meant that if he did get married, it would be difficult to support his wife back home.

Not surprisingly, Eva tried to persuade Henson to decline Peary's offer and stay on at the navy yard. Henson in turn tried to convince Eva that if he made the journey with this ambitious young white man, not only would he achieve personal fame, but Peary would take care of him in the future, as well. Such were the arrangements that white men had with their loyal "colored" assistants in those days. Eva was skeptical; her family, even more so. They urged Eva to refuse to marry Henson, at least until he returned.

But Eva and Matthew were in love, and they both thought it was time to make a decision. Henson consulted Peary and his wife, Josephine, and they were encouraging. Peary felt that marriage would give Henson stability, although he was privately concerned about its impact on Henson's flexibility. Already, it seems, he had special plans for young Henson on future Arctic expeditions.

On April 13, 1891, Eva Helen Flint and Matthew Alexander Henson filled out an application for marriage before the clerk of Orphan's

Court in Philadelphia. Three days later they were joined in marriage in the presence of a few friends and family members. During the next two months they lived with Eva's family, drawing up plans for the future and awaiting the departure of Peary's expedition.

In early June, Henson bade his wife farewell and traveled to Brooklyn, where he boarded the barkentine *Kite* and assumed his duties as Peary's assistant. In the late afternoon of June 6, 1891, the *Kite* set sail from Brooklyn. Throngs of well-wishers stood on the docks, waving white handkerchiefs, as the ship moved out to sea via the East River, en route to northwest Greenland.

In addition to Henson, the hand-picked expeditionary team included four other assistants, each selected on the basis of his "mental and physical well-being" as well as for the particular skill he offered: Frederick A. Cook, an affable young physician from New York; Eivind Astrup, an experienced Norwegian Arctic traveler; Langdon Gibson, an ornithologist from Long Island; and John M. Verhoeff, a mineralogist from Kentucky. Also among the passengers was Josephine Peary. As far as the American public was concerned, the presence of "the woman," as Mrs. Peary was commonly referred to, was no less unusual than that of Peary's black "manservant."

Henson, of course, was no mere servant. In addition to his skills as a carpenter and mechanic, he had more experience at sea than any other member of the expedition, including naval lieutenant Peary. He loved sailing in the open sea, and the 280-ton *Kite*, with its vast white sails and seven-knot steam engines, was his kind of ship. During the seven-week voyage, Henson spent most of his time doing inventories of the expedition's equipment and supplies, preparing for the landing.

After struggling through the frozen waters of Disco Bay and Baffin Bay, the *Kite* reached Wolstenholm Sound near the area of Itilleq. On July 26, Peary's party went ashore with pickaxes, shovels, and lumber and began to set up camp at the base of red-brown cliffs near the mouth of an inlet. The burden of work fell chiefly to Henson, whose carpentry skills were called upon to build a spacious two-room house that would serve as the expedition's headquarters. Henson and the other assistants labored long and hard to erect the large rectangular dwelling before the winter set in. Incapacitated by a

broken ankle, Peary could only observe and supervise the construction of "Red Cliff House," as it came to be called.

Completion of construction happened to coincide with Matthew
Henson's twenty-fifth birthday on August 8. In commemoration of
both events, Josephine Peary threw a party at which Henson was the
guest of honor. For his present, he was permitted to select the dinner
menu from their stores and to eat as much as he wished. In *A Negro
Explorer at the North Pole*, Henson later described the occasion as
among the most memorable of his life.

The group spent the fall and winter acclimating themselves to
Arctic conditions and exploring the surrounding area, in the vicinity
of present-day Thule. In the spring of 1892, Peary and his men,
including Henson, set out to accomplish the principal mission of the
expedition, a crossing of northern Greenland from west to east.
Though the ostensible goal was to locate the northernmost terminus
of Greenland, in actuality Peary wanted to determine the shortest
route to the North Pole.

Josephine Peary remained behind at Red Cliff House, as did John
Verhoeff, whom Robert Peary considered to be insubordinate and
undependable in the field. Verhoeff, in fact, had been trouble from
the start, not only for Peary but also for Matthew Henson. A Ken-
tuckian unaccustomed to interacting with blacks as equals, he resented the respect and relatively impartial treatment that the Pearys
accorded their "manservant." He repeatedly harassed Henson, calling him by the most vulgar of American racial epithets and occasionally threatening him.[7] Friction between the two men came to a head
after Henson hurt his heel during the early stages of the trans-
Greenland crossing and was forced to return to Red Cliff. At one
point Verhoeff attacked Henson for resting his injured foot on a table.
On another occasion Verhoeff became infuriated when he discovered, after oversleeping, that Henson had taken over one of his
duties. So frequently did the two men clash that the otherwise placid
Mrs. Peary eventually ordered them out of the house to "fight it out."

In the meantime Gibson and Cook also returned to the camp,
leaving only Peary and Astrup to complete the crossing. Both Gibson
and Cook seemed to share Verhoeff's sentiments about Henson, even
if they didn't imitate his tactics. When Henson asserted in their

presence that black Americans should have the right to vote, for example, they were quick to remind him of his proper "place." Similarly, they joined Verhoeff in deriding Henson's efforts to befriend the Eskimos and learn their skills.

None of this deterred Henson from standing up for his beliefs, however, or from learning as much as he could about Polar Eskimo culture. He hunted with the Eskimos, visited their villages, and eventually became the only member of any of Peary's expeditionary teams to master their language.

By contrast, the other men at Red Cliff seemed to have no interest in the Eskimos beyond taking advantage of the women. According to Verhoeff's diary, Cook and Gibson regularly flirted with the Eskimo women, at times engaging in the practice of "cooney," which involved "putting their faces to the women's faces and smelling them." This intimate behavior apparently offended the local Eskimo men, some to the point of threatening violence. On one occasion Cook and Gibson cited such a threat to convince Henson to take Mrs. Peary farther inland for a few days to a safe, remote location that Lieutenant Peary had arranged for her in case of danger. While she and Henson were away, Cook and Gibson gave a "dinner party" for four Eskimo women, during which they engaged in "cooney," according to Verhoeff, who claimed he was a reluctant participant in the dinner and that he did not take part in the other activities.[8]

Yet in spite of his differences with the other men, Henson enjoyed life in the Arctic. In many ways, he was freer and more independent there than his fellow African Americans were back home. So unusual was Henson's position in Peary's Arctic work that T. S. Dedrick, a white assistant on a later expedition, felt compelled to voice his outrage at Henson's "freedom and insolence" and Peary's apparent "indifference" to it.[9]

The truth of the matter was that Henson had time and again proven his worth and earned Peary's admiration and respect. Henson even managed to win over Frederick Cook, who would later become Peary's archenemy. After their return to the United States, Cook invited Henson to live in his mother's New York apartment while an eye injury suffered during the expedition healed satisfactorily. Ironically, Henson's own chief nemesis, John Verhoeff, never made it back from

Greenland. He was said to have been killed in an accident while exploring a glacier just a few days before *Kite* set sail for America.

Henson spent the better part of the next eighteen years of his life exploring the Arctic with Robert Peary. He returned to Greenland with Peary in 1893 and remained there with him for another year after the other members of the team abandoned the mission and went home. He marched across the entire ice cap of Greenland with Peary and Hugh J. Lee in 1895 and joined in the discovery of the island's northern terminus. He also participated in the 1896 and 1897 expeditions, when Peary removed some of the Eskimos' sacred meteorites and only source of metal, which he later sold to the American Museum of Natural History in New York to finance his subsequent explorations.

Henson also helped raise money between expeditions by donning his Eskimo regalia and accompanying Peary on cross-country lecture tours. He even toured the United States alone in a play of Peary's creation titled *Under the Polar Star.* This latter work proved so physically and psychologically exhausting that on November 7, 1896, Henson wrote Peary complaining of the difficulty in managing the dogs onstage and of poor health. "Mr. Peary," he pleaded, ". . . I don't think that I could stand going around this winter, I have been sick ever since I have been in Chicago and now I am hardly able to get to the theater—but I have to do it, or walk home. Will you please let me know if you can get me a place at the American Museum [of Natural History], for I am afraid that I have to give this job up."

Understandably, Henson's travels put a severe strain on his marriage. Unwilling to play the classic role of the sailor's wife, Eva Henson refused to tolerate her husband's long absences. Henson tried to mollify her, chiefly by requesting more money from Peary "to send home to my wife." But he had no intention of changing his ways. Having established himself as a permanent member of Peary's expeditionary team and, in the process, having acquired a degree of personal fame, he was determined to share in the achievement of Peary's ultimate goal—the conquest of the North Pole. To put it another way, his love for his work eventually surpassed his love of his domestic life in Philadelphia and, apparently, Eva. By 1896, the couple was on the verge of a divorce.

A terse letter that Eva wrote to Robert Peary in June 1896 reflects the lack of communication between Henson and his wife as well as Eva's growing impatience.

Dear Sir,
   I hear you are going to Greenland again. Will you please inform me when you expect to go and how long you are going to stay and oblige yours truly

Mrs. Eva Henson
1240 Rodman St,
Phila. Pa

p.s.
as Matt says he is going with you again.

Henson later accused his wife of infidelity in his absence. She and her family in turn accused him of negligence. The relationship became so bitter that Henson wrote Peary on April 5, 1897, saying that he would like to stay in Greenland "for five or ten years . . . anything to get away from this town."

Peary and Henson returned to Greenland that summer to collect the last and largest of the Inuit's sacred meteorites, which the Eskimos called "The Woman." When they returned to the United States in October 1897, Eva requested a divorce. Henson agreed, and their relationship ended that year.

The years between 1897 and 1902 were the toughest for Henson and Peary. Determined to reach the North Pole, they remained in the Arctic for four uninterrupted years of exploration. During this time they developed the first map of the northern boundaries of Greenland and for the first time traveled out on the Arctic Ocean, reaching a record 84° 17′ north. But they did not attain their goal.

In the summer of 1900, Josephine Peary made an unplanned visit to the Thule area aboard a relief ship. To her utter surprise, she found Ahlikahsingwah with a part-white baby that was said to be Peary's. It was probably Anaukaq-Hammy, Robert Peary's first-born Amer-Eskimo son. A woman of great stoicism and devotion to her husband, Josephine accepted the painful reality of the child and kept her marriage intact.

From 1902, when the expedition returned to the United States until 1905, Matthew Henson worked at a variety of odd jobs, first as a porter on the New York Central Railroad and later as a janitor in New York City. Although the cross-country train rides appealed to his love of travel, and his work in New York kept him close to friends, Henson could find little satisfaction in the mundane routines of workaday life. At one point he did seek a job with his old employer, the American Museum of Natural History, but he was unsuccessful. He could only find work as a janitor.

In the summer of 1905 Henson and now "Commander" Peary returned to the Arctic, where they undertook preparations for their historic spring 1906 assault on the North Pole. Though they managed to get as far as 87° 6' north, a new record, delays at open water and dwindling food supplies forced them to turn back about one hundred miles short of their goal. The failure of the expedition crushed both men. Peary, at age fifty, and Henson, forty, knew they were getting too old for the rigors of Arctic work. They also knew that the public was becoming less interested in and tolerant of their misadventures.

Returning to New York in the late fall of 1906 on the badly damaged *Roosevelt*, Peary and Henson agreed to make one final attempt to reach the North Pole the following year. Peary then set out to raise money for the expedition while Henson remained on the docked ship, directing repairs and readying equipment. It was during this period that Henson proposed to Lucy Jane Ross, whom he had been courting for two years while he was a tenant at her mother's house on West 35th Street. Not long before the *Roosevelt* set sail for the last time, Matthew and Lucy were married in a quiet ceremony, with only Lucy's mother and a few friends present.

On June 21, 1908, Henson wrote to Peary.

> *Mr. Peary, Dear Sir*
>   *I am going to ask you for a raise in wages as I think that 40 dollars a month is rather small to maintain a family. I have never asked you before as I did not have any encumbrance. I would like to have sixty dollars a month if that is not asking too much of you.*
>
> *Respt.*
> *M.A. Henson*

Peary split the difference and agreed to pay Henson "$50 a month and keep." In the interest of the greater mission, Henson accepted.

CHAPTER SEVEN

✳ ✳ ✳

The Struggle for the Pole

On July 6, 1908, after a year's delay for repairs to the USS *Roosevelt* and amid much fanfare, Henson and Peary departed New York for a final attempt at the Pole. President Theodore Roosevelt was on hand to see the men off, declaring that if any man could succeed, it would be Peary. This time Peary had his finest hand-picked team: Dr. John W. Goodsell, a physician from Pennsylvania; Donald B. MacMillan, an instructor of mathematics and physical training at Worcester Academy in Massachusetts; Ross G. Marvin, professor of engineering at Cornell University; George Borup, a recent graduate of Groton and Yale and an outstanding athlete; Robert Bartlett, the ship's captain; and Matthew Henson, the most experienced Arctic explorer in the group other than Peary.

By the first week of August the expedition had reached Etah, where they took on Eskimo helpers and collected enough coal and freshly killed seal, walrus, and narwhal to last through the winter. The *Roosevelt* then headed farther north, struggling against the barriers of Kennedy and Robeson channels like a modern icebreaker, finally reaching its destination—Cape Sheridan on the northernmost tip of Ellesmere Island, Canada—on September 5, 1908. There the expeditionary team disembarked and prepared for the relay assault on the Pole. Henson and the other men were busy all winter, hunting for musk-ox, deer, and arctic hare, and readying the equipment for the journey north. Team member Donald B. MacMillan would later say that Henson, "with years of experience equal to that of Peary himself, was indispensable to Peary and of more real value than the combined services of all four white men. . . . He made all the sledges, he made all the camp equipment, he talked the language like a native."[1]

On February 18, 1909, Henson, accompanied by a group of Eskimos and laden with supplies, left the *Roosevelt* for Cape Columbia, which had been selected as the jumping-off point for the strike at the Pole. When they reached the tip of the cape, Henson and the Eskimos set about building several large igloos that would serve as a base camp. Then they waited until the entire team could be assembled at "Crane City," as the encampment was named.

On the morning of March 1, 1909, Peary ordered Henson and three Eskimos to take the lead in breaking the trail north to the Pole. For an entire month the Americans and their Eskimo assistants acted as relay teams, setting up caches of supplies along the trail that would support the journey to the Pole and back. Henson and Bartlett did most of the trailbreaking, with Peary's and Marvin's sled teams following.

The American members of the team knew that they could not all accompany Peary to the Pole. Eventually someone would be selected to make the final leg of the journey, and the choice would be made by Peary alone. Donald MacMillan would later say that Peary had remarked to him before they even left the ship that "Henson must go all the way. I can't make it without him."[2]

There were, of course, a variety of considerations weighing in Henson's favor, beginning with his uncommon skills and long experience as an Arctic explorer. For twenty years he had used his talents to support Peary's ventures, proving his loyalty time and again. He knew Peary better, perhaps, than any man living: his likes and his dislikes, his virtues as well as his idiosyncrasies. He also shared one of Peary's most intimate secrets, knowledge of the children Peary had fathered with the Eskimo woman Ahlikahsingwah. Henson and Peary undoubtedly saw their Amer-Eskimo sons when they returned to Etah in 1908, but Henson never breathed a word of this in public, then or ever.

No matter how much he may have deserved the honor of sharing in the discovery of the North Pole, however, Henson himself did not count on it. He remembered that on the historic march across Greenland in 1895, when he had literally saved the lives of Peary and Hugh Lee, Peary had promised both men that they would be with him if he ever reached the Pole. Now there was no Lee, only Henson. But as Henson well knew, even if Peary still intended to keep that pledge, any decision was subject to change out on the treacherous and unforgiving polar ice. Injury, illness, anxiety, or a dozen other things could force a complete rearrangement of even the best-laid plans.

MacMillan and Goodsell were the first to turn back, after ferrying supplies to 84° 29'. MacMillan most likely would have been permitted to travel farther north, but he had injured his heel. Borup and his Eskimo assistants took the next leg, to 85° 23', then returned to the ship behind MacMillan and Goodsell.

The ranks of the expeditionary team were thinned further on March 27, when Peary ordered Marvin back after reaching 86° 30' north. At that moment, Henson later recalled, his "heart stopped palpitating, I breathed easier, and my mind was relieved. It was not my turn yet, I was to continue onward and there only remained one person between me and the Pole—the Captain [Bartlett]." In keeping with his reputation for being a gentleman, Henson "went over to Marvin's igloo to bid him good-by." According to Henson, "In his quiet, earnest manner, he [Marvin] advised me to keep on, and hoped for our success; he congratulated me and we gave each other the strong fraternal grip of our honored fraternity and we confidently expected to see each other again at the ship."[3]

Unfortunately, the anticipated reunion would never take place. Marvin's two Eskimo companions, Kudlooktoo and "Harrigan" (a nickname given Inighito by Peary's group because of his frequent attempts to sing the popular song of the same name), returned to the ship without Marvin, saying that he had fallen through thin ice and drowned out on the Arctic Ocean. Henson, the only man aboard the ship who could speak their language well enough to interrogate them, believed their plausible story. Some years later, however, it was learned during a confession at a Christian confirmation that Marvin had been killed on the return march when he apparently became emotionally distressed after suffering a seriously frostbitten foot and threatened Kudlooktoo and Harrigan for not carrying him on the sled.

The version of the story told among the Polar Eskimos today is that Marvin treated their people brutally and even tried to get Harrigan, the younger of his two companions, to leave Kudlooktoo behind on the ice when their food ran low. Rather than leave his fellow Eskimo out to die, Harrigan shot and killed Marvin, and the two men buried his body under the snow and ice. It is ironic that both Peary and Henson (who knew the tribe even better) had always described the Polar Eskimos as an innocent, childlike people who were incapable of violence. Yet as early as their first expedition in 1891, they had encountered the threat of violence from some of the natives. It is even more ironic that the only other violent incident recorded on the entire North Pole expedition of 1909 occurred aboard ship during the tense months they wintered in Cape Sheridan, waiting for the spring journey to the Pole. This incident involved Harrigan, who was severely beaten by one of the more irascible members of Peary's crew who had tired of his "practical jokes." Harrigan protested this physical assault to Peary, but he and his men laughed the matter off and gave the angered Eskimo a cloth shirt to calm him down and make him forget the incident. Apparently, he did not forget about it. He had learned his violence well from the *kahdonah*.

Bartlett broke camp on March 27, and Henson followed about an hour later. After six days of "marches" over treacherous ice, each involving up to fourteen hours of travel from start to rest, the group reached 87° 46′ 49″ north. It was at this latitude, on April 1, that Henson learned for certain that he had gotten the call. Peary ordered Bartlett back to the ship, leaving Henson as the only other American on the final leg of the historic journey. Recalling the occasion, Henson wrote: "I knew at this time that he was to go back, and that I was to continue, so I had no misgivings and neither had he."[4] Bartlett would later say, however, "I don't deny that it would have been a great thrill to have stood at the peak of our globe. . . . It was a bitter disappointment. I don't know, perhaps I cried a little. But . . . Henson was a better dog driver than I."[5] As a kind of consolation prize, Peary let Bartlett travel on five or six miles to 88° north, putting him farther north than any other European explorer had traveled. Peary later explained his decision by saying that "in view of the noble work of Great Britain in artic exploration, a British subject [Bartlett was a Canadian from Nova Scotia] should, next to an American, be able to say that he had stood nearest the Pole."[6] Henson recollected that "Captain Bartlett was glad to turn back when he did. He frankly told me several times that he had little expectation of ever returning alive."[7]

Under pressure to defend his choice of Henson, Peary later wrote that "Henson was the best man I had with me for this kind of work, with the exception of the Eskimos." At the same time, however, he undercut that explanation by asserting that "Henson . . . would not have been so competent as the white members of the expedition in getting himself and his party back to land" because "he had not as a racial inheritance, the daring and initiative of Bartlett or Marvin, MacMillan or Borup. . . . I owed it to him not to subject him to the dangers and responsibilities which he was temperamentally unfit to face."[8]

What prompted Peary to offer such a fundamentally racist rationale for his decision? Did Peary really believe that the man who had spent close to twenty years traveling around the Arctic with him could not find his way back to land—the man who had brought him home safely so many times before? And what about the Eskimos? Did their "racial inheritance" preclude them, too, from following the trail back home on their own?

Perhaps Peary simply intended to mollify those critics who derided his choice of a black man as codiscoverer of the North Pole. Some have speculated that an editor or ghostwriter inserted the statement to make Peary's decision more palatable to the reading public. Still others have suggested that the reason Peary chose Henson in the first place was because he knew a black man would never be accorded equal recognition for discovery of the North Pole. The implicit, though glaring, racism of his subsequent explanation was thus consistent with his intentions.[9]

Whatever one may conclude about Peary's rationale for his decision, his reasons at the time were clear to every man on the expedition, including the Eskimos. As MacMillan, who later became a famous Arctic explorer in his own right, wrote in a 1920 article for *National Geographic:* "And the Negro? . . . With years of experience equal to that of Peary himself . . . clean, full of grit, he went to the Pole with Peary because he was easily the most efficient of all Peary's assistants."[10]

After Bartlett and his Eskimo team turned back, Henson, Peary, and four Eskimos—Ootah, Seegloo, Egingwah, and Ooqueah— were all left alone on the frozen Arctic Ocean, more than three hundred miles from land and more than one hundred miles from the Pole. For the next five days they raced toward their goal, rarely sleeping, and stopping only long enough for Peary to take readings on his chronometer-watch and sextant and to make depth soundings through the Arctic ice. His calculations confirmed those of Henson who, knowing the distance and direction they had to travel and the average distance covered per march, judged from dead reckoning that they were heading in a straight line toward the Pole.

The almost reckless pace of the final thrust toward the Pole was dictated as much by fear as by anticipation. The men knew that they could freeze to death, that they could fall through the thin ice at any moment and drown or die of hypothermia. Perhaps most terrifying of all, they faced the possibility that a large lane of water would open like a river and leave them stranded on the other side to starve to death.

What happened during the last few days is a matter of some dispute. Peary reported that it was he who broke trail and reached the Pole first. Yet after the expedition returned to the United States, Henson said that it was he, Ootah, and Seegloo who first reached the point they later determined to be the North Pole. In fact, Henson maintained that he reached the Pole some forty-five minutes ahead of Peary after inadvertently disobeying the commander's orders to stop short of what they judged to be the actual spot. There he was to wait so that Peary could travel on alone and lay claim to the honor of being the first person to stand at the North Pole.

According to Henson, Peary became so angry with him for denying him this long-awaited privilege that he refused to speak to him all the way back to the ship. "It was my boy Ootah who disclosed to me that Peary was to leave me behind in the final few miles of the Pole," Henson recalled, and with Egingwah he witnessed "the disappointment of Commander Peary when a few miles from camp, his observations told the lieutenant that he had overstepped and gone past the Pole, which we had reached the night before. Our camp itself was practically situated at the 'top of the earth.' For the crime of being present when the Pole was reached Commander Peary has ignored me ever since. . . . It nearly broke my heart on the return journey from the Pole that he would rise in the morning and slip away on the homeward trail without rapping on the tent for me as was the established custom. . . . On board ship, he addressed me a very few times. When we left the ship he did not speak. I wrote him twice and sent him a telegram, but received no reply from him."[11]

After studying the personality of both men from documents spanning some fifty years, I would not be surprised if the aggressive and self-assured Henson deliberately charged ahead to beat his old friend and boss to the Pole. Henson might well have reasoned that since he and Peary lived in separate worlds back home anyway, why should he not go for the glory that would be known only among his race back in the segregated America of 1909? After all, this was clearly their last polar expedition. Moreover, at that moment—and for the first time in their twenty-three-year relationship—they were equals. It was no longer them against the world. It was man to man. Peary was crippled and weak. He had lost all but two of his toes to severe frostbite some years earlier and found walking very difficult, especially on the jagged ice trail. He later admitted, in fact, that he had traveled the last hundred miles of the expedition on a sled driven by his Eskimo assistants. Henson, on the other hand, traveled on foot with the Eskimos all the way to the Pole, driving the sled with all the scientific equipment. Ironically, while one of the prevailing "scientific" theories of that period held that dark-skinned people could not tolerate the Arctic climate and conditions, Henson never suffered a permanent injury in all his years in the Arctic.

While we may never know exactly what happened in those last days, we do know that two Americans, one black and the other white, held the United States ensign at the top of our planet long before anyone else or any other nation. And in the minds of African Americans, at least, Matthew Henson was the "Co-Discoverer of the North Pole."

* * *

It was a sad moment for the Eskimos when they learned that Henson and Peary would leave Greenland, never to return. Ootah later told Danish explorer Peter Freuchen:

> "If it had not been for Mahri-Pahluk, Peary might have been quite another man. Because as both of them came from far away white man's country, there were so many things they did not understand.
>
> "Mahri-Pahluk was the only man from Peeuree's land who could learn to talk our language without using his tongue like a baby. If a strange man walks during the winter when everything is dark and some meet him, and ask who is there, the American will always answer so one is glad it is dark—because it is difficult not to laugh. But Mahri-Pahluk could talk like a full-grown, intelligent person. Besides, Mahri-Pahluk showed all his days that he did not look down upon people from up here. Therefore, he wanted to learn our ways and he sure did. Nobody has ever driven dogs better than he has. And not only swing the whip . . . whenever the sled broke down, he could fix it like any of us. He could repair the harness or make new ones—and none has ever made a snowhouse [igloo] faster and better and bigger than him.
>
> "But Mahri-Pahluk could also sing like us, dance like us, and his mouth was always full of stories none had heard before.
>
> "Therefore, we liked him, and we all felt sorry when we understood that we should never see him again. . . . But we will always tell our children about him and we will sing songs about him."[12]

In contrast to Matthew Henson's legendary status among the Polar Eskimos, his treatment in America was one of "benign neglect" at best. Few men have given so much to the honor of their country and received so little in return. When Henson returned to America after the North Pole discovery, there was, to be sure, a small level of mainstream press coverage for "Peary's colored servant." But the America of 1909 found it hard to accept the fact that Peary had selected a black man over his five white assistants to share in the conquest of the North Pole.

Peary's decision to take Henson to the Pole certainly did not help his case when he returned home to find that Frederick Cook, the former assistant turned archrival, had laid claim to having discovered the Pole a year earlier. Cook took full advantage of the honor system that governed Arctic exploration, where a man's word regarding his achievement was accepted as fact—unless that man happened to be black, or an Eskimo. Cook's two Eskimo companions, Etookahshoo and Ahpellah, later told Danish officials that he had taken them on a circuitous trek around the islands of northwest Canada, not to the Pole. In fact, they reported, they had never traveled beyond the sight of land during the entire trip. There is no land within four hundred miles of the North Pole. The Eskimos added that they had spent most of the year holed up in an earthen shelter in northern Canada with plenty of food stores.[13]

Henson also suspected that Cook's claims were preposterous, not just because of the Eskimos' testimony but because of other, earlier experiences with Cook that had proved him amateurish in the serious business of Arctic exploration. Nevertheless, the conflicting claims created a personal dilemma for Henson. Cook had treated and cared for Henson in his family's home in New York back in 1892, when the latter had temporarily lost much of his vision to snow blindness. Henson never forgot this kind gesture and for a while found it difficult to criticize Cook publicly.

Even when several international scientific societies sided with Peary and denounced Cook as a charlatan, many people refused to accept their verdict. Some still do. Compared to the pompous, if misunderstood, Robert Peary, the charming Dr. Cook would always be a more acceptable American hero.

Eventually, however, Peary received the recognition he sought and deserved. Most of the leading scientific organizations at home and abroad acknowledged him as the "discoverer" of the North Pole, and the National Geographic Society of Washington gave him their highest award, a special gold medal struck in his honor. Henson, on the other hand, was completely ignored by the geographic societies and other prominent mainstream groups. In fact, it must have been very painful for Henson when the National Geographic Society skipped over him and gave their second highest award, another gold medal, to the white man on Peary's North Pole expedition who, next to Peary, got closest to the Pole. That man was Robert Bartlett, who admitted that he never got within 130 miles of the Pole.

Yet if white America ignored Henson, black America certainly did not. By the time the expedition returned to New York City on October 2, 1909, the New York newspapers had named Matthew Henson as Peary's American companion at the Pole. Black leaders around the country who had been following accounts of Henson's explorations sent him telegrams and letters of congratulations for "representing his race well" and organized a celebration in his honor.

On October 19 a group of the most prominent black American intellectuals, politicians, and religious leaders from across the country gathered at the prestigious Tuxedo Club on Madison Avenue in midtown Manhattan for a special dinner to honor Matthew Henson's achievement. There, amid speeches and great fanfare, they presented their hero with a gold watch and chain. The organizers and guests of this impressive affair included Booker T. Washington; the Reverend Adam Clayton Powell, Sr.; John E. Bruce, noted publisher and author; Charles W. Anderson, the highest-ranking black civil service official in New York; Judge M. W. Gibbs of Arkansas; Assistant U.S. Attorney W. H. Lewis of Boston; and many other distinguished leaders. Seldom in the nation's history has such a collection of African-American leaders come together to honor a single person. These men were to the black American community of their day what the highest U.S. government and cultural figures were to the white community. The *New York Times* of October 13, 1909, reported the affair under the heading: "DINNER TO MATTHEW HENSON: Leaders among Colored Race to Give Peary's Aide a Watch and Chain."

Like Peary, Henson had at last achieved his goal: recognition from the leaders of his race. He had risen from the lowly background of a sharecropper with only six grades of schooling to a permanent place in history for his contributions to polar exploration.

Unfortunately, Henson's fame brought him nothing in the way of material reward. In fact, after twenty-three years of service to his nation and to Peary, he found himself without a job or even the prospect of employment. No one came forward to offer the black American hero even a minor position or appointment. For a time he tried to take advantage of the public interest in polar discovery by giving lectures on his North Pole journey with Peary, during which he would challenge Cook's claims. But Peary, fearing that the publicity would cause his adversaries to continually raise the issue of Henson's race, restricted his lecture activities and stopped Henson from showing his own photographs publicly.[14] Henson later wrote, "In my letters [to Peary] I hoped for some understanding. . . . But no reply came until I signed for a series of lectures. When I had given my first lecture I received a telegram from Commander Peary warning me not to use the pictures. At once I sat down and wrote him another long letter. He never replied to it."[15]

On October 15, 1909, Peary wrote H. L. Bridgeman, secretary of the Peary Arctic Club (which had financed his polar expeditions) and the man who had paid Henson his salary:

> "My dear Bridgeman
>
> I have not happened to come across the so called Henson challenge to Cook [Cook's claim of a North Pole discovery], though I note reference to it in the papers.
>
> While I can only infer from these references what the challenge really is, it strikes me that anything of the kind would be unwise for three reasons. It is likely to make a fool of Henson by giving him pronounced megalomania; it will put him in a position to be tangled up and made to say anything by emissaries of the Herald [newspaper], and it will introduce into this matter the race issue."

During much of this time, Henson was working on his own book, which he entitled *A Negro Explorer at the North Pole*. Peary's agreement with members of his expeditionary team precluded the writing of memoirs or other accounts of their Arctic experiences without his approval. After a year or so, as public interest in the subject waned, Peary decided that Henson could publish his book without stirring up too much controversy, but only after Peary had first reviewed the manuscript. Henson was the only member of the 1909 team granted permission to publish an account of the historic expedition. The book was not a best-seller.

In 1912, deeply frustrated and jobless, Henson wrote Peary to request that he use his influence to help him find a job as a "chauffeur or messenger or some other position that I could fill. . . . I am in need of work." Peary responded by writing the secretary of the treasury to recommend Henson for a federal position that carried a lifetime pension. Securing such sinecures was a standard practice among the explorers' fraternity, a way to reward loyal assistants by providing them a measure of long-term security. At about the same time, some of Henson's friends and black politicians were petitioning President William Taft on his behalf for a federal appointment similar to those traditionally given to European American heroes.

About a year later, President Taft signed an executive order granting permission to appoint Henson to "any suitable position in the classified service." Henson was appointed "messenger" in the federal customs house in New York. He remained at the customs house until his retirement in 1937 at the age of seventy. From then until his death in 1955, he and his wife Lucy lived mainly on his small pension of about one thousand dollars a year.

When Peary died in 1920, Henson read about it in the New York papers and, according to a friend, got up, went into his bathroom for privacy, and ran the tap water to mask the sound of his weeping. In spite of their differences of race, status, and condition, Matthew Henson and Robert Peary had become so close during their years of struggle and hardship in the Arctic that they were more like brothers than just friends.

Peary was given a hero's burial in Arlington National Cemetery. The National Geographic Society purchased a magnificent monument to mark his grave. The monument, which was conceived by Peary before he died, is a giant white granite globe mounted on a broad-based pedestal, with a bronze star marking the North Pole. On the base, beneath the globe, is the inscription "ROBERT EDWIN PEARY DISCOVERER OF THE NORTH POLE." Inscribed on another side of the base is a Latin line from Seneca, which his daughter called "his guiding motto": *Inveniam Viam Aut Faciam* (I shall find a way or make one). The monument commands its own hill in the cemetery.

President Warren G. Harding joined hundreds of other dignitaries at the Arlington ceremony. Officials of the U.S. government have said that Henson was also invited to the burial, but he cannot be seen in any of the scores of archival photographs taken of the ceremony that day. If Henson or any other black American was present at the burial ceremony, he must have been seated far away from the official guests.

Yet Henson was not completely forgotten. In 1937, twenty-eight years after the North Pole discovery, he was made an honorary member of the famed Explorers Club in New York City of which Peary had once been president. He was the first and for decades the only black African American so recognized by the club. In 1946, he received a medal from the U.S. Navy in recognition of his contributions to the North Pole discovery. The same medal was given to all members of Peary's 1909 expedition and did not single Henson out for reaching the Pole. Also, Morgan State College in Baltimore and Howard University of Washington, D.C., two predominantly African-American institutions, awarded him honorary master's degrees. Dillard College of New Orleans, to whom he gave the Eskimo clothing he wore at the North Pole, named a hall after him.

By his own account, however, his most prized possession was the gold medal he received from the Chicago Geographical Society. The Chicago award was the work of Henson's old friend Donald B. MacMillan and Comdr. Eugene F. McDonald, Jr., president of the Zenith Radio Corporation and a longtime admirer. To Henson, this medal represented the ultimate tribute to an explorer: recognition by a geographic society. For the entire forty-six years between the discovery of the Pole and his death, he was virtually ignored by the National Geographic Society, a group that had honored and paid numerous tributes to Peary and the other white men on the North Pole expedition.

In 1948 Matthew Henson was "rediscovered" by mainstream America when author Bradley Robinson wrote a biography titled *Dark Companion*. This marked the first time Americans were given a true picture of the role Henson played in the polar discoveries of Robert Peary. Robinson, the liberal son of a member of the Explorers Club, decided to write Henson's story after learning of his crucial role in the conquest of the Pole through extensive interviews and research. Published at a time when American racial attitudes were

becoming more enlightened, the book was well reviewed and became a big seller. Henson, now in his eighties, suddenly found
himself the object of much attention. Newspapers and magazines interviewed him, and he made guest appearances on radio. He talked
about his years in the Arctic and his contributions to the North Pole
discovery. Although he had little contact with the Peary family after
the admiral's death and felt bitter about the way they had ignored
him, he never spoke disparagingly about his old comrade. Throughout his life he would remain faithful to Peary's memory and to their
friendship, traveling nearly every year to Arlington Cemetery to
place a wreath at Peary's grave.

Matthew Henson died of a cerebral hemorrhage on March 9, 1955,
at the age of eighty-eight. Thousands turned out for the funeral five
days later at the historic Abyssinian Baptist Church in Harlem, where
the Reverend Adam Clayton Powell, Jr., conducted the memorial
service. In his eulogy, Powell told Henson's widow Lucy and the
large funeral gathering that the "achievements of Henson are as
important as those performed by Marco Polo and Ferdinand Magel-
lan." His pallbearers included Arctic explorer Peter Freuchen and
other members of the Explorers Club.[16]

No geographic society or Arctic club or any other group offered to
help bury Henson among other American heroes in Arlington National Cemetery. With only a modest, fixed income to draw on, Lucy
Henson buried her husband on top of her mother, Susan Ross, in the
small plot they owned in Woodlawn Cemetery in the Bronx.

Matthew Alexander Henson (1909). *Courtesy of the Explorers Club*

Comdr. Robert Edwin Peary in full Arctic gear (c. 1909). *Peary Collection, National Archives*

Matthew Henson aboard Peary's ship, the USS *Roosevelt*. This photograph is believed to have been taken in March 1909, shortly before Henson and Peary launched their final assault on the North Pole. *Courtesy of Johnson Publishing Co.*

Ahlikasingwah and her baby, Kali, the younger of Robert Peary's two Amer-Eskimo sons (c. 1907). *From* My Attainment of the Pole *by Frederick Cook*

Akatingwah carrying a baby believed to be Matthew Henson's son, Anaukaq (c. 1907). *Peary Collection, National Archives*

Navy lieutenant Peary and his daughter Marie Ahnighito Peary (c. 1899). *Peary Collection, National Archives*

Matthew Henson (*front row, center*) and a group of Polar Eskimo villagers (c. 1900). Deeply interested in the ways of the native population, Henson was the only member of Peary's expeditionary teams who learned to speak the Inuit language. *Courtesy of the Explorers Club*

OPPOSITE:
Taking a break from cleaning a fresh supply of fish, members of Peary's expeditionary team pose alongside their ship, the *Kite*, en route to northwest Greenland in 1891. *Peary Collection, National Archives*

The 1891 North Greenland Expedition. *Left to right:* Frederick Cook, Matthew Henson, John M. Verhoeff, Eivind Astrup, Josephine Peary, Lt. Robert E. Peary, Langdon Gibson. *Peary Collection, National Archives*

GIBSON.

VERHOEFF.

DR. COOK.

ASTRÜP.

HENSON.

Portraits of the members of the 1891 expedition as they appeared in Robert Peary's book, *Northward over the "Great Ice."* What is perhaps most noteworthy about the arrangement of the photographs is the implicitly equal status that Peary accorded to Henson.

Dozens of sled dogs crowd the deck of the USS *Roosevelt* as it steams toward Cape Sheridan, the staging point for the historic 1909 assault on the North Pole. *Courtesy of the National Geographic Society*

Matthew Henson and Polar Eskimos repair a sled used to transport food, supplies, and scientific equipment during the 1909 polar journey. *Courtesy of the Explorers Club*

Particularly during the early stages of the 1909 expedition, the rugged Arctic surface caused repeated delays. Here, members of the team struggle to pull their supply sleds over a small ridge of jagged ice. *Courtesy of the National Geographic Society*

Matthew Henson (*center*) and four Polar Eskimos at the North Pole, April 6, 1909. This photograph was taken by Comdr. Robert E. Peary. *Courtesy of the National Geographic Society*

The four Polar Eskimos who accompanied Henson and Peary to the North Pole. *Left to right:* gingwah, Ootah, Ooqueah, and Seegloo. *Peary Collection, National Archives*

ive months after the Peary Expedition reached the North Pole, newspapers widely circulated he story that Frederick Cook had accomplished the same feat a year earlier. The front-page hotograph shown below purported to confirm Cook's claim, but subsequent investigation roved otherwise. *From* To Stand at the Pole *by William R. Hunt*

THE EVENING MAIL

HOME EDITION · HOME EDITION

NEW YORK, WEDNESDAY, SEPTEMBER 1, 1909.

DR. COOK REACHES NORTH POLE

EXTRA

News of Cook's success was worth an "Extra."

Cook's photograph of his companions at the Pole

GOAL LONG COVETED B' WORLD'S EXPLORERS WO FINALLY BY AMERICA

Dispatch Received at the Dani Colonial Office from Lervik, Nor way, Says Cook Accomplishe His Great Feat, More Than Year Ago, on April 21, 1908.

The first black to be elected to the exclusive Explorers Club, Matthew Henson poses with other members for the official club portrait in 1947. Next to Henson, in the center of the front row, is the noted Danish Arctic explorer, Peter Freuchen. *Courtesy of the Explorers Club*

Matthew Henson displays a watch and gold chain awarded to him by black American leaders after his return from the North Pole. A medal presented to him by the U.S. Navy in recognition of his achievement is pinned to his lapel (1947).

CHAPTER EIGHT

* * *

"Now I know I have relatives"

The trip had not been uneventful. It almost never is. The lumbering C-141 military transport lifted off the runway at McGuire Air Force Base in New Jersey at 2300 hours, en route to Thule, Greenland. Before long the aircraft gained cruising altitude, and the military crew, a few other scientists, and I settled into our seats for the long haul. Although the flight sergeant had provided us with ear plugs, the absence of any windows or insulation intensified the high-pitched whine of the jet's engines. Adding to our discomfort, tons of cargo teetered menacingly just ahead of us in the open hold.

Several hours into the trip, I was awakened by the flight sergeant tugging at my arm. He told me that we had developed engine trouble and would be landing at a nearby air base. Despite the momentary surge of adrenaline one feels upon hearing this kind of news, I was more worried about my scheduled connections in Greenland. If we arrived too late, I would be unable to get a helicopter to take me over the mountain range. I would have to travel over the frozen sea by dogsled, a more exciting but more time-consuming means of transportation.

It was pitch black when we landed and disembarked at the air base in Canada. We rushed through the cold night air and huddled into what looked like a small brick bunker while the plane underwent repairs. After a while, the flight sergeant came in to inform us that the mechanics could not repair the plane and we would be returning to the American air base on the next available flight. The news was depressing. It was more than an inconvenience because even a few hours of delay here could result in a layover of several days in Greenland. "Such is life," I reflected, as I began to rearrange in my schedule book my plans to visit Moriussaq. There is probably no sadder or lonelier feeling than being stranded in a bunker on an isolated air base.

A few hours later—just as the full implications of what had happened began to sink in—the flight sergeant reappeared. "I have good news," he said. "The mechanics have repaired the plane and the flight crew is ready to take us to Thule."

"All right!" I shouted. Everyone else in the room just stared at me. Thule, Greenland, it seems, is not the favorite station of our military men and women.

Subzero temperatures and howling winds greeted us on our arrival in northwest Greenland. To minimize our exposure to the dangerous cold, we rushed from the giant green plane into a nearby hangar. I knew that even in the unlikely event that the helicopter was still at the base, it could not take off in these strong winds. I would have to try to get a dogteam to travel north.

＊　＊　＊

By late fall, the sun disappears at the top of the world, not to be seen again until spring. A kind of twilight appears for several hours during the day, but since the sun never breaks the horizon, the short day resembles an extended gray-blue dusk. By early December, the last vestige of daylight has disappeared altogether, and the area is thrust into total darkness until the sun begins to reappear briefly in mid-February. From March through July, the sun rises higher and higher, eventually circling the sky for twenty-four hours.

The entire settlement appeared deserted as I approached Moriussaq that fall. Although most of the food stores had already been gathered for the winter, I wondered whether the men were out hunting and had taken their families with them. But as I neared the center of the settlement, I spotted several children playing with a bobsled on a small hill. The children rushed forward to greet the visitor, with Ajako's daughter—and Matthew Henson's ten-year-old great-granddaughter—Aviaq leading the bunch.

"Allen," Aviaq shouted, as she and the other children and sled-dog pups ran through the snow toward me. I immediately recognized several of the children whose ears I had examined during my previous visit. I greeted them and Aviaq with big hugs. Hearing the commotion, several older children and adults came out of their igloos to see what was going on. The area came alive. After exchanging greetings of affection, the children and adults helped me with my small packages and bags as I headed off toward the home of Anaukaq Henson.

From a distance, I could make out the figure of a man wearing a heavy blue winter jacket. He walked toward us with the help of a cane in rapid, solid steps. I knew at once it was Anaukaq. I walked forward at a hurried pace, hand extended to meet my old friend. From several yards away, his unmistakable laugh cracked through the cold, crisp air. It lifted my spirits. As we approached each other, he shouted, "Allen, you came back. I did not think you would come back." He then burst into laughter as we shook hands and embraced. The crowd of children and young people gathering around us seemed vicariously to share the old man's delight as they giggled and chuckled shyly at our joyful reunion. We all headed for Anaukaq's igloo.

As we stepped into the warm house, I was greeted by the odor of fresh meat. Just inside the door, a large, freshly skinned bearded seal hung from a rope attached to a ceiling timber. The fleshy mammal was about the size of a small human. A huge bowl on the floor, directly under the seal, collected the blood that slowly dripped from the thawing carcass. Several of the family members cut off small pieces of the raw meat and ate them as snacks as we settled into the central room of the house.

Anaukaq made the usual gesture of offering me tea, which seems to be brewing in almost every Eskimo home one visits. He was all smiles. I had brought along some freshly ground coffee and some spiced tea for him. He suggested that we start with the spiced tea he had been so fond of during my last visit. They don't have such tea in Greenland.

"I am very happy to see you, Allen," Anaukaq said. "We missed your laugh."

"Thank you, Anaukaq, I am happy to see you and your family again," I said, charmed by the idea that Anaukaq and the other Eskimos had discovered my essence and persona in, of all things, my laugh.

"I am so glad you came back," Anaukaq repeated. "Many times I have said to myself and to my children that you would probably not return to this cold land. But you kept your word," he said, patting my shoulder.

By now, all the Amer-Eskimo Hensons were gathering around us in the central room, each greeting me warmly. They were much too modest to ask me questions right away, but I knew what was on their minds.

I had brought along small gifts for the entire family, mainly hunting knives for the men, as well as wool caps and other useful items. I distributed the gifts to the children, and then to the older family members. They accepted the gifts with gracious smiles and soft *kooyounahs* [thank yous]. The polar Eskimos are generally not a very expressive people. Even in joyous moments they typically exhibit a quiet reserve. Anaukaq seemed to be somewhat exceptional in this respect. He was more outgoing, more expressive than the other Eskimos, and endowed with a great sense of humor.

A short time later, Anaukaq asked the question on everyone's mind. "Did you find any of my relatives over there in Mahri-Pahluk's homeland?"

"Yes," I replied. "I have found several of your relatives in America—and they were very pleased to learn about you and your family." The room lit up with a cheer and smiles from the entire family.

"Do I have any brothers and sisters still alive?" Anaukaq asked pointedly.

"No, I'm afraid I did not locate any brothers or sisters, but I found several of Mahri-Pahluk's brothers' and sisters' children and grandchildren in Maryland, in Washington, D.C., and in Boston, Massachusetts, and they are very excited about meeting your family." Again, when my sentence was translated for them, Anaukaq and the family clapped their hands with pleasure.

"Do you mean Mahri-Pahluk and his American wife had no children that I could call brother or sister?" Anaukaq asked.

"No, not that I could find. Matthew and your stepmother Lucy Jane Ross Henson never had children, according to the records I found. But his brothers and sisters had plenty, and you have several first and second cousins still alive and well."

Anaukaq gave a momentary sigh of sadness, partially masked by a smile and a soft chuckle. "It seems so strange to me sometimes—that I have so many parents and yet no brothers or sisters."

Sometimes Anaukaq would say the profoundest things with such simplicity. I felt his sadness even in this moment of joy. He had really hoped for a brother or sister—some close, tangible evidence of a connection to his father. His mother, Akatingwah, had no other children, so he had grown up in Greenland without siblings. In fact, "Cousin Kali" had been the closest to a brother he had known. A true biological brother or sister, albeit a half brother or sister, might even look something like his father, whom he had not seen since he was three years old. A real brother or sister could tell him something about the father he had never known—what he was really like. Anaukaq had always dreamed of meeting a brother or sister. And now, I had to tell him he had none, living or dead.

I did not know at the time, but learned later, that in the spring of 1896, Matthew Henson's first wife, Eva, had given birth to a child, but that Henson had disowned the infant. He later complained to Robert and Josephine Peary that he was "only home [from Greenland] for seven months when the child was born in my family, and they want to say that it was my child. . . . Do you think I ought to live with that woman any longer? I will ask you and Mrs. Peary for your advice." This prompted Eva's brother "Flint" to threaten Henson with plans to write his employers at the American Museum of Natural History in New York and Peary to complain that Henson "did not treat Eva right." Henson continued to support Eva for about another year, but he never claimed the child as his own biological offspring. His belief in her infidelity during his absence caused him to leave her in the spring of 1897.

That summer, Henson went back to Greenland to help Peary collect the last of the Eskimos' sacred meteorites. On October 8, 1897,

Eva wrote to Robert Peary too and asked, "Will you please inform me of the whereabouts of my husband? . . . I did not know that he had been away with you, until I read his name among the crew [of Peary's expeditionary ship]." She asked Peary to "please excuse the liberty," but indicated that she sought no further aid from Henson, only Peary's help in getting Henson to give her a "bill of divorce."

✳   ✳   ✳

I reached into my backpack and pulled out the colorful blanket that Olive had sent Anaukaq. "It's from your cousin Olive," I said.

"My cousin?" Anaukaq echoed, with a big smile.

"Yes, your cousin Olive in Boston sent you this blanket. She made it herself."

"*Irriahnocktoe, irriahnocktoe* [Beautiful, beautiful]," Anaukaq declared with a wide grin. "Pretty good," he shouted as he looked around the room, holding up the blanket for the family to see. He patted my shoulder several times with the strong hands of an old hunter, and said, "*Kooyounah,* this is a wonderful day for me. Now I know I have relatives over there!" He passed the gift around the room to his children and grandchildren. They too marveled at the handsome blanket, made even lovelier by the fact that it came from one of their heretofore only imagined relatives in America.

When the blanket came back to Anaukaq, he wrapped it around his shoulders like a shawl, then quietly rocked from side to side and from front to back, humming to himself as if meditating, relishing the moment.

"I also brought along some photographs of your relatives," I said, pulling a stack of old and new photographs out of my backpack. The rest of the family quickly crowded around Anaukaq and me, chattering away excitedly. "This is a photo of your cousin Olive, who sent you the blanket," I said.

"This is my cousin?" Anaukaq asked, holding the photo close to his face and gazing at it with his better eye. "She looks very good. She could be an Eskimo woman," he said with a chuckle.

"Yes, and this is her father David, Mahri-Pahluk's brother."

"Ooh, look at them. They are very good—very beautiful." After examining each print carefully, the old patriarch passed the photos down the line among his children. He continued to rock back and forth, chuckling all the while, as he reached for the next photo.

I had even brought along a few photos of the most recent American Hensons, babies born to Matthew Henson's brothers' and sisters' grandchildren. "Look at them, they are so fat—so cute. They look like Eskimo babies," Anaukaq and his granddaughters were saying. "Oh this baby is so beautiful. I want to keep her," Malina said of one of the American Henson babies.

But one old photograph that I pulled from my collection really caught Anaukaq's eye. It was one of his father at the age of eighty-one—almost Anaukaq's own age—taken in 1947 by the Urban League of New York as part of a new magazine series on black heroes. The photograph showed a distinguished-looking Matthew Henson in a dark three-piece suit, showing an issue of *Negro Heroes* to an African-American boy of about ten, who is sitting on his knee.

"Who is this boy?" Anaukaq inquired right away. "Is he related to Mahri-Pahluk?"

"I really don't know, but I am still trying to locate him through old records," I said. "If he still is alive, he would be about fifty years old now."

"Maybe he is the son of one of my uncles," Anaukaq offered.

"Perhaps. But I shall try to find out who he is when I return to America."

He looked at the photograph, then back at me, and laughed, "My father was a good-looking man."

Anaukaq took this photograph and put it on a shelf behind him in a "special place."

"Do you have a picture of my father's grave?" he asked.

"No. Unfortunately, I did not take a photograph of his grave site. But I can tell you that he is buried in a place called Woodlawn Cemetery, in the city where he spent most of his life, New York."

"Is he buried alone or among others?" he asked softly.

"He is buried among many others, in a large burial ground," I replied.

Anaukaq thought for a moment, looking back at the photograph on the shelf.

"Is he buried next to his wife?" Anaukaq asked.

"No, not exactly," I answered. "She died thirteen years after Mahri-Pahluk's death and was buried in the nearest space available, about thirty meters from Mahri-Pahluk's grave."

"A man and his wife should be buried beside each other. So they can be together again as in old times. So that they can talk about old times. When I die, I will be buried next to my Aviaq."

"I agree," I said. "But I believe Mahri-Pahluk and his wife were poor in their old age. When he died, she had just enough money to bury him in the same grave as her mother, Susan Ross. Then when she died some years later, her friends and relatives buried her in the nearest gravesite available."

Anaukaq sat quietly for a moment, taking this all in. The others in the room, who had been quietly but intently listening to our conversation, now began to talk softly among themselves.

"I would like very much to see my father's grave one day," Anaukaq said, as he took the 1947 photo from the shelf and stared at it again. "I would also like to see my relatives. But I haven't much time. I am an old man now. I have been ill in recent years. I hope I live to see some of my relatives and Mahri-Pahluk's grave. I hope I live to see the day."

"I too hope that you will someday meet your American relatives and see your father's grave. I can only promise you that I will do all that I can to help you."

"Did you find Cousin Kali's relatives too," Anaukaq inquired.

"Yes, I found some of Kali's relatives in the United States also," I responded, somewhat hesitantly.

"Then they must have been happy to learn of Kali," he said, questioningly, then continued. "They say that some of Peeuree's family came up here many years ago, but we never saw them."

"Well, I never really met any of Kali's relatives, but I spoke with them by phone, and they seemed surprised to learn that I had found you and Kali," I said, trying to skirt the issue.

"Did Kali have any living brothers and sisters?" Anaukaq asked.

"Oh, yes," I replied. "Peary had one son in America, and he is still living. He is now eighty-three years old."

"He is eighty-three years old? That is wonderful," Anaukaq responded. "I know Kali will be very happy to meet his brother."

"Well, Robert Peary had a big family in America," I said. "Two children, seven grandchildren, and many great-grandchildren. I told the family about Kali, and I am sure that he will meet some of them."

In spite of my efforts to disguise the reaction of Kali's American family, I had a feeling that Anaukaq detected my reservations. He ended the conversation by saying, "It is good that Kali has a living brother. They should meet. They are brothers and should know one another."

* * *

Over the next few weeks, I followed Anaukaq all about the village, filming him and just observing him as he visited his Eskimo relatives, old friends, and some of the young people of the settlement. He was immensely popular.

He showed the photos of his relatives to almost everyone he met. "These are my cousins from Mahri-Pahluk's homeland," he would say with a big grin. "I'm going to go over there to meet them one day."

His neighbors were invariably gracious. "Oh, what a beautiful family you have," they would say, after looking at the photos. "You must be very happy to have such a beautiful family."

Anaukaq's sister-in-law Mikkisuk Minge, now in her eighties, still wore traditional Polar Eskimo clothing, including hip-length, cream-colored sealskin boots. "Of course, I have known Anaukaq since we were very young," she told me. "Anaukaq has always been known for his very special laugh. No matter how unhappy one felt, when Anaukaq came around and laughed that special laugh of his, your spirits were just lifted in the air."

"One day, when we were young," she went on to say, "I was sitting out in front of the igloo with his wife, Aviaq, cutting some whale meat, when Anaukaq came up and gave her a bottle of wine that he had bought at the Danish trade station. He did not give me one, so I was very jealous. I said to myself, she is married to a *kulnocktooko* man and he treats her very special. He comes here and gives her some good drink. He treats her special, but gives nothing to his sister-in-law. I was jealous." She burst into laughter.

This was an opportunity for me to find out more about the significance of Anaukaq's and Kali's racial differences among the Eskimos, especially among the older people, who were not so much influenced by the world beyond. "You mentioned that Anaukaq was a black man, Mikkisuk. Did the Eskimo people feel that he was different from everyone else because he is dark skinned?"

"Well, yes, of course," she responded, with a big smile. "Up here we all say that Anaukaq and family are a little different from the other Eskimos. Not in a bad way. But different in a good way."

"You mean different because he is darker than the other Eskimos and has curly hair?" I asked.

"Ha, ha! Different in many ways. We always say that it must be because he is Mahri-Pahluk's son."

"How are Anaukaq and his family different? Give me an example," I asked.

"Well, up here we say that his whole family walks different from the other Eskimos."

"Walks differently?" I repeated.

"Yes! You can distinguish a member of Anaukaq's family walking from a great distance. We say that they walk like they are gliding on ice."

Another woman in the room joined in. "It's true what she says. Up here everyone knows this about Anaukaq's family."

Mikkisuk continued. "Anaukaq and his sons could also dance better than the other Eskimos. When we would have our dances, they were always the best dancers."

By now I could no longer contain my laughter. How could these people, who had little or no knowledge of black people, harbor this comical stereotype? I knew they meant no disrespect to Anaukaq and his family. Quite the contrary. They saw these characteristics as desirable traits.

"Most of Anaukaq's family can play musical instruments too. When the *kadoona* missionaries brought musical instruments up here through the trading post, Anaukaq and his family were the only Eskimos to get them and play them well, even his grandchildren."

"Do you really think they dance better than other Eskimos, or did you learn this from the Danes?" I asked, jokingly.

"No! It is true. Everyone up here knows that Anaukaq and his children are the best dancers and the fastest runners among our people—and they walk nicer, so smoothly."

She got up to demonstrate. "See, Eskimos walk like this," she said, taking short, soft steps to imitate their stride and pace. "And the *kahdonah* walk like a stone—like this," she said, now moving from side to side taking long, wide, stomping strides. "Anaukaq and his family walk like this." Her steps were now light touches on the ground, as she glided across the room, slightly twisting her body from side to side, as if riding on a breeze.

Even in my laughter, I had to admit that her imitation of the Amer-Eskimo Henson's walk was unmistakably African-American. Could this be true? I wondered. Amazing! I too had observed that some of Anaukaq's gestures, such as his frequent hand-clapping when he laughed, reminded me of behavior of some older African Americans.

"What about Kali, was he different also?" I asked.

"Yes. Kali was somewhat different from the other Eskimos too. He could dance too, but he could not dance like Anaukaq," she said.

"Well, how was he different from the other Eskimos?" I inquired.

"Kali?" she said, as if rethinking my question. "Kali was a very funny man when he was young. He had a great sense of humor and loved to tell jokes. He also loved to brag about being a good hunter. But he was a good hunter. When he used to have a drink, he would sing and try to dance like Anaukaq."

"What about Kali's children?" I asked. "Were they good dancers and runners like Anaukaq's?"

"Not really. Kali's family is very nice, but they are different—maybe not as friendly as Anaukaq's family. I think when Kali was young he was not as popular as Anaukaq. But everybody up here liked Kali and thought that he and his family were very nice."

* * *

When Anaukaq learned of my plans to travel up to Qeqertarsaaq to visit Kali, he reminded me that he too would like to see his "cousin Kali." "We haven't spent any time together since we were fifteen years old," he said.

I offered to take Anaukaq to Qeqertarsaaq with me, but then thought better of it when I remembered that Kali's island home is not accessible by helicopter. We would have to travel about seventy-five miles over the frozen bay to Qeqertarsaaq. Although Anaukaq appeared in good physical condition, he was still walking with a cane and could tire over long distances. Kali, on the other hand, was in excellent condition. He still frequently traveled by dogsled with his son and grandsons. And yet, I thought, it would be great to see the two old hunters together again after so many years. The stories they could tell would be fascinating, and I could learn much more about their growing up half-Eskimo in Greenland, one half-black, the other half-white.

Anaukaq solved the problem for me. "Why don't you tell Kali that he is welcome to come back with you to visit me? I have plenty of food and tea."

CHAPTER NINE

※ ※ ※

Growing Up Eskimo

Kali and his son, Talilanguaq, welcomed me back as warmly as had Anaukaq and his family.

"Did you have a good trip?" Kali asked.

"Yes. It was a long but safe trip," I replied. "I flew in the big military *cheemeahktoe* [man-made bird] to Thule. I didn't realize it would be so cold up here until we landed. It was warmer the last time I was here."

"Oh, it's only cold outside the igloo," he said with a chuckle. "You just have to stay inside the igloo as much as you can."

"Then I must build my own snow igloo, like in the old days, so that I can really keep warm," I said to his obvious delight.

"Did you find Cousin Anaukaq's relatives over there where you live?" he asked.

I told him that I had located several of Anaukaq's relatives and that they were pleased to learn of their Eskimo relatives.

"That is very good," Kali replied cheerfully. "Does he have many relatives over there—any brothers and sisters?"

"He has many relatives all over the United States, mostly cousins, but no brothers or sisters," I replied.

"I hope they are well," Kali said.

"They are well indeed," I said. "I only met a few of Anaukaq's folks personally, but I talked with most of them by phone. I hope to meet more of them when I return to my country."

There was a long, pregnant pause before Kali posed the inevitable question, "What about my people? Did I have any relatives over there?"

"Yes!" I answered, trying to muster as much enthusiasm as I could in my voice and smile. "I located several of your American relatives, and they all wished you well."

Kali smiled but said nothing.

I told him that I had not met any of his relatives face to face yet, because they all lived in different parts of the country, but that I had talked with some of his nephews by telephone and learned from them that he had an eighty-three-year-old brother living in Maine. "That is in another territory, north of the place where I live," I explained, "and I have not had the opportunity to meet him yet."

"Eighty-three years old," Kali repeated. "We are about the same age."

"That's right," I said. "He is your second big brother."

Kali laughed. "*Eeee* [Yes]! He was born between Hammy and me. What is his name?"

"Robert Peary, Jr.," I replied. "He was given the name of his father."

"He was named for Peeuree?" Kali asked.

"Yes," I replied. "That is a common practice in my country. He has a son named Robert Peary III and a grandson named Robert Peary IV. He has several children and grandchildren, just as you have, but I can't remember how many. He lives with his wife and son in Augusta, Maine, Peary's old home area."

"I hope that he is in good health. I would like to meet him," Kali said. "But we are both getting old."

"I hope you will have the chance to meet soon," I replied.

Since I had received no gifts for Kali from his American relatives, I had brought along a few of my own. I reached into my pocket, pulled out a Swiss Army knife, and handed it to him.

"This is a gift for you," I said.

"For me?" Kali responded.

"Yes, it is for you," I said. "A great hunter always needs a good hunting knife."

"*Kooyounah!*" Kali said with a big smile.

"*Iddigdoo* [You are welcome]," I replied in my best Eskimo.

"Who is this gift from?" he asked.

"It is a gift from me," I said.

"*Kooyounah*," he said again as he examined the knife. I suspected that he would like this gift because such knives are prized among the Polar Eskimos, especially the hunters.

"I have another gift that I brought from America for you," I said, handing him an eight-by-ten black-and-white photograph. "It is a photograph of your father, Commander Peeuree."

"Commander Peeuree," Kali repeated, as if imitating my English.

He studied the photograph for a while. "He looks like he is growing old in this picture."

"I think he was only in his fifties when this photo was taken," I responded, leaning over to look at the photograph again.

"Mmmm. This is my father, Peeuree," Kali said thoughtfully. "It is a good-looking photograph of my father. But I don't remember how he looked. He left when I was a small child. I do remember my mother saying to me that when I was a child, I would hit him about the legs whenever I was near him. I don't know why I would do a thing like that, and I don't remember hitting him," he chortled. "I also remember something else my mother told me many times. She said that when Peeuree was worried, he would take himself like this." Kali grasped the bridge of his nose with his index finger and thumb as he bowed his head over a closed fist and swayed from side to side. "I think maybe I do that, too, sometimes."

Kali continued to stare at the photograph. I wondered whether he could see the remarkable resemblance to himself that was so clear to me. I wondered just how many times during his eighty years he had thought about his real father, or imagined how different his life might have been had Peary claimed him as his son and contributed to his upbringing. I wondered, but I did not ask.

I told Kali that his cousin Anaukaq hoped that he would return with me to Moriussaq. Much to my delight, Kali accepted the invitation. Joined by his son, Talilanguaq, he crossed the bay to Qaanaaq, where he boarded a helicopter. Kali was at first skeptical of the *chemeahktoe,* but once aloft he seemed to enjoy the ride. He grudgingly admitted that this form of travel had its advantages, even if it lacked the adventure and romance of traditional dogsled travel. Even by the fastest dogsled, the trip from Qaanaaq around the mountainous coast to Moriussaq normally took a day. By helicopter it took only an hour.

When he landed in Moriussaq, Anaukaq was there to greet him. As Talilanguaq helped his father from the helicopter, the two old friends began laughing joyously. They shook hands, grabbed each other's shoulders, and stared each other in the eye, chuckling all the while like two young boys.

"*Hinaynukwhonay* [Hello, how are you], my cousin? It is good to see you," said Kali.

"*Aheewhoghia* [I am fine]," Anaukaq replied. "It is good to see you, too, my cousin. Welcome to Moriussaq. You look great!"

"I am good for an old seal hunter. It must be that shot of whiskey that I take once in a while," Kali replied. Again they broke into laughter. "You look well to me," Kali continued. "I had heard from my children that you had been very ill a while back."

"I was very ill last year, but I am much better now," Anaukaq replied. "My granddaughter Malina acts as a nurse for me, and my sons hunt for me. So I am well fed and very *peeshahhah* [strong] today."

"Good," Kali said, as we hurried from under the whirring blades of the departing helicopter, which was blowing swirls of snowflakes all around us.

We collected the bags and headed off in the direction of Anaukaq's igloo. Together for the first time in many years, the two men chatted away. They were a striking sight walking together, proudly leading the small entourage of villagers toward the center of the settlement, ever conscious of my camera recording their interaction. As I watched them step surefootedly over the packed snow—one dark in complexion, the other much lighter—I could imagine that I was looking at Matthew Henson and Robert Peary themselves, hiking together across this frozen land nearly a century ago.

When we reached Anaukaq's home, his sons came out to greet Kali and Talilanguaq and invited all of us into the central room of the house.

"Aah, *keyettoe* [warm]," Kali said. "*Irriahnocktoe* [beautiful] igloo."

Everyone exchanged pleasantries and talked about the two families. Kali was particularly charmed by Magssanguaq, Anaukaq's ten-year-old grandson, who had just returned from a hunting trip wearing his traditional polar bear fur pants and carrying a rifle.

"This is my grandson, Magssanguaq," Anaukaq said proudly, rubbing the boy's head. "He is a *peeneeahktoe* [hunter] at age ten."

"A *peeneeahktoe* already?" asked Kali, making an obvious effort to show the boy that he was impressed. "Maybe he will grow up to be a *peeneeahktoe wah* like his grandfather."

"I hope so," Anaukaq said. "I think he will be a great hunter when he grows up."

Young Magssanguaq smiled, shyly proud at this praise from his revered elders.

Anaukaq served *cobve* [coffee], and the two old-timers sat across from each other, drinking and talking. Later, as a special treat for his guest, Anaukaq brought out their favorite delicacy.

"*Cheemeuhk* [Birds]!" Anaukaq announced, displaying a pair of white kittiwakes. These birds, which look like moderate-sized seagulls, are stored in closed sealskin pouches under a rock pile for about a year. During that time they become fully fermented, allowing the Eskimos to eat them raw.

"Aah, *cheemeahk*," Kali exclaimed. "*Kooyounah*. I haven't had any *cheemeahk* since last summer."

"*Iddigdoo*," Anaukaq said. "There is plenty, so eat much. My grandson Magssanguaq shot them."

"Oh, that is wonderful," Kali responded. "That grandson of yours is really a good *peeneeahktoe*."

Anaukaq and Kali skillfully peeled away the birds' feathers and skin, much as one peels an orange, to expose the red, fleshy meat. Eventually each retrieved from his bird a walnut-sized, membranous sac that looked like a small plastic bag. The sacs were filled with seeds eaten by the bird and stored in its crop. They held the sacs up and commented on their size and contents, which told the old hunters many things about the origin, health, fertility, and general condition of the kittiwake population.

"Here," Kali said to me. "Smell this." He opened the top of the little sac and held it to my nose. It had a fragrance similar to that of fresh flowers, or maybe jasmine.

"It smells very pleasant," I said.

Anaukaq then got up and found a small string of sealskin. He tied one end of the string around the top of the membranous sac and attached the other to the timber in the ceiling. "It will make my igloo smell very good," he explained.

"That is wonderful," I said, once again amazed at the resourcefulness of my hosts. "You have taught me so many things about the Eskimo ways." Both men chuckled with pride.

With their pocket knives, they began to carve their birds in much the same way that we slice apples, putting slivers of the raw, bloody meat in their mouths in between words. Before long their mouths and hands were stained a deep red.

"*Mahmaktoe*," Kali said with a grin, as he handed me a small slice of the delicacy.

Actually, the meat was quite flavorful—somewhat vinegary, but not bad. "Kali. Anaukaq. Which one of you was the better *peeneeahktoe* in your younger days?" I asked. The two men continued eating in silence for a moment, thinking over my question.

"This one!" Anaukaq said, pointing at Kali. "This one! He is probably the greatest hunter of all the Inuit people."

Anaukaq had barely finished when Kali pointed at him and said, "This one! Anaukaq. He is the greatest hunter of all the Inuit people. Before he injured his eye cutting a seal, no one was better."

"Ooh, no," Anaukaq protested. "You used to hunt *pooeehee* [seal] and *kahlayleewah* much better than any of us. You enjoyed it so much."

"Oh, I really enjoyed hunting *kahlayleewah* more than anything," Kali said. "I can remember when I got my first kayak. I was so happy because then I was able to take care of myself. I could be on my own. I liked to sneak up on the *kahlayleewah* by paddling silently," he continued, dramatically imitating the twirling motions of a kayaker.

"Then I would lift my harpoon and thrust it into the *kahlayleewah*, like this." He demonstrated. "All of a sudden, the rope attached to the harpoon tip would start to unwind, and the sealskin float would jump from the kayak into the water as the big *kahlayleewah* struggled against me. We would fight until one of us won. Oh, that was the greatest thrill. I enjoyed that very much."

"You were the best," Anaukaq said, chuckling at Kali's histrionics. "I really miss the old hunting days."

"But you were good at everything, my cousin. I remember how you could run across the ice faster than anyone we had ever seen," Kali said, laughing. "You were the fastest of all the Inuit boys."

Anaukaq's son Ajako, who had just entered the room, chimed in, "Up here they say the men in our family have the fastest legs of all the Inuit, and my *ahtahtah* [father] was the fastest runner."

Kali then turned to me. "Anaukaq could run so fast that I once saw him run after a big *chairreeinyah* [fox], and not only did he catch the fox, but he began kicking him, too, as they ran along."

The old men laughed uproariously at this story.

Changing the subject, I asked Anaukaq and Kali about their up-bringing. "Did you attend missionary schools when you were young-sters?"

"No," Anaukaq replied immediately. "There were no missionary schools in those days when we were young. We could only become hunters. There was nothing else we could do. The women became hunter-wives. Nowadays, the young men and women can go to school and take jobs with the Danes. They can become mechanics, like my fourth son, Vittus. But we enjoyed being hunters. I think a hunter is the best thing a man can be."

"When the missionary schools came along, did you want your children to go to school?" I asked.

"*Eeee*," said Kali.

"Oh, yes," Anaukaq agreed. "We wanted them to have the best advantages. We knew that our traditional world was changing with more of the Danish people coming up here and more modern things reaching this area by ship. But we also wanted them to keep the old ways, too, to become hunters."

"All of our oldest sons were still hunters first," Kali interjected, "even if they attended the missionary schools. But we old hunters had no opportunity to attend school."

"That is right," said Anaukaq. "Even after the air base was built in the 1950s and we saw some modern things come into this area, we were still hunters on the move, so that we could all eat. And our children traveled on the hunt with us."

"Sometimes we would have to take our children out of school so that they could join us on the hunt. We had to have enough food," Kali said. "But we would try not to disturb them while school was in."

"We were happy to be hunters," Anaukaq said. "We could write our names, and we could read our names. That was good. Our children could read and write, so they helped us. But we taught our sons to be hunters so they could survive on their own, look after their families in the traditional ways."

"Didn't the Danes and the Americans provide you with modern food supplies?" I asked.

"They provided some things like canned foods and fish, even frozen chicken lately," Anaukaq answered. "But we preferred our own native foods, like *nanook, kahlayleewah, cheemeahk, ahvuk, pooeehee, tooktoo,* and *ahkahlik,*" he said, listing them in order of Polar Eskimo preference.

"Anaukaq, were you ever treated any differently by the other Eskimos because you were of mixed race?" I asked.

He laughed. "*Nahahn* [No]. Not really. The people up here are too nice for that kind of thing. When I was a youngster, though, if I was too rough with other children, sometimes they would shout, 'You are black! You are black and not clean-faced!' But they didn't mean anything by it, and it was usually my fault for making them say such."

"Did everyone know why you looked different? I mean, why you were darker than the other Eskimos, and why you had curly *newyah* [hair]?" I asked.

"Yes, of course," Anaukaq replied. "All of the Inuit knew I was the son of Mahri-Pahluk and that he was *kulnocktooko.* But I was very happy for that, for being *kulnocktooko* like my father. For many years, though, I was ashamed of my curly *newyah*."

"Ashamed?" I was puzzled. "How so?"

"Yes," he laughed. "As a child, even as a man, I wanted straight hair, like my mother and later my wife. I would say to my wife that 'straight hair is so beautiful, why do I have this unruly curly hair?' Then later all of the young Inuit women started trying to curl their hair. Many of them started to use curlers. I said to them, 'Your straight hair is so beautiful. Why do you mess it up by making it curly?' But they said to me, 'No, your curly hair is beautiful. We want hair like yours.' I was so surprised at them. I thought the idea was kind of silly."

"What about you, Kali? Did the other Inuit treat you very differently as a youngster because you were part white?" I asked.

"Well, sometimes," he replied.

"How so?" I asked.

Kali seemed a bit more reluctant to talk about this subject than Anaukaq had been. "Mmmm, sometimes the other children would taunt my brother and me, call us names, things like that," Kali said.

"What kind of names?" I asked.

"Sometimes they would tell me and my older brother Hammy that we were more *kahdonah* than Eskimo, and that we thought we were better than others. Other times they would point to us and say, 'There, the *kahdonah* ones.'" Kali chuckled. "We used to get very angry, especially Hammy. But our mother protected us."

Kali continued. "This really affected Hammy more than it did me. He used to get so upset inside. He was always very active, doing things to keep his mind off his hurt. Hammy and I tried to be the best hunters we possibly could. That way, we could show them that we were as good as everyone else."

"You mean that you were as much Inuit as everyone else?" I said.

"Yes, that is right," said Kali.

"Do you feel different from other Eskimos because you are part white?" I asked.

"I am Eskimo," he affirmed proudly, still chewing on a piece of raw bird. "I was born and raised Eskimo. I think Eskimo. I was an Eskimo hunter. I did not grow up in the ways of the *kahdonah*. All my children were raised as Inuit. My sons Talilanguaq and Peter and my grandson, Ole, are all Eskimo hunters. My *ahnahnna* [mother] and my adoptive *ahtahtah*, Peeahwahto, raised me to be a good Eskimo," he continued. "That is what they knew. They never told me that I should try to be different from other Inuit because I looked different. And Peeuree did nothing for my brother Hammy and me. There were no other *kahdonah* around. We lived only with other Inuit, traveling from place to place with other families, with the seasons."

"That is right," Anaukaq chimed in. "We are both Inuit Eskimos and we have known only the Inuit life. We had no contact with the *kahdonah* except for the few Danish missionaries at Thule Station, and we would only see them about once a year."

"Sometimes during the summers, whaling ships from different lands would come to Cape York, south of here," Kali added. "Then we would see *kahdonah*, some even from Peeuree's homeland."

"Yes," said Anaukaq. "That reminds me. When we were young boys, MacMillan, who had worked on the North Pole trip, used to come up here to work and travel north on the ice. He would find Cousin Kali and me, and give us gifts and candy. He was very kind to us. He would tell us that our fathers were well and bring us greetings from them."

"MacMillan was good," Kali agreed. "We never saw our fathers up here, but MacMillan came up here several times when we were boys. He was very nice. He always gave us something. It kind of made us feel that we were not forgotten. He gave candy and gifts to other children as well."

"Did he ever give your mothers gifts or anything sent from America personally from Mahri-Pahluk and Peeuree?" I asked, looking at both men.

"Oh, *nahdoohhoyah* [I don't know]," answered Kali. "I can't remember." Anaukaq could not recall either but thought he remembered MacMillan bringing some things from Mahri-Pahluk for his mother, Akatingwah.

Their recollections were certainly consistent with MacMillan's reputation. By all accounts, he was among the kinder, more open-minded members of Peary's party. We also know that after Peary's

last expedition, MacMillan became the preeminent American explorer of the Arctic and made several visits to the area in which
Anaukaq and Kali lived. As one of the few people who knew for
certain of Peary and Henson's "North Pole secret," and as a loyal
friend of both men, MacMillan might well have been asked to look in
discreetly on the explorers' Amer-Eskimo "orphans."

"Did MacMillan ever offer to take you to America?" I asked.

"No," Anaukaq answered. "We were too young then, and we had
to stay with our parents. But later we wanted very much to go to
America and see our fathers and other relatives."

Kali added that when they were young boys, his brother Hammy
used to tell people, especially when they taunted him, that he was
going to go to America to find "Peeuree." And when he found him,
he would stay with his *ahtahtah* in a big igloo. But he and Hammy
were frightened, Kali said, because everyone had heard about the
bad things that had happened to Mene and his family when they
went to Peary's homeland.

"The Eskimos," Kali said, "felt that Mene and his group were all
overcome by bad spirits and died."

Kali was referring to the tragic story of the young Polar Eskimo,
Mene, who, with his father, Kes-shoo, and four other Inuit, was
taken to the United States by Peary in 1897 and later "exhibited" at
the American Museum of Natural History in New York. Some of the
Eskimos had been with Peary that year when he confiscated the last
of the sacred Polar Eskimo meteorites, or "heaven stones," which he
later sold to the museum. Soon after they arrived in the United
States, most of the Eskimos fell ill with pneumonia and other afflic-
tions. Peary and the museum director promptly summoned Matthew
Henson, the only person in the United States known to speak their
language, but there was nothing he or anyone else could do. All but
the eight-year-old Mene and one other Eskimo were hospitalized and
eventually died. Compounding the tragedy, the museum defleshed
the remains of the dead Eskimos and put their articulated skeletons
on display. Upon seeing his father's skeleton in public, the forlorn
Mene became enraged. With the help of others, including some
journalists, he fought to remove his father's remains from the exhibit
for proper burial. Although the noted anthropologist Franz Boas had

come up with the idea of displaying the Eskimos, Robert Peary was roundly criticized for his role in the affair.

After twelve difficult years in America, Mene returned of his own volition to northwest Greenland in 1909 aboard Peary's relief ship, the *Jeanie*. Fortunately, he met Peary and Henson just as they were preparing to depart for the United States. According to Henson, "[Mene] was almost destitute, having positively nothing in the way of an equipment to enable him to withstand the rigors of the country, and was no more fitted for the life he was to take up than any boy of eighteen or twenty would be. . . . However, Commander Peary ordered that he be given a plentiful supply of furs to keep him warm, food, ammunition and loading outfit, traps and guns."[1]

Mene slowly and painfully tried to reacclimate himself to the Eskimo life he had known as a child. He became a pretty good hunter and, with the help of friends and relatives, learned to look after himself. But eventually he abandoned any hope of fully readjusting to his native culture. In the summer of 1916, seven years after his return, he hitched a ride on an expeditionary relief ship bound for the United States and left Greenland for the last time. Unable to reestablish his old contacts, he wandered around the eastern United States for two years, working as an itinerant laborer. Some speculate that he may have been trying to work his way up to Peary's residence in Maine. In any event, in 1918 Mene died of bronchial pneumonia while working at a lumber camp in Pittsburg, New Hampshire. He was buried by friends in a local cemetery, where his body remains today.

"Did anyone besides MacMillan ever bring you word from your fathers?" I asked.

"No," replied Kali. "After MacMillan stopped coming up here, we heard nothing about our fathers. We gave up all hope of ever visiting Peeuree's homeland."

"Did the other white men who came up here know that you were the sons of Mahri-Pahluk and Peeuree?" I asked.

"*Nahdoohhoyah*," said Anaukaq. "No one ever said so. We were treated by outsiders just like other Eskimos. We did not have last names in those days, before the missionaries asked us to take last names in the late 1960s. We were only known by our first names."

"There are other half-white Inuit up here," Kali added. "Maybe they did not know which of us were the children of Peeuree."

"That is possible in your case, Kali," I said. "But Mahri-Pahluk was the only *kulnocktooko* to visit Polar Eskimo lands at that time, and any dark offspring would have to be his."

Both men laughed. "You are right."

"When they built the military base at Umanak," Anaukaq said, "many men came up here from Mahri-Pahluk and Peary's homeland. But they did not know who we were or that we were their [Henson's and Peary's] sons. They just told all Inuit people that they had to move much farther north or south of Umanak mountain because they were going to build a base there. The people did not want to move but were forced to do so."

"One day we heard that some of the Inuit had seen a *kulnocktooko* man while traveling past the base on the way to Savissivik," Anaukaq continued. "My family became very excited because we thought that he might be one of Mahri-Pahluk's descendants—one of our relatives. Maybe he had come up here to find us, we thought. We wanted him to come and visit us, but he never came. A short time later, he left Greenland. We don't know why, but some said that maybe the chiefs at the base would not let him come to see us."

I spent the next few days listening to and recording the two men's stories. They seemed to delight in the opportunity to talk with someone who showed interest in their lives and cultural heritage. The younger family members who joined us also learned from these revelations about their past and ancestry.

I followed them all about the settlement. Anaukaq showed Kali around his settlement much as one does a guest in any culture. Anaukaq proudly presented his eight sled dogs and talked about their strength and breeding. He took Kali to the little general store at the edge of the settlement run by his fourth son, Ajako, and to the grave of his wife, Aviaq.

Too soon the time came for me to return to the United States. I would have to leave the settlement by helicopter while the unpredictable weather was calm, so that I could reach Thule in time for my scheduled flight to McGuire Air Force Base.

On my last evening in Moriussaq, I prepared a big dinner for

Anaukaq, Kali, and their families. The bill of fare was all my remaining food. Though they loved my canned tuna, ham, and other meats, they found other offerings less than appetizing.

"What do you call this stuff?" asked Kali. "It tastes like paper."

"Oatmeal," I replied. "It's a kind of grain, like a bread."

"Why do you have so much of it?" Anaukaq inquired.

"Well, it's easy to carry, it's filling, and it's good for you. All you have to do is add water."

"It is good for people with no teeth," Kali interjected.

Everyone laughed.

In a more serious tone, Anaukaq asked, "Allen, do you think you will be able to arrange for us to go to America?"

"I hope so, Anaukaq," I answered. "But I cannot promise anything, other than that I will try my best to arrange such a trip. There are many difficulties, you know. It will be very expensive. Transportation alone from Greenland to the United States is a big problem. Then we must have food, lodging, and transportation in the United States. It is very difficult and very expensive. I don't know how I can do it, but maybe I can raise the money from your American families. And perhaps I can get the Danish government to help us. I'm just speculating now," I quickly added. "I don't want to get your hopes up only to fail. But I promise you that I will try my best."

"I know you will. We have faith in you," Anaukaq said with uncharacteristic sadness in his voice. "I hope this dream becomes real. It is the last dream I have before I die. You see, I have been ill lately, and I will not live much longer. So if I am ever to see my American relatives and my father's grave, it must be soon."

"I understand, my friend," I said.

"I hope I live to see the day, but if I die before you can arrange such a trip, I hope that you will help my sons and their children meet their American relatives and see Mahri-Pahluk's grave site. That is very important to me."

"You have my word that I will try my best," I said. "Just keep the faith."

"*Eeee*," Kali added. "My cousin has been very ill lately. I now worry for him. I hope we can both go to our fathers' homeland before he becomes more gravely ill. I will help to look after him."

I was deeply moved by Kali's concern for Anaukaq. During the time I had spent with the two of them I had come to believe that they were more like brothers than friends or "cousins." At eighty years of age they were still looking after each other. Their fathers, who also shared a special bond, would be happy to see this, I thought.

"If I can arrange this trip to the United States, how many of your family would you want to go along with you?" I asked both men.

Anaukaq spoke up first. "I would be very happy if my sons could go with me: Avataq, Ajako, Ussarkaq, and Kitdlaq. My other son Vittus is not here. He is in southern Greenland working for the Danes and maybe cannot join us. But I would like to see him."

Then Anaukaq's granddaughter Malina, who had been dancing in African-American fashion to a soul music tape on my recorder, said, "I would like to go, too."

"Me, too," added Anaukaq's ten-year-old granddaughter, Aviaq. "If Malina goes I want to go also."

"What about you, Kali?" I asked. "Which of your children do you want to travel with you to America if we have the opportunity to go there?"

"Oh, I don't know. But I think I would like for my son, Talilanguaq, and my grandson Ole to go with me."

"Let me see," I said, counting on my fingers. "That's Anaukaq, Kali, Avataq, Talilanguaq, Ajako, Ussarkaq, Kitdlaq, Ole, Malina, Aviaq, and possibly Vittus—a total of thirteen, counting myself and Navarana Qavigaq, the translator. That is quite a few people. It will be very expensive. But we shall see. If we have to take fewer people on the first trip, I will let Anaukaq and Kali decide who will join them."

"Maybe we can aim for a date next fall [1987], about a year from now," I said. "But I promise you I will be back in the spring to let you know about my progress in arranging a visit. Just keep the faith."

"Yes, the fall or winter would be a good time because it might be very hot in the other seasons," Anaukaq said.

"I agree with my cousin," Kali chuckled. "You know, Eskimos don't like heat."

Everyone laughed, and on that cheerful note we ended our dinner.

In spite of the enthusiasm I had shown in the presence of Kali and

Anaukaq, privately I was less optimistic. I knew that it would be an enormous task to arrange a trip to America for both families. Just how I was going to do it, I did not know.

As we stepped out into the cold darkness, we witnessed a final, unexpected salute to the end of my visit. At first I was startled. The scene before my eyes seemed surreal, even magical. In the pitch black of the night, as if by some theatrical orchestration, the sky suddenly lit up with lights so bright that I thought they came from unnatural or artificial sources. The lights formed radiant streams of white ghostlike figures, descending from a large circle in the sky directly above me. Some of these luminous apparitions seemed to have long tails and faces on their cometlike heads. As if on cue, the brilliant streams of light would drop straight down toward the ground and then sail back up again. Before long the light forms were all around us, dancing and moving in all directions, like special effects in a Steven Spielberg movie.

Several of the young people ran out of their houses to enjoy what to them must be similar to our Fourth of July fireworks. But I was uneasy. For the first few moments, the lights looked so unnatural that I thought they might be exploding rockets. The fact that we were so close to the air base at Thule, the "northern defense line" of the Pentagon's Early Warning System, only intensified my anxiety. I shivered as my imagination conjured up the ultimate conflagration while I stood at the top of the planet, staring at the night sky.

It took several minutes for Anaukaq and Kali to convince me that I was actually witnessing the aurora borealis. They said that while they regularly see these northern lights, this was one of the grandest exhibitions they had ever experienced. As they explained it, the aurora borealis is a special game played by the spirits of their ancestors, a sport akin to football in which the ancestors kick a walrus's head across the sky.

Curiously and somewhat eerily, Anaukaq and Kali whistled when some especially bright lights appeared in the sky. Several of the youngsters who had joined us also whistled. To my amazement, the sound seemed to bring the lights down like comets, toward the whistler. In each instance, it looked as though there were a direct relation between the whistling and the movement of the light toward

Earth. Groping for some explanation, I thought that perhaps the pitch of the whistle caused the cold air particles to move closer together in such a way as to create a temporarily denser conductive medium of lower resistance for sound and light. Kali and Anaukaq had a simpler explanation. They said that the ancestral spirits simply came to them when they called.

When they were children, walking through a village alone, Kali said, they often were frightened by the aurora borealis if it came too close when they whistled. They thought that the ancestral spirits might come down from the sky and take them away to a strange place.

"Maybe it is a good omen," I said. "Maybe the spirits are telling us something."

The next morning Anaukaq and Kali bade me farewell as I left by helicopter for the Thule air base.

CHAPTER TEN

* * *

Keeping the Faith

Nestled in a fjord surrounded by snow-covered mountains, Dundas Air Force Base at Thule is a colossal sprawl of nondescript military buildings and airplane hangars. Although its strange appearance restores a measure of primal fright even to the most jaded observer, it offers certain conveniences otherwise unknown in this remote corner of the earth. After weeks of melting ice in my "igloo" just to take a "bath," it was therapeutic to step into a shower at the base. The hot, powerful cascade seemed to melt away the dirt, seal oil, and other vestiges of the unusual world I had just left. I let the water run for over an hour, all the while thinking about how I could help Anaukaq and Kali get to the United States—and once there, how I would arrange for their stay and their travel.

Finding transportation to the United States was the first problem. There seemed to be only two possibilities. One was to obtain seats on the weekly, sometimes monthly, military flight from Thule to Copenhagen, and then take a commercial airliner from Copenhagen to the United States. As far as I knew, however, the Copenhagen flight was restricted to the Danish military and staff personnel serving at Thule. Traveling by such a circuitous route, moreover, promised to be not only time consuming but also prohibitively expensive.

The second possibility was to hitch a ride on one of the American

C-141 transports that regularly shuttled between the United States and Thule. Like the Danish flights, however, these too were strictly for military, scientific, and other personnel serving the base. The only difference was that the U.S. Air Force had contracted with the Ministry of Greenland to transport Eskimos between Thule and Sondre Stromfiord Air Base in southern Greenland. Perhaps they could extend this policy to flights destined for the United States, I thought. I decided to meet with both the American and Danish base commanders to explore these options.

In the dining hall at the base, I had a chance meeting with Maj. Quincy Sharp, director of base operations. A tall, statuesque, soft-spoken man in his early forties, Sharp was the lead pilot in a fleet of B-52 bombers. He had flown numerous missions over the North Pole and knew about Matthew Henson and Robert Peary, but he did not know about Anaukaq and Kali, and their story fascinated him. He agreed to help me arrange a meeting with base commander Col. James Knapp, whom I had written earlier for permission to use base facilities.

The next day Colonel Knapp greeted me warmly at base headquarters. He too found the story of the two Amer-Eskimo men fascinating and advised me on the procedures for obtaining official permission from the Department of Defense to use military aircraft. Things were looking up.

I hoped that the Danish authorities would react similarly to my proposal, recognizing it as an opportunity to show some good will toward the native population. Denmark has governed Greenland since 1916, when American control of the territory, first claimed by Peary and Henson, was relinquished as part of a trade for the Danish (now American) Virgin Islands. Yet even before then relations between the Danes and the Eskimos were strained. Early Danish explorers, for example, captured Polar Eskimos and took them back to Denmark for exhibition. To the astonishment of many Danes, some of the Eskimos would steal away from Denmark in canoes in an effort to return overseas to their homeland, only to drown far out at sea.

Some Eskimos still complain, not without reason, about what they regard as a condescending attitude on the part of the Greenlandic Danes. One day during my visit to Moriussaq, I met a Danish technician who had been sent from Thule to repair some downed communication lines in the area. I shared some of my tea with him and inquired about his feelings toward the Eskimos. He said that he and many of the other Danes in Greenland called the Eskimos "junkyard Indians." When I asked why, he said it was because the Eskimos were frequently seen around the refuse and junk heaps of the Danish and American military installations, sorting through the discarded material for wood, metal, and other things. This, he said, was one of the many things that lowered them in his eyes.

But other Danes I met in Greenland, particularly those with whom I collaborated, sincerely cared about the welfare of the Polar Eskimos and treated them as equals.

In the end, the Danish authorities at Thule referred my inquiries about transporting Anaukaq and Kali to their government offices in Copenhagen and Washington.

＊　＊　＊

When I arrived in Cambridge, an autumn snow had given the old Harvard Yard a picture-postcard beauty. The branches of the huge elm trees strained from the thick, cottonlike snow, and large icicles hung from the roofs of the gracefully aging red-brick buildings.

In my University Hall office, I found stacks of letters inquiring about Anaukaq and Kali. Many of the letters were from Matthew Henson's relatives all over the country. They had read the stories in newspapers and journals about my encounter with their Amer-Eskimo kin, and they wanted to meet them too. I was reminded of the statement Matthew Henson made in 1947, following the appearance of a series of articles highlighting his life. He said that he heard from relatives he didn't even know he had.

I contacted each of the family members and explained my hopes of arranging a visit to the United States for Anaukaq and Kali the following fall. All the American Hensons I spoke with expressed a strong desire to receive their Eskimo kin and to be a part of a general reunion. Some lived in Boston, some in New York, some in Maryland, others in Washington D.C., the Midwest, even California. I later learned that Matthew Henson's eighty-three-year-old niece, Virginia Carter Brannum, the last living offspring of his closest sister,

Eliza Carter, was living in Washington, D.C. A delightful woman of great poise and remarkable memory, she told me how her Uncle Matthew used to send her money to help take care of her mother. When I met and interviewed her, she shared with me her personal letters and other memorabilia from Henson.

In the meantime, following up on my conversations in Thule, I contacted the U.S. offices of the Danish government about possible support for my plans. The Danish officials with whom I spoke expressed complete surprise to learn of Anaukaq's and Kali's existence. I was told that my request would be considered by the proper authorities, who would contact me when a decision was reached.

I also wrote to the U.S. Air Force and the Department of Defense and requested permission to fly Anaukaq, Kali, and their families to America free of charge aboard one of the regularly scheduled C-141 transports. This kind of project, I was told, was unprecedented and would require special consideration.

Anaukaq and Kali had essentially defined an itinerary for their trip when they said that they wanted to visit their fathers' grave sites and meet their American relatives. Matthew Henson was buried in Woodlawn Cemetery in the Bronx, New York. He had lived mainly in New York City, Philadelphia, Washington, D.C., the Maryland area, and, for a brief time, Boston. Most of his closest relatives were in those cities. Robert Peary was buried in Arlington National Cemetery, just outside Washington, D.C. His surviving descendants lived for the most part in Maine, New York City, the Washington, D.C. area, and Maryland.

Though I hadn't heard from any of the American Pearys since my return, I still hoped that eventually they would agree to meet with their Amer-Eskimo relatives. Even if they didn't, I suspected that Kali would want to come and visit his father's grave.

Anaukaq and Kali had given no time limit for their visit but agreed with their sons that about two weeks would be all the time the group could spend away from their families, dogs, and work. This would allow us time only to tour the most important family sites on the East Coast and give receptions at each place.

By now I had determined that the major expenses in the United States would be room and board in each city. If all the Greenlandic family members that Kali and Anaukaq had requested were to come along, this would be a very costly proposition. Most of the American Hensons were working people who had big hearts and a lot of pride but did not have much extra money. They wanted to do all that they could to help me make the Eskimos' visit to America a pleasant one. They offered to contribute what they could to help me bring their relatives to the United States and to transport and house them.

My only complication with the Hensons was that relatives at each location wanted the Eskimos to stay with them longer than with the other kin. In response to this problem, I recommended that we hold a single large family get-together in one city and, from that base, take short excursions into the other cities. I left the choice of the city for the American Hensons to decide, but the relatives and friends could not agree. I then recommended Washington, because it was the city where Henson and Peary first met and it is readily accessible to anyone living along the eastern seaboard.

About a month later, I received a letter from the Danish government indicating that they would not provide support for Anaukaq and Kali's trip to America. This was disappointing. I had thought that at the very least the Danish authorities would have provided us with transportation from Thule to Copenhagen.

Some weeks later, I heard from the U.S. Air Force, my last hope. I nervously opened the letter to read that my request had been turned down. This was a crushing blow. I sat for minutes, just staring at the letter, remembering how optimistic Anaukaq and Kali had been when I last saw them and trying to decide how I would break the news. But after a while, I pulled myself out of my depression and started to write to the air force and the secretary of defense, this time with an offer to pay for seats on one of the C-141 transport jets. I still had faith.

Meanwhile, I decided the time had come to contact the American Pearys and find out whether they had had a change of heart. When I reached the family representative, I was once again met with a polite but cold tone. I talked about my recent visit with Kali and made it clear that he still hoped to meet his American relatives. After an extended silence, the spokesman said, "I guess if you give them free transportation, they would go anywhere with you."

"I don't think Kali and his family are looking for anything free, sir," I responded. "They just don't have the resources to pay for such a trip. The only way they will ever get to the United States to see Admiral Peary's grave is for us to help them."

"Well, we won't help," he replied. "You give them the free transportation if you want, but we will not help you bring them here."

I was disappointed that the Peary-Staffords had not softened their position and sad that I might inadvertently be hurting their family by insisting on inviting Kali to come along with Anaukaq. Nevertheless, I could not understand how they could reject Kali outright.

Around the same time, I heard from the Amer-Eskimos Hensons through the translator in Greenland. Anaukaq had taken ill and was being kept in the tiny Danish and Eskimo-run infirmary at Qaanaaq. The diagnosis was prostate cancer. Like most elderly people, Anaukaq hated hospitals and wanted to go back home to his family. When he entered the hospital, he told the translator that he would be well enough to return to his family in a short time but added, "Tell Allen if I am going to visit America, it will have to be soon. Please don't you leave the area before I get out of the infirmary, because I want you to go to America with Kali and me as our translator when Allen comes to get us."

When I contacted a Danish physician who had treated Anaukaq to inquire about his condition, he told me that his prostate cancer, like other cancers, was fairly unpredictable. "It is difficult to tell," he said. "In his present condition, he could go on living for years, or he could succumb earlier. I think he has a strong will to live now."

Understandably, Anaukaq's family also felt a greater sense of urgency about the trip. Fearful that Anaukaq's health might deteriorate quickly in the months ahead, they suggested that we plan the visit for the spring of 1987 rather than the ensuing fall. I agreed, even though the new timetable would make it even more difficult to work out our plans.

As a result of the nationwide publicity about my meeting with Anaukaq and Kali, I was receiving dozens of letters and telephone calls from journalists and film crews—all wanting me to tell them how to reach Anaukaq and Kali. From the articles that appeared in *Newsweek*, the *Boston Globe*, the *New York Times*, and other newspapers, Anaukaq and Kali had attained a kind of celebrity, and many in the media simply wanted to get their story. I could just imagine some of the callers descending upon their villages with their note pads, tape recorders, and cameras. Some reporters and photographers all but demanded that I reveal to them Kali's and Anaukaq's whereabouts. In fact, one U.S. wire-service reporter called me to say that he had received permission to travel to Thule by convincing the air force that he was going to do a story on the military in Greenland, but that he really wanted to do a story on Anaukaq and Kali. He insisted that I tell him how to locate the Amer-Eskimo families and expressed anger when I refused.

Even in Denmark, a number of newspapers carried articles on Anaukaq and Kali for the first time, prompting new interest in the Polar Eskimos. Some Danes tried to contact them. Others claimed that they had known of Anaukaq and Kali all along, but apparently never thought the information of interest to the public.

Perhaps the most disturbing news I received from Greenland during this depressing period, however, came a few weeks later. I learned from the Amer-Eskimo families in Greenland that some of the American Pearys had contacted them and had tried to dissuade them from traveling to America with Anaukaq and his family. The Amer-Eskimo Pearys were shocked, confused, and eventually angered by this effort. The American Pearys had never reached out to make contact with or even to acknowledge them as relatives in over eighty years. Now these same people, who had earlier tried to convince me that Kali was not Robert Peary's son, claimed to be acting with Kali's best interests in mind. The irony of this was not lost on the Eskimos.

The Amer-Eskimos told me that the Peary-Stafford family had enlisted the help of an adventurer who traveled to the area for Arctic photographic work. It appears that this man, like so many others, became aware of Anaukaq and Kali only after they had come to national and international attention in 1986. Eventually he put together a team of filmmakers from England and traveled to the area to film Anaukaq and Kali in the spring of 1987, just before they were to leave for America.

The Peary-Stafford family representative also sent letters and other materials to one of the Eskimo Pearys who spoke some English, suggesting that if Kali and his family came to America with me, they would be abused and midhandled, particularly by the news media. Even more disruptive, the family representative and his collaborator brought up the issue of race in an apparent effort to create a rift between the Eskimo Hensons and Pearys. According to the Eskimos, they suggested that my efforts in this project would only exalt Henson and discredit Peary, and that although they were part Eskimo, they were also part white. It would therefore be better if they waited and came to the United States at some future date. Kali later informed me that the explorer had tried to get him to wait and visit America with him.

Naturally, I became deeply concerned about the Pearys' interference with the plans that I had made with Anaukaq and Kali. The intervention of the Pearys and their associate had ended up pitting members of the Amer-Eskimo Peary family against one another, and I could see the potential for further confusion and discord if such meddling persisted. I felt I had no alternative but to call the family spokesman to investigate the allegations.

When the Peary-Stafford representative confirmed that he had been in touch with Kali and his family, I asked him why. He responded by saying that he and his family remained convinced that if Kali and his children came here, they would bring negative publicity on themselves as well as on the American Pearys, and he thought it was within his right to say this to them.

"Well, if you cared as much about this family as you're suggesting now, why haven't you been in touch with them before, just to introduce yourself or acknowledge them as family?" I asked. He seemed to squirm about for an answer, suggesting that the American side of the family might have done so one day in the future but that my efforts had really added impetus to their desire to talk to the Arctic Pearys.

"Well, just a few weeks ago you indicated to me that the Peary family members were not certain that Kali was in fact Robert E. Peary's son, and now you're contacting them and asking them not to come to America," I said. He struggled uncomfortably for a reply.

It became quite clear to me that this man was in fact attempting to sabotage Kali and Anaukaq's plans to visit America. It took all the strength I could muster to control myself. I assured him that I was responding to Anaukaq's and Kali's wishes in bringing them to America and that they were both elderly men who simply wanted this opportunity now because they did not know what the future held for them.

He suggested that it would be fine for Anaukaq and his family to come to the United States but that he still felt the need to let the Arctic Pearys know that they were probably being exploited. "If you felt there was exploitation," I responded, "then why were you not concerned about the Amer-Eskimo Hensons being exploited as well? Why didn't you contact the Eskimo Hensons as well to indicate that they too might be exploited?" Again he was unable to come up with an adequate reply.

He then explained his collaborator's role by saying that he had been working with him on a new project about Robert Peary's polar explorations and that the family was providing him with certain information from the Admiral's private papers. He admitted that he had asked this man to intervene on behalf of the Peary family in America with "the Eskimos who say they are Pearys."

Despite my anger, there was little I could do except urge him to stop interfering with our plans. I assured him that every activity I had planned for Anaukaq, Kali, and their families would be carried out with great dignity and respect for them, their privacy, and their well-being. I ended the conversation.

At this point so many issues and problems confronted me that I simply did not know which way to turn. I still hadn't been able to line up transportation to the United States for Anaukaq, Kali, and their families. I was uncertain just how successful the Peary-Staffords and their emissary had been in undermining my efforts. And, further complicating matters, I was receiving reports that the publicity surrounding the trip had attracted the attention of a number of influential people in Greenland who felt that they should be included in our plans.

There was, moreover, another matter that bothered me—and had bothered me for some time. Robert Peary had been buried with full military honors and had a beautiful monument in Arlington National

Cemetery, while Matthew Henson was buried in a simple grave in Woodlawn Cemetery. In many ways their graves symbolized the disparate treatment they had received in life from their fellow Americans. Peary's grave site boasted a massive monument from the National Geographic Society. Henson had received nothing from the society, which had ignored him in death as in life. Peary's grave site was situated on a hill carefully selected for its commanding position in Arlington National Cemetery. Henson's small gray headstone was simply placed in a common row of other equally simple grave sites. If Henson's service to his country had been given proper consideration at the time of his death, he too would have been buried in our most prestigious national cemetery. This was a tragic wrong that needed to be righted. I felt that moving Henson's remains to Arlington National Cemetery would in some measure make up for the lack of recognition he had received from his country during his life.

I shared my idea of the reinterment with several of the American Hensons, and they fully agreed. Next, I contacted Washington officials who could help me to arrange to have Matthew Henson's remains removed from the Woodlawn Cemetery and reintered at Arlington. I learned that only two people can assign individuals to burial sites in Arlington National Cemetery. One is the secretary of the army, who makes decisions about former military personnel whose families wish to have them buried in Arlington. The other person is the President of the United States.

At the very mention of this idea, some of my colleagues and friends laughed in disbelief. "You'll probably have to wait for another administration. This administration is not known for doing this kind of thing," one friend told me. Others suggested that such an effort would be virtually impossible under the present army hierarchy and that it was futile for me to try. But, as usual, such comments only hardened my resolve.

One evening in late 1986 I sat down and composed a letter to President Reagan requesting permission to reinter Matthew Henson among other American heroes in Arlington National Cemetery.

Later in the spring, I received word that Anaukaq had left the infirmary in Qaanaaq of his own volition, telling the nurses and translator that he was fine and ready to travel to the United States.

"Please don't forget that I want you to travel to Mahri-Pahluk's homeland with me and my family to serve as our translator, when Allen comes," he reminded the translator.

What Anaukaq did not know was that I still had not found a way of transporting the families. I had begun to explore the incredibly expensive option of using a Canadian charter airline, which hops from island to island across northern Canada, when I again heard from the Department of Defense. This time the news was good. The U.S. Air Force had granted my request to transport Anaukaq, Kali, and their families from Dundas Air Force Base in Thule to McGuire Air Force Base, provided that each passenger paid a fee covering air transport and lodging on the base. The cost of transporting all prospective passengers would run to at least ten thousand dollars. At this point, I was so thrilled at having surmounted a major obstacle that I did not worry about the money. I simply heaved a great sigh of relief and then ran through University Hall telling my students the good news.

Several of my students, fellow faculty, and friends at Harvard had been very helpful and supportive throughout my involvement with this project. Even the president of the university had met with me to express his special interest in my efforts and to offer his encouragement. But the students were a tremendous source of inspiration from the moment they heard the story. They saw this effort as a kind of victory for Anaukaq and Kali—a victory over prejudice and abandonment and the fulfillment of a lifelong wish. And they wanted to be actively involved in making that dream come true. I drew much of my inner strength from the enthusiasm of these young people.

We decided to form the "North Pole Family Reunion Committee," a group of Harvard students, faculty, and staff, along with members of the American Henson and, we still hoped, Peary families. As we began to organize the visit, we soon realized that the costs would be much greater than originally anticipated, and the complications manifold. In addition to the cost of air transportation from Thule, we would have to pay for air- and ground-travel in the United States as well as for food, lodging, guides, translators, and security in every city. We also needed medical and health insurance along with traveling medical personnel, in case of an emergency. We estimated the total costs to be in the tens of thousands of dollars. Like typical academics, we turned to granting agencies.

I approached several such agencies and known philanthropists about possible support for the project. While they all found the idea interesting, each had other funding priorities at the time. No support materialized. I had already decided that I would pay Anaukaq's and Kali's transportation and other expenses from my personal funds, but I was unsure about how to cover the other costs of bringing several members of their families along. Some of the committee recommended that we cut costs by reducing the number of family members traveling on this first trip. But we all agreed Anaukaq wanted his five sons with him and Kali wanted his only son and one grandson to join him. This meant a minimum of nine family members plus the translator. Also, Malina served as Anaukaq's nurse, so she would have to come along. And Aviaq did not want Malina and her father to leave without her. Reluctant as I was to leave Anaukaq's and Kali's sons and grandchildren behind, I had to concede it was unlikely that I could raise the thousands of dollars necessary to bring them along. The committee suggested a more modest plan of bringing Anaukaq, Kali, a translator, and one assistant on the first U.S. visit. We could try to bring other family members sometime later.

Just when we had all but given up hope of finding outside financial support, I remembered a chance encounter I had had some ten years earlier with a man who shared my admiration for Matthew Henson. This man, too, is one of my heroes, and he had told me about the role Matthew Henson had played in his own successful career. I had filed this remarkable story away in the back of my mind years ago. Now, as if by divine intervention, I retrieved it at a critical juncture.

The man was John H. Johnson, chairman of the Johnson Publishing Company and publisher of *Ebony* and *Jet*. Johnson and his publishing empire represent a historical institution in America. He is an icon in the black communities of the world. From very humble beginnings like Henson's he has risen to become one of the wealthiest and most accomplished men in America.

After fleeing racially oppressive Arkansas in the thirties, Johnson and his mother moved to Chicago. His mother encouraged him to become a businessman and, when he reached adulthood, she helped him borrow five hundred dollars to support his idea of starting the new magazine he named *Ebony*. Johnson launched his publishing venture in 1945, when postwar America was beginning to deal with civil rights, and black Americans were in the incipient stages of developing a substantial middle class.

Like all magazines, *Ebony* needed business advertisements to survive. But all the large wholesale and retail businesses in Chicago were owned by whites. So Johnson and his wife, Eunice, would go from business to business, door to door in Chicago, trying to obtain the necessary advertising to keep his magazine afloat. This kind of effort was unprecedented in 1945, and Johnson, like most black entrepreneurs, was unable to establish substantive business relationships with the white establishments of Chicago. He went as far as hiring white ethnics to try to sell the ads to white businesses in Chicago, but without success. He found that even those businesses that had a large black clientele would not purchase advertising space from him. In many ways, Chicago was as racially biased as his native Arkansas.

But Johnson and his wife persevered. She would often wait in the car while he tried, usually without success, to get past a secretary and meet with the head of a corporation to discuss advertising space in *Ebony*.

As Johnson tells the story, his luck changed one day in 1946 when he entered the headquarters of Zenith Radio Corporation in Chicago to meet with its chairman, retired commander Eugene F. McDonald. McDonald had agreed to give Johnson a brief audience to hear about his business venture.

When he entered the office, McDonald stood, extended his hand, and cordially welcomed the well-dressed young entrepreneur. He offered Johnson a seat in one of the dark leather chairs in his office. "Do you see those snowshoes there on my wall, Johnson?" McDonald asked. "Those snowshoes were given to me by one of the greatest explorers in the history of Arctic exploration. He was a better man than any three white men put together—and he happens to be of your race." McDonald explained that the snowshoes had been given to him by Matthew Henson after he returned from the North Pole with Peary. Rubbing the walrus-skin strings of the snowshoes as if they were precious gems, he asked Johnson if he had ever heard of Matthew Henson.

Johnson told McDonald that he had just done a story on Henson in his new magazine, *Ebony*. He handed McDonald a copy of the magazine, feeling proud that he had carefully researched McDonald's interests before the meeting and learned that Arctic exploration was one of his passions.

McDonald skimmed through the magazine until he reached the story on Henson. He quickly read over parts of the story, then looked up at Johnson. McDonald was impressed. He mentioned that Henson had written an autobiographical account of his North Pole experiences, which he had been unable to find anywhere. He asked Johnson if he would help him locate a copy, whereupon the well-prepared young publisher handed McDonald an autographed, hardcover edition of *A Negro Explorer at the North Pole* by Matthew Alexander Henson.

McDonald was flabbergasted. He thanked Johnson profusely as he thumbed through the book.

"Mr. Johnson, how can I help you?" McDonald asked.

Johnson told him that he wanted to sell Zenith some advertising space in his new magazine. He described *Ebony* as a human-interest magazine that featured educational, social, cultural, and political articles by and about blacks in America and other parts of the world, and he expressed confidence in its potential for success. Johnson had actually been trying for months to get ads from Zenith, but on each occasion he had been turned away, usually by McDonald's secretary.

McDonald pressed his intercom and asked his secretary to step into his office. To Johnson's—and the secretary's—surprise, he asked her to arrange to have Zenith ads placed in *Ebony* on a regular basis. McDonald also agreed to ask some of his business associates to have their companies buy advertising space in *Ebony*.

Johnson thanked McDonald and left. A few days later, he received his first substantial advertising account from Zenith. Soon other large white-owned Chicago businesses bought advertising space as well. Johnson Publishing Company was off and running, and Matthew Henson had unwittingly played a major role in another historic moment.

I wrote John H. Johnson and reminded him of our meeting and mentioned my recollection of this remarkable story. I told him about Anaukaq and Kali and asked whether he would consider defraying some of the costs of the North Pole Family Reunion.

Johnson telephoned me immediately upon receiving my letter. "Amazing," he said. "Dr. Counter, have you actually found a son that Matthew Henson fathered in the Arctic?" he asked.

"That's right, Mr. Johnson—and Henson's five grandsons, and twenty-two great-grandchildren."

"That is incredible!" he said. "How on earth did you find them?"

I told him the story from the beginning. I could tell from his voice that he was deeply moved.

"How can I help you, Dr. Counter?"

"Well, sir, I am trying to raise money to pay for the North Pole Family Reunion project. I am using my own funds for some things, but I need more money to make the project a memorable success. I wondered if you would be willing to make a contribution to the effort?"

"Dr. Counter, I support what you are trying to do. Matthew Henson is our hero, and it is just great to know that you are trying to keep his memory alive. You have brought this project this far, and I have all the faith in the world that you will carry it through. I want to help you in any way that I can. Just write me and tell me what you need."

"Thank you, Mr. Johnson."

I was bursting with joy and pride—joy that I had finally secured the necessary funds, pride that John H. Johnson, a man I greatly admired, had agreed to cosponsor the project. I drew up a budget and sent it off. A short time later I received a check and Johnson's best wishes for success. The North Pole Family Reunion was now closer to reality.

*　*　*

Anaukaq and his family wanted to visit in the late spring of 1987, and we agreed upon late May to early June as the best time for everyone. The only problem now was that this date gave us very little time for preparation. We needed passports, visas, and other documents that would normally take months to process. So we wasted no time in organizing the tour.

At our next committee meeting, we planned the official North Pole Family Reunion itinerary. We carefully selected the cities and sites that held special significance in the lives of Anaukaq's and Kali's fathers. Formal ceremonies were planned for each stop on the tour, involving local family and officials. Several students were selected as hosts and escorts for the tour, and other committee members were assigned various tasks. I would spend the next weeks on the telephone or in writing letters in an effort to implement our plans.

Perhaps our most important decision was to start the North Pole Family Reunion at Harvard. Our committee felt that we had such widespread support for the project in the Harvard community that it would be a good idea to hold the welcoming reception at the university. Such an arrangement would also protect Anaukaq and Kali from the uncertainties of a more public reception, where we would be less able to control events and people. In addition, we decided that a single North Pole Family Reunion Banquet involving Hensons, Pearys, and friends from all over the nation would be more practical than trying to hold several small banquets in different cities. This "neutral" venue was agreeable to most of the family members, although some still wanted small banquets in their hometowns. We chose Harvard's historic Memorial Hall as the banquet site.

Our committee raised concerns about possible actions of the American Peary family. We still had received no expression of interest from them, and we wondered if their apparent efforts to sabotage our plans in Greenland portended similar behavior once Kali and his family arrived in the United States. We were not even certain whether Kali and his sons would still want to make the trip in the wake of the family conflicts and dissension that the American Pearys and their associate had caused. But the committee shared my belief that if Kali still wanted to come along, we should bring him and his family, regardless of whether the Pearys would receive him. We would receive him and would see to it that he visited his father's grave site in Washington as well as Peary's old summer home on Eagle Island, Maine. Although we also knew that the American Hensons were prepared to welcome Peary's Eskimo family as their own, we agreed that I should try once more to reach other members of the American Peary family to see whether they might receive Kali or at least greet him at the Harvard reception.

By now, I had an extensive list of immediate Peary family members living all over the United States. I reached a few of them, but they all indicated that they did not want to meet Kali or take any part in our activities. One of the most revealing encounters occurred while I spoke with one of Robert Peary's great-granddaughters. We spoke by telephone and her voice suggested a very pleasant and kind person. I introduced myself and told her about the plans for Kali's visit. I also told her that Kali was a Peary and simply wanted to visit America and meet some of his relatives. She listened attentively, occasionally responding with polite remarks.

"I understand what you're doing, Dr. Counter, and I would like to participate, but I have to stick with the family." I implored her to consider Kali's feelings and his lifelong desire to meet his American family. I invited her to meet him at Harvard or in the privacy of her home.

"This is the first time I ever heard of any Greenlandic Pearys," she said. "I would like very much to have my children meet them."

I could feel her wavering a bit. I became hopeful. "I would be happy to bring Kali and his children to your home to meet you and your children," I offered, probably with too much enthusiasm.

"Mmm, I don't know," she said. "But there is something I would like to know. What is the name of the young man with the beautiful smile?"

"I beg your pardon?"

"You know, the young man in the *Newsweek* article—the one with the very beautiful smile. What's his name?"

I pulled out the copy of the *Newsweek* that featured my first visit with Anaukaq and Kali. "Oh, yes. You must mean Ole, Kali's nineteen-year-old grandson. He is a wonderful person—a little shy but very friendly. You and your family would enjoy meeting him, and he you."

The woman at the other end of the line seemed to acquiesce for a moment. "Yes, I would like very much for my children to meet him."

Then she added, "But no, I can't do that. I'm sorry, I have to stick with my family on this one. Good-bye."

* * *

Obtaining passports and visas for thirteen Greenlandic Eskimos to visit the United States was a formidable task. It involved coordinating activities with authorities in Greenland, Denmark, and the United States. The police inspector at Thule agreed to help me obtain passports for each of the Hensons and Pearys traveling to the United States, provided I could get photographs of each. Fortunately, I had taken photographs of each of the Hensons and Pearys when I was in Greenland. With the help of my translator Navarana and the police inspector, I managed to get the paperwork completed and passport applications for the thirteen members of the traveling party sent to Copenhagen. This effort was complicated by the fact that most of the men were away from the settlement for weeks on hunts.

The next hurdle was the visa office of the U.S. embassy in Denmark. Because of the unusual nature of the project and the use of military transportation, I had to request special visas for the group. I wrote the U.S. ambassador to Denmark, asking for his help in obtaining special short-term visas. Within about two weeks, the consulate had agreed to grant the group special entry visas. To save time, and because the members of the traveling party had no experience in this process, they even permitted me to complete the visa applications for each member of the group.

"In all my years of foreign service, I have never received a visa application on which the applicant's profession is listed as 'retired hunter,'" said Lynn Schiveley of the U.S. consulate office in Denmark, when he called to confirm that the applications were being processed. "We all have been very moved by your project, and we have taken a special interest in it here at the embassy. The ambassador and staff want to offer you all the assistance you need."

"Thank you, Mr. Schiveley. And please thank the ambassador for me."

CHAPTER ELEVEN

❋ ❋ ❋

Defeating Tornarsuk

In Polar Eskimo culture, when something goes wrong or when something interferes with the best-laid plans, it is often attributed to the evil spirit Tornarsuk. Such, of course, is the stuff of myth and legend, one of those features of traditional societies we find quaint and colorful. Or so I thought as I prepared to bring Anaukaq, Kali, and their families to the advanced technological world that is the United States of the late twentieth century. By the time our trip was over, however, I would become as much a believer in Tornarsuk as any of my Eskimo friends.

❋ ❋ ❋

The surface of the heavily packed snow glistened like ground glass under the bright May sun over Moriussaq. Even at a temperature of −20°F, the twenty-four-hour day gave a feeling of warmth. Dogs throughout the settlement barked at the crunch of my boots as I made my way through the snow toward Anaukaq's igloo.

Anaukaq met me along the path looking somehow different—younger and more vibrant than on my earlier visits. At first I could not figure out just what it was that made him look so changed. He greeted me with a big smile and his characteristic laugh. Then it dawned on me—Anaukaq had new teeth. While in the infirmary that winter, he had asked the Greenlandic health authorities to give him a set of dentures in preparation for his big trip. The infirmary had also provided him with glasses and a hearing aid to help overcome his typical hunter's hearing loss.

"Allen, I am ready to go with you to Mahri-Pahluk's homeland now. I look like a younger man now that I have teeth—and a haircut," he chuckled, rubbing his hand through his newly cropped hair.

"You look great, my friend. Your American relatives will be impressed with your new youthful appearance," I said, giving my first hint that the trip to America was imminent.

Anaukaq laughed and grabbed my hand. "Welcome back to Moriussaq, Allen. I have been waiting for you every day. Our settlement becomes so quiet when you leave."

There was a special excitement in the air throughout the settlement. Everyone knew that Anaukaq and his family were going to America, and they were happy for him. Yet Anaukaq was cautious in his optimism. His sealskin bag had been packed for weeks. But after waiting three-quarters of a century for this moment, he would not be certain of the reality of this trip until he set foot on American soil.

Little Aviaq and her favorite cousin, Malina, were also packed and ready to go. Everywhere I went around the settlement, Aviaq tagged along to be certain that I did not leave for America without her.

Anaukaq's sons Avataq, Ussarkaq, and Ajako were miles from the settlement, hunting for food that would supply their families and dogs during their absence. We had no way of contacting them or knowing when they would return. Kitdlaq and Vittus, the other two sons, were rushing to complete their work in time for the trip.

I hadn't the slightest idea about Kali's plans. I wondered whether the Pearys and their English associate had persuaded him not to travel to America after all or, worse, whether they had hurt his feelings. Anaukaq too was concerned about Kali. He had received word of conflicts among the Amer-Eskimo Pearys caused by the outside intervention, and he too had been approached by the Pearys' associate after my last visit to his settlement.

"No one has ever taken any interest in us up here. Now that you are taking us to Mahri-Pahluk's homeland to see our relatives, some have come up here to photograph us and to ask Kali and his family not to go with you. I do not understand this," Anaukaq said.

A week passed by without any word from Kali and his family. Anaukaq was also becoming anxious because his sons had not returned from the hunt. We bided our time recording stories of Anaukaq's impressions of his youth and explanations of Eskimo life.

Several days later, while outside stretching sealskins, we spotted a dogsled on the horizon, mushing toward us at great speed. Normally, the Eskimo children will recognize the driver of the sled hundreds of yards away, from his manner of driving or his dogs or his yells, and shout out his name for the other youngsters and villagers. In this case, however, the children of Moriussaq did not know the sled driver or dogteam.

As the dogsled came closer, we could see that the driver was dressed in full, traditional Eskimo garb, including polar bear skin trousers, anorak, sealskin boots, and a combination of sealskin and polar bear fur mittens. He was raising his whip high and cracking it just above the ears of his dogs. "*Wock, wock, wock,*" he yelled as he mushed the dogs up the hillside toward the village. When he reached us, he brought the excited dogs to a halt. "*Ha-shhh.*"

The driver turned to Anaukaq and me and smiled. Even before he pulled back the hood of his anorak, I could tell from his radiant smile that it was Ole, Kali's grandson. "Whew! I thought I might be too late," he said, out of breath. "I was out hunting for food for my family and our dogs. Are we still going to America?"

"Of course we are," I responded, hardly concealing my delight at this first indication that Kali and his family would join us. "Where is Kali?"

"My grandfather left Qeqertarsaaq by dogsled some days ago. He is in Qaanaaq now, but he is coming," Ole replied.

"Great! *Ahunggweelok* [Fine]" I said, shaking his hand vigorously. "I am so happy that you are going to join us."

"Talilanguaq, my father, is coming here also. He wants to travel to America with you, but he is many days out, hunting for seals and walrus, and has not had much success. I hope we can wait for him."

"We'll wait for him," I said with a sigh of relief. "I am just happy that you are going to join us."

Anaukaq was ecstatic about the news. "I am so happy that my cousin Kali will join us," he told Ole. "We have waited for this opportunity all of our lives, and now the time is here."

When Ole parked his sled and secured his dogteam, we all went to Anaukaq's igloo and sat down to some hot tea, fresh soup, and seal meat.

A few days later, Avataq returned by dogsled to Moriussaq with his ten-year-old son Magssanguaq riding atop several seals they had killed on the hunt. Magssanguaq cuddled his pet puppy as he rode into the settlement.

"Allen!" Avataq shouted, as he and Magssanguaq unloaded the seals and about a dozen kittiwakes tied together. "I am ready to travel to Mahri-Pahluk's homeland. But Ajako is still out on the ice hunting seals. He should be here in a few days."

I noticed that the usually active and friendly Magssanguaq appeared sullen and distant. Though already an accomplished hunter, Magssanguaq was still a child at heart. Dressed in his polar bear pants and anorak, he looked like a miniature image of his father. He had taken his one-month-old puppy with him to the hunting grounds for company, and he was now focusing all of his attention on the pup in play and ignoring the people around him entirely. "What's wrong with Magssanguaq?" I asked Avataq.

"He is sad because I have told him that he cannot go to America with us on this trip," Avataq said. "I told him maybe he could go on some future trip."

I knelt down and tried to cheer up little Magssanguaq, but he was not in the best of moods. He did not want his father and grandfather to go away without him and he was sad. "My *ahtahtah* and my *ahtah* [grandfather] are going far away, over there," Magssanguaq said pointing toward Umanak mountain in the south, "and they may not come back."

"Oh, they will come back," I reassured him. "They will only be away for about two weeks, and then they will come right back to Moriussaq," I told him.

"Aviaq is going," he said, referring to his ten-year-old cousin.

"I know," I said sympathetically. "She was selected by your family to make this trip. But there will be other trips, and I promise to take you to America to meet your relatives on the next trip. Okay, my little friend?"

Magssanguaq nodded his head, staring down at the puppy in his lap, and softly, but unconvincingly mumbled, *"Eee."*

Anaukaq put his arm on Magssanguaq's shoulder and said, "Come with me, my little *peeneeahktoe*." He walked Magssanguaq behind the igloo, out of his father's sight, where the two of them sat down in old broken chairs. Anaukaq was very fond of little Magssanguaq, who lived in his igloo and whom he had helped to rear.

"Magssanguaq, you are a very good hunter. Your *ahtah* wants you to become a full-time hunter when you grow up," Anaukaq told the boy. "You should not try to work for the Danish people in any of these trade jobs—that would not suit you. You must promise me you will be a full-time hunter when you grow up, just like your grandfather and now your father."

"Eee, ahtah," Magssanguaq murmured, still looking toward the ground and pulling at the polar bear fur on his trousers.

"Now the first thing a great hunter must learn, no matter how young, is responsibility," Anaukaq continued. "We would like to take you on this trip, but we cannot. I want you to stay behind this time and take care of the family and look after our dogs. That is a big responsibility."

"Yes, Grandfather," he responded.

"We won't be away long," Anaukaq said. "Do you think you can look after the rest of the family and the dogteams until your father and I return?"

"Yes, Grandfather," Magssanguaq replied.

"Allen has said that he will take you to Mahri-Pahluk's homeland on a future trip. He will keep his word with you just as he did with me."

Still looking down at the snow, Magssanguaq pulled anxiously at his polar bear fur. Anaukaq rubbed Magssanguaq's head. "You are a fine grandson," he said.

* * *

While we waited for Kali and the hunters to arrive, I went around the settlement and out to the hunting grounds conducting audiological tests on all the villagers. Everyone was cooperative and enthusiastic about the tests. It was common knowledge among the villagers that the hunters in particular had problems hearing, even in their twenties and thirties. Some young fathers complained about not being able to hear their children's voices well, a complaint most often made by grandfathers in our society. My results bore them out. I was finding that permanent, high-frequency, "nerve" hearing loss began in the teenage years and became progressively worse through age sixty. Many had severe hearing impairment in both ears by age forty. These were noise-induced hearing losses due primarily to the men's regular hunting activities with high-caliber rifles. The Polar Eskimo women I tested, who generally do not hunt with rifles, did not have such hearing losses.

I had brought along some special earplugs attached to a necklace that could be hung around the hunter's neck until he was ready to use them. When he spotted game and was about to shoot, he could put the plugs in his ears to attenuate the gunshot noise reaching his inner ear, then remove the plugs after each shot. By introducing this simple hearing conservation measure, I felt that I could reduce the incidence of hearing impairment in present and future generations of Polar Eskimos.

One afternoon some days later, while I was out on the hunting grounds conducting one of my tests, Ajako's sons Nukka and Jens came flying across the ice with their father's dogteam. "Allen, Kali has arrived in Moriussaq," they shouted as they approached me. "He is with Anaukaq."

"Fantastic!" I shouted back. "Let's go back to the settlement to greet your grandfather," I said to Ole, who had brought me out on his dogsled.

We packed my audiometer and other apparatus, and in no time we were off, sledding across the ice at high speed behind eight big running dogs.

Ole was beaming with happiness. He was pleased that his grandfather had chosen to join Anaukaq. On our way back to Moriussaq, he vented his excitement by racing Nukka and Jen's dogteam.

When we reached Moriussaq, Anaukaq and Kali were sitting outside on a log, basking in the sun and enjoying a cup of coffee. An older woman and friend from the neighborhood had joined them. As I jumped off the sled and ran toward Kali, he greeted me with his outstretched hands and a huge grin. We shook hands and embraced before Kali pulled back and looked me in the eye, saying nothing, just grinning from ear to ear.

"Oh my goodness! Kali, you have new teeth," I shouted as I finally grasped what he was trying to show me.

We all laughed.

"You didn't think I was going to let Anaukaq get new teeth and not get some for myself, did you?" Kali chuckled. "We might meet some new wives over there in the United States, and we have to look our best."

Kali continued to joke, and Anaukaq loved every minute of it. This was the old Kali he had known since childhood—his friend, his cousin. And now he knew for certain that they would fulfill their lifelong dream together.

Kali explained that he had stopped at the infirmary in Qaanaaq en route to Moriussaq to get his new dentures. That was the reason his arrival had been delayed.

"They ship these from Denmark for the old people up here, and the nurses shape them to fit our mouths."

They both grinned to show each other their new chompers.

*   *   *

Most members of the traveling party were now gathered in Moriussaq. The only ones missing at this point were Kali's son, Talilanguaq, and Anaukaq's sons Ussarkaq, Kitdlaq, and Vittus.

"I would only hope that all five of my sons can go to America with me," Anaukaq said. "This may be the last time we will all be together again."

"*Eeee,*" Kali agreed. "I want my son to travel with us also. Maybe he will like it over there and take my other children and grandchildren someday."

I had arranged for a flexible departure schedule because of the unpredictable weather and other possible unforeseen circumstances. Nevertheless, we had only a small window of opportunity for travel.

We could not request the delay of a U.S. Air Force plane. If the sons did not show up in time, we would be forced to leave without them. I hoped that this would not be necessary.

Later that evening, we discussed our American itinerary.

"Our trip to our fathers' homeland now looks as if it is going to be a reality," Anaukaq said to Kali. "I don't know if I am prepared to meet such fine people. Allen, you will have to advise me on how to act," he said mischievously.

"Just be yourselves," I said. "Just be Anaukaq and Kali and everything will be fine."

"When we get to America and meet such fine people as our relatives, we will have to take off our hats and bow—like this," Anaukaq chuckled, removing an imaginary hat and bowing. He fell back on the bed, laughing. We all laughed. I had never seen Anaukaq in such a jocular mood.

"What about you, Kali?" I asked. "How will you act at our big family reunion banquet?"

Kali thought for a moment. "Oh, I get very emotional at gatherings, especially when there are speeches being made. I can't help that. I think when I meet my relatives and see my father's grave, I will get very emotional.

Kali showed us a small wreath of dried flowers he and his family had made for his father's grave. He was quite proud of the wreath. Only a few species of tiny flowers grow in northwest Greenland, but he and his children had collected many of them, along with shrubs, and tied them together to form a lovely oval.

While we waited for the rest of our traveling party, Anaukaq entertained Kali by showing him some of his prized possessions. One was a massive polar bear skin, which looked as if it had been pulled off the bear in one piece. Avataq had killed the bear not far from the settlement earlier that winter. But he said that his favorite new possession was a banner I had given him as a gift on an earlier visit. It was an Afro-American flag that I had designed some years earlier in the interest of instilling cultural and historical pride in young black Americans. I had used the flag on lecture tours and in classrooms to teach Americans of all races about the origins, history, and present-day makeup of Americans of black African ancestry. Anaukaq had put the flag up on the wall of his igloo so that his family and visitors could view it.

Like a teacher, he walked Kali through the symbols of the flag. "The dark brown represents the color of Mahri-Pahluk's people," he told Kali. "The red borders represent the blood of their ancestors who died to build their country; the green tree speaks of their ancestry from a place called Africa." And so on through each symbol, just as I had explained to him almost a year earlier. I was touched that this gift had meant so much to him and amazed that he had actually memorized everything I had told him.

Kali showed his interest in the flag by asking Anaukaq questions about each symbol.

"What does the star stand for?" he asked.

"That is the star the *kulnocktooko* people used to find their way to freedom," replied Anaukaq.

"And what is this?"

"That is *herrkahnook* [the sun]," Anaukaq answered. "It gave life and skin color to the first *kulnocktooko*."

Whether they fully understood what they were discussing, I shall never know.

*   *   *

The police inspector had received all the visas and passports from Denmark but one. Malina's passport had been lost. She was shaken by the news, which dampened everyone's spirits. Malina had been looking forward to this trip, especially since she was her grandfather's caretaker and personally very close to him. She did not want him to be far from her care.

Using the lone battery-operated telephone in the settlement, I reached the police inspector at Thule. He had no idea where Malina's passport was or whether it could be found in time for her to make the trip. The next flight from Copenhagen was over two weeks away. I asked him to wire Lynn Schiveley of the American embassy in Copenhagen and request a special visa for Malina in lieu of a passport.

A few days later, Schiveley sent word that the embassy would wire ahead to our U.S. point of entry to explain that if Malina had proper, official identification, she could enter the country on a short-term visitor's visa for the two-week visit.

The police inspector informed me that the only person in the area authorized to draw up identification papers for Greenlandic citizens was the Danish military commander at Thule. We made arrangements for me to meet with the commander as soon as we reached the air base.

Four days before we were to depart from Thule, we still had not heard from Talilanguaq or Anaukaq's other sons. We were all getting worried. Anaukaq went outside and walked through the village. A short time later he returned and told Kali and me, "We're in for some bad weather. It looks to me like a big storm is coming. It could last for several days."

We just looked at each other, knowing that we were powerless to do anything about it. We could only wait—wait out the storm, wait for the others to reach Moriussaq.

Everyone was packed and ready to go. The men busied themselves with chores, one of which was feeding the dogs. Both Avataq and Ajako were out stuffing their dogs with seal innards and blubber. When the dogteams were fully fed, the residual food was then taken to some of the female dogs with puppies. The nursing females were kept in small shelters built to protect the puppies from the extreme cold. It is not uncommon to find the carcasses of small pups that have wandered off from their mother frozen solid in the snow. With most of the chores completed, we were ready to travel to Thule.

The storm rolled in later that day, with heavy, wet snow and howling winds. It rapidly became a blizzard. We were trapped. Only Magssanguaq seemed oblivious to the storm and its implications for our trip, as he played with his puppy and ran around in the igloo. Outside, even the short distances between the little houses were difficult to negotiate in the blinding, wind-driven snow. The dogs, curled up into balls and totally covered by snow, posed another danger. If you accidentally stepped on a snow-covered dog, it was likely to tear off a piece of your ankle.

As the blizzard roared on into its second day, our hopes sank in the deepening snow. We wondered whether the storm had trapped the hunters out on the ice. The Polar Eskimos are accustomed to unpredictable snowstorms and generally seem undisturbed by weather-induced delays. This time, though, everyone was hoping for a rapid improvement in the weather.

It was three days before our scheduled departure from the air base, and the storm was still raging. The helicopter would certainly not come for us in this weather. Wearing my heaviest clothes, I stumbled through the blizzard to the government-run shop near the edge of the settlement. I wanted to call the police inspector to get a weather forecast and some word on the helicopter schedule. But the telephone—the only one in the village—was out of order. The batteries were dead. We now had no way of communicating with the outside world. Tornarsuk, it seemed, had put another hurdle in our way.

The telephone batteries were three massive, 10-volt units, like those used in large trucks. They were encased in a huge wooden box. New batteries would have to be brought in by helicopter; there were no replacements in the village. If the storm continued another day and the helicopter couldn't come to get us, dogsleds were our only hope for reaching the base.

I broached the idea of traveling by dogsled with the group, and they all agreed that this might be our only means. Dogsled travel, however, was not easy. It would require a mobilization of the entire Moriussaq community.

Then we discovered that Ajako had a large box of new 1.5-volt flashlight batteries. We tried connecting twenty of these standard D batteries in a series to get the equivalent of thirty volts and attached them to the telephone wires. It worked!

When I reached the helicopter control office, I was told that the storm was expected to leave the area in the next twenty-four hours, but the winds were forecast to be too strong for the helicopter to go aloft. Dogsleds it would be, then.

I also reached Qaanaaq by phone and learned that the other members of the traveling party had returned safely from the hunting grounds but could not leave the village because of the storm. I urged them to travel to Moriussaq by dogsled, but they pointed out that it would be difficult to bring their dogs there and leave them in the care of the others. Dogs are a very private and personal possession among Polar Eskimos.

The next day the storm finally blew over, and a period of calm descended. We were now only two days from our scheduled flight from Thule. I made a quick decision to transport the group already at Moriussaq to the air base a day before our scheduled helicopter flight, to avoid the possibility of being trapped there by another storm.

All day, we waited near our bags, ready to go. But the helicopter never came. When I telephoned the helicopter flight director at Thule, he said that the winds were still too strong for the helicopter to fly to Moriussaq, but that the moment the winds died down, they would come in for us. We waited for several more hours, and I called the helicopter pad again, only to be told the same thing. It was now four o'clock in the afternoon. I knew that the helicopter pad would close at five. Yet by this point, I had become concerned about the judgment of the helicopter control post. It appeared to us that the weather had calmed down enough to fly the helicopter in. I shared the helicopter people's concern for safety, but the Eskimos and I felt there was no reason why the helicopter couldn't fly in to get us while the weather was calm, even after regular work hours. After all, there were twenty-four hours of daylight this time of year.

Five o'clock. No word from the helicopter base. I tried to reach helicopter control, but no one answered. The managers had left the post for the day and would not be reachable until the next day. By now, everyone worried that we would not make our plane. It seemed that old Tornarsuk had done his worst.

Nukka, Jens, and a neighbor offered to take the ten of us to the air base on three large dogsleds, but we decided that this would be risky. We were contemplating their offer, however, when I remembered that I had met the helicopter pilot on an earlier trip and he had given me his telephone number at the pilot's barracks. The pilot was Swedish and used to enjoy my surprising facility with the Swedish language, something he seldom heard in Danish Greenland.

It's worth a try, I thought, as I dialed the number. To my surprise, the Swedish pilot answered the phone.

"Hej! Jag heterer, Allen. Hur star det till? [Hello, this is Allen. How are you?]"

He too was surprised to hear from me.

"Jag mar bra, tack [I am fine, thank you]."

I described our desperate situation and explained the special nature of our project, mixing in a little Swedish wherever I could.

The winds had been too strong to permit the helicopter to fly over the mountains into our area earlier that day, he said. But it was now after work hours, he reminded me, and the pilots were not expected to fly into areas such as ours unless there was an emergency.

He paused. "I will come to fetch you."

"Great! Tack sa mycket! [Thank you very much]," I said.

"I will call back in an hour or so to let you know when I am leaving Thule, so that you can be ready at the landing area. I must get in and out quickly while the weather is good."

I was ecstatic. I had taken a chance and something positive had happened. This was typical of Greenland. It seemed that nothing happened unless someone made it happen, and everything required a bit of luck. Clearly, had I not made the effort to reach the pilot that afternoon, we would have been stranded in Moriussaq for another day or two and would probably have missed our jet to America.

The phone rang. "We are on our way to Moriussaq," the pilot said.

I ran about the village and notified everyone that the helicopter was on its way. The news created quite a stir. We all grabbed our bags and put them on the sled for transport to the landing site. Everyone, including Anaukaq, said their good-byes and made last minute bag checks.

About forty-five minutes later, we heard the roar of the helicopter off in the distance. As always, the children of the village heard it first and started running about, yelling that the helicopter was coming.

Anaukaq and Kali led the crowd as we walked toward the landing area. Anaukaq, with his cane, moved through the snow as quickly as everyone else. Our bags and camping gear were being pushed to the landing site on a large sled.

As the helicopter landed, we had to turn our head to protect our faces from the heavy snow blown up by the blades. The Swedish pilot got off the helicopter and headed straight for me. "Hej, Allen. Der ar kallt [It is cold]," he said in the accent of northern Sweden.

"Ja, mycket kallt [Yes, very cold]," I replied.

"It looks like the weather has cooperated with us," he added.

"Yes! But I want to thank you for your special efforts in coming out to pick us up. You have contributed greatly to the success of this project."

"Don't mention it. I am glad to help you," he said. "I think you are doing a good thing. But we must hurry and board the helicopter," he added. "With the amount of luggage you have and the number of passengers, we will have to make two trips."

He had been in the area for a number of years but he had never heard of the Henson-Peary story or of the sons of Henson and Peary. But once he heard the story, he said, he was touched by my efforts to help Anaukaq and Kali, and he offered what help he could.

Unfortunately, the weather north of Moriussaq was still too inclement for him to fly up to Qaanaaq to pick up the other three members of our traveling party. He would fly our Moriussaq group on to Thule and wait for a chance to pick up the rest of the group the next day.

After we packed the luggage securely in the helicopter, Anaukaq and Kali were the first to board. They were grinning like two young boys. Seven of us, including Aviaq and Malina, left on the first shuttle. When the pilot lifted the helicopter above the ground, everyone looked at one another and smiled.

In the noisy chopper, everyone sat silently, staring out the window. I wondered what each person was thinking about. The silence was occasionally broken by the excitement of spotting a dogsled down on the ice, traveling at what appeared to be, in relation to a helicopter, an incredibly high speed. As we neared our destination, Kali pointed with excitement to the unusual mountain called Umanak, saying it looked to him like a teacup turned upside-down. This mountain had special significance to the older men. It had been the traditional home of many of their people before the air base was built at Thule, and the two old hunters had spent many of their eighty years in its shadows. Some of the young Polar Eskimos had begun to talk about reclaiming the area around the base. This, of course, did not sit very well with the military establishment.

Once we passed over Umanak, the military base came into view. The sight of the sprawling air base caused quite a stir among the passengers. As they marveled at its enormous size, I thought about how very different much of the outside world still must appear to the Polar Eskimos. They, more than any other Eskimo group, had adhered to the old cultural ways of hunting, preparing food, and making clothing. They still spoke their special Polar Eskimo language, and they think of themselves as true Eskimos. While nothing about the outside world seemed to overwhelm them, they were still awed by many things they saw. I could only wonder how they would react to New York City, Boston, and Washington, D.C.

"You are clear to land," we heard the military air-traffic controller tell our pilot. Very soon he was hovering just above the landing pad and slowly putting the helicopter down in its center. Everyone smiled as the rotary blades wound to a halt.

Anaukaq seemed especially cheerful. He looked happy and as healthy and strong as ever. We all helped each other down from the helicopter pad and headed off for our quarters. The pilot lost no time in unpacking baggage and heading back to pick up the others left behind in Moriussaq.

*   *   *

The huge dining hall was a novel sight for the Eskimos, and our group was something of a strange sight for the military staff too. Many wanted to know who we were and what we were doing there. When I explained who Anaukaq and Kali were and the purpose of our trip, everyone wanted to meet the "celebrities."

To my chagrin, the helicopter pilot told me that evening that the winds were still too strong up in Qaanaaq to pick up Talilanguaq, Ussarkaq, and Kitdlaq. I reached Kitdlaq by phone and told him that it looked as though the only way for his group to reach the air base was to travel by dogsled. Kitdlaq said this would be impossible, since they could find no one who could take time off to bring their dogs back. Moreover, they could not be assured of having enough food for the dogs' round trip, since their latest hunt had not been so successful as they had hoped. It now looked as if I would have to put them on a later U.S.-bound military jet or have them wait for another trip in the distant future.

The pilot said that regulations required him to get a certain number of hours of sleep before flying, but he would make another attempt at 4 or 5 A.M., weather permitting. I told him that I would go to my quarters and pray for good weather. And I did.

Later that evening, I received an urgent call from Maj. Quincy Sharp, chief of operations. He told me that the base commander wanted to meet with me, but that I had to wait until seven o'clock the next morning because he would be in meetings until late that night.

"Is there something wrong?" I asked.

Sharp said he was not sure, but it must be important if the commander had requested a meeting. He did, however, mention that the adventurer had visited the base. Understandably, I began to worry that some of the Peary family's powerful friends had convinced the commander to rescind our flight orders. I knew that such a decision would devastate the Eskimo families. Unfortunately, I could not find out for sure until the next morning, just before our scheduled departure.

I invited Major Sharp to meet Anaukaq, Kali, and their families at the residence hall where we were staying. When we entered the door, a loud cheer went up from the Eskimos, who all rushed forward to greet the major. Several crowded around him and asked that I take their photographs with him. They were thrilled to meet this impressive black American officer, and he in turn was charmed by their sincere warmth. They seemed to think that all blacks they met were in some way relatives. I sensed that he represented for them the first symbol of what their trip to America would be like. As the major left, he assured me that he would do everything he could to make certain that our flight orders were okay.

Despite his encouragement, I stayed up all night worrying. While my Eskimo friends slept, I busied myself with packing and various other tasks. I prayed that our flight orders had not been changed and that the weather would permit the helicopter to get through and pick up the rest of the traveling party at Qaanaaq.

At 3:30 A.M., I walked about a mile through the cold morning air and waited outside the hangar for the helicopter pilot. True to his word, he arrived at precisely 4 A.M. It was a go. The weather had miraculously opened a brief window of time for him to fly over the mountains to Qaanaaq and back, a trip of about two and a half hours. We had beaten Tornarsuk again, I thought.

The pilot lost no time getting the helicopter airborne. I left for the base commander's office.

Upon my arrival at 7 A.M., I was immediately escorted in and offered a cup of coffee. The commander greeted me as warmly as always. First, he said, he wanted to confirm the names of everyone in my traveling party. After we discussed this matter, he informed me that our flight to McGuire Air Force Base would be delayed because of activities there involving the secretary of defense. We talked about the reunion project in relation to the Thule air base, and he assured me of his support for the project. At last I could relax. He invited me next door to meet the air force public relations staff, who would do a story on its role in the North Pole Family Reunion.

I was relieved that my worst fears had not materialized. As I was saying good-bye, the commander said he would join us at the departure terminal to meet Anaukaq and Kali and to see our group off.

When I arrived at the hangar, I saw the helicopter sitting on the landing pad. I knew then that the other members of the traveling party had arrived. I ran up to the pilot, grabbed his hand, shook it, looked him in the eye, and said, "Tack sa mycket! [Thank you very much]." He looked me back in the eye and said in Swedish, "ingen orsak, ingen orsak [You're welcome, you're welcome]." We had just enough time to get the group together and over to the military airlift command hangar for the jet flight to the United States.

The waiting room at the military airlift command is rather austere in comparison to the waiting rooms at commercial airline terminals in the United States. When we arrived with our many bags, we were asked to stack them with others in a large pile in one area of the terminal. The bags would be taken and placed with the rest of the freight in the cargo section of the plane, just ahead of the seats. We waited and took our seats among thirty or so air force servicemen who were also traveling to the United States. As promised, Major Sharp and Colonel Knapp came out to bid us farewell.

Walking from the hangar onto the frozen tarmac, we saw the camouflaged green C-141 that would carry us to America. Its small tires and very low-slung profile made it look more like a large bomber than a conventional jet, while its large wings, extending from the top of the fuselage, seemed to droop like those of a giant vulture.

In no time we were all aboard and strapped into our seats facing backward, away from the cockpit. Everybody seemed very comfortable, and no one seemed especially frightened or uneasy about the flight. The flight sergeant started blaring instructions over the loud intercom system, which is designed to overcome the attenuation of the earplugs each passenger receives on the uninsulated jet. I had to get up with the translator and go from person to person to make certain that seat belts were fastened and earplugs were in.

The crew treated the Eskimo travelers rather like celebrities, passing out extra fruit and juice. The pilots invited us to the large panoramic flight deck, which is about four times the size of the cockpit of a regular commercial aircraft. Anaukaq and Kali enthusiastically accepted the invitation, and we headed up the steep stairs. Once in the room-sized flight deck, they were thrilled to see the sky around them at forty thousand feet and the vast snow-covered flatlands and mountain peaks below. The pilots and other officers on the flight deck were so impressed with the two old men that they pulled the military insignia from their uniforms and gave them to Anaukaq and Kali as a gift. The two old hunters accepted graciously the first gifts from their American journey.

"*Kooyounah, kooyounah,*" they repeated as they tried to stick the velcro insignia to the shoulders of their coats.

After seven hours of smooth, restful flying we started our descent for McGuire Air Force Base in the center of New Jersey.

On Friday, May 29, 1987, Matthew Henson's and Robert Peary's sons set foot on American soil for the first time. They stood together on the tarmac for a moment, surveying their surroundings in silence. Their faces registered pleasure and awe.

"It is now a reality. We have reached our fathers' land," Anaukaq said.

"Yes, after so many years," replied Kali. "But it sure is *Keyettoe* [hot]!"

As we feared, the temperature was a steamy ninety degrees, a hundred-degree differential from the temperature we had left in Greenland. The East Coast was experiencing one of the worst heat waves in decades, and the air was oppressive. But the group didn't seem to mind. We all just shed our coats as we stepped aboard an air force van bound for the terminal.

The air-conditioned terminal came as a relief. We filed through customs to the comfort of a waiting room. Everything appeared in order as the unsmiling, tough-looking customs official checked us through, one by one. There were thirteen Eskimos in the group, nine Hensons, three Pearys, and the translator. The Hensons included Anaukaq and his sons Avataq, Ussarkaq, Ajako, and Kitdlaq, who were all together for the first time in years. (I made separate, special arrangements to bring Vittus, the fifth son, into the United States from southern Greenland.) Also, Anaukaq's grandson Massauna-Matthew and his granddaughters Malina and Aviaq were with us. Kali had invited only his son, Talilanguaq, and his grandson Ole along.

Just when we thought it was going well, we hit a snag. The customs official called me over to say that Malina did not have proper identification and could not be permitted to enter the country. This could not be so, I assured him. After all, we had received special permission from the U.S. consulate in Denmark for her to use the document signed by the commander of the Danish military at Thule. But the customs agent showed me that the commander's document read in small print that it was valid only if the said Malina Henson could prove her identity with a birth certificate or other form of Danish/Greenlandic identification. Malina had no such identification. She had never been outside the Moriussaq region and had no need for it. No one had told us she needed further identification.

"I am sorry. The others may go through, but I cannot let her enter the country without proper identification," the customs officer said.

When the translator explained the problem to the group, Malina dropped in a chair and lowered her head. Tornarsuk had a long reach.

I pleaded with the customs officer, but to no avail.

"Well, she can't stay here at the base. What can we do?" I asked.

"We'll have to send her back on the next available plane," he replied. In the meantime, she would have to be confined to base.

I knew that the next plane would leave for Thule at 8 A.M. the following Monday. If that flight had no seats, she would have to remain on base until the air force could find her a seat on yet another returning flight.

The other members of the group, having cleared customs, sat in a second waiting room, separated from us by a large glass enclosure. They could see Malina slumped in her chair, staring at the floor. Their momentary joy had turned to despair.

I went over to console Malina, who was shaking with fear. She was hurt and embarrassed that she might have caused complications for her grandfather. I tried to reassure her that everything would be fine.

I asked for permission to call the State Department to request special approval for Malina to enter the country. My request was granted, but I knew that this would probably involve a great deal of red tape—and our staying on the base until the matter was resolved.

Returning to the customs officer, who by now had observed the sadness that had swept over the entire group, I appealed for understanding. I told him the story of Matthew Henson and Robert Peary, and the significance of their sons' visit. I showed him copies of the visa applications which I had brought along, including Malina's. I even shared with him reprints of newspaper and magazine articles about the planned reunion. He seemed unmoved.

"There is no way I can permit her to enter the country without the documentation called for in the commander's identification papers," he said. "I'm sorry, but I must put her on the next flight to Thule."

"Please sir," I implored. "Don't break this young woman's heart. Let her join her family for this two-week visit. I give you my word that I will have her back at this gate, ready to return to Greenland on schedule."

He did not respond. In fact he began to talk with others around the terminal.

I was on my way to the phone to call the State Department, when I turned to him and asked, "When will you be able to put her on a flight back to Thule?"

"In two weeks," he replied, smiling for the first time. "Take her on through—and good luck on your project."

We just looked each other in the eye for a moment and acknowledged our mutual appreciation. The gruff old guy had a heart after all. "We all thank you, sir," I said.

The group cheered Malina when she came through the customs door. Avataq and Ajako ran up to the customs officer and shook his hand saying, *"Kooyounah."*

CHAPTER TWELVE

✳ ✳ ✳

The North Pole Family Reunion

Outside the terminal, my students were waiting in a large, air-conditioned chartered bus. Our committee had chosen the bus over other forms of transportation because we felt it offered us the greatest flexibility and, in the long run, would cost less. The driver, a seasoned veteran, and the student escorts who had driven down from Cambridge earlier that day helped our guests get comfortable. Before long we were on our way to Harvard. Trying to avoid the big-city traffic, the driver took as many back roads as possible. Our Eskimo friends glowed with excitement as they gazed out the windows in utter amazement at their surroundings.

"Incredible," said Ussarkaq. "Look at all of these plants," he said pointing to the trees and shrubbery along the road. "I have seen these plants ever since we arrived. They're everywhere! I have never seen so many plants in my entire life."

"The pathways go on forever," said Kali, referring to the maze of highways. "They never end! Are they manmade? Maybe they were here when the earth was formed."

"*Eemuckkah* [Maybe]," responded Anaukaq, sitting beside him. "But look at the *pedde* [cars]—so many *pedde*. They look like a flock of little *cheemeahk*—little auks, flying all around you. They just keep coming toward us and coming toward us," he shouted, gesturing with his hands. "Endless! They never stop. So many *pedde*—it's just too much."

"Igloo, igloo, igloo, igloo, *quah, quah, quah, pah che* [So many igloos]," said Kali.

"*Eeee*, I see them," said Anaukaq. "Look! The tall ones have many little igloos inside where people live—like the cliffs above Moriussaq where the birds live in holes on the face of the mountain."

"Look at that large white igloo. I could live in that one," Ussarkaq shouted, pointing to a large white Victorian home.

Everyone laughed.

"It is hard to believe that we are now in America. A little while ago I was sleeping in Qaanaaq," Ussarkaq said.

As we passed through one town, Ole shouted, "Look at all of the people—where do so many people come from?"

"I don't know. They come and go down large streets which look like canyons," Talilanguaq commented.

"So this is America," said Kitdlaq. "The place we have always dreamed about. I can't believe we are here."

After a few hours of travel, we pulled into a highway rest stop. We all got off to stretch our legs and get a bite to eat while the bus refueled. The only restaurant at the stop was part of a well-known hamburger chain, so the Eskimos were treated to a classic American meal: a large hamburger, french fries, and a cola. They loved it. This would be just the beginning of many such roadside stops as we moved up and down the East Coast during the next two weeks.

We arrived at Harvard early that evening and were greeted by students, family members, and friends at Leverett House, where I had previously made lodging arrangements. After dinner in the Leverett dining room, we joined other students in the courtyard. The trees, birds, and squirrels around the courtyard all fascinated the Eskimos. No one wanted to turn in. They were all too excited about the strange new world around them.

Eventually we convinced Kali and Anaukaq that they should retire to their room and get some sleep. We then took the rest of the group to Harvard Square. The lights and sounds of the square dazzled them. There were people and cars everywhere. And now they were no longer viewing them from the window of the bus, but mingling among them. The Eskimos spoke with curious passers-by and sampled pizza, sausages, sandwiches, ice cream, and about every other tasty delight the Square had to offer.

When we returned to Leverett with late-night snacks to talk about the planned events, we found Anaukaq and Kali still up, talking in their room. Only utter exhaustion forced the group to retire in the wee hours of the morning.

The next day, everyone was up at six o'clock. For over an hour, the entire group stood in the courtyard and watched two squirrels put on what was, for the Eskimos, a fantastic show. The lively squirrels ran about the Leverett courtyard, climbing trees and scampering across telephone wires. Back in Greenland, no wild animal runs about so freely, especially if there are hunters around. Little things that we take for granted fascinated my Eskimo friends.

Anaukaq noticed a slight swelling in his leg and brought it to my attention. I had him examined immediately by our project physician, Dr. Louis C. Brown, who had served for many years as a physician to the Harvard University Health Services. Dr. Brown, assisted by Ann J. C. Daniels, R.N., determined that Anaukaq's leg was not draining properly. Like many elderly folks, he had a slight swelling in his legs from time to time because of poor circulation. His legs had been in one position for several hours during the long flight and later during the bus ride, and this had adversely affected his circulation and drainage. They also found that he had never removed the tight wool long underwear that he had worn since we left Greenland. They treated him and elevated his leg in a comfortable position for several hours. Dr. Brown and Nurse Daniels would spend the next ten days with us, checking Anaukaq's and Kali's blood pressure, heart, lungs, body temperature, sweat levels, and just about everything else on a daily basis.

The following morning, while Anaukaq rested his leg, we took the group shopping for clothes. We bought summer shirts, pants, jackets, shoes, and accessories for everyone. Aviaq and Malina bought dresses, along with earrings, headbands, sunglasses, and watches.

Our plans called for us to visit the Peary-MacMillan Arctic Museum in Brunswick, Maine, that afternoon. Since the museum is not far from the home of Robert Peary, Jr., before we boarded the bus I decided to make one final plea to the Pearys to see if they would meet Kali. This time, however, I bypassed the family spokesperson and telephoned Robert Jr. directly. His wife answered the phone. She listened patiently as I explained how much it would mean to Kali to meet his half brother, that we didn't mean to intrude but had planned to be in the area anyway, and so forth.

"Oh, all right," she said finally, in a grandmotherly way. "Bring him up to meet us."

I was no less delighted than I was surprised by her response. How ironic, I thought, that the two people who ostensibly needed to be "protected" most from the sensitive news of Kali's existence were the ones who first agreed to see him.

When we arrived, the Pearys, along with their son, Robert III, came out to greet us. Robert Jr. walked up to Kali with a big, warm smile and extended his hand. With an equally big grin, Kali shook his hand. They stared at each other for a moment.

"Now, are you my half brother?" Robert Jr. asked.

"Yes, I am Peeuree's son," Kali replied.

"And your name is Kali?"

"Yes, Kali Peeuree."

"Well, I'm a bit confused," Robert Jr. admitted. "I have never met you, but when I was up in Greenland back in twenty-six, I saw some Eskimos that were said to be related to me. I didn't meet them, but the name I remember is Anaukaq. Now I hear from my son that Anaukaq is colored—Matt Henson's son. I'm confused."

"You are confusing me with my older brother Anaukaq!" Kali explained through the translator. "He too was Peeuree's son. But he is dead now."

"Now I understand," said Robert Jr. "Now I understand."

"And who are all these fine people?" asked Mrs. Peary.

"Well, this is your brother-in-law," Robert Jr. said to his wife.

"How nice to meet you," she responded warmly.

Kali introduced his son and grandson, and we introduced ourselves.

"Well, come on inside," Mrs. Peary said. "I had my son go out to get some cool lemonade for you."

The house was filled with Peary memorabilia. Bearskins and other

Arctic trophies lined the walls of the rustic New England home. Robert Jr. took Kali on a complete tour of the house, explaining each item. Kali too explained some of the items that were indigenous to Greenland, such as old Eskimo implements.

"Do you have the classic Peary gap between your two front teeth?" Robert Jr. asked Kali at one point. "All Peary men must have the trademark of the family," he chuckled.

"Well," Kali thought for a moment. "I think I used to have that gap when I had my own teeth. But I can't rightly say that the ones I have now are mine."

Everyone burst into laughter.

As we all gathered in the living room to drink our lemonade, the joviality of the atmosphere moved Robert Jr. to play the old upright piano that was taken from Peary's ship, the *Roosevelt*—the piano that had been on the ship when Kali was born there.

After playing a delightful song for a few minutes, Robert Jr. cheerfully raised his hands to show Kali and the others that he had not been playing the piano after all. It was a player piano.

Kali and the rest of us laughed uproariously.

At Robert Jr.'s invitation, Kali, Talilanguaq, and Ole sat down at the piano to play as well. Three generations of Pearys, playing the admiral's piano. Talilanguaq and Ole beamed with pride at the warmth of the reception for their father.

With his hand on Kali's shoulder, Robert Jr. explained the piano to his half brother. They have finally come together, I thought, and they were enjoying each other like the long-lost brothers they were. I wondered just how much of the resistance to letting Kali meet his American relatives had come from family members who were out of touch with Robert Jr.'s feelings. Like many elderly people, Robert did not seem to care about all the fuss being made over what Kali might do to his father's image or family name. He seemed only to want to enjoy people and every moment of the rest of his life.

Robert Jr. and his wife were gracious hosts. The visit was brief, but it meant the world to Kali and his children. "For the first time in my life," Kali said to his brother, "I feel like a Peary." Robert Jr. stared at him but said nothing.

We gathered on the lawn for photographs before departing for the Peary-MacMillan Arctic Museum in nearby Brunswick.

* * *

On Sunday morning, we rose early and dressed for services at Harvard's Memorial Church. The Amer-Eskimo Hensons and Pearys looked quite spiffy in their new clothes. Anaukaq wore his new trousers, but not the shirt we had bought. He insisted on wearing the traditional white Polar Eskimo anorak he had brought with him from Moriussaq.

Knowing that Anaukaq and Kali had embraced Christianity and from time to time attended the missionary church in Greenland, I had asked my dear friend Peter J. Gomes, minister of Memorial Church, for a special "Service of Welcome" for the Eskimos and their American families. As a member of our committee, Gomes had expressed both concern and compassion for the Amer-Eskimo Hensons and Pearys, and he shared my desire to make their first American reception special.

The church steps were crowded with American Hensons who had come to meet Anaukaq and his family. Several of them ran forward to greet Anaukaq, including his cousin Olive, who warmly embraced him. Emotions poured forth from both sides.

"These are your American family members," the translator told Anaukaq and his sons.

"My family?" Anaukaq said, now glassy-eyed.

"Yes, they are all Hensons—and this is Olive, your cousin who sent you the blanket."

"This is Olive?" Anaukaq said. "I am happy to meet you. Thank you for the beautiful blanket."

"Oh, is this your cousin?" Kali asked Anaukaq. The American Hensons embraced Kali and his sons as if they were part of their own family.

At the sound of the bell, we moved from the enervating outdoor heat into the shady comfort of Memorial Church. Hundreds of students, faculty, and other regular parishioners stood as we took seats in the first pews.

With hands raised above the congregation, Peter Gomes declared a day of celebration and welcome in honor of our guests from Greenland.

"We are particularly honored and happy to welcome as visitors to this congregation this morning, members of the Henson and Peary families, who come to us from very far distant places indeed. We have done our best to provide you with as opposite and different weather as it is your custom to experience—we hope you will forgive us if it is too hot. We trust that should we in turn visit you, you would return the favor. . . .

"Now the books have long celebrated the achievements and discovery of your fathers, Matthew Henson and Robert Peary. They live in the pages of history. . . . And by dint of imagination and great courage landed at the top of the world. And one would like to think that it is their example of colleagueship and indeed fellowship that trickles down from the top of the world and embraces all the rest of us today. But what we celebrate today is not a mere geological survey or Arctic adventure—a simple cover story for *National Geographic*. Rather, we celebrate the story of an enormous human achievement and adventure, a tale of collaboration between black and white when that was neither fashionable nor familiar. And we celebrate as well the human spirit that knows no boundaries, either of race or place— a spirit that in the faces of these men and women unknown to us and each other for so long says we are all related, we are all your brothers and sisters. The distance between us is bridged by the human fellowship we now share with one another. We are all cousins. Dare we aspire to anything less than this? . . .

"We know the risks and charges of our history. The burden of it is with us every day of our lives. That is why it is so wonderful when we can celebrate a discovery whose human dimension enriches us all and redefines in the most appropriate and useful way, the whole meaning of the human family. That is why your visit to America is not purely a private matter—though that it is. It is a matter of the most immense public interest. For you by your presence help us define anew, and more generously, who we are and who you are. . . .

"And so in the spirit of that reunion, I am delighted that our brothers and sisters from the top of the world have taken the risk of reunion—have taken the risk of the journey, have taken the risk of the heat—to be with us today. And to help us celebrate with you the unity of the human family, under God. You are proof that it works— as are we to you. Why did it take you so long to come home?"

Peter preached eloquently throughout a service mixed with Scripture, poetry, humor, and wit. At one point, he reminded the congregation that "the Eskimos were in some ways like the Indians at Plymouth Rock. They had their own culture and history. And when they first came into contact with outsiders who claimed to have discovered them, they exclaimed, 'What do you mean "discovered" us? We were never lost in the first place!'" It was what we call at Harvard a classic Gomes sermon, at once fitting and deeply moving.

Following the service, the church held a brief outdoor reception attended by family, friends, students, and, of course, the press. Although the fierce midday heat forced us to cut it short, it was here that Kali met some of his other American relatives, albeit distant ones. The couple and their son were descendants of one of Robert Peary's paternal uncles. This line of Pearys had moved to Pennsylvania along with Robert Peary's father to set up a wood and barrel business in the mid-1800s, and they had remained there when Robert's mother moved back to Maine after her husband's death. Upon learning of my meeting with Kali in Greenland and my plans to bring him to the United States, the Pennsylvania descendants had written to ask if they might participate in the reunion activities. The committee, of course, was delighted to oblige. Before Kali's arrival in the United States, they were the only members of the Peary family who had shown any interest in meeting Kali and his family.

* * *

Later that afternoon, we headed to the town of Milton, a suburb of Boston, where the American Hensons had arranged a traditional backyard barbeque for their Eskimo kin. As I drove Anaukaq, Kali, and their families to Milton in a large rented van, they all sang traditional Eskimo songs—songs of joy and happiness.

To locate the family gathering, we had to find our way through the maze of curving streets and rotaries common to the Boston area. But the American Hensons provided very special directions. For the last few miles, all the way to the door of the house, they had tied yellow ribbons around the trees along the road to mark the way. The Eskimo families had never heard of this practice and were profoundly touched when I explained it to them. They delighted in helping me spot the trees with the yellow ribbons, cheering each as it came into view.

When we reached the Henson's home, there were the usual introductions, along with music, dancing, and, of course, lots of food—"soul food"—on the lawn of the beautifully landscaped backyard. Our hosts served barbequed chicken, cornbread, collard greens, black-eyed peas, yams, ham, corn, rice, okra, cakes, and even homemade ice cream.

"This is the special food of the *kulnocktooko* people," Ussarkaq announced to the others. " 'Soul' food—that is what they told me."

"What are collard greens?" Avataq asked.

"That is a traditional black American vegetable," I told him.

"Mmmm, it tastes good," he responded.

"Try a little vinegar on them," I told him.

"This is some of the best food I have ever tasted," Avataq offered.

"*Eeee*," Anaukaq replied. "This chicken tastes a little like our *cheemeahk* in Moriussaq—and the ham is a little sweet, like *nanook*."

To show their appreciation, the Amer-Eskimos sang several songs, after which Anaukaq and his children held a ceremony to present gifts they had brought from Greenland for their family and friends. They handed out authentic native carvings and other traditional Eskimo handiwork. Anaukaq and Kali surprised me with a gift they knew I really wanted: a beautiful pair of handmade, traditional sealskin hunter's mittens with polar bear fur tops. Nothing is more suited to the Arctic cold, not even the expensive synthetic gloves they saw me wearing in Greenland. Receiving these from Anaukaq and Kali, two *peeneeahktoe wah*, was a great tribute indeed.

Olive and the American Hensons presented Anaukaq and Kali each with a combination radio–tape recorder, with shortwave and AM-FM—something I knew they would enjoy back in their homeland. Greenland now has a radio station broadcasting in the Polar Eskimo language. Anaukaq, Kali, and their families were quite fond of listening to such radio programs.

"I am so happy to be here today—to look around me and see so many of Mahri-Pahluk's family here. I am also happy that my children and their children could come here to meet their relatives. We always thought we had relatives over here—and now we know. We are here now, and we can see you, and we feel good. We thank you for this celebration. I hope you will come to see us in our land. *Kooyounah*."

Everyone cheered and applauded.

The celebration continued into the evening, with some family members retiring to the house, where they played the piano and sang.

One of the Hensons had a fancy van with dramatic designs on the exterior and an interior that looked more like an elegant studio than an automobile. The Eskimos were captivated by this unusual *pedde*, with its carpeted floors, colorful lights, and multistereo sound. And to their utter delight, they all got a ride in it—several times each.

As the reunion party continued into the evening, I overheard Kitdlaq say to his brothers, "This has been a great day for our family—perhaps the greatest ever. And the *kulnocktooko* people are very special—they have so much feeling." Talilanguaq, who was among the Amer-Eskimo Hensons, nodded approvingly, "Yes, they are very special."

* * *

The following evening, Harvard University sponsored the North Pole Family Reunion Banquet for Hensons and Pearys from all over the country. Anaukaq and Kali were the guests of honor in a gathering of some two hundred people at Harvard's historical Memorial Hall. I had initially planned a smaller get-together, but as word of the reception spread, more and more people wanted to come, and we had to increase the size of the function. Among those in attendance were Robert Peary III and Robert Peary IV, who at the last minute accepted our long-standing invitation to join in the festivities. They said Kali's brother, Robert Peary, Jr., was unable to make the trip from Maine to attend the banquet. Kali was, however, delighted to see his nephew and great nephew there, and so were the members of our organizing committee.

In spite of the heat and the formality of the occasion, the two retired hunters were gregarious and at times looked like royalty, as they were fanned and otherwise attended by family and friends. They sat at the head table with Harvard's president Derek C. Bok, and they spoke eloquently when introduced to the audience. Bok had earlier expressed a personal interest in the Amer-Eskimo families and was most helpful to the North Pole Family Reunion Committee. At my request, he agreed to act as host of the affair and present awards of recognition to Anaukaq and Kali, to herald their visit to the university and to honor their fathers.

At the podium, Bok addressed the gathering. "It is a great privilege to welcome to Harvard the sons of Robert Peary and Matthew Henson—Anaukaq Henson and Kali Peary—and the members of their families. This trip, as many of you know, represents the realization of a wish to see the land in which their fathers lived and died." His warm presentation was punctuated with spirited applause.

This was followed by a stirring speech from the keynote speaker of the evening, John H. Johnson, who several times brought the audience to its feet.

"I am delighted to be here tonight," Johnson began. "I usually have a speechwriter—and I had one this time. And I have a speech, but I'm not going to give it. I feel too much from my heart. This has touched me. I feel as if history has come alive here tonight."

Johnson was at his best, evoking both laughter and tears as he told us what Matthew Henson meant to his life and to the success of his business. "When they were trying to decide on who was going to go with him [Peary] on the last lap to the North Pole, Peary said 'I can't make it without Henson.' This is a man who had been with him for eighteen years—who had made eight trips with him. Imagine, eight trips. I think I would have dropped out at seven! But he made eight. This is a man who believed in his leader. I also think this says something good about Admiral Peary. It says that he was the kind of man who dared in 1909 to say that the best man for the job was a black man. That was a daring thing to do in 1909! Frankly, it's daring sometimes now."

Olive represented the Henson family. "I want to welcome everybody to this beautiful, happy feeling that I have in my heart right now," Olive said with choked voice and tearful eyes. "And I just wish everybody could feel the way I do. Thank you."

University marshal Richard Hunt joined Bok in making the presentations to Anaukaq and Kali.

"This award is presented to Mr. Anaukaq Henson to mark his visit to Harvard University and to salute his father's contributions to the discovery of the North Pole. Given this day, June 1, 1987."

Anaukaq, his pride not permitting any of us to assist him in walking, stepped up to the podium without his cane to receive his award.

"Also, from Harvard University, to mark his visit to the university and to salute the contributions of his father to the discovery of the North Pole, we present this award to Mr. Kali Peary."

The two old hunters were clearly moved. They stood together, erect with poise and dignity after walking up to the podium to receive the large, elegant engravings of the old Harvard Yard, with their names etched in shiny brass. They would gladly have accepted even the smallest token of recognition from any American, regardless of his or her position. They did not understand or even care about American hierarchy. But here they were tonight, being recognized by the president of the oldest and most distinguished university in America, receiving the same plaques customarily presented to royalty and heads of state.

Anaukaq never failed to amaze me. This little big man from the tiny village of Moriussaq addressed the Harvard gathering like a practiced statesman.

"I thank all of you for this reception you have given me and my family and Kali this evening. This is a special night for me," he said. "I thought that I would never have the opportunity to visit Mahri-Pahluk's homeland. And I believed that I would never have a chance to see my relatives in America. We are here now, and we are very pleased to be with our relatives."

The audience applauded. Thinking he had finished, I started to pass the microphone to Kali, only to be stopped by the translator, who reminded me that Anaukaq was "not finished yet."

"When people up in Greenland used to talk of Peeuree and Mahri-Pahluk, I would think about whether I had relatives over here. I used to tell my children, 'Maybe we have some relatives over there in Mahri-Pahluk's homeland. Maybe I have a brother or sister down there,' I would say. I had no brother or sister in Greenland. I was alone. And now I know that Mahri-Pahluk had no other children, and that I have no sisters or brothers in America. But I have lots of other wonderful relatives down here. I am just as happy to meet Olive and my other American relatives.

"I thank everyone who helped make this trip possible for me, my sons, and some of my grandchildren. I have finally made it to America, and here I am—Matthew Henson's son, Anaukaq, who has been hiding up in Greenland all these years." Then with a big laugh, he raised his arms, clenched fists above his head, and waved them defiantly. "I have finally come home in 1987 to proudly show everyone that I am the son of Matthew Henson."

His animation surprised everyone. During his long life, Anaukaq must have dreamed this scene over and over, many times. He must have fantasized about coming to his father's land and being received as a hero by family and admirers. He was ecstatic.

Kali spoke with confidence and eloquence. "I don't have words to express myself tonight. But I am reminded of the time when I was much younger and working in politics among my people. I learned an important thing. I learned the importance of cooperation among people. And I am thankful for that. Later, I was amazed when the first ships came up to the Thule air base, and we met other people. They wanted to cooperate with us, and we with them. And I thought that maybe the people have finally heard my words when I said that people must work together as people. It is very important for people to work together in achieving something. I can't keep going now because this is more than I can handle," he said with tears in his eyes. "Let some of the others take over. We are here with you tonight because we have all worked together—because of our cooperation. *Kooyounah*."

The sustained applause testified to the powerful emotions that swept over the gathering. In a community where people typically depart quickly after a social affair, we were all surprised to see that most of the guests remained to talk with our Eskimo visitors and with each other long after the ceremony had ended.

The celebration continued at my house, where Anaukaq and Kali were later inspired to get up and dance to music they heard while watching television. They had everyone in stitches as they did old Eskimo dances to modern music.

The next morning, after a hefty breakfast, we boarded the bus for Charles County, Maryland, and Washington, D.C. A small group of friends gathered to see us off. I knew that Anaukaq and Kali charmed all who met them. But I never realized just how deeply the two men and their families had affected our community until I saw *Harvard Gazette* senior writer Marvin Hightower standing at the roadside, crying, as the bus pulled away. As a member of our committee, Marvin had helped us organize activities and chaperon the family. Like others who were involved with Anaukaq and Kali, he had also become emotionally very close to both families. The Eskimos fell silent when they saw Marvin's tears. Staring back through the windows, they slowly waved good-bye to him as the bus pulled off. He, like the other Americans, had had a profound effect on them as well.

* * *

In some sections, Charles County, Maryland, is as bucolic and verdant today as it was when Matthew Henson was born here in 1866. We were met at the county line by members of the Charles County Afro-American Heritage Society, with whom I had earlier arranged a public reception. The group's president, Mary Louise Webb, pinned black-eyed Susans on every member of our entourage and, with a motorcycle police escort, directed our long motorcade into the county seat. With sirens blaring, the police and motorcade led us down the main street to the town center. The Eskimo family sensed that this would be an important ceremony for them when they saw the parade of cars behind our bus, and the motorcycle police with lights flashing, in front.

"This is how they treat important people," Avataq said to Kali, who was sitting beside him. "This is to show us how much they appreciate that we are here."

I had also written the county commissioners to request an official reception for Anaukaq and his family. They welcomed us with a band and a flag-waving ceremony. The conductor led the band in "76 Trombones" as our entourage arrived.

Anaukaq and Kali stepped off the bus to loud applause from a gathering of more than two hundred citizens. Each of us received a small American flag from local officials as we were led to our seats behind the podium on the steps of the antebellum, white-pillared county courthouse.

Speeches by government officials and singing by local citizens rounded out the welcome.

"As a token of our appreciation for Mr. Henson's visit, we are presenting his family with the county flag," said the county commissioner, as she handed Anaukaq a large yellow banner with the Charles County insignia in its center.

"*Kooyounah,*" Anaukaq said, graciously accepting the flag and shaking the commissioner's hand.

In the tiny town of Nanjemoy, in the center of Charles County, we walked deep into the thick woods so that Anaukaq could view the spot where his father was born. We were guided by long-time resident William Diggs who, along with other members of the Charles County Afro-American Heritage Society, had located and marked the spot for posterity. Diggs had met Matthew Henson on some of his visits to Charles County to see his family.

"I thought that I would see the igloo where my father Mahri-Pahluk was born," Anaukaq said.

"Unfortunately, it is long gone," Diggs replied. "It was a log cabin. Only parts of the fireplace remain."

"It was over one hundred years old and made of wood," I added. "It simply deteriorated over time."

Anaukaq said he was pleased just to stand on the ground where his father was born. He took two bricks, part of the original fireplace, from the ruins of his father's home. These he would take back to Greenland as mementos.

As we drove along the narrow, rustic back roads, Anaukaq sat alone on the bus, staring out the window at the thick green forest around us.

"What a beautiful country!" he said. "This is Mahri-Pahluk's land.

I can see that he lived in a beautiful area. It seems like I am dreaming, but I'm not. I have never been to such a beautiful place."

* * *

Next, we traveled to Washington to commemorate the meeting of Anaukaq's and Kali's fathers in that city a century earlier and to visit Robert Peary's grave in Arlington National Cemetery.

A few months earlier, I had contacted Mr. Raymond Costanzo, superintendent of Arlington National Cemetery, and told him about my plans. From the outset, Costanzo showed sincere interest in the subject and wanted to know how he could help. I requested that a small ceremony be held at Peary's grave, with a navy honor guard and chaplain to salute both Kali's visit and the memory of Robert Peary. Costanzo promptly contacted me to say that my request had been approved and that he would help arrange the ceremony. I then sent a letter to the White House, inviting the president or one of his representatives to join us for the ceremony.

About the same time, I contacted the Woodlawn Cemetery. Assuming that the president would not grant permission to transfer Henson's remains to Arlington in time for Anaukaq's visit, I requested a similar ceremony at Woodlawn, with a military honor guard, a minister, and a formal wreath-laying ceremony.

When our bus arrived at the gates of Arlington, uniformed soldiers snapped to attention and directed us up the winding road to Peary's grave. The stately tombs lining the pastoral lanes entranced everyone on the bus as we made our way up the curving hill. The monument marking Peary's grave sits alone on a spacious, hilltop site that commands a view of much of the cemetery.

About seventy-five Henson family members and friends greeted us when we reached the grave. The assembled guests were seated in front of the monument, under the branches of a large tree that shaded us from the afternoon sun. Standing to our left, behind a roped-off area, were some thirty members of the press, with cameras and sound equipment. Their cameras had started clicking the moment we stepped from the bus.

Costanzo greeted us with a warm smile. A man of gentle but firm demeanor, he had a special reverence for this cemetery, and he conveyed that feeling as he gave us a briefing on the procedures of the ceremony. Costanzo introduced me to Chase Untermeyer, assistant secretary of the navy, who attended the ceremony on behalf of the president of the United States, who was attending a summit meeting.

"I was sent to represent the president of the United States in the ceremony today. He has sent you a special message," Untermeyer told me. I was very pleased.

Next to Untermeyer was Comdr. Stanley DeLong, navy chaplain of Arlington National Cemetery. I could see many other high-ranking military officials in attendance as well. DeLong, Untermeyer, and Costanzo gave Kali and Anaukaq small gifts with military insignia.

Costanzo called the gathering to order. "We gather here today to honor Admiral Peary and Matthew Henson. Peary's and Henson's accolades were not won on the battlefield, but they were no less gallant. Their daring sacrifices in uncharted and treacherous territories rank them among our nation's most celebrated men of courage. They are linked to a long list of explorers and scientists who have been laid to rest here at Arlington. We are here to pay tribute to their immense contributions."

The ceremony was now under way. Dressed in white uniforms, a five-man navy honor guard marched before the assembly carrying the ceremonial U.S. flag, the U.S. Navy flag, and rifles. At Costanzo's signal, the entire gathering stood as the honor guard paraded before us. They stopped in front of Peary's monument. "Abou-uuut face! Attennn-hut!"

After DeLong delivered the invocation, the cemetery historian told the gathering about Peary's burial and the subsequent monument dedication. Although Peary was buried in Arlington in 1920 with full military honors, including airplane flights over his grave, the monument was given by the National Geographic Society and dedicated at an even larger ceremony by the president of the United States in 1922.

When my turn to speak came, I thanked the government officials for making this a special day for Kali. But I also reminded the gathering that we could not forget that Matthew Henson belonged in Arlington as well.

"Admiral Peary, the great explorer, deserves to be buried here. But Matthew Henson also deserves to be buried here among other American heroes. Henson and Peary were inseparable in their Arctic lives and accomplishments. They should be together in their resting places. I have written a letter to the president of the United States, asking him to consider reinterring the remains of Matthew Henson near those of his close friend and colleague Robert E. Peary here in the Arlington National Cemetery. This act would be appreciated by fair and patriotic Americans of all races, creeds, and colors."

Next, Chase Untermeyer stepped up to the podium and read a letter from the president:

> *Greetings to everyone gathered at Arlington National Cemetery for a service honoring the memory of Matthew Henson and Robert Peary, and a very special welcome to Anaukaq Henson and Kali Peary and their families, who have made the long journey from Greenland for the occasion.*
>
> *I am proud and happy to join with you in saluting the achievements of these Arctic explorers, who, with four Polar Eskimo companions, planted the American flag at the North Pole on April 6, 1909. Matthew Henson and Robert Peary worked together for twenty-three years and made eight Arctic voyages, during which Peary's leadership and Henson's interpreting and survival skills proved invaluable. The descendants and all the countrymen of these great Americans can be truly proud of their legacy of heroism and accomplishment in the service of science and our country.*
>
> *You have my very best wishes. God bless you.*
> *[signed] Ronald Reagan.*

After a round of grateful applause, Kali spoke from the podium.

"I thank the people here for this day. I have come this far to see the burial place of my *ahtahtah*, and here he sleeps in this beautiful place that I could not have imagined back in my homeland. My son and my grandson are here with me to share this day. And I have brought this wreath that my oldest daughter helped me make, so that our family and the Hensons of Greenland could honor Peeuree by putting it on his grave today. *Kooyounah*."

A lone officer dressed in navy whites and standing among the tombstones some distance away, played a soft "taps" as Kali stepped up to Peary's monument and gently placed the wreath he had made for the occasion just beneath his father's name. Talilanguaq, Ole, and

Cousin Anaukaq then placed a second, larger wreath alongside the first. Kali asked me to walk to the monument with them. An honor guard escorted us.

After the ceremony, Kali bent over to try to read the inscription on the tombstone. I had it translated for him. It read: "Robert Edwin Peary—Discoverer of the North Pole—April 6, 1909." The side inscription read: "His beloved wife—Josephine Diebitsch Peary."

"This is Peary's wife's name," I told Kali and Anaukaq, who had joined him. "She is buried here also." He made no comment as he stared at the inscription.

This was the central ceremony planned for Kali in the itinerary. None of the American Pearys showed up. After the ceremony, he walked up to almost all the whites at the gathering, asking them one by one whether they were his relatives. They all said no. Sensing his loneliness, my Harvard students became very protective of him. They huddled around him and became his family. He never talked about it, but we hoped the Arlington ceremony was still a special event for him.

* * *

Between all the ceremonies, our guests had plenty of rest and relaxation. Their favorite pastime was playing in the swimming pool. The word "playing" is more appropriate than "swimming," even for the adults, since no one swims in polar Greenland. In fact, to the Eskimos, the very idea of plunging into a body of water is associated with death. This was especially evident from the face of Anaukaq, who had lost his eldest son to the icy northern sea. He watched with trepidation as Talilinguaq, Ole, Avataq, and the others entered the water for the first time and began thrashing about. They screamed and yelled at the thrill of their own buoyancy and their surprising ability to move about in water. Ajako, who was afraid to enter the pool, kept sticking his foot in the water to allay his fears, until he was finally pushed in. After this, it was difficult to get him to come out.

Eventually Anaukaq, too, overcame his fears. Although he never braved the water himself, he and Kali sat at the poolside, directing the others and laughing deliriously at their antics.

"Look at that!" Anaukaq said. "How can they move about in the water like that?"

"Ole looks like a big *pooeehee* under the water," Kali commented. "Look at him move," he chuckled, as his grandson dove beneath the surface in the three-foot section.

"Move your arms more like this," Anaukaq shouted to Malina, as he imitated swimming strokes.

With instructions from the experienced swimmers among our student escorts, Massauna-Matthew, Ole, Malina, and Aviaq, the youngest members of the group, quickly learned some strokes.

* * *

At 1237 Pennsylvania Avenue in Washington, a towering office building now stands where H. Stinemetz & Sons, Hatters and Furriers, stood a century earlier. As we passed the location, I pointed out to Anaukaq and Kali that this was the spot where their fathers had met a hundred years before.

The mayor had agreed to act as host at a reception for us at the Washington, D.C., Convention Center. Over a hundred guests, including American Hensons and friends, greeted us as we entered one of the reception areas of the massive building. In the center of the room stood a large ice sculpture of an igloo, surrounded by a profusion of elegant hors d'ouevres. The Eskimos cheerfully sampled everything until they were full.

We were officially welcomed by Washington Convention Center board chairman, and my old friend, Kent T. Cushenberry, who had arranged this affair at my request and who had been tremendously helpful to me throughout the project.

I had written Mayor Marion Barry about Matthew Henson's Washington roots and his contributions to the discovery of the North Pole, and I asked that Barry name the day of Anaukaq's first visit to Washington "Matthew Henson Day."

"I had never heard of the name Matthew A. Henson, to be frank with you, because it was left out of our history books," said Barry, surrounded onstage by Anaukaq, Kali, and their families. "And so I learned that Matthew Henson was a part of the North Pole expedition, that he was in fact chosen by Admiral Peary to actually, physically plant the flag at the North Pole. Never would I have thought in my wildest moments of fantasizing dreams that I would be here in Washington, D.C., today, as mayor of our nation's capital, meeting the sons of Peary and Henson. Now that is history being made. Actually, I really can't even write words to express what I'm talking about, I feel so touched."

The gathering erupted in emotional applause.

The mayor read from the proclamation. "And therefore I, the mayor of the District of Columbia, do hereby proclaim Wednesday June 3, 1987, as Matthew A. Henson Day in Washington, D.C., and call upon all the residents of this city in saluting this famous explorer. Signed Marion Barry, Jr., Mayor."

When the interpreter translated the mayor's words for the Eskimos, Ajako, who was holding his daughter Aviaq close to him, started to cry.

Detecting these feelings, the translator added a little humor to her translations.

"This day is Matthew Henson Day in Washington, D.C., until the great earthquake comes [Eskimo talk for the day of the end of the earth]. *"Bikdaoahgee* [Congratulations]," she shouted to the family.

Anaukaq, Kali, and their families cheered.

The mayor handed the proclamation to a happy and very appreciative Anaukaq.

Kent Cushenberry presented Anaukaq and Kali with U.S. flags that had been flown over the Capitol in their names at the request of Walter Fauntroy, congressman from Washington, D.C. The two Eskimo patriarchs and their children were visibly overwhelmed by these gestures.

I watched as Anaukaq and Kali, swarmed by family, friends, and well-wishers reveled in the moment. I recalled that a century before this day, Matthew Henson had sat down, not far from where we stood at the Washington Convention Center, and written Peary a letter expressing his desire to continue working with him in the future. He signed the letter, "From a friend—Matthew Henson." The friends who had met here in 1887 could never have dreamed that their sons, two very close friends, would be standing in Washington one hundred years later, being honored by the president of the United States, the mayor of the nation's capital, and a member of Congress.

* * *

Although Matthew Henson was born in Charles County, Maryland, and spent much of his youth in Washington, he lived for most of his life in New York City. He first moved there temporarily in 1892, when he rented a room at the home of Frederick Cook's mother while recovering from an Arctic eye ailment. Henson became enamored of the city and, after his estrangement from his first wife in 1897, he moved there permanently, remaining a New Yorker until his death in 1955. His last residence at 246 West 150th Street often buzzed with activity. A fireman who worked at a station near Henson's house in the 1950s recalled that one day, after having seen so many people visit the home, he was forced to ask the station chief who lived there. "In that home, my boy, resides the great Matthew Henson, who went to the North Pole with Peary," the chief told him.

Others remember Henson's legendary long walks, particularly those from his West 150th Street apartment to the Explorers Club on East 70th, in the dead of winter, without a topcoat. Henson enjoyed demonstrating his stamina and extraordinary ability to tolerate the cold.

I had told Anaukaq and Kali about the Explorers Club and their fathers' involvement with this select body. Peary served as president of the club from 1909 to 1911 and from 1913 to 1916, and Henson was elected to honorary membership in 1937. I arranged for the Eskimo families to have a tour of the club's house.

Just inside the entrance of the stately Tudor-style building, we were met by a ten-foot-high polar bear, standing on his hind legs, claws outstretched and teeth bared in a menacing snarl. The sight thrilled the old hunters, who rubbed the fur in amazement. They had never seen a stuffed polar bear, and the superb taxidermy made the animal look startlingly real.

"*Nanook*," Anaukaq said to Kali. "What a huge thing. I don't think I have ever killed one this large. Have you?"

"No, not this large. And look at its *kokeet* [claws]," Kali replied.

Avataq, a hunter who has killed and eaten many polar bears, also marveled at the size of this "lion of the Arctic" that towered over him. "Look at the size of that mouth," he remarked, examining the stuffed beast as though he thought it might come to life at any moment. Even as Avataq walked away, he continued looking back at the bear in disbelief.

The bell taken from the *Roosevelt* is mounted on the wall of the club's main entrance. The family cheered as Anaukaq and Kali took turns ringing the bell, something they were too young to have done when the ship left Greenland for the last time in 1909.

Kali was particularly fascinated by the artifacts from his father's ship. During our visit to the Peary-MacMillan Arctic Museum in Maine, he spotted a replica of the *Roosevelt* and became very excited. "Is that the *Roosevelt*?" he asked. When the translator confirmed that it was, he became even more animated. "That is where I was born," he told me, gesturing toward the model. "Really, it is the truth. I'm not telling you a joke. That is what my parents told me. I was born in the *Roosevelt*'s machine room, and cousin Anaukaq was born in the coal room."

"Did you say Anaukaq was born in the coal room?" I asked in jest.

"*Eeee*," Kali replied. "We have known this since we were boys."

"Is that why Anaukaq is so dark?" I asked.

Kali and the other Eskimos burst into laughter. "Must be!"

On the walls, among the framed photographs of past presidents and honorary members of the club, were classic pictures of their fathers that made Kali and Anaukaq pause: Peary in a grand pose, wearing his military uniform and hat and sporting a thick, curled moustache; Henson, equally striking in his trademark anorak, the wind-blown fur of the hood outlining his features.

"Our *ahtahtah*," Kali said to Anaukaq, pointing at the photographs.

"*Eeee*," Anaukaq said solemnly.

"Who are all of these other men?" Kali asked.

"Past Explorers Club presidents," our guide told us.

"They all look so important," Kali said with a chuckle.

Yet what excited them most was the sight of one of the original sleds that Peary and Henson had used on their North Pole journey in 1909. Given to the club by the Peary family, the dark oak sledge (as sleds were once called) was about twelve feet long, two feet wide, seven inches off the ground, with three-foot upstanders. It was lashed together with sealskin thongs for flexibility and strength.

"Oh, this is a beauty. It suits this place," said Anaukaq. "It is the kind we had in the old days."

"Ahhh, look at this. This is very good workmanship," said Kali.

"Maybe Mahri-Pahluk used this one to give his boss a ride to the North Pole," Anaukaq said, teasing Kali.

"Maybe!" Kali laughed. "What are these bindings made of?" he asked Anaukaq as he rolled the lashings in his fingers.

"Aren't these thongs made of bearded seal?" Anaukaq replied, examining the tough leather cords with his experienced hands.

"I don't know," Kali said, still feeling the bindings. "Maybe they are made of something from this country."

The two old hunters explored every inch of the sled, like two old-timers examining an antique car from their youth.

After an extended tour of the club's several floors we departed, but not before Anaukaq and Kali had put their signatures on Explorers Club stationery, which I had dated to record their visit in the historical archives of their fathers' mutual fraternity.

* * *

Only the mountains of the Eskimos' world compared with the giant skyscrapers of New York City. Like all newcomers to the city, the two families were awed by the scale of everything around them.

"Igloo, igloo, igloo, *quah, quah, quah, pah che* [So many, many houses]," was again the cry of everyone on the bus. Ajako called his daughter Aviaq over to his seat and pointed out the tall buildings on his side. She lay on his lap, facing upward toward the ceiling of the bus so that she could appreciate the height of the skyscrapers.

After a shopping spree at Macy's and other stores, we pounded the pavement for blocks so that our friends could get a feel for Matthew Henson's city. At times their faces suggested that we were on another planet, as we crossed crowded streets, moved up and down elevators, looked down from skyscrapers, and stopped to touch police horses.

* * *

The sights, sounds, and smells of Broadway on a summer night are wildly alive and enticing. My Eskimo friends were taking it all in as we walked past street vendors and street hustler after gaudy street hustler.

"Hey, man! You wanna buy a watch?"

"Hey, you! Come here! See this ace of hearts? Now you find it among the three cards I just dealt on the table, and I will give you twenty dollars. If you don't select the right one, you give *me* twenty dollars. Deal?"

"Look here! I got some gold necklaces over here—cheap. I'll give you a good deal. What do you say?"

Some of the Eskimos bought items as gifts for their wives, children, and other relatives back in Greenland. Though they seemed somewhat puzzled by my efforts to bargain with the ravenous vendors, as we haggled over prices they were dazzled by the vast array of flashing neon lights and the open display of money—not to mention the legions of colorful, unusual-looking people.

"Look at all the people," Talilanguaq remarked. "Where do all the people come from? They are like huge flocks of birds."

On the next block, several young black and Puerto Rican teenagers danced to rap music blasting from a "boom box." Malina and Massauna-Matthew were spellbound by this impromptu street show. Excellent dancers themselves, the two eighteen-year-olds studied the steps intently and then mimicked them playfully.

The video arcade on Broadway was a big hit with everyone, youngsters and adults alike. The people playing the flashy electronic machines were as interesting to the Eskimos as the games themselves. And the old-fashioned mechanical claw that can be manipulated to pick up rings, watches, and other gifts behind a glass enclosure proved universally popular. I had never seen Ole or his father, Talilanguaq, laugh so much as when they tried, time and time again, to grab a prize with the claw. They became even more delighted when, to the cheers of the group, each succeeded in picking up a new watch.

As our group proceeded down the avenue, I felt Malina tugging vigorously at my arm. I turned to see sheer horror on her face as she mumbled something in Eskimo that I did not understand. Shaking visibly, she pulled me back to a spot we had just passed. She pointed to the ground, where an apparently homeless black man lay against the side of the building, his eyes glazed and fixed. The others watched in silence as Malina tugged at my pockets, beseeching me to give her some money, something she had never done before. I reached into my pocket, pulled out a five-dollar bill, and handed it to her. She stepped up to the man on the ground and handed him the money. He accepted, then looked up at Malina with a wide-eyed, blank stare and nodded his appreciation. She smiled slightly.

"Come along, Malina," one of the students said, pulling her along as she kept looking back over her shoulder.

As we continued along the busy New York streets, I could not help thinking of how Malina and the others must regard the stunning contrast of wealth and poverty in our country. She could not understand how people could walk past the obviously disabled man and not even acknowledge his presence, not to mention fail to help him. No one in her homeland would ever walk over a person in need.

* * *

Sunday morning. We are driving through Harlem. On one corner we see two apparently drunk young black men fighting. On the other corner stands an impeccably attired, elderly black woman in white dress and large white hat, seemingly oblivious to the violent clash across the street as she waits for her ride to church. Inside the bus, which has stopped at a traffic light, the Eskimos watch the incongruous scene in silence.

We were on our way to New York's historic Abyssinian Baptist Church. This was Matthew and Lucy Henson's church. They attended Abyssinian services regularly, and Lucy did civic and social work there. When Matthew died in 1955 and Lucy in 1968, their funerals were held at Abyssinian.

Knowing of the Hensons' long association with the church and two of its past ministers—Adam Clayton Powell, Sr. and Jr.—I contacted the current pastor, the Reverend Dr. Samuel Proctor, and asked whether he would hold a special service of recognition for my Greenlandic friends. Proctor enthusiastically agreed.

Anaukaq and his children had spoken frequently about their desire to experience various aspects of the culture of the *kulnocktooko* people, with whom they so strongly identified. I wanted them to experience the most enduring institution in the black community, the African-American church.

Abyssinian is a large Gothic church in the heart of the predominantly black community of Harlem, with a seating capacity of more than a thousand. The church was filled on this day. Two large choirs in flowing gowns stood in different balconies, singing a gospel song, when we entered the church. The uniformed ushers escorted us to reserved seats in the center of the congregation. By now the Eskimos were accustomed to large gatherings, but not so large or animated as this one. In our pews, the Eskimos sat in complete wonder throughout the service. There was singing and hand-clapping and foot-patting and contagious spirituality.

Proctor delivered a powerful sermon, his gravelly voice resounding throughout the church.

"Our circle is widening today, isn't it, Abyssinian?"

"Oh, yes! Yes, Lord," answered members of the congregation.

"We have people here today all the way from *Greenland*," Proctor stressed. "People who live in ice all the time. Speak another language. Eat another kind of diet. Dress differently. People whose lifestyle is different from our own. But here they are, smiling in our midst because Abyssinian has widened the circle today, and thank God for the friends who have helped us to widen our circle today."

"Amen," shouted the congregation in unison.

"Peacemaker, peacemaker. Learn how to be fair!" Proctor thundered. "You don't have to be so smart. You don't need to have a Ph.D. degree. Just have some *sensitivity* to what you are doing to people."

"Yes, Lord! Amen."

After the sermon, Proctor officially recognized and welcomed Anaukaq, Kali, and their families to the church.

"We welcome to Abyssinian today the son of Matthew Henson, who was a member of our church. Mr. Henson and his family are from Greenland. Will you bring Mr. Henson forward to speak with the congregation?" Proctor asked, his arm raised high in a magnanimous gesture.

As I escorted Anaukaq to the pulpit, I noticed that he moved swiftly, without reservation or discomfort about speaking before the congregation. At the pulpit, he stood proudly erect and addressed the congregation like a preacher.

"I am happy to be here, to share this ceremony with you today, in such a beautiful way. I am only a very ordinary person from far, far away, visiting the church of my father, Matthew Henson. And I thank you for receiving me and my family. *Kooyounah.*"

When the translation ended, the congregation erupted into applause. Anaukaq smiled in appreciation.

"We also welcome to our church this morning the son of Admiral Robert Peary. Will you please stand, sir?"

At the translator's signal, Kali stood to loud welcoming applause.

Following Proctor's lead, the congregation broke into one of the classic black American spirituals, accompanied by the choir and rhythmic hand-clapping.

I'm—so—proud that Jesus lifted me,
I'm—so—proud that Jesus lifted me,
I'm—so—proud that Jesus lifted me
Singing glory hallelujah,
Jesus lifted me.

This was a traditional Sunday song of fellowship. Members of the congregation turned to their neighbors to shake hands or embrace during the singing. Many came over to greet Anaukaq, Kali, and their families, welcoming them with a warm handshake or an embrace.

The congregation of the all-black church treated Kali and his sons with kindness and respect, as if they were longtime members of their spiritual community. Kali was moved to comment that he "felt good

with the *kulnocktooko* people—like I'm one of them—and they treat
me like I am one of them."

After the service, we were the church's guests at a lunch attended
by hundreds of other parishioners in Abyssinian's large dining area.
There we met many older church members who had known Anaukaq's father personally, one a well-known sculptor who had had
Matthew Henson pose for a bust forty years earlier. To Anaukaq's
delight, the old parishioners shared with him many stories about his
uniformly admired father.

*   *   *

Our last stop was Woodlawn Cemetery in the Bronx. This would be
our last ceremony on the tour. As in Washington, the ceremony was
attended by ministers, political dignitaries, Henson family members,
and friends. Letters from the governor of New York and the mayor of
New York City were read by their representatives. The Fordham
College Choir sang and speeches were delivered. Four U.S. Marines
in ceremonial dark-blue uniforms and white hats marched toward
Matthew Henson's headstone in slow lockstep, then stood at attention with rifles shouldered and flagstaffs held high. Somehow a
marine honor guard was fitting, I thought. Whereas the clean-cut,
tailored, and suave Robert Peary in many ways epitomized the navy,
the rugged and intrepid Matthew Henson seemed better suited to
the navy's celebrated assault troops.

As Anaukaq and his family walked forward to lay a wreath at the
grave, they were almost stampeded by a pack of disrespectful reporters and photographers. Although we had to stop the ceremony to
move them back and give the family some privacy, Anaukaq remained unfazed. He placed the wreath on his father's grave and
stared down at the headstone. After a long silence, he spoke aloud to
himself.

"So it is here that my father is buried. . . . He must have had a
tough life up in our land. . . . He must have been very cold up there
at times. . . . My father. . . . My father."

He turned to us. "I too will be *sinnegbo* [asleep] soon. I am now
ready to go back home to die and rest near my wife, Aviaq."

None of us knew what to say. Finally, I turned to him. "Anaukaq, when I visit Greenland next year or even five years from now, you will still be racing around Moriussaq with that old cane and laughing up a storm." He laughed.

* * *

The North Pole Family Reunion ended where it had begun ten days earlier, at McGuire Air Force Base. There was both joy and sadness as we all embraced and said our good-byes. Joy that the two worlds had been reunited—reconnected in both tangible and spiritual ways. Sadness that new friends and loved ones were about to be separated by vast distances and time.

Anaukaq and Kali were still in high spirits. Just about everything they could have imagined they had accomplished in the previous two weeks. Most important to them was meeting their American kinfolk and visiting their fathers' graves. They were now ready to return to the only world they had ever known.

But much had happened over the previous ten days. Eighteen-year-old Massauna-Matthew had become deeply infatuated with Suzanne Malveaux, one of the Harvard student escorts. He talked about her incessantly. When he reached the airplane, he started crying openly and did not want to leave. His father, Ussarkaq, had to persuade him to get on the plane.

Ole, the nineteen-year-old full-time hunter, had become equally enamored of Mariana Ortiz-Blanes, another student escort, who, upon sensing the Amer-Eskimo Pearys' loneliness in the absence of their American kin, had become a kind of protective mother and sister to them.

And Malina had been greatly taken with Kermit Alexander, the first young *kulnocktooko* man she had ever met. She joked that she wanted to marry him.

Both Eskimo families had fallen in love with Camille Holmes and Sean Brady and wanted to take them back to Greenland.

Ten-year-old Aviaq, who was already beyond her years in maturity, had grown tremendously. Entering the plane, she sported new sunglasses, watches, and other gifts she had received. She had always asked many questions about her American great-grandfather. Now she had some answers.

We had all become one big family.

As a final gesture, Anaukaq came up to me before boarding and handed me an official red-and-white Greenlandic flag, the recently inaugurated first flag of his nation. "This is a gift for you, Allen, from me and my family, and Kali and his family, to show you how much we appreciate what you have done for us. We hope you will come back to us in Greenland. *Kooyounah*, Allen, my friend."

"*Iddigdoo* Anaukaq, my friend."

We embraced and said good-bye.

Left to right: Kali Peary, S. Allen Counter, Anaukaq Henson, and Kali's son, Talilanquaq, in the village of Moriussaq, Greenland, in 1986.

Ajako Henson leads his sled dogs through Moriussaq on the way to the hunting grounds.

A Polar Eskimo family at a hunting camp in northwest Greenland (c. 1900). Though it is no longer a common practice, Polar Eskimo families traditionally traveled together during the hunting season, moving by dogsled from camp to camp across hundreds of miles of ice and frozen terrain. *Courtesy of the Explorers Club*

Ussarkaq Henson, Matthew Henson's grandson, hurls his harpoon at a narwhal. While most Polar Eskimos now hunt with rifles, many still resort to more traditional methods.

Ole Peary, great-grandson of Robert E. Peary, hunts for seals off the coast of northwest Greenland. The apparatus attached to his rifle is a white cloth blind, designed to conceal the hunter as he approaches his prey.

Avataq Henson and his son Massanguaq pack their dogsled for a hunt.

Returning from the hunt, Avataq Henson displays the tusks from a large walrus he killed. The ivory tusks will be sold to the government of Greenland, with all proceeds shared by the community of Moriussaq. The walrus meat will also be distributed among the villagers, although the best portions will be reserved for Avataq and his family.

Puto, wife of Ajako Henson, teaches her niece, Malina, to scrape the fat from the skin of a polar bear with a utility knife called an *ulu*.

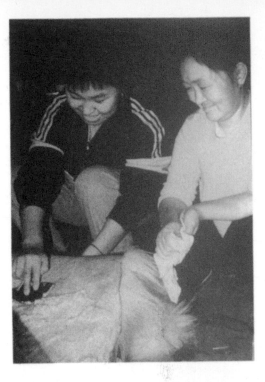

After dipping the bear skin in icy water and then covering it with snow, Ajako and Puto beat it with a stick to remove the ice. The skin will later be stretched and made into trousers for their son, Nukka, whose slaying of the bear entitles him to wear this traditional hunter's attire.

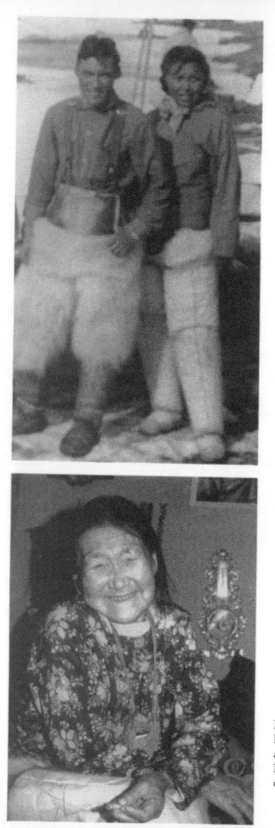

The late Peter Peary, Kali's oldest son, and his wife (c. 1960).

Mikkisuk Minge, Anaukaq's sister-in-law and close friend, who provided the author with an account of life in Moriussaq in the early decades of the century.

Kali and Anaukaq aboard the helicopter that will take them to Thule air base. From there they will fly by military transport to the United States (May 1987).

Anaukaq, Kali, and their families gather in Harvard Yard, May 1987. *Left to right*: Ole (*foreground*), Vittus (*background*), Ajako, Talilanguaq, Ussarkaq, Massauna, Malina, Avataq. Kali (*left*) and Anaukaq, wearing traditional Polar Eskimo anorak, sit in the front row.

Robert E. Peary, Jr., and his half brother Kali meet for the first time at Peary's home in Augusta, Maine (May 1987). In the center is Robert E. Peary III; to the left, the author.

Harvard's president Derek C. Bok (*second from left*) welcomes Anaukaq (*standing, center*) and Kali (*seated at far right*) at a banquet held in their honor. Seated between Anaukaq and Kali is translator Navarana Qavigaq Harper. Publisher John H. Johnson (*far left*), who co-sponsored the North Pole Family Reunion, and the author (*standing, right*) join in the applause. The banquet was attended by some 200 guests, including American members of the Henson and Peary families. *Photo by Hans P. Biemann*

Olive Henson Fulton displays a gift from Anaukaq at the Henson family picnic in suburban Boston (May 1987).

The Reverend Dr. Samuel Proctor welcomes Anaukaq, Kali, and their families to Abyssinian Baptist Church in Harlem.

Anaukaq Henson acknowledges the applause of the Abyssinian congregation. Seated to his right are Kali Peary and other members of the Amer-Eskimo Henson and Peary families.

Anaukaq Henson with Allen Counter at the grave site of Matthew Henson in Woodlawn Cemetery in the Bronx. When this photograph was taken, Anaukaq was telling the author that he had fulfilled his life's ambition and could now go home and join his wife, who had died several years earlier.

Accompanied by his wife Lucy and friends, Matthew Henson prepares to lay a wreath at the grave of Robert E. Peary in Arlington National Cemetery in 1954. Henson regularly visited the tomb of his longtime Arctic companion. *Courtesy of Virginia Carter Brannum*

Members of the Henson family join friends and officials at formal ceremonies marking the reinterment of Matthew Henson at Arlington National Cemetery on April 6, 1988. *James P. Blair, courtesy of National Geographic Society*

Matthew Henson's niece, Virginia Carter Brannum, poses near her uncle's newly installed monument in Arlington National Cemetery, adjacent to the grave site of Robert E. Peary.

U.S. postage stamp issued in 1986 to commemorate the conquest of the North Pole by Peary and Henson. *Copyright © 1986, U.S. Postal Service, Dennis Lyall, Designer*

Anaukaq Henson and his "cousin" Kali Peary in Moriussaq, Greenland (1986).

CHAPTER THIRTEEN

❊ ❊ ❊

Back Home in Greenland

The miracle of modern transportation again bridged two worlds in one day. Ten hours from the time they left America, Anaukaq, Kali, and their families were back in remote northwest Greenland. I did not relax until I received word that they had arrived safely.

They returned to families eagerly awaiting a full accounting of the American adventure, not to mention the distribution of all the gifts brought back from the United States. Avataq brought Magssanguaq a leather pilot's jacket. Kitdlaq brought his wife some jewelry. Ussarkaq and Ajako brought their wives dresses. Aviaq brought her mother a pair of sunglasses, and so on.

But they had also returned to the reality of their world, which even in modern times is a harsh one. They had many vital chores awaiting them: taking care of their dogs, hunting for seals, and, in this season, *kahlayleewah* to feed their families, readying themselves for the approaching fall and winter.

The Eskimos quickly readjusted to their customary way of life. Anaukaq went about Moriussaq as he had always done, visiting friends, eating fresh seal, drinking tea and coffee, and sharing stories, although they were now of his visit to America. His sons successfully hunted seals and birds, while Malina and Aviaq collected eider-duck down and eggs. The down would be sold to the government for communal income. The eggs would be consumed.

After a brief visit with other family members in Qaanaaq, Kali, Talilanguaq, and Ole returned to Qeqertarsaaq. Within a week, Ole had gone out to sea and slain his first narwhal of the season.

When I contacted Navarana, my former translator, a few weeks later, I learned that everyone was doing well.

* * *

One morning, about three weeks after returning to Moriussaq, Anaukaq got up, ate, did a few chores about the igloo, and followed his usual routine. Sometime later, he told his son that he felt like getting some fresh air. He put on his heavy coat, went outside, and walked around the entire settlement. He walked to the sea to look at Avataq's boat. He went to Ajako's little general store. He saw his grandchildren Malina, Aviaq, and Magssanguaq.

He returned to his igloo, walked up to Avataq, and told him that he had done everything that he wanted to do in his life and was now ready to sleep next to his wife, Aviaq. Anaukaq lay down on his bed. A few hours later he died of complications from prostate cancer.

The translator reached me at four o'clock in the morning to tell me the news. All telephone rings at 4 A.M. signal bad news. One reaches for the receiver with a numbing apprehension, knowing that something tragic has taken place. As I lifted the phone, I was prepared to receive sad tidings about someone in my own family. When I learned it was Anaukaq, the effect was the same.

I got up and started making arrangements to travel to Greenland. I had received the call on Thursday. The earliest available air force flight to Thule would leave the following Monday. I confirmed my reservations and made plans to travel to McGuire. But on Friday night, I learned that Anaukaq's family and friends had decided on an earlier burial. They would bury him the next day. I canceled my plans.

In a combination of traditional Eskimo and Christian funeral ceremonies, Anaukaq Henson was laid to rest under a white Christian cross next to his wife, Aviaq, in the little cemetery where he and I had stood just a few months earlier. Covering him was the African-

American flag that I had given him and that he cherished so dearly. He had asked his sons that the flag be draped over him when he died.

The weather in Moriussaq that day was extraordinarily beautiful, and the sun shone brighter than anyone could ever remember, the family said. After the ceremony, family and friends gathered outdoors to celebrate Anaukaq's life. They all felt he had lived a long, happy life, and they wanted no sadness because Anaukaq had rarely been sad.

At Woodlawn Cemetery, he had told us that he was going back home to die and join Aviaq. We hadn't believed him. Yet the Danish physician who had treated him in the past and Dr. Brown, the reunion committee's consulting physician, both said they were surprised he had lived as long as he had, given the advanced state of his prostate cancer. They shared with others a belief that the hope of fulfilling his lifelong dream had sustained him in recent months.

His sons said that Anaukaq had not shown any signs of illness before his death. In fact, he was actively looking after his dogs and doing other chores around the settlement. Had he been visibly ill, they said, they would have taken him to the nearby infirmary at Qaanaaq, but no one noticed any change in him. One Eskimo woman who had seen him back home in Greenland put it another way. "When I looked in Anaukaq's face, I could see that he was ready to go," she said. "I have seen that look before on the faces of the old ones who have done what they wanted to do in life and wanted nothing more than the final rest."

Anaukaq was not forgotten in the United States. The obituary pages of several American newspapers carried the announcement of his passing under the heading "Anaukaq Henson dies in Greenland."

Anaukaq's sons had anticipated his death. They asked Navarana to convey a special message to me from all of them: "Thank you for bringing all five of us together with our father for one last time."

"It was my privilege," I responded. "I am honored to have known Anaukaq."

* * *

A few weeks after his death, I received a somewhat unsettling message from some of the Eskimo Hensons. Anaukaq, they said, had come back to them. At first I did not understand. Then I was told that Anaukaq's twenty-five-year-old granddaughter Equilana had just given birth to a boy and named him Anaukaq. In the Polar Eskimo tradition, Anaukaq had truly returned to them.

CHAPTER FOURTEEN

❊ ❊ ❊

Welcome Home, Matthew Henson

W<small>hy</small> did Peeuree have an impressive tomb in Arlington National Cemetery and Mahri-Pahluk a simple grave in New York? I had the difficult task of explaining to my Eskimo friends the nature of American racial prejudice and the disparate treatment of their respective fathers. Rarely has a man given so much of his life to the honor of his country and received so little in return as had Matthew Henson. Rising from the lowly background of a sharecropper with only six grades of schooling, he had become one of the most accomplished explorers of all time. He deserved a permanent place of honor in recognition of his achievements.

Before our final parting, I told Anaukaq that I had written to President Reagan and requested permission to transfer Matthew Henson's remains to Arlington National Cemetery. I promised that even if I were at first turned down, I would continue to petition until I succeeded.

"If you do move him, I want my children to see it," Anaukaq said.

Several weeks after I sent my first letter to President Reagan, I received a reply from the office of the secretary of the army. The letter explained that the White House had passed along my request to those military officials responsible for burials in Arlington National

Cemetery. An extensive discussion of the regulations governing burials at Arlington followed. Then came the verdict:

> Although Mr. Henson rendered great service to this country, I regret that the established criteria preclude me from granting your request. I am sorry that my response cannot be more positive. It is no reflection on Mr. Henson to say that to make an exception in his case would be unfair to the many others who have been denied burial at Arlington under today's restrictive criteria. Undoubtedly, he contributed much to the nation, but the Army is obliged to administer the rules of eligibility strictly and consistently. We do appreciate your bringing this matter to our attention.

Unwilling to accept this routine response, I continued my campaign by sending letters to cabinet members, prominent members of Congress, and even the First Lady. But the outcome did not change.

In the meantime, my efforts attracted the attention of the *Boston Globe*, which printed an excellent story, "Seeking Honor for an Explorer," on the treatment of Matthew Henson (April 22, 1987). This article stimulated so much interest that people of all races wrote me to offer their support. On April 27, 1987 the *Globe* also followed up with a lead editorial on the subject, "An Explorer's Overdue Tribute," suggesting that the president should make a special effort to reinter Henson's remains in Arlington. Several other newspapers ran similar stories as well.

In response to this spate of publicity, officials at Woodlawn Cemetery contacted me to express their displeasure at what they perceived to be my "complaints" about Matthew Henson's present grave site. Understandably, the Woodlawn staff took great pride in having Matthew Henson in their cemetery and, indeed, took care that the plot remained tidy and had flowers planted around it. I assured the Woodlawn people that I had not intended to belittle their cemetery or the condition of Henson's grave. But I also told them that I thought it only fair to try to have him buried in our most prestigious national cemetery. They seemed to understand.

My research on the proposed reinterment revealed several interesting things. I learned, for example, that some people had been working to have Matthew Henson buried in Arlington ever since

Peary was buried there in 1920. After his death in 1955, a number of people had recommended that he be buried in Arlington instead of Woodlawn. But, then as now, some people in the military opposed reinterment because Henson had never officially served in the armed forces of the United States. Others objected because they did not believe that Peary had ever reached the North Pole and consequently felt that neither he nor Henson deserved to be buried at Arlington. Still others seemed to have had no other reason for opposing Henson's reinterment except considerations of race.

As I pointed out in my letters to the White House, to disqualify Matthew Henson from burial at Arlington because he had never served in the military was to perpetuate a past injustice in the guise of a bureaucratic technicality. During the period that Henson worked for Commander Peary (1887–1909), the U.S. Navy severely restricted, as a matter of official policy, the jobs and ranks that African Americans could hold. As someone who had served as a valet for a naval officer in the field and as a messenger at the Philadelphia Navy Yard, Henson had filled two of the few roles reserved for blacks in the navy at that time. Moreover, he had served his nation no less courageously than Peary and had brought it honor.

Whether such reasoning proved persuasive, I will never know. But in October 1987 I finally received word from the Department of the Army that President Reagan had granted my request to move Henson's remains to Arlington. I immediately wrote the president to thank him.

My joy was tempered only by the fact that Anaukaq would not be there to see it. Nevertheless, I was determined to fulfill my promise and bring his children back to America to witness the reinterment. I notified the Greenlandic and American Hensons of the good news. We all found it hard to believe.

I now had to deal with a host of problems raised by the prospect of the reinterment. First, I was told that the expense of the reinterment would not be handled by the government. I would have to pay the costs of disinterment and reinterment. Second, I had to go through the courts to obtain legal permission to disinter the remains from Woodlawn Cemetery. Third, I would have to recommend a burial site. Fourth, there were regulation caskets to be obtained. And so on.

I began by contacting Superintendent Raymond Costanzo at Arlington. As always, he was cordial and encouraging. He agreed to meet with me to discuss a burial site and headstone.

In the interim, I set in motion the legal proceedings for Henson's disinterment. New York law requires special permits from the city's Department of Health and the local court before any disinterment can take place. While the staff of Woodlawn Cemetery understood that I had the president's permission to transfer Henson's remains, they informed me that they would contest the disinterment in court. This, they explained, was simply a matter of policy, something they did with all disinterment cases, to protect the cemetery. I was left with the impression that they would not strenuously oppose the removal.

When I arrived at Arlington, I met Costanzo and his assistants at the marble administration building just inside the gates. I requested that Matthew Henson be buried with full military honors, his civilian status notwithstanding. I also asked that Matthew and Lucy Ross Henson be buried next to Peary and his wife, Josephine. This site, I felt, would give them equality in their resting places. Anaukaq and Kali too had said that "the old friends should be together."

I wanted to erect a fitting headstone, one that would make all Americans knowledgeable and proud of Matthew Henson. Costanzo and his staff listened carefully to my proposals but pointed out that there were new rules governing the size of all headstones in the cemetery. No longer were grave sites permitted to have the giant monuments of the past, such as the one the National Geographic Society had erected for Peary. All new monuments were restricted to a height of five feet, a width of four feet, and a thickness of one foot. Moreover, he noted, the cemetery preferred that the new headstones be even smaller.

Back in Cambridge, several members of the North Pole Family Reunion Committee, including Henson relatives and others, joined me in forming a new committee to oversee the reinterment. I was chosen to chair the committee, and John H. Johnson was elected honorary chairman. The "Matthew Alexander Henson–Arlington National Cemetery Reinterment Committee" met weekly to discuss every aspect of the project, including the possible dates for the disinterment and reinterment, guest lists, the program, the invitations, the headstone funds, and so on. Because the military was to be involved, officials at Arlington took responsibility for organizing the memorial ceremony. But the committee would be responsible for planning the memorial service.

My next task was to arrange for the return of the Amer-Eskimo Hensons to the United States to participate in the ceremony. The experience of the North Pole Family Reunion helped, but the requirements of obtaining special visas, arranging helicopter and air force flights and American accommodations were no less exhausting than the first time around. Committee members, students especially, also helped with the voluminous paperwork involved in getting the Amer-Eskimo Hensons back down to the United States.

A few weeks later, Costanzo wrote to say that the burial site next to Peary had been approved along with my request for full military honors. Lucy could also be buried next to Matthew. I would have to return to Washington to discuss the memorial service and the design of the headstone.

The committee decided that the monument should be as large as the current regulations would allow. I recommended a five-foot-high, four-foot-wide, one-foot-thick slab of polished black Vermont granite, with gold lettering and an attached three-foot-square gold-colored brass plaque with Henson's face in bas-relief. Both Arlington National Cemetery and the reinterment committee approved.

I spent the next several weeks drawing the design for the bas-relief, checking it over each night before I went to bed. For the facial bas-relief, I drew from the classic photograph of Henson in his Eskimo anorak. Just beneath the face on both sides of the bronze plaque, I included a globe showing the "American route" to the Pole, with a bronze star at the top.

I also felt that Henson would have wanted the Eskimos who traveled with him and Peary to the Pole included on the monument as well. For the Eskimos, I selected a photograph of them standing with Henson on a mound of ice at the North Pole, with an American flag in the background.

Last, I thought there should be a dramatic depiction of the struggle to reach the North Pole that included Peary and the other five men on the last leg of the journey. The opposite side of the headstone would read:

MATTHEW ALEXANDER HENSON
Co-Discoverer of the North Pole
His Beloved Wife Lucy Ross Henson

As I have mentioned, one of the memorable statements attributed to Peary and etched in Latin on his monument reads: "I shall find a way or make one." For Henson's headstone, I selected the last statement in his book of 1912: "The lure of the Arctic is tugging at my heart/To me the trail is calling/The old trail/The trail that is always new."

When I completed my drawings and proposal, I submitted them to the committee for review. They were approved unanimously. None of us, however, was prepared for the cost of high-quality headstones and caskets. The cost of the headstone alone would run into the tens of thousands of dollars. The cost of disinterment, transportation of the remains, and new caskets would also be in the thousands. I had already committed a substantial amount of my own money to the effort, but we needed more help to cover the rest. Unfortunately, the Henson family was in no position to help defray such expenses. But our honorary chairman, John H. Johnson, offered a contribution that made possible the reinterment and the monument we hoped for.

We chose April 6, 1988, as the date of the reinterment—the seventy-ninth anniversary of the North Pole discovery.

Rev. Peter J. Gomes would serve as our reinterment ceremony minister. Col. Guion S. Bluford, America's first black astronaut in space, agreed to deliver a memorial salute. Bluford, like Henson, was an explorer of uncharted worlds. John H. Johnson was selected to deliver the memorial address. Dorothy Height, head of the National Council of Negro Women and an old friend of Lucy Henson (who belonged to that organization), was asked to eulogize Lucy during the service. I was asked to deliver the eulogy for Matthew. Hampton University, a traditionally African-American university in Virginia, offered to provide the ceremonial band and choir.

Meanwhile, the Vermont granite cutters and the company making the bronze bas-relief rushed to meet our deadline. Several models of the bas-relief were sent to the committee for review and modification before final approval.

My court appearance in New York City was nothing short of bewildering. My attorney, a young Harvard graduate, ran into stronger-than-expected opposition from the three Woodlawn attorneys, one of whom was a Yale graduate who seemed eager to carry out the traditional rivalry of Harvard and Yale. The two men fought in legalese and postured for what seemed an eternity, both in and out of the courtroom. After listening to all the arguments, the judge, who happened to be black, ruled that he saw no reason why Matthew and Lucy should not be removed from Woodlawn and reinterred in Arlington. The Woodlawn lawyer tried to appeal the ruling, but to no avail. As he spoke, the judge looked over at me and, almost imperceptibly, nodded his head. In a silent expression of gratitude, I nodded back.

To represent the family at the ceremony, the Amer-Eskimo Hensons chose Mahri-Pahluk's oldest living grandson, Avataq; his youngest grandson, Kitdlaq; Ajako and his oldest son, Jens; and Magssanguaq, the ten-year-old son of Avataq and Anaukaq's favorite little hunter.

As he had been promised, Magssanguaq got to travel to America. After he and his family arrived at McGuire Air Force Base, we proceeded by train to Washington. It was now Magssanguaq's turn to stare at the new world. He was glued to the window of the train. Large lakes and boats astounded him—not to mention all the cars, igloos, and people.

In the days before the ceremony, Magssanguaq and his family toured the nation's capital. We took him and the family to the Cherry Blossom Festival, watched a large parade, and, to the family's extreme delight, saw a circus.

At the Air and Space Museum, the Eskimos were particularly interested in the Black Aviators section. But over at the Museum of Natural History, Magssanguaq and Avataq were utterly surprised to see life-size models of Polar Eskimos in kayaks.

"They look so real!" Magssanguaq said.

"Yes, but their kayaks are poorly built," said Avataq. Seeing their culture represented in lifelike mannequins behind glass was very strange to them. It gave them a chance to evaluate and criticize an exhibit about which they as Eskimos were the authorities.

On a visit to the Washington Zoo, Magssanguaq saw seals in captivity for the first time. He was mesmerized by their antics. Instinctively the hunter, he several times raised an imaginary gun, took aim, and "fired" at the seals.

* * *

April 6 arrived quickly, but with everyone and everything in place. At noon on that day, we were picked up by limousines and driven to the administration building at Arlington, where everyone on the program gathered for the preceremony check. The assembled group included the Greenlandic Hensons, Olive Henson Fulton, the honorary pallbearers, John H. Johnson and Col. Guion Bluford, Rev. Peter Gomes, and Superintendent Costanzo.

At 1:45 P.M. the limousines and hearses left the administration building for the site. Some two hundred people, mostly family and committee members, awaited our processional in the private guest area. Across the road were another fifty or so invited guests and a platform filled with members of the press.

We walked the last yards to the grave, with the Henson family leading the way. When we reached the monument at two o'clock, the reinterment ceremony officially began.

Magssanguaq and I each took a rope on top of the velvet cloth and on cue unveiled the new monument. Everyone applauded. The cloth draping the Henson monument had also been used for the monument to the astronauts who died in the Challenger disaster.

Ushers led the family and other official participants to the site of the open graves, where Matthew's and Lucy's caskets were to be suspended on cords. We held our hands over our hearts while the military pallbearers, wearing dark navy dress uniforms and white caps, removed the caskets from the hearses and marched them to the graves.

Peter Gomes performed the act of committal. "We have brought the explorer home. For here is where he belongs. To all of us, and to the nation."

I then stepped up on the platform next to Matthew Henson's casket and delivered the eulogy. "Welcome home, Matthew Henson. Welcome to the hearts of black Americans, and persons of all races who beam with pride in the knowledge that you are finally here.

"May your presence here inspire generations of explorers yet unborn as they seek new horizons. Welcome home, Brother Matthew. Welcome home."

After I had delivered the eulogy, ceremonial volleys from a twenty-one-gun salute echoed through the stillness of the cemetery. With the playing of "Taps," the honor guard ceremoniously folded the U.S. flag that had covered Matthew Henson's casket. The triangular, folded flag was then given to Comdr. Charles W. Marvin, the presiding navy chaplain, who presented it to Avataq.

"On behalf of the president of the United States, the nation is grateful for Matthew Henson's service and patriotism," the chaplain said to Avatak. "We present this flag to show our great appreciation for his faithful and loyal service."

Following the initial ceremony, the memorial service began with welcoming remarks by Gen. Julius Becton, representing the president of the United States.

Next, Johnson delivered the memorial address:

> Matthew Henson taught us all a great deal. He taught us to be independent. He taught us to achieve. He taught us to make the most out of whatever opportunities are before us, while trying at all times to improve those opportunities.
>
> Henson was a proud man. He did not receive the recognition that he deserved, but he never complained. I remember reading about his speech to the Chicago Geographical Society in which he said he had only sought to serve—that he was not bitter—that he knew what he had done—and that he had his own particular kind of pride. And so I would say, the world is better for Henson. The world has a better feeling about achievement—about a man who was willing to pay the price—a man who once said nothing had ever been given to him. He had always earned it. Matthew Henson has earned the recognition he is receiving today.

"Today, a grateful nation salutes Matthew Alexander Henson,"
Col. Guion Bluford said, "an Arctic explorer and a black American.
May all future explorers follow in his footsteps."

Kitdlaq represented the Hensons.

"We Hensons from Greenland are very proud and honored to be
here among our relatives and other people from the United States on
this very important day in the history of America. We are thankful
from our hearts. We are sure the Eskimos Egingwah, Ootah, Ooqueah, and Seegloo would be very proud if they knew Matthew
Henson was being buried here in Arlington. They are the Inuit who
went to the North Pole with Peary and Henson. Thank you."

The Hampton University band played "The Battle Hymn of the
Republic" while the wreaths were placed at the grave.

The ceremony ended with the playing of "Lift Every Voice and
Sing."

"Now the old friends are together again. They can talk about old
times," Kitdlaq said.

Welcome home, Matthew Henson.

EPILOGUE

※ ※ ※

The Controversy: Did Peary and Henson Reach the North Pole First?

Perhaps no other claim in the history of modern exploration has been so controversial as the 1909 announcement by navy commander Robert Edwin Peary that he, Matthew A. Henson, and four Polar Eskimos had reached the North Pole on April 6 of that year. Some questioned the navigational accuracy and validity of the distances Peary claimed to have covered. Others dismissed his claim because he did not have any "reliable" witnesses. Still others believed that Frederick Cook, Peary's onetime assistant, had successfully reached the Pole a year earlier than Peary.

The dispute was never resolved. As a result, the widespread publicity surrounding the North Pole Family Reunion project in 1987 and the reinterment of Matthew Henson in 1988 sparked the controversy anew. Within months after the reinterment, articles appeared in national periodicals once again seriously questioning whether Peary and Henson had really made it to the North Pole.

The most direct challenge came from Dennis Rawlins, a Baltimore-based writer and longtime Peary critic. Rawlins claimed to have found a previously unexamined slip of paper in the National Archives with Peary's actual 1909 calculations as well as references to it hidden among the private papers of former Johns Hopkins and American Geographic Society president Isaiah Bowman. Rawlins

189

maintained that this evidence proved that Peary never got within a latitude 121 miles of the Pole. Even more contentiously, he argued that when Peary realized his navigational error, he faked his records to show that he had reached the actual Pole.

It was not the first time that Rawlins, who is not a field explorer or navigator, had made such accusations. As far back as 1970, Rawlins claimed to have found conclusive evidence that Peary had never reached the North Pole.[1] Even though his alleged evidence of Peary's "hoax" was later shown to be nothing more than unsubstantiated conjecture, his 1988 challenge was taken seriously by some. Most notably, Boyce Rensberger of the *Washington Post* gave Rawlins's interpretation extensive coverage on several occasions, even after it had been questioned by professional scientists.[2] In defense of Rawlins's position, Rensberger quoted one expert, who said: "Rawlins has cracked a code that's been sitting there for eighty years. I couldn't be more convinced that he's right."[3]

A second, more widely publicized challenge to Peary's claim appeared in an article by Wally Herbert, a British explorer, in the September 1988 issue of *National Geographic*. The magazine's publication of this challenge ("Robert E. Peary: Did He Reach the Pole?") came as a surprise to many because the National Geographic Society has long been viewed as the main bastion of Peary's support. But when one considers the widespread interest in the topic, coupled with long-held suspicions that the society was "hiding" some of the facts in this case, it is understandable that the magazine's editors would permit another point of view to be aired in that, their centennial year. Nevertheless, to some the article seemed to signal the official abandonment of Peary after nearly eighty years of steadfast support.

Many African Americans were also troubled by the new challenges to Peary and Henson's claims. They could not help wondering whether it was pure coincidence that the new, "damaging evidence" against Peary just happened to surface some six months after the president of the United States had granted permission to reinter Henson in Arlington National Cemetery as "co-discoverer" of the North Pole. It was as if someone had said, "Okay, we'll show you that neither of them made it."

Wally Herbert, the author of the 1988 *National Geographic* article, had himself traveled to the North Pole in 1969, using back-up airlift support and airplane navigation for verification. Like Rawlins, Herbert had long held the view that Peary and Henson did not make it all the way to the exact Pole. In preparing for the article, however, he examined Peary's written records of the 1909 expedition, which are housed in the National Archives in Washington.

Although Herbert found "no simple yes or no" answer to the question of whether Peary reached the pole, the tone of the article and the character of the evidence he puts forth leave no doubt about his verdict. "The burden of proof . . . generally lies with the explorer," Herbert writes, and "Robert E. Peary failed to provide conclusive evidence that he had reached the North Pole." Herbert places particular emphasis on Peary's personal diary of the final expedition, which has "blank pages, an inserted leaf, and an incomplete cover title" and on "Peary's astonishingly slack navigation." He also expresses doubts about the distances Peary claimed to have covered on his final series of "marches" and subsequent return journey from the Pole.

In the end, Herbert characterizes Peary as a man so obsessed by his quest for worldly renown that he simply could not face the fact of his failure. "In all probability," Herbert writes, "during those last five marches northward Peary was being driven not by the rational mind but by a conviction that the Pole was his and that he had the divine right to discover it and return to proclaim his achievement."

* * *

I also contributed an article to the same one-hundredth anniversary edition of *National Geographic* in which Herbert's essay appeared. Although my piece did not directly address the issue of Peary's claim, I too had access to Peary's diary and other expeditionary records in the National Archives. The conclusions I reached, however, were quite different from those of Herbert and Rawlins.

Herbert's charge of "astonishingly slack navigation," for example, rests heavily on the fact that Peary did not take longitude readings, or at least did not record them in his diary, during much of the 1909 expedition. As a result, Herbert hypothesizes, he was probably detoured from the actual Pole some "30 to 60 miles."

What Herbert fails to point out is that Peary and Henson recorded navigational information in several places, not just in the small pocket diary on which Herbert bases his conclusion. Further, and more important, he does not sufficiently take into account the circumstances in which they found themselves. Racing against the elements, in constant danger of finding themselves marooned by a break in the ice, they could not afford to stop to take unnecessary measurements—and longitude readings were unnecessary.

On the morning of March 1, 1909, Peary, along with six American assistants and eighteen Polar Eskimo assistants, left his land base at Ellesmere Island, Canada, for the North Pole, which lay 413 nautical miles (475 statute miles) ahead of them. This is approximately the same as the distance between Richmond, Virginia, and Boston, Massachusetts. Once they set their line of travel along the seventieth meridian of west longitude, Peary and Henson used a simplified navigational technique that experience had taught them was equally accurate and much less time-consuming than conventional marine navigation, which involves ex-meridian observations and longitude sights. In fact, there is evidence that they had used the latter method on the unsuccessful 1906 North Pole expedition, when it nearly cost them their lives.

Using their compasses, sextants, and heated mercury sinks as an artificial horizon, the two men made frequent latitude observations and azimuth observations. Their navigational technique for steering north was based on the simple fact that the sun is due south at its noon high point and due north at its midnight low point, and that it is virtually impossible to steer a sledge closer than five degrees to a compass. They made midday latitude determinations, noting when upper culmination (the maximum elevation angle) of the sun occurred as it passed the meridian; the position of the sun is lower earlier and later in the day. Longitude lines narrow to within a few miles apart at latitudes near the Pole and are not critical to measurements of location. They checked their compasses for deviation every noon and midnight. The margin of error using this technique is self-correcting, not cumulative. In describing this navigational system, which is well known to professional explorers, *Polar Record*, a publication of Scott Polar Research Institute of Cambridge University, observed that it demonstrated "precision and elegance."[4]

There is also considerable evidence that Peary and his assistants calculated for ice drift due to the changing winds. Although we have only recently gained enough bathymetric (ocean-depth) data to predict Arctic ice drift with any precision, Peary and Henson were both aware of the "Nansen rule," which has long been used by navigators to provide a rough estimate of drift.

For a more objective assessment of my conclusions, I consulted several established authorities in the field of navigation. One of my primary sources was Terris Moore, former president of the University of Alaska, a decorated pilot, a navigator, and an Arctic bush pilot with the Canadian International Geophysical Year. Moore has studied Peary's navigational techniques for years and has written extensively on the subject. According to him, "Even if you have no idea what longitude meridian you're on, you can still continue to steer north in this way, wandering five to ten degrees in your 'pointing' back and forth, but pulled back constantly to averaging true north by your compass and by the periodic check of the sun to correct for any observed change in the magnetic deviation." Moore added, "I have done it innumerable times."

It is interesting to note that Peary's simplified navigational technique was precisely the same as that used by the Norwegian Roald Amundsen and his navigators in their attainment of the South Pole on December 14, 1911. Yet Amundsen's feat is today accepted universally. In fact, Amundsen "borrowed" Peary's system of navigation. Amundsen had planned to join the race for the North Pole, but when he received word in 1909 that it had already been claimed, he changed his plans and aimed for the South Pole. When Amundsen reached the South Pole, like Peary at ninety degrees north, he also measured his position with a "sextant" and an "artificial horizon" (a tray of mercury).[5]

Like Peary, Amundsen met with disbelief when he first reported that he had reached the South Pole. Like Peary, too (and all other polar explorers, for that matter), he had only his own word as proof. From the time of his announcement on March 7, 1912, in Hobart,

Tasmania, until months later, Amundsen's claim was treated with great suspicion and distrust, especially by the British, whose favorite son, Captain Robert Falcon Scott, was in a race with Amundsen (similar to that between Peary and Cook) for the national prestige and personal honor of reaching the South Pole first. Scott's wife publicly scoffed at Amundsen's claim, and much of Europe simply refused to accept his records or proofs as authentic. This treatment so angered Amundsen that he publicly charged that the British "are bad losers" who "feel obligated to detract from the success of an explorer just because he is not of their own nation."[6] Amundsen wrote in his autobiography: "The year after the capture of the Pole, the son of a prominent Norwegian in London came home from his classes at an English school one evening, protesting to his father that he was being taught that Scott was the discoverer of the South Pole."[7]

The scientific article in the January 1979 edition of *Polar Record* reported that with his "system of navigation" Amundsen "took no longitude sights during the whole polar journey, depending instead on a single longitude fix. . . . Thereafter he trusted to latitude observations alone, combined with dead reckoning based on compass courses and distances run."[8] *Polar Record* goes on to point out that "in contrast, Scott used conventional marine navigation as employed at lower latitudes, . . . made ex-meridian observations and longitude sights, spending considerable time and effort on calculations for a few kilometers, sometimes a few hundred metres of meaningless accuracy."

When Scott finally reached the South Pole, he found Amundsen's Norwegian flag and a tent containing jettisoned paraphernalia, a letter for the king of Norway, and a message addressed to Captain Robert Falcon Scott. Fortunately for Amundsen, the South Pole has stable, solid terrain and does not shift like the ever-changing ice floes of the North Pole. Amundsen's flag and other materials left behind as proof remained permanently in place.

Tragically, Scott and his men perished on their return journey. It was only after a search party found his body and his diary, along with some of the proof Amundsen left behind at the Pole, that the explorers and scientific societies accepted Amundsen's claim. It is ironic that the deceased Englishman became the verifier of Amundsen's

South Pole discovery. If Scott's remains had not been found, it is possible that there might have been years of bitter dispute about whether Amundsen reached the South Pole with such an "astonishingly slack" navigational system.

The second argument used by Peary's critics since 1909 is that it was impossible for him to have covered the distances he claimed— more than 296 miles from Bartlett's farthest north camp to the Pole and back—in the time he was gone. This charge is also erroneous.

Let us examine the points on which most observers agree. First, Peary had five "credible" witnesses on the North Pole trek, in addition to Henson and the Eskimos. Dr. J. W. Goodsell, the surgeon from Kensington, Pennsylvania, and Donald B. MacMillan, a mathematics and physical training instructor from Worcester Academy in Massachusetts, verified that they traveled north with the Peary expedition on the first leg, along the Cape Columbia meridian, for two weeks, ferrying Peary's supplies to 84° 29' (about the distance from Richmond to Washington, D.C.). MacMillan, who later became a U.S. naval commander and a famous explorer in his own right, never recanted his support of Peary's North Pole claim. MacMillan might have been permitted to travel with Peary and Henson closer to the Pole had he not injured his foot. George Borup, a recent graduate of Yale and an outstanding athlete, testified that he and his Eskimo assistants traveled with the expedition farther north, carrying supplies to 85° 23' (about the distance from Washington to Philadelphia). Ross Marvin and his Eskimo assistants then took fuel, food, and other supplies to 86° 38' (say, Philadelphia to New York), where he wrote and signed a message for Peary saying he had taken a measurement showing "Latitude at noon March 25th 86 degrees 38' north. Distance made in three marches, 50 minutes of latitude, an average of 16 2/3 nautical miles per march. The weather is fine, going good, and improving each day."[9] Unfortunately, Marvin lost his life on the return trip.

Finally, on April 1, 1909, Robert Bartlett, captain of Peary's ship the *Roosevelt* and an experienced navigator who had been a member of Peary's 1906 expedition (which came within 175 miles [87° 6'] of the Pole) wrote, "I have today personally determined our latitude by sextant observations. 87 degrees 46 minutes 49 seconds north. I return from here in command of the fourth supporting party. I leave Commander Peary with five men, five sledges with full loads, and forty picked dogs. The going fair, the weather good. At the same average as our last eight marches Commander Peary should reach the Pole in eight days."[10] This meant that according to the best instrument readings of that time and at the end of a line of five reliable witnesses, they were "133 nautical miles [153 statute miles] from the Pole." This is about the distance from Stamford, Connecticut, to Boston.

It is unlikely that all five men would falsify their records. Moreover, even if the expedition had traveled no farther north than Bartlett's position, they would still have achieved the record for "farthest north."

From this point, Peary and Henson—each with two Eskimo associates and with five sleds loaded with food, fuel, and scientific instruments—headed north. They traveled as rapidly as possible, with Henson leading and breaking the trail most of the way. On April 5, 1909, after several "marches" (uninterrupted sledge travel before rest) north, Peary "took a latitude sight and indicated [their] position to be 89° 25′, or thirty-five miles from the Pole" (about the distance from North Providence, Rhode Island, to Boston).[11]

After a rest and before midnight on April 5, they "were again on trail." According to Peary, "In twelve hours of actual traveling time we made thirty miles. The last march northward ended at ten o'clock on the forenoon of April 6. I had now made the five marches planned from the point at which Bartlett turned back. Our average for five marches was about twenty-six miles." In other words, since leaving the point where Bartlett turned back, they had covered about 130 miles in about six days. Then Peary noted, "at approximate local noon, of the Columbia meridian, I made my first observation at our polar camp. It indicated 89° 57′."[12] He called this reading out to Henson, who wrote it down. According to Peary's records, they were now only three miles south of the theoretical exact spot of the North Pole (or the distance from South Boston to, say, Beacon Hill, a point they would have seen from such a distance). Peary and his team then traveled five to ten miles in different directions, taking latitude and meridian observations with what was then state-of-the-art technol-

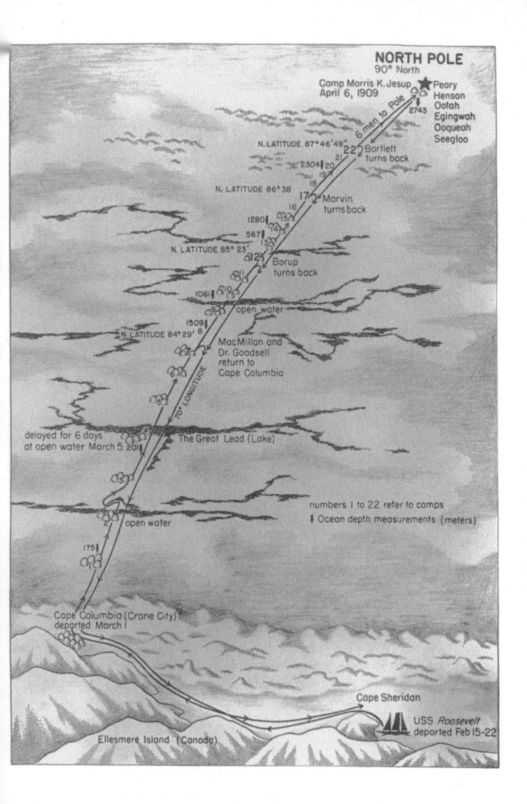

NORTH POLE
90° North

Camp Morris K. Jesup
April 6, 1909

Peary
Henson
Ootah
Egingwah
Ooqueah
Seegloo

6 men to Pole

2743

N. LATITUDE 87°46'49"

22 Bartlett
turns back

21

2304 20

19

18

N. LATITUDE 86°38

17 Marvin
turns back

16

1280 15

14

567 13

N. LATITUDE 85°23'

12 Borup
turns back

11

1061 10

9 open water

1509 8

N. LATITUDE 84°29'

7 MacMillan and
Dr. Goodsell
return to
Cape Columbia

6

5

70° LONGITUDE

4

delayed for 6 days
at open water March 5 20 The Great Lead (Lake)

3

numbers 1 to 22 refer to camps
Ocean depth measurements (meters)

2 open water

175 1

Cape Columbia (Crane City)
departed March 1

Cape Sheridan

USS *Roosevelt*
departed Feb 15-22

Ellesmere Island (Canada)

ogy (a sextant and an artificial horizon). With the sextant one can measure positions to an accuracy of one to three minutes of arc (or nautical miles). Peary and Henson were both quite capable of using a sextant proficiently.

At this point, the two Americans and four Eskimos had literally reached the top of our planet. If the North Pole were a fixed geographic feature, as Hispaniola was for Columbus, Robert Peary, Matthew Henson, Ootah, Seeglo, Egingwah, and Ooqueah would have been the first human beings to lay eyes on it. But, of course, this is the problem. The North Pole is a point on a vast, ever-shifting expanse of ice—a sort unverifiable by the human eye. Its exact position can only be measured by modern electronic instruments. Any other measurement is imprecise. Yet if, as Wally Herbert surmises, Peary and his party were some thirty or so miles from the actual Pole, they were still the first Americans (and Greenlanders) to have reached the very top of the globe. Or, as retired glaciologist William O. Field told me, "I feel that Peary and his group got close enough to the Pole to be given credit for reaching it first." Field, a member of the American Geographic Society, a scientific group, has conducted research in the Arctic regions for many years. In personal communication with me George Michanowsky, a historian-explorer and member of the Explorers Club, added, "as a partisan of the concept of sufficiency, I would say that the Peary expedition came close enough to the exact North Pole to be credited with discovering it."

After about thirty-six hours of measurements and rest at the Pole, the expedition set out at about four o'clock on the afternoon of April 7 for the land base at Camp Columbia. According to Henson, they traveled at "the break-neck pace that enabled us to cover three of our upward marches on one of our return marches."[13] On much of the return trip, they simply had to follow their outward tracks back to the next camp, which made their travel comparatively easier and faster. According to some experienced explorers, there are fewer pressure ridges (giant hills of broken ice blocks) and more smooth ice in the area near the Pole than near land, thus making it easier to travel at faster sledge speeds far out in the Arctic Ocean. "Our return from the Pole was accomplished in sixteen marches," wrote Peary, "and the entire journey from land to the Pole and back again occupied fifty-three days, or forty-three marches." This means that Peary, Henson, and the Polar Eskimos, using five sleds, covered about twenty-six nautical (twenty-nine statute miles) per march on the return trip and approximately nineteen miles per march for the entire round-trip to the Pole and back. Each march involved eight to fourteen hours without rest.

These figures are not as unreasonable or unprecedented as Peary's critics would have us believe. In a 1983 article in the *American Alpine Journal*, Terris Moore points out that the Alaskan "Iditarod" race of 1,047 miles from Anchorage to Nome is in some ways comparable to the thousand-mile distance the Peary expedition traveled from Cape Columbia and back, and that "many drivers . . . including women, have consistently done over 75 miles per day carrying sleeping gear, tent, and the necessary food provisions" in this race. Moore also points out that the 1981 Iditarod winner, "Rick Swenson, set the course record of 12 days, 8 hours, 45 minutes and 2 seconds. This would seem to be 84.8 miles per day, day after day. The times and distances have all been publicly verified."[14]

There are still other examples, such as one dogsled driver who traveled fifty-two miles in thirteen hours while rushing diphtheria serum to Nome in 1925. More recently, American explorer Will Steger, leading his first expedition on the Arctic ice, reported making thirty-eight miles in eighteen hours en route to the North Pole.[15] Again, Herbert seems to have overlooked or ignored these facts and figures in the course of his research.

Another equally important factor is that in 1909, Peary, Henson, and the four Polar Eskimos had more experience in dogsledging across the Arctic ice than probably anyone else on earth. During their years in the Arctic, Peary and Henson each had covered over ten thousand miles by dogsledge, under some of the worst conditions imaginable, and sometimes in complete darkness. Moreover, Peary, Henson, Ootah, Seegloo, and Bartlett had had the experience of traveling out on the Arctic Ocean in an attempt to reach the Pole in 1906, and had come within 175 miles (87° 6') of their goal, only to be turned back by shortages of food and supplies. Certainly, this extraordinary experience at sledging lends some credence to Peary and Henson's distance claims.

Most of Peary's modern-day critics simply ignore or fail to mention Henson's or the Eskimos' navigational skills. Henson was never treated as a "reliable" witness in the entire North Pole affair. Because of the racial attitudes of the times, he and the Eskimos were viewed by many whites as incapable of comprehending even the most fundamental technical concepts of navigation. This belief, often expressed in his presence by whites, hurt Henson deeply. He was particularly demoralized when the well-known general Adolphus W. Greely said in a major newspaper article that he did not believe Peary had made it to the Pole, especially since his only witness was an "ignorant Negro."[16] Greely, who had led an Arctic expedition to Fort Conger in northern Canada to set up a research station during the first International Geographical Congress in 1881, loathed Peary. Greely and his twenty-seven crewmen were left marooned for two years in the Arctic when, because of ice and other difficulties, the relief ships could not reach them. Most of his men perished of starvation as they traveled south on foot, trying to reach the rescue ships. When they were finally rescued, it was learned that the seven who survived had resorted to cannibalism. Peary (and Henson) later criticized Greely by suggesting that had he been a competent Arctic explorer, he would have found abundant game in the area to keep the group alive. Greely's racial attitudes may have prevented him from working with the local Polar Eskimos, who could have helped his men survive the ordeal. Greely never forgave Peary or Henson for this criticism.

But Henson knew how to determine latitude and longitude, and he confirmed Peary's sledging distances. Terris Moore, who knew Henson for close to twenty years, interviewed Henson on several occasions about his knowledge of navigation and the expedition's journey from Bartlett's farthest point north, at 87° 47', to the Pole. I asked Moore, "Are you fully satisfied from your many discussions with Matthew Henson that he knew enough about navigation to have gotten to the North Pole and back, and to have confirmed Peary's sledging distances and direction?"

"Yes, absolutely," Moore replied. "Matt knew how to determine latitude and longitude from solar sights at the noon and midnight meridian passages. He fully understood the use of Greenwich Mean Time, Greenwich Hour Angle [G-H-A], and the equation of time to obtain longitude at simple meridian passages. The Eskimos too knew that the sun is due south at its noon high point and due north at its midnight low point." Moore added that Henson had been taught navigational skills aboard the *Roosevelt* by Ross Marvin, a professor of engineering at Cornell University.

Unfortunately, through his own racial naivete, Peary may have contributed to the credibility gap that has plagued him since the North Pole discovery. For example, he wrote in *The North Pole* that Henson "would not have been so competent as the white members of the expedition in getting himself and his party back to land. . . . He had not, as a racial inheritance, the daring initiative of Bartlett, or MacMillan, or Borup."

Comdr. Donald B. MacMillan, on the other hand, would later write in *National Geographic* (1920) that Matthew Henson "was indispensable to Peary and of more real value than the combined services of all four white men."

What made the public so incredulous of Peary? There were several reasons, but a summary answer may be that Peary made so many wrong moves. He knew, for example, that Bartlett, a skilled navigator as well as a white man, was an especially "credible" witness. So he permitted Bartlett, rather than one of the four young white Americans, to lead the last support party and travel to a record north which surpassed that of the then-current record holders, Fridtjof Nansen of Norway and Umberto Cagni [under Duke Abruzzi] of Italy. This put Bartlett in the record books. But why did he not let Bartlett travel above the eighty-eighth parallel, say, to within seventy-five miles of the Pole—or fifty miles or twenty-five miles?

Peary said that Bartlett would have been nothing more than a "passenger" if he had taken him farther. But Peary also felt that no one would ever question his ability to travel the last one hundred miles, especially with Matthew Henson, Ootah, and the three loyal, younger Eskimos.

Peary was also well aware that any distance beyond the eighty-eighth parallel would not only establish a record distance north; it would also essentially put him at the top of Earth. Thus, to carry Bartlett farther meant that he would have to share the glory of the victory with him. The same did not apply to Henson. Like the four

Eskimos, he would never be accorded the status of "co-discoverer," on racial grounds alone.

Yet that was not the principal reason why Peary selected Henson to accompany him on the final leg of the journey. As Peary confided in MacMillan at the outset of the 1909 expedition: "Henson must not turn back. I cannot get along without him."[17] This was true for several reasons. First, Henson had more sledging and Arctic navigation experience than any of the other Americans. Second, he was the man who built and repaired sledges and alcohol stoves and who drove the dogteams with the skill of an Eskimo. Third, he was the only man on the expedition who could speak the Eskimo language fluently and who could persuade the Eskimos to travel so far out on the ice. The Eskimos trusted him thoroughly.

Much has been made of the fact that on the return trip to Cape Columbia, Peary barely spoke to Henson. Wally Herbert, for example, interpreted this silence as evidence of Peary's bitter disappointment and personal "anguish"—a tacit admission, as it were, that he had failed to reach the Pole. But Henson himself offered a different explanation for Peary's behavior. In a 1910 article in the *Boston American*, he revealed that on the last leg of the journey he and two of the Eskimos had pushed on to the final campsite in defiance of Peary's specific orders. Although they thought they had stopped at a point just short of their ultimate goal, Peary's subsequent calculations showed that the camp was situated virtually at the Pole itself. It was this realization that left Peary despondent and provoked his anger toward Henson. "For the crime of being present when the Pole was reached Commander Peary has ignored me ever since," Henson explained.

In any event, looking back, it seems clear that Peary would have been better off had he taken both Bartlett and Henson to the Pole. In this way, he would have had his "credible" white witness to satisfy the Americans and Europeans, and Henson, the master explorer and expert in Eskimo sledging, culture, and language, to get them there.

Yet of all the sources of mistrust in Peary, none looms larger than Frederick Cook, the affable doctor who had served as Peary's assistant on an earlier expedition and who claimed to have reached the North Pole in 1908. Cook was a popular and charismatic all-American boy. By contrast, Peary was viewed as arrogant, distant, well connected, and heavy-handed. The great Danish explorer Peter Freuchen, who knew both men, once remarked that "Cook was a gentleman and liar; Peary was neither."

Objective examination of Cook's records would lead even his most ardent supporters to conclude that he never got within several hundred miles of the North Pole. It took four support groups, 133 dogs in seven teams, and tons of food, fuel, and other supplies to get Peary, Henson and the four Eskimos to the Pole. Cook would have us believe that he reached the North Pole and returned with two Eskimo assistants, two dogteams, and two sleds of food and fuel.

One is hard put to find any serious scholar, explorer, or scientist who believes that Cook came within four hundred miles of the North Pole. But strangely, some of Cook's supporters are willing to overlook his many inexplicable and weak excuses for acts unbecoming of a serious explorer. Cook's explanations for his lack of proof of his "attainment of the Pole" always seemed a little too convenient. For example, he claimed to have left the "proof" of his attainment of the Pole (i.e., papers and instruments) behind in Greenland in the care of a friend, while he traveled to Denmark to celebrate his victory. In the minds of the world public of that time, reaching the North Pole was tantamount to reaching the moon in our time. And how much "proof" was required? Notebook? Compasses? Peary is today being challenged on the basis of his "proofs" in a small pocket-sized notebook kept in the National Archives. Rawlins even used scribbles of Peary's notes on a single scrap of paper as "proof" for his claim that Peary faked the discovery. And yet Cook did not have in his possession even a single pad of navigational measurements. He "left them behind," where they are said to have been buried (and later destroyed by the elements) by his friend because Peary would not let him bring them to the United States aboard his ship.

Rather than attempt here to present the numerous other reasons that make it extremely improbable that Cook reached the Pole (many arguments have already been presented by Arctic historians), I will cite what in my opinion is one of the strongest arguments against his claim.

One of Cook's biggest mistakes was that he, like Peary, thought of the Eskimos as an inferior race of people. He was convinced that they would be unable to understand or report his movements around the islands of northern Canada in his so-called attainment of the Pole and that they would not be credible witnesses among white people. Cook, who had maintained little or no contact with the Polar Eskimos since his visit to Greenland in 1891, would also have us believe that he simply appeared in their villages seventeen years later and convinced them to travel with him on foot and by dogteam some 300 nautical miles from their village at Etah to the northern tip of Canada and an additional 413 miles to the North Pole (a round-trip of about 1,800 miles). Even Peary and Henson, who had known every Eskimo member of their team since they were youngsters, had great difficulty getting them to travel out on the dreaded Arctic Ocean ice. The Eskimos almost never traveled out of view of land on the sea ice, and they feared the ever-present danger of accidents on the ice, which they referred to as being swallowed up by the evil spirit of Tornarsuk. Although Peary paid each man handsomely with material goods and promises, a number of the Eskimo assistants deserted the expedition after a few days out on the ice. Others tried to abandon Peary as the expedition traveled farther north, but were persuaded by Henson and MacMillan, through promises of exorbitant pay, to remain.

By all accounts, Cook could not even speak Eskimo except to babble a few words, let alone enough to persuade them to travel out on the Arctic Ocean. Also, for some strange reason, after being dropped off near Etah by a fishing schooner, Cook left his single white assistant, Rudolph Francke, behind in an Eskimo village. He then set off "for the Pole with four Eskimos." After traveling about twelve miles out on the Arctic Ocean, two of the Eskimos returned to their village, leaving Cook, Etookahshoo, and Ahpellah alone in a snow house (igloo) they had built. There, Cook is believed to have raised the American flag over the snow house and taken a photograph of what he later called the North Pole. Cook then traveled south to one of the upper Canadian islands and found an old abandoned earthen igloo, where he and the two Eskimos wintered. In early spring, he made his way back to Etah to announce his "Attainment of the North Pole." His two Eskimo assistants later said during questioning that they did not know whether they had traveled to the North Pole with Cook, but they were certain that wherever they traveled they were "never out of sight of land." No land can be seen from the North Pole.

The two Eskimos were later interviewed by the Eskimo–Danish explorer and anthropologist Knud Rasmussen, who reported their story. The highly respected Rasmussen had initially believed Cook's claim of having reached the North Pole, but after talking with Cook's Eskimo hirees and reviewing the records of his journey, he concluded, "I realized it was a scandal." Rasmussen's interview of Peary and Henson's Eskimo assistants, on the other hand, corroborated their report of the polar journey.

It is worth nothing that Cook may have first conceived the idea of challenging Peary for the Pole around 1901 when, at the request of Peary's friends, he gave Peary a medical examination and found him in such poor health that he was not likely to be able to continue his polar quest. In any event, he did more than anyone to deprive Peary and Henson of the North Pole prize they rightly earned.

Peary also alienated many Americans with his aloofness and his catering to narrow, special-interest groups. For example, he carried the flags of the Daughters of the American Revolution and his Bowdoin College fraternity to the Pole, and he raised them along with the American flag. Some have even suggested that Peary was perceived by many Americans as being too closely allied with big-name Republican interests, making him a target for Democrats who traditionally supported underdogs like Cook. Predictably, he also overreacted to Cook's ruse, appearing to the American public to be mean-spirited and despotic, while Cook came off looking magnanimous. "Two records are better than one," said Cook when he heard that Peary had reached the Pole. Peary responded by calling Cook a "liar" who had "sold the American public a gold brick."

Some of Peary's critics also charge him with treating the North Pole as if it were "his domain" and calling the Greenland–Canadian route to the Pole "his" route. Indeed, Peary and Henson had spent eighteen years searching for and reporting in public journals the best route to the Pole. Moreover, Peary was not unusual or irrational in his insistence that he was the American representative in the race to the North Pole and that the Cape Columbia meridian route was his. Every nation involved in the race usually had one man who was by reputation and experience its sole representative in the North Pole contest, and that nation threw its support behind its man. In Italy, for example, the duke of Abruzzi with his associate Umberto Cagni were the "official" contestants for the North Pole. In Norway, until 1900, it was Fridtjof Nansen. One cannot imagine any other Italian attempting to compete with Cagni and the duke for the prestige of the North Pole or any other Englishman challenging Scott for the South Pole. In the explorers' world of that era, it was considered dishonorable for one explorer to invade the ongoing exploration of another. But in America, the land of opportunity (and opportunists), Cook did not have to adhere to these unwritten gentlemen's rules.

Most of Peary's detractors use a simplistic and time-tested formula: if you discredit Peary's character and motives and make him appear to have been an irrational, dishonest, and blindly ambitious man, and you then eliminate Henson and the Eskimos as "credible" witnesses, you can sow enough "reasonable doubt" to deprive Peary of his claim.

No one, however, can impugn the courage of the men who undertook the historic 1909 expedition. Every successful polar expedition since that time has required the use of aircraft or other advanced technology for backup and resupply. It is well known to psychologists and physiologists that such security serves as a source of comfort and physical resilience, enabling a person to husband special psychic and somatic resources for a dangerous and difficult task. This was an advantage that Peary, Henson, and the other members of the team did not enjoy. They knew that once they ventured out onto the Arctic they could not be rescued. The loss of a supply sled through a break in the ice, the opening of an impassable sea lane, a sudden violent storm, a broken or frostbitten limb—any of these or countless other accidents could result not only in disappointment and delay but in death. Yet somehow they overcame these obstacles, found their way to the Pole, and returned to the same spot on land.

* * *

Or did they? To settle the dispute once and for all, the National Geographic Society commissioned the Navigation Foundation, a highly respected private association of navigation specialists based in Rockville, Maryland, to review all the evidence related to Robert Peary's claim. The foundation spent more than a year poring over some 225 cubic feet of documents contained in the Peary Collection at the National Archives as well as other relevant papers collected at the American Geographical Society, the National Geographic Society, the Explorers Club in New York, and other institutions. It also solicited testimony from a range of experts who had studied the evidence. I, too, submitted my findings.

Among the first conclusions reached by the Navigation Foundation was that Dennis Rawlins's analysis of Peary's data was "completely erroneous."[18] Far from cracking some hidden "code," the foundation reported, the equations Rawlins used to prove Peary's failure were actually drawn from the serial numbers of Peary's three navigational watches. The report went on to suggest that anyone with even a modicum of navigational experience would not have made such errors in analyzing Peary's notes, which were apparently taken on an earlier expedition and from land.

William E. Mollett, a navigation expert who flew ninety-one polar missions with the U.S.A.F. Weather Service between 1952 and 1955, delivered an even more stinging indictment. In material submitted to the National Geographic and the Navigation Foundation as part of their investigation, the retired U.S. Air Force colonel wrote:

> The complete amateur, Dennis Rawlins, and the Polar stunt man Wally Herbert were very critical of Peary for not taking transverse sextant sightings (unnecessary), frequent soundings of ocean depth, variation figures, constant wind speed and direction of cloud conditions. Peary was intent on only one thing: reaching the Pole. To call his efforts to obtain a lot of scientific data perfunctory would be an exaggeration. Soundings and unnecessary sextant sightings when the temperatures were so cold to say the least are activities that can easily be skipped. . . . There was a serious error made in the September 1988 article [in *National Geographic*] when it was assumed that Peary was attempting to navigate the Pole without any celestial references for longitude. His celestial reference was almost constantly available, and only slightly less accurate than references made with a sextant. They could be done without bothering with logarithms and spherical trig-

onometry and a miserably cold sextant operation. Why use a bubble horizon when the sun is right on the real horizon?[19]

The Navigation Foundation agreed with Mollett. "We are persuaded," the foundation reported, after systematically presenting the available evidence, "that Peary's system of navigation was adequate to get him to the near vicinity of the Pole without taking longitude observations along the way."[20]

The foundation also found that the distance and speed Peary claimed to have traveled during the expedition, including the final dash to the Pole, "are entirely credible. Dogs and sleds with far less skillful drivers than Matthew Henson and Peary's Eskimos have often maintained or exceeded these claimed speeds over much longer distances."[21]

Additional confirmation of Peary's claims was provided by a comparison of recently established Arctic Ocean depths along the seventieth meridian with measurements recorded during the expedition and by "photogrammetric rectification"—a technique involving the mathematical analysis of shadows on photographs to determine the sun's elevation when the picture was taken. After applying this technique to a series of photographs that Peary claimed to have taken at the Pole, the foundation concluded: "The pictures were taken very close to the vicinity of the Pole. . . . probably within four or five miles of the reported position." This the foundation regarded as its "final and most conclusive" evidence that Peary, Henson, and the four Eskimos were "essentially at the Pole."[22]

Several months later, in April 1990, the foundation issued a "Supplemental Report" after discovering two more photographs from the 1909 expedition.[23] Unlike the other thirteen pictures that had been analyzed through photogrammetry, these photographs showed the position of both the sun and the horizon, making it possible to determine even more precisely the position of the photographer. Analysis of the new photographs moved Peary and Henson's probable location even closer to the exact Pole.

The Navigation Foundation's reports should put the matter to rest. But somehow I doubt it. As Robert Peary himself observed, the North Pole was the "Last Great Geographical Prize." Yet unlike so many other such "prizes"—the South Pole, Mount Everest, even the moon—the North Pole remains shrouded in uncertainty and mystery, a point surrounded by an ever-shifting sea of ice and unidentifiable by the human eye. Perhaps that is its most enduring legacy: it continues to represent human striving for what is approachable but never fully attainable.

NOTES

Chapter 6. Black and White Partners

1. Matthew Henson's date of birth is commonly believed to be August 8, 1866, but is listed as August 8, 1868, on his marriage license issued on April 13, 1891, by the Clerk of the Orphans' Court of Philadelphia County, Pennsylvania.
2. Robert E. Peary diary entry, in Robert E. Peary Collection, Record Group 401-1, National Archives, Washington, D.C.
3. Robert E. Peary, *Northward over the "Great Ice"* (n.p., n.d.), p. 508.
4. Ibid., p. 47.
5. Matthew Alexander Henson, *A Negro Explorer at the North Pole* (New York: Frederick A. Stokes, 1912), p. 3.
6. Robert E. Peary Collection, Record Group 401-1, National Archives, Washington, D.C. Unless otherwise noted, all personal letters that I quote from in the text can be found in this collection.
7. John M. Verhoeff diaries, in Robert E. Peary Collection, National Archives, Washington, D.C.
8. Ibid.
9. T. S. Dedrick, Jr., diaries, in Robert E. Peary Collection, National Archives, Washington, D.C.

Chapter 7. The Struggle for the Pole

1. Donald B. MacMillan, "Peary as a Leader," *National Geographic,* April 1920; and Donald B. MacMillan, "Matthew Henson," *The Explorers Journal* (official journal of the Explorers Club), Fall 1955.
2. MacMillan, "Matthew Henson"; and Bradley Robinson, *Dark Companion* (New York: Robert M. McBride, 1947), p. viii.
3. Henson, *Negro Explorer*, pp. 113, 114.
4. Ibid., p. 124.
5. Robinson, *Dark Companion*, pp. 261–62; Harold Harwood, *Bartlett: The Great Explorer* (Toronto: Doubleday Canada, 1977), p. 87.
6. Robert E. Peary, *The North Pole* (New York: Frederick A. Stokes, 1910), p. 269.

7. "Matt Henson Tells the Real Story of Peary's Trip to the Pole," *Boston American*, July 17, 1910.
8. Peary, *North Pole*, p. 273.
9. Robert H. Fowler, "The Negro Who Went to the Pole with Peary," *American History Illustrated*, May 1966 (this article was based on interviews with Henson that Fowler conducted in 1953). Also, personal communication to author from Terris Moore.
10. MacMillan, "Peary as a Leader."
11. "Matt Henson Tells the Real Story."
12. Letter-article by Peter Freuchen, "Ahdolo, Ahdolo!" dated March 18, 1947. Sent to James Zarlock, Robert McBride Co. (publishers), New York.
13. "Cook's Route Far from Pole, His Eskimos Say" and "Map of Cook's Arctic Voyage Containing No Dash to the Pole—Traced by His Two Eskimos," *New York Times*, October 13, 1909.
14. Telegram from Peary to Henson, October 17, 1909: "If, as papers state, you have pictures of North Pole and sledge journey they must not be shown. Wire me"; and letter from Peary to H. C. Bumpus. Both in Robert E. Peary Collection, Record Group 401-1, National Archives.
15. "Matt Henson Tells the Real Story."
16. "Matt Henson Mourned by Thousands," *New York Amsterdam News*, March 19, 1955.

Chapter 9. Growing Up Eskimo

1. Henson, *Negro Explorer*, p. 183.

Epilogue

1. Boyce Rensberger, "Debunking Peary Myth," *Washington Post*, September 18, 1988. According to Rensberger, Dennis Rawlins had put forth his case against Peary in a report to the Navy Institute Proceedings in 1970 and had reiterated his challenge three years later in *Peary at the North Pole: Fact or Fiction* (Washington, D.C.: Luce, 1973).
2. Boyce Rensberger, "Peary's Notes Show He Faked Claim: Suppressed Document Places Explorer Far from North Pole," *Washington Post*, October 12, 1988.
3. Boyce Rensberger, "Explorer Bolsters Case against Peary," *Washington Post*, November 2, 1988.
4. D. J. Drewry and R. Huntford, "Amundsen's Route to the South Pole," *Polar Record* 19, no. 121 (1979): 329–36.
5. Roald Amundsen, *The South Pole* (London: John Murray, 1912), p. 112; and Roald Amundsen, "Expedition to the South Pole," *Annual Report of the Smithsonian Institution*, 1912, pp. 701–16.

6. Roald Amundsen, *My Life as an Explorer* (New York: Doubleday, Doran & Co., 1928), p. 72.
7. Amundsen, *South Pole*, p. 112.
8. Drewry and Huntford, "Amundsen's Route," pp. 329–36.
9. Peary, *North Pole*, pp. 319, 356. Marvin's note was found in a small canvas pouch attached to the upstanders of his sledge when it was returned to the ship by his Eskimo companions, Kudlooktoo and Harrigan. They had apparently overlooked this item when they pushed his body and all his personal belongings into the Arctic Ocean to hide the evidence of his murder.
10. Ibid., p. 360.
11. Ibid.
12. Ibid., pp. 285, 286.
13. Henson, *Negro Explorer*, p. 140.
14. Terris Moore, "Charge of Hoax against Robert E. Peary Examined," *American Alpine Journal*, 1983, pp. 114–22.
15. Will Steger and Paul Schurke, *North to the Pole* (New York: Times Books, 1987).
16. "Neither Peary nor Cook Found Pole, Is Gen. Greely's Belief," *Washington Star*, January 25, 1926.
17. MacMillan, "Matthew Henson"; also Robinson, *Dark Companion*, p. viii.
18. Peary North Pole Interim Report, No. 1, January 13, 1989, Navigation Foundation, Rockville, Maryland.
19. Letter/report, October 1988, from Lt. Col. William E. Mollett, submitted to National Geographic and Navigation Foundation.
20. "Robert E. Peary at the North Pole," report of Navigation Foundation, December 11, 1989. See also "New Evidence Places Peary at the Pole," *National Geographic*, January 1990.
21. "Robert E. Peary at the North Pole."
22. Ibid.
23. "Robert E. Peary at the North Pole: A Supplemental Report," Navigation Foundation, April 16, 1990.

GLOSSARY

This glossary gives the phonetic spellings of common Polar Eskimo words and phrases used by Matthew Henson. These spellings and their pronunciations served Henson well in his dealings with the Eskimos, and he was the only American on the Peary expeditions who was able to communicate with the Eskimos in their own language. Not all the words given in this list appear in the text, but the sampling is intended to offer the reader an introduction to words in everyday use. The selection proved helpful to the students and staff involved in the North Pole Reunion Committee.

Ah-dok	Bottom of feet
Ah-ee-who-ghia	I am fine
Ah-hahn-nah	Aurora borealis
Ah-hock key-et-toe	Hot summer
Ah-kah-lik	Rabbit
Ah-kai-gu	Tomorrow
Ahk-duk	Killer whale
Ah-key-show	Ptarmigan or grouse
Ah-mak-de-hee-oh	Many
Ah-muck-kah	Maybe
Ah-nah-kah-ting-woot	Sister
Ah-nah-kah-ting-woot-neeya	My sister
Ah-nahn-na	Mother
Ahn-nah	Woman
Ah-poot	Snow
Ah-she-de-shot	Camera

Ah-tah	Grandfather
At-tah-tah	Father
Ah-tow-toe	Yawn
Ah-ung-gwee-lok (Greenlandic)	Fine
Ah-vuk	Walrus
Ah-who-ghia	Fine, okay
Ak-day-you-ahk-toe	Shy
Ang-goot	Man
An-new-ee	Wind
An-no-wah	Hooded jacket, anorak
Bik-check	Good
Bik-doo-ah-gee	Congratulations
Cah-nock-toe	Falling snow
Cah-nook	Mouth
Chair-ree-in-yah	Fox
Chee-me-ahk	Bird (general)
Chee-me-ahk-toe	Airplane
Chee-tok-we	Cup
Chi-bag-ee	Tobacco
Ching-mia	Bird (general)
Cobve	Coffee
Dah-ho	Fighting between two people; a fight
Day-mah	It is finished
Dough-ko	Dead
Du-wah-hok	To hear
Ear-ee-ah-nock-toe	Beautiful
Ed-de-hahm-ah-neet-cho	Crazy
Eeee	Yes

Ee-hee-kah-kah	[My] feet
Ee-helk	Eye
Ee-nuk	Person
Eh-nah-hock-toe	Yawn
Err-nahk	Son
Foo-he-ah	Membranous sack in bird's throat; crop
Foo-who-chee	What are you doing? What's happening with you?
Ha-ah-chew-go	Ouch
Hah-vik	Iron or metal
Hav-oc	Sheep
He-ah-wah-whah	Sugar
Hee-ah-ko	Knee
Hee-oou-nee	Ear
Herr-kah-nook	Sun
He-tak-toe	Sling shot
Hi-nay [Hi-nah]	Hello; Hi
Hi-nay-nuk-who-nay	Hello. How are you?
Hi-nic-toe	Sleeping person
Hin-nik-doo-ah-gee	Good night
Hin-nik-toe	Sleep
Hu-qua-gah	Candy
Id-dig-doo	You are welcome
I-ding-nook	Bad (weather)
I-du-di-ah	Iceberg
I-hee-ga	Foot
I-hook-ko	Little finger
Ik-kil-nock-toe	Cold, or to be cold

Ik-pill-nah	Mosquito
Ing-mung-wah	A little, as in "a little coffee"
In-nook	Water
In-nuit	Person
I-nook-du-yak	Good-bye
Ir-riah-nock-toe	Beautiful
Kaa-be-ho	Coffee
Kah-do-nah	White-skinned person
Kah-kok-tok kah-lay-lee-wah	White whale (Beluga)
Kah-lay-lee-wah	Narwhal
Kahl-nock-tok kah-lay-lee-wah	Black narwhal
Kah-mah-toe	Angry
Kah-tuk	Cup
Kah-ou	Forehead
Ka-miks	Boots (made of animal skin)
Kang-wah-chee	Binoculars
Kar-rah-hah	Brain
Ka-toong-wah	Children
Kay-cheek-toe	Dancing
Kee-chuck-dah	Middle finger
Keen-yah	Nose
Key-ah-see-oak-dua	I'm sweating.
Key-et-toe	Warm, hot, heat
Key-net-chee	What is your name?
Key-you-tee	Teeth
Kim-milk	Dog
Kod-dee-pah-luk	Stove
Ko-do	Thumb
Ko-keet	Claws

Kong-new-we-ho	Snore
Koo-you-nah	Thank you
Kul-nock-to	The color black
Kul-nock-too-ko	Dark-skinned or black [person]
Ku-mah-ah-ho	Puppy
Kute (cute)	Tooth
Nah-mak-toe	Good tasting or tasty
Mee-kee-lil-rahk	Ring finger
Nah-ahn	No
Nah-do-oh-hoy-ah	I don't know
Nah-mock-toe	Fine, as in okay
Nah-pah-ham-a-wick	Infirmary; hospital
Na-nook	Polar bear
Nay-goo-hock	Doctor
Nee-shock-toe	Great, as in "a great person"
Neh-we-ah	Seagull
Net-do-ve	When were you born?
New-nah	Earth, land
New-yah	Hair
Nock-toe-ho	Pregnant
No-dia	Wife
No-low	Rear end; buttocks
Oh-mia-hahm-me	On board ship
Oh-mia-hock	Big ship
Oh-you-ah-hock	Rock
O-miak	Ship or boat
O-ming-mak	Musk ox
Om-mik	Moustache
On-ee-yee-cheech	Stop here

Ooh-kah	Tongue
Ooh-wang-gah	I
Peed-de	Car
Pee-nee-ahk-toe	Hunter
Pee-nee-ahk-toe wah	Great or master hunter
Pee-shah-hah	Strong
Poo-ee-hee	Seal
Puto	Hole
Pu-you-tee	Pipe
Qeqertarsaaq	Herbert Island
Quah, quah, quah, pah che	So many
She-neck-tah-ko	To sleep forever; to die
She-neg-boo	Sleep
She-you-tee	Ears
Tad-dok	Chin
Tah-ku-huk	To see
Tah-tah-rah	Black-legged kittiwake
Tee-de-ord	Teapot
Teek-yuk	Index finger
Tee-nee-vok	To fly or flying (as in "the bird is flying")
Tie-ee-ok-toe	Sneeze
Tock-toe	Dark, darkness
Took-too	Caribou
Too-lu-gah	Crow
Tu-pik	Tent
U-lu or Ooh-lu	Small utility knife
Who-we	Husband

ACKNOWLEDGMENTS

Many fine people of all races, colors, and backgrounds contributed to the success of the North Pole Family Reunion and the reinterment of Matthew Henson. I have named some in the text; here I wish to thank them and others who made exceptional contributions to this project.

I am especially grateful to John H. Johnson, chairman of Johnson Publishing Company. The North Pole Family Reunion and the reinterment of Matthew Henson were made possible by his moral and financial support.

I thank the members of the Amer-Eskimo Henson and Peary families, especially Anaukaq and Kali, for their friendship and supportive efforts. I also thank the members of the Polar Eskimo communities of Moriussaq and Qaanaaq, northwest Greenland.

I thank the members of the Harvard community, the North Pole Family Reunion Committee, and the Matthew A. Henson Reinterment Committee for their support and encouragement, especially President Derek C. Bok, Rev. Peter J. Gomes, L. Fred Jewett, dean of Harvard College, Marvin Alvert Hightower, David L. Evans, Dudley Herschbach, Kent Taylor Cushenberry, Chester Pierce, Richard Hunt, Josephus Long, Lynn Thompson Long, Edwin H. Kolodny, John E. Dowling, Sisella Myrdal Bok, Erik Borg, Mimi Aloian, Kermit Alexander, Sean T. Brady, Mariana Ortiz-Blanes, Camille Holmes, and Suzanne Malveaux.

I am also grateful to the government and military officials who contributed to this project, including President Ronald Reagan, Samuel R. Pierce, Frederick J. Ryan, Jr., Raymond J. Costanzo, Gen. Julius Becton, Marion Barry, Jr., Col. Guion S. Bluford, Navy Chaplain Charles W. Marvin, Col. Philip Bracher, Col. James Knapp, Maj. Quincy Sharp, Sgt. Theodora Hart, Kay Cormier, the Department of Defense, the Military Airlift Command (MAC), and the U.S. Air Force.

I owe special thanks to the project associates and the Henson family: Ann J. C. Daniels, R.N., project nurse; Dr. Louis C. Brown, project physician; Regina O. Counter, project assistant; Navarana Harper, primary translator in Greenland and America; Ned Johnston, cinematographer; Anthony B. Jacobs, sound recordist and technician; Hans P. Biemann, photographer; Olive Henson Fulton; Virginia Carter Brannum; and Audrey C. Mebane.

I would also like to thank the following individuals and organizations for their special efforts and contributions to the project: Rev. Samuel D. Proctor and Abyssinian Baptist Church, Thobius Danielsen (second translator), Ruth Hamilton, Dr. Robert Screen, William R. Harvey and the Hampton University Band and Choir, Dr. Bo Klarskov, Police Inspector Karl Peterson, Carlos Vallechio, Cherie Cushenberry, Ann Willoughby, Mr. and Mrs. Marvin Hightower, Sr., the Washington, D.C., Convention Center, the Afro-American Heritage Society of Charles County, Maryland (especially Louise Webb and William Diggs), Terris Moore, Nicholas Sullivan, William F. Looney, Robert C. Barber, Jeanne Capodilupo, John, Jean, and Brian Powell, Melvin B. Miller, the Fordham College Choir, the National Archives, First Air of Canada, and the Explorers Club.

I wish to thank Bruce Wilcox and the University of Massachusetts Press for their genuine interest in *North Pole Legacy*, and especially Clark Dougan for his excellent editorial advice.

CREATING A
Positive School Culture

CREATING A
Positive School
Culture
How Principals and Teachers
Can Solve Problems Together

MARIE-NATHALIE BEAUDOIN
MAUREEN TAYLOR

Skyhorse Publishing

First Skyhorse Publishing edition 2015.

Skyhorse Publishing books may be purchased in bulk at special discounts for sales promotion, corporate gifts, fund-raising, or educational purposes. Special editions can also be created to specifications. For details, contact the Special Sales Department, Skyhorse Publishing, 307 West 36th Street, 11th Floor, New York, NY 10018 or info@skyhorsepublishing.com.

Skyhorse® and Skyhorse Publishing® are registered trademarks of Skyhorse Publishing, Inc.®, a Delaware corporation.

Visit our website at www.skyhorsepublishing.com.

10 9 8 7 6 5 4 3 2 1

Library of Congress Cataloging-in-Publication Data is available on file.

Cover design by Anthony Paular

Print ISBN: 978-1-63220-554-4
Ebook ISBN: 978-1-63220-971-9

Printed in the United States of America

Contents

Preface

In the past decade, an increasing amount of pressure has been placed on school staffs to teach an expanding curriculum. At the same time, resources were decreased, responsibilities grew, and less time was made available for teachers to support each other.

As a result, issues often develop among staff members, such as negativity, isolation, or censure. This can cause principals and teachers to spend a tremendous amount of time and energy addressing these problems instead of focusing on academia, their initial goal. Educators and students alike may suffer.

Our intention in this book is to assist principals, with the collaboration of teachers, support staff, and parents, to form a school culture in which rich, supportive, and energizing relationships will be enhanced. Specifically, the purpose of this book is to help educators find efficient ways to understand and solve staff problems, prevent conflicts, and generally enrich their school culture. With that in mind, we gently invite readers to reflect on somewhat controversial questions and make visible the challenges of the current school system. Once visible, these challenges can be contained and practices can be developed to bring forth each person's wisdom and compassionate self. Narrative therapy, considered the cutting edge in systemic approaches, has been a very relevant theoretical framework to understand and address school culture issues. It offers a contextual perspective that fosters respect and awareness, and contributes to bringing the best out in everyone.

We have made every possible effort to write this book in a practical, clear, and creative way. Tutorials, exercises, common questions and answers, transcripts of conversations, illustrations, cartoons, dialogues between the authors, and numerous examples are used to keep the readers engaged with the material. This work is the result of many years of successful collaboration between a narrative therapist, consulting with several school principals, and a dedicated elementary school teacher. By combining therapeutic knowledge with day-to-day educational experience, the text provides a rich and comprehensive approach to a vast array of staff-related problems.

This book is *not* intended as an introduction to narrative therapy but rather as the application of narrative and social constructionist ideas to the field of education. For that reason narrative concepts are only covered in their relevance to teachers and principals, and the clinical practices associated with the ideas are not thoroughly examined. The interested reader can easily find further information on the subject in the many excellent introduction to narrative therapy books readily available (Bird, 2000; Freeman & Combs, 1996; Freeman, Epston, & Lobovits, 1997; Madsen, 1999; Winslade & Monk, 1999; White & Epston, 1990; Winslade & Monk, 2000; Zimmerman & Dickerson, 1996).

Embedded in the spirit of the narrative approach is the belief in local knowledges and in the wisdom of lived experience. Expertise is assumed to develop from the handling of everyday life and not simply from theoretical conceptualization. With that in mind, we could write a book marrying the narrative approach and education only by recruiting educators to share their experiences. We believe this has significantly enriched the material that we present and certainly inspired us greatly in the ideas that we propose. As a result, we have interviewed and/or surveyed well over 200 educators from a wide range of elementary and middle public schools in Northern California. The populations in these schools varied in terms of socioeconomic status, race, and ethnicity. Schools were visited in rural and suburban areas as well as in the city. Four schools involved parent participation, while the remaining were general public schools. The questionnaires, surveys, and interview format for this research are included in Resources D and E.

From those conversations we have extracted pressures, struggles, solutions, and reflections that color each individual's journey in schools. We have integrated all of the emerging themes into different sections. The first chapter of the book explores the experiences of principals and teachers in the subculture of the school system. Our intention in writing this section is to foster a greater understanding of people's struggles and experiences in schools, regardless of their respective roles. It covers in particular the pressures that constrain their ways of being and includes quotes from our research that reveal both the humor and hardship of the job. Chapter 2 presents a few fundamental principles and practices inspired by the narrative approach. A careful attempt has been made to eliminate most of the jargon embedded in the theory to render it accessible and relevant to educators. Chapter 3 details the climate problems that can emerge in systems under pressure such as schools. It covers, for example, the numerous problems presented to us by educators, such as gossip, cliques, and union conflicts, as well as more educational themes, such as competition, hierarchy, and evaluation. Chapter 4 offers a complete case analysis of the development of a climate problem and its solution. Chapter 5 engages the reader in the step-by-step process of inviting a group of staff members to change without triggering conflicts. Chapter 6 summarizes the ingredients of a strong school culture. Chapter 7 offers words of wisdom, ideas, suggestions, and strategies shared by principals to prevent or solve problems. Finally, Chapter 8 offers brief suggestions and perspectives for working with other adults in the school, such as parents and yard duty volunteers.

We hope that all readers will be inspired by at least one of the ideas exposed and will finish their reading energized to explore new possibilities with their colleagues. Above all, we hope that the book will bring forth more appreciation and compassion for yourself and the dedicated members of your community.

Acknowledgments

As in our first book of this project, *Breaking the Culture of Bullying and Disrespect, Grades K–8,* we would like to express our gratitude to all the educators who have participated in our research. In particular, we would like to acknowledge the staff from the following schools who have taken the time to kindly answer our lengthy surveys: Anderson School, Baker School, Country Lane School, Easterbrook School, Moreland Discovery School, and Rogers Middle School. Heartfelt acknowledgments are sent to those teachers from other schools across California who opened their classrooms to us: Sequoia Baioni, Maria Diaz-Albertini, Melissa Freeberg, Mariah Howe, Cathy Klein, Karen Lam, Kayla Meadows, Peter Murdock, Mary Robson, Sara Saldana, Chris Telles, the staff at Christa McAuliffe, Stuart Williams, and the staff at Cedarwood Sudbury School.

Interviews and e-mails with the following educators were also invaluable in that they provided a rich forum for personal stories and for in-depth accounts of their experiences in the education system. Given that some of these interviews were lengthy, often from one to two hours, we are eternally thankful for their trust, honesty, and generosity of time despite their busy schedules:

Les Adelson, Carolyn Barrett, Ann Dubois, Honey Berg, Martha Cirata, Nancy Cisler, Denise Clay, Carin Contreras, Harry Davis, Mindy Dirks, Bob Geddes, Maria Hansen-Kivijarvi, Faith Johnson, Tom Kennedy, Mary Anne Landis, Rick Ito, Sue Healy, Dale Jones, Debbie Judge, Barbara Lateer, Michele Mandarino, Heidi Meade, Bill Menkin, Alison Moser, Cleo Osborn, Joe Pacheco, Beverly Prinz, Herb Quon, Jim Richie, Lorie Rizzo, Kathleen Ryan, Louise Santos, Maria Simon, Bitsey Stark, Gary Stebbins, Mary Alice Tallahan, Stephany Tyson, Tiffany White, John Wise, and Jenny Wishnac.

We wish to thank the numerous other principals, teachers, and students who greatly contributed to this project and yet wish to remain anonymous.

Our gratitude goes daily to those creative, inspiring folks from the Bay Area Family Therapy Training Associates

(BAFTTA) who have kindly reviewed and edited the manuscript for narrative congruency as well as contributed to the statistical analysis:

Jeff Zimmerman, Ph.D.

Sonja Bogumill, Ph.D.

We are also indebted to the gracious individuals who have provided wisdom, support, and a variety of ideas during the length of this project:

Leisha Boek, Susan Brown, Kristi Busch, Fritz Dern, Erin Devinchenzi, Miles Gordon, Suzanne Hicklin, Krista Poston, Annie Prozan, Mari Rodin, Linda Rough, Sherry Stack, Judy Volta, May Walters, and Anne Woida.

We are grateful to the following professionals: Melanie Birdsall, our production editor, who was quite efficient and very refreshing to work with; Debbie Bruce, our cartoonist, who had a remarkable knack for creating delightful expressions of our ideas; and Rachel Livsey, our acquisitions editor, who was patient, skilled, and sincere.

Finally, last but not least, we offer great thanks and affection to the following generous, loving, and patient souls . . .

Amelia, Brian, David, Francine,
Jack, Jeff, Judy, Magnolia,
Marlene, Meika, and Paul.

The contributions of the following reviewers are gratefully acknowledged:

RoseAnne O'Brien Vojtek, Ph.D.
Principal
Ivy Drive Elementary School
Bristol, CT

Charles F. Adamchik, Jr.
Teacher/Educational Consultant
Blairsville High School and Learning Sciences International
Blairsville, PA

Gerald Monk
Professor
San Diego State University
San Diego, CA

John Winslade, Ph.D.
California State University, San Bernardino
San Bernardino, CA

About the Authors

Marie-Nathalie Beaudoin, Ph.D., is the training director at Bay Area Family Therapy Training Associates (BAFTTA) and supervises the counseling work in several schools in Silicon Valley, California. She has devoted much of her career to working with children, teaching tolerance projects, and improving staff relationships in public schools. Marie-Nathalie has been invited as a consultant to Bright House and Boston Consulting Group to assist them in improving the internal climate of an established Fortune 100 company. She is also an adjunct professor at John F. Kennedy University, where she teaches cross-cultural awareness, family therapies, and group dynamics. Marie-Nathalie has presented at numerous conferences and has published articles on narrative therapy, the *Silencing Critical Voices* journal (www.voices.com), and two other books, *Breaking the Culture of Bullying and Disrespect, Grades K–8*, and *Working With Groups to Enhance Relationships*.

Maureen Taylor is an educator in Northern California. Her background is in teaching preschool through sixth grade and being an environmental educator. Her main interests lie in teaching science and writing, two subjects that gently unfold for the learner. Maureen is currently developing a program for children blending art, environmental education, and social issues. She has coauthored *Breaking the Culture of Bullying and Disrespect, Grades K–8*, with Marie-Nathalie.

*To all the educators of the world who commit their hearts and spirits
to the blossoming of young minds*

—MNB

With love to the Estherettes, Teapot Quincy y mi chunketue

—MT

CHAPTER ONE

Understanding the Different Experiences of Teachers and Principals

M ost educators can probably relate to the following three scenarios.

Everyone thinks of Karen as the Mother Teresa of the school. She is well known for going the extra mile, helping students at recess, bringing in items for needy families, and spending evenings in her classroom hosting parent gatherings. She attended the latest conferences on character education and positive discipline, and held a staff workshop to share the latest information from the conferences. Karen, however, feels like a fraud. She knows that she often yells at her students, and she feels guilty because she recognizes it reduces her classroom's morale. She finds herself yelling anyway.

Why does Karen yell, against her intentions and better judgment?

John enjoys his job as a principal. He likes to lead by example and makes great effort to visit classrooms daily. He has received many kudos for his dedication to his community. Recently, however, staff members have become upset by his absences during lunch. John has been going off campus more and more often to have lunch alone; for the staff, this means he is gone when they most need support and time to run ideas by him. Many perceive this act as a reflection of a deep lack of care, and question his reliability and authenticity.

Why does John "run away" despite the pleas of his staff?

Chris is the newest teacher on staff. He is well respected for having good control of his class and being enthusiastic about curriculum development. The mostly female staff appreciate having such a compassionate, masculine figure on site, especially one who is so kind and devoted to his work in education. To everyone's amazement, Chris is noticeably shy with the elderly woman who volunteers for lunchtime yard duty and seems to avoid her whenever possible. Some staff are beginning to question why Chris would act in this manner.

Why is Chris so distant with this woman, when he is so good with colleagues and children?

Why? Why? Why? is the question that many educators, principals and teachers alike, strive to answer when faced with an interpersonal challenge. There is a belief that we should understand the cause of a problem before we can even attempt to solve it: You can't fight an enemy you don't know. Yet many of the explanations we usually come up with focus on individuals, their believed personality, their "strengths" and "weaknesses."[1] In so doing, the personal and professional context of those people's lives is often forgotten. Often, the context of people's lives has at least an equal or greater influence on people's actions than any individual choice (see Beaudoin & Taylor, 2004, for more information). The context will determine if you are your outgoing and funny self or your more shy and reserved self. It is important to understand context because it:

1. Has the power to shape each individual's action

2. Colors how people expect others to behave

3. Is the backdrop against which problems develop

Consequently, no school culture can be truly addressed in any significant way until the context and the experiences of people are well understood. The more you know about the context and its unique impact on the individuals involved, the more power you have to address the situation effectively.

Whether you are a principal or a teacher, this chapter will:

- Assist you in articulating your own experience and depersonalize the struggles associated with your role
- Give you an insider's view into the responsibilities and pressures experienced by your colleagues
- Connect you further with compassion for others' responsibilities (compassion is always handy when addressing interpersonal tensions!)
- Allow you to use the ideas presented in the rest of the book successfully!

Principals often think they understand teachers' experiences because most of them "have been there"; in our research that has not proven to be true, as the leadership demands on principals often take precedence over remembering what it was like to be in a classroom. In addition, we tend to forget the nuances of experiences that have not been specifically named. For example, you may remember feeling generally overwhelmed at the end of the year but you may not (especially when overwhelmed) have actually articulated, named, and reflected upon exactly what happened. This makes it difficult to remember the details and implications of the experience. Finally, people's experiences on a principal career path can be distinct from those of other teachers in subtle ways. Your reference point provides only one perspective; certainly a valuable one, but it may overlap in limited ways with the integrated feedback of large numbers of educators.

This being said, let us now explore briefly the experience and work context of

a. Principals
b. Teachers

PRINCIPALS[2]

- What are the stories you have about who principals are as people?
- What comes to your mind when thinking "principals should . . ."?
- Which ones of these "shoulds" may be unrealistic?

These are some of the main questions we sought to understand as we interviewed a large number of administrators from a variety of districts and communities. What we found over and over again was that principals' daily lives were dominated by three experiences:

- Being mistaken for God
- Doing more, more, more
- Being everything for everyone all the time

Being Mistaken for God

People almost expect the principal to supply them everything they need, as if you were a counselor or a mommy or had a magic wand. I realized they wanted me to be God. I thought, "Oh, I didn't apply for that job. I think the position is already filled!"

—Elementary School Principal

What are the implications of being mistaken for God? When someone places you on a pedestal or overestimates your authority, you become trapped into a role where you cannot be your preferred self and must instead:

- Never make mistakes
- Know all the answers
- Be able to solve everything
- Control everything at will (parents, students, cafeteria issues, etc.)
- Predict the future (e.g., school enrollment or even the weather)

An elementary school principal spoke of this:

The teachers expect that you will never make a mistake. That is an unreasonable expectation. I once had a teacher say, "You called a rainy day lunch and it did not rain. You ruined my whole week!"

Principals are often assumed to have unlimited amounts of authority in controlling students, parents, teachers, circumstances, and the school environment. The pressure of being powerful takes on a life of its own, becoming a story. It is then repetitively confirmed by the noticing of only certain events over which the principal actually does have a certain power.

Those events are, in reality, of a limited nature. Upon closer analysis, three words distinguish a principal's actual power: narrow, solitary, and visible.

First, the power is narrow, limited in scope, and applied to only very specific issues. People experiencing a principal's power may experience it as intense, but on a broader scale of time and school culture it may have only a small effect. For example, a principal may have the choice to transfer or lay off a teacher, an action that has an intense effect for that teacher, but that same principal may be unable to affect a broader issue, such as changing a school's culture.

Second, the power is solitary, meaning that it is held by one individual in the face of a larger group of subordinates. Although it may seem as though the principal holds more power than a group of adults, regardless of the group's size and whether it is made up of teachers or parents, this solitary voice in reality can become very insignificant. We have spoken to many principals who wish they could implement a new practice, yet have been turned down by the majority. Ultimately there may be a popular and/or vocal teacher on staff who may hold more influential power over such items.

Third, the power is visible to all in the community. Because of the distinct nature of his or her role in the school, the principal is also the civic representative and the one to lead publicly. This visible power can lead to an inflated, unrealistic perception or story of the principal as a person and as a professional. Following are some comments from principals:

I was promoted to assistant principal, and soon teachers who had twenty or thirty years' experience were asking me for advice, though I felt they had been teaching much longer than I had.

—Middle School Assistant Principal

When you go from the classroom into that office, all of sudden people look at you different, as if you have been gifted with all the answers in education. Sometimes we feel like we should; they expect us to! They don't realize we are just human, just like them.

—Middle School Principal

Teachers feel they personally have limited amounts of power and know that the principal has somewhat more power, without knowing the limit of that power. The power is visible, yet the limit is often invisible.

Principals don't have a lot of power, and anyone going into a principalship for power is in for a rude awakening. If there is power, it's shared power. You're in between a rock and a hard place, meaning you have to keep the parents happy, the teachers happy and the district office happy. Sometimes these are at opposing places. I don't think I have power. I say "sorry" a lot and "what do you want me to do?" If you say to [people], "Is there something you want me to do?", many times they don't know, but they feel better that you listened to them.

—Elementary School Principal

There is a disconnection that may exist between teachers and principals in terms of understanding each other's realities. This is particularly true in regard to principals' lives, which may appear much more unpredictable and multifaceted to others than the known and visible routine of teachers. In other words, people get only a glimpse of a principal's day and may remain totally unaware of the full story. The pressure placed on principals to be powerful can have a whole set of undesirable consequences. This distorted story can, on one hand, create a context where teachers feel less capable than they actually are, engage in relationships in a disempowered way, and avoid responsibility on issues they could significantly affect. Teachers may end up taking a more passive role and expect principals to solve problems that pertain to everyone: "You have the power here . . . what are you going to do?"

As for principals, it can leave them with a false sense of entitlement and trying to impose demands on their staff (which typically backfires). Enormous amounts of responsibility can also bear heavily on one person's shoulders and create a context where mistakes are not only unavoidable but also accentuated by the community and difficult to forgive.

When teachers put you too high up it changes the way they treat you and ask questions. It puts the decision on you, which is bad because then you are responsible for everything. If you think someone is way up there, then you can't have honest conversations.

—Middle School Principal

Finally, the unrealistic story of principals as super powerful can create a false impression of them as invulnerable, without any particular human "needs" of their own and able to take in a lot of grief without being seriously affected.

Doing More, More, More

When the school year starts in August, you hit the ground running and you never stop. The school year is one big sprint.

—Middle School Principal

In most school districts, principals are responsible for: planning student assessments, class placement, discipline, student study teams, clubs, sports, yard duty, lunch duty, administrative paperwork, observations, district meetings, planning, staff development, staff evaluation, grants, leading staff meetings, spreading information, memo writing, facilities, traffic, buses, cafeteria, food delivery, parents, Home and School Club, homework center meetings, community programs, counselor, planning assemblies, grade-level meetings, coordinating prep times, evaluate absentee rates, test scores, research, fundraising, supervising, conferencing, teaching, modeling, coordinating parent help, hiring process, firing process, conferences, professional growth, accommodating visitors, emergency contact, financial work/budget, staff cheerleader . . . and so on.

This pressure places an enormous amount of responsibilities on principals and can be unrealistic. Over the past hundred years, schools have been increasingly institutionalized and have faced more complex sets of requirements. The educational system has been facing more demands while being burdened with a limited budget. As a result the government has simply resorted to increasing the principal's workload. Given that, in many states, administrators do not have the luxury of an organized union's protection, they often feel forced to subject themselves to those demands with little possibility of protest. As discussed by two California principals:

If you don't know how to work with the superintendent, you're out. [In my area] there is no union to back you up. You work at the pleasure of the superintendent.

—Middle School Principal

A teacher once asked me when I was going to get tenure! I told her that [here] we don't get tenure. We don't even have a year-to-year contract. Our work is day to day. You simply have to do the best job you can for your people.

—Middle School Principal

In other words, if educators are really committed to the work of leadership, their only real option is to do so with all the additional tasks. This can remind us of the situation a century ago, when employers subjected workers without job security to excessive amounts of work. The biggest difference in this situation is that there is practically no one to replace principals if they decide to leave.

How far can this go? How many more demands can be placed on principals? Current data reveal there may soon be a principal shortage, as people are less willing to work an average of 54 hours a week, in stressful conditions, with lack of resources, increasing responsibilities, and a sense that the compensation, in certain districts, can result in a pay cut when actual hours of work are factored in (Education Writers Association, 2002). In the meantime, current principals have the sense that they never can do enough.

Such a high level of accountability, to many different groups with different goals and preferences, also means that you can never satisfy everyone; you always receive some criticism and very little appreciation.

Having to let go a teacher, for example, is very difficult. If you keep the person, the staff may be upset because you are keeping a bad apple; if you ask them to leave, those who have bonded with the teacher will be upset. And then you have to live with this situation 'till the end of the year.

—Elementary School Principal

Our middle school team has worked hard with the union to organize a late-morning start on Wednesdays so that teachers can meet and collaborate with each other. We were very pleased to make that possible for teachers, and it is certainly in the best interest of students. Parents, however, started calling and were upset thinking that their children might miss out on academics. We really can never satisfy everyone.

—Middle School Principal

Other effects of this pressure may be: exhaustion, imbalance of personal and professional life, feeling over-whelmed, and depression.

I know it will never be enough even if I stay here every night until 10. It has tremendous effect on family life. Sometimes I don't see my children for several days, and, even when I am sitting home on a Sunday thinking "it's me time," I'm not able to be present. My mind is still at school.

—Middle School Principal

Finally this pressure demands such an extreme amount of work focused on the community's children and families that, ironically, very little time can be left for one's own. It is not sur-prising that the turnover rate for principals between 1988 and 1998 was 42% and that approximately 40% of principals leave the field because of politics, bureaucracy, and unreasonable demands (Education Writers Association, 2002).

Being Everything for Everyone All the Time

The principal is often perceived as the person to go to if you have a problem, particularly if it is a big problem. People are aware of their own needs and do not necessarily realize that their demands are multiplied by at least 30 other staff and countless families. We have heard teachers and parents wonder what a principal does with his or her time, especially if the principal does not respond that very day to a question or request.

We once met with a principal at 1 P.M. We walked in as she was just finishing checking her e-mail. She announced to us that while she was busy on lunch duty, the district office had sent an e-mail, expecting all administrative staff to meet at the district office at 1 P.M. We stood there, stunned that a district could possibly mandate principals to be at a meeting an hour and a half after an e-mail had been sent.

Principals clearly experience a pressure to be available. Principals have to be willing to drop everything and do what the district prioritizes for them. They have to be at the beck and call of the system and able to meet many multiple demands. Principals have to ensure that everyone is happy, the school is running smoothly, and all the paperwork is completed.

The implications of this pressure are great. First, principals can never fully know in the morning how their day will go—will they have to be prepared for a life-threatening emergency or have a peaceful day? They have to be somewhat on guard all the time and can never totally relax or achieve a sense of control over their day.

My biggest "Aha!" when I went from a being a teacher to being a principal was that I can never control my day. As a teacher, I would spend hours planning for every hour of every day. However, as a principal, I could have nothing on my planner for a particular day and that day will end up being crazy!

—Elementary School Principal

Second, such bombardments of requests by many people require that decisions be made quickly. This may result in decisions that are not always ideal and may not even represent what the principals themselves would have preferred, given a chance to reflect, as illustrated in the following comments:

You have to make these quick decisions and then later on you realize . . . Oh . . . no . . . did I really say that?

—Elementary School Principal

At school you have to make so many decisions so quickly that you end up not being as collaborative as you'd like. Things come back from your staff to bite you if you make too many decisions in isolation.

—Elementary School Principal

Third, principals not only have to be everything for everyone all the time at school, but this pressure carries into their personal lives. Specifically, numerous principals have shared how any public appearance has the possibility of turning into a school conversation, whether they want it to or not. This is particularly true of principals living in or near the community served by their school.

In many ways, this pressure does not allow principals the freedom to perform other identities in their public community, or the space to enjoy the richness of their lives and the multiple roles they wish to fulfill.

I live in this community. It's 24–7. When I go out, for example to a softball game, all the parents approach me and want to talk about their kids. I don't mind sometimes, but sometimes I'm with my godchildren or I'm coaching, and I don't get to just be a person. My principal friend and I laugh because you never go out in shorts and sandals with messy hair. I can't be seen buying beer. You feel like you have to explain that you really still are a good role model.

—Elementary School Principal

It would be nicer if more people got that I'm a person, I'm not just the administrator. There is a tendency on the part of people to think that the administrator is a different animal. I am a parent, I am a human being, I am a mother, I am a wife, I am a runner, I'm a lot of things. What I do here is another skill that I have, and I'm a person underneath it all.

—Elementary School Principal

In Sum . . .

These three pressures (being mistaken for God; doing more, more, more; and being everything for everyone all the time) have the effect of rendering a principal's life highly stressful, can create a sense of inadequacy in the face of unrealistic demands, can be isolating, and may lead to burnout. We were inspired by a middle school principal's description of the experience of this role (Figure 1.1): "A principal has to walk this difficult obstacle course with a beach blanket Babylon hat, with everything attached on it—school safety, scores, budget, buses, traffic, cafeteria, etc. They have to keep everything balanced while everybody is watching you, evaluating how you're solving problems, and wondering if you're going to fall into crocodile-infested waters."

Figure 1.1   Principals have to keep everything balanced while they walk an obstacle course and are evaluated for their performance

As will be discussed later in this book, many principals remain in the profession for their commitment to children and find ways to deal with these pressures. As illustrated in the following box, humor keeps many of them going!

Box 1.1   Creative Metaphors About the Role of Principal

- "When you are the principal, sometimes you"re the bug, sometimes you're the windshield!"
- "A principal has to keep on swimming upstream, despite the current, the storms, and the dams."
- "Being a principal is like being a sewing machine, stitching things together and joining the different fabrics."
- "Being a principal sometimes feels like acting in a Shakespearean play . . . you can't leave during one of the tragic parts, only when the play is completed."
- "Being a principal is like operating a TV remote control. If used unconsciously, one can get trapped into spinning through all the choices that are available and never focusing on one important thing. If used for its intent (to be more efficient), it can be seen as a way to maneuver through a lot of information and make a choice that saves time and brings a focus to time spent."
- "Principals can act as manure or fertilizer. The potential is there for them to do things that stink a lot, but you can also very much help things grow."
- "A principal is like a Cuisinart. It does all the different tasks with the different attachments. It takes different ingredients, mixes them all together, and makes a new product. It's really fast, so you are dizzy all the time."
- "When you are a principal, you act as a watering can. You fill it up and nurture everyone to grow: parents, teachers, and kids. One seed won't grow alone and you have to give them all water. You also have to find out how to fill up your watering can."

- "Being a principal is like being a mom . . . you are everything to everybody. You are always reminding people to do things and console them when they are hurt. You are trying to please everybody but you can't."
- "Being principal is like being Don Quixote. In the face of all the obstacles, you just stay hopeful, believe in your people, and believe that the best is possible."
- "A principal is like an underwater juggler. You hold your breath, hoping everything goes where it is supposed to, but everything floats away. Sometimes you come up for air, see land, and things are the way you thought they would be. So you think, 'Oh, I'll just go back on down; it's all right.'"
- "Being a principal is like being a car going down the highway ninety miles an hour."
- "Being a principal is like being Jiminy Cricket. You are always showing up at the right times saying all the right things to keep them going."
- "A principal is like a butterfly . . . people do mistake you for a Godlike creature but you are simply fluttering around campus, hoping to help someone have a better day and doing your best to make people's lives more productive."

TEACHERS

As most groups in any given culture, teachers receive pressure to be a certain way. These standards are often unspoken and are assumed to come naturally with the profession. It is interesting to explore how these pressures evolve over time and how they differ or continue. Here is an amusing look at published rules for teachers at the beginning of the 20th century.

Rules for Teachers—1915

1. You will not marry during the term of your contract.

2. You are not to keep company with men.

3. You must be home between the hours of 8 P.M. and 6 A.M. unless attending a school function.

4. You may not loiter downtown at ice cream shops.

5. You may not travel outside the city limits unless you have permission of the chairman of the board.

6. You may not ride in a carriage or an automobile with any man unless he is your father or brother.

7. You may not smoke cigars.

8. You may not wear bright colors.

9. You may under no circumstances dye your hair.

10. You must wear at least two petticoats.

11. Your dresses must not be any shorter than 2 inches above the ankles.

12. To keep the schoolroom neat and clean, you must sweep the floor at least once daily, scrub the floor at least once a week with hot soapy water, clean the blackboard at least once a day, and start the fire at 7 A.M. so the room will be warm by 8 A.M.

SOURCE: Cabell County West Virginia Board of Education, Old Sacramento Schoolhouse Museum.

- Which one of these pressures still exists for teachers in the 21st century?
- If you were to write the rules for the present time, what would come to mind?
- Do you find current pressures to be very different from the rules published in 1915?
- What are the effects of these pressures on teachers' job satisfaction, relations with each other, and performance as educators?

Intrigued by these questions, we surveyed and/or interviewed 240 teachers from a variety of public schools in California. These teachers have various degrees of experience and work in school districts with a wide range of population, ideologies, and socioeconomic status.[3]

In our research most teachers reported that the pressures to be a certain way were very strong (4 or 5 on a scale of 1 to 5). Four main pressures were identified as placing significant stress on teachers. The pressures were to (1) sacrifice personal time; (2) be super responsible; (3) always be in control; and (4) be perfect role models. As such, the current rules for teachers at the turn of the 21st century could be playfully written as follows:

Rules for Teachers—2004

1. You will do constant "little" extras
2. You will embody responsibility and be "on," always
3. You will never smile before Christmas
4. You will be 100% pure and conservative

While reading this section, some readers will relate more than others to certain pressures. These reactions can be based on their personal experience of race, class, gender, subculture of current school, and various other life occurrences. Also, pressures may vary in how they are expressed from one school environment to another. Let us now explore each one of these pressures in more detail.

You Will Do Constant "Little" Extras

Most teachers are hard-working professionals and feel the pressure to work long hours. Society expects teachers to sacrifice and overwork in the name of dedication. In many schools there is a pressure, an unspoken message, that working long hours and doing "little" extras proves your commitment to students. While dedication in itself is a beautiful way of being, the problem lies in that there is no limit to the amount of work that needs to be done. The possibility of dedication becomes unlimited. You could always:

Create a new lesson

Clean your classroom

Change decorations in your classroom

Write more anecdotal records on your students

Write another parent newsletter

Plan another field trip

Surf the Internet for resources

Head up a new committee

Answer e-mail messages from parents

Call a parent

Write more feedback on papers

Learn something new

Support a new teacher

Develop new curriculum

Take an online course

Mentor a student

Collaborate with a colleague

Add to this list

In our survey, systematically all teachers, when asked directly, reported having to sacrifice personal time to get the job done, and 83% of those teachers said they sacrificed personal time to complete their job most of the time or always. As stated by one teacher,

> *You could work as many hours as you want. You would never find an end to your time. Even when I go places and do activities with my family, I see [everything] as a teacher. I'm always thinking, "What can I use? This would be neat."*

—Fifth Grade Teacher

Teachers are expected not only to teach their curriculum but also to tend to the extra needs of families and students, often during personal time. Teachers who work at a school with financially privileged families shared with us that a great deal of pressure was based around constantly providing more academic curriculum for students. This requires the preparation of challenging academic exercises and a richer curriculum. Other teachers find themselves working long hours focused on after-school activities and clubs, mentoring, tutoring, and socially caring for underprivileged neighborhood children.

Again, while a certain amount of dedication and little extras in one's work are not bad in themselves, in excess they have two major implications. They imply that teachers are pushed into sacrificing some of their personal time for their work. This may be a painful dilemma, costly both to family relationships and well-needed self-care activities. As illustrated by the following teacher comment:

Sometimes I feel so rushed and so tired and I think I come to school looking tired and drained. I feel like some parents want me to be perfect and perky with nylons and dressed to a T. I can't do that when I stay up until 11 grading and get here early in the morning to do something. I am so tired and I have no time for me. I look like I got hit. I can't go work out; I have to get this done. I find I don't have that balance for the gym and eating right. I am a better teacher when I do that. I'm nicer. I have more patience.

—Fifth Grade Teacher

Box 1.2   In Their Own Words

Teachers Speak of the Pressures of Dedication and Sacrifice

- "Give 100% of your time to your class."
- "Keep a cute and immaculately clean classroom."
- "Accept the fact and do not complain about how little salaries are, and apologize for having summers off."
- "Pay for all cool classroom materials and buy things for your students."
- "Do not complain: teaching is an 'easy' job."
- "Don't take personal days off because the kids are depending on you, and there's a shortage of subs."
- "Provide students with tons of homework at levels above grade level."
- "Do all the necessary paperwork all the time and have exciting lessons planned for your students so that all students are busy all the time."
- "Solve *all* student learning and behavior problems."

Third, problems can develop when teachers chose not to fulfill the pressure of sacrifice and feel stigmatized by that difference. In the eyes of their school community, these teachers may be perceived as underperforming or less committed to the profession, even though they actually are, just not in that particular way. Teachers who are parents cannot win. If they put teaching above parenting, they may be questioned as a neglectful parent. If they put their family above teaching, they are in danger of not appearing as professional as others appear.

> *I had a difficult time balancing career and my son, mostly because of my feelings of hypocrisy. I felt that I was always trying to implement "best practice" for kids and then wasn't able to apply the same principles for my own. I felt that leaving him all day at the day care center was too long, and when I expressed wanting to leave our staff meeting early, it was met with strong objection. My principal told me that others resented it and said that we all had commitments (kids, appointments, personal lives) and I shouldn't be allowed to leave early if no on else could. I found this colored my outlook, and I scrutinized all demands on my time. I became really frustrated when we would be discussing, at length, a situation that was only applicable to one or two people (e.g., I can't get my e-mail to work. What do we serve for the brunch?). I think that my feelings were interpreted by others. They thought I was not caring enough for my students and school, that I was putting my child first and really didn't have a vested interest in that staff. I have never felt that the amount of time a teacher is at school (e.g., until 7 P.M. and on the weekends) is a just indicator of how effective or dedicated they are.*
>
> —Third Grade Teacher

In sum, the pressure of doing too many "little" extras and overly sacrificing personal time can have negative effects on individuals, school culture, and students. Common effects of this pressure on teachers include:

- Sacrificing their own needs for health, family, and personal space, which can eventually lead to dissatisfaction in their lives, family conflicts, and resentment against giving so much and not necessarily receiving significant appreciation in return
- Being drained of energy and, in some situations, facing professional burnout
- Feeling guilt and frustration. Teachers commonly worry that there is never enough time and that what is done is never enough or as much as one would like to do
- Doubting yourself and questioning your worth as an educator when you do set limits or try to be dedicated in ways that are different from those privileged by the pressure

Ironically, this pressure can also have negative effects on the teacher-student relationship. Although it may seem that students would gain from an overly dedicated teacher, it is questionable whether they gain on a level that is meaningful for them. Students may become more attached to and perform better for a teacher who is present, relaxed, and energetic than for a tired teacher who has prepared extra assignments. Teachers who spend enormous amounts of time and energy preparing as much as they can may sometimes become resentful of the lack of recognition and appreciation they get in return from students, principals, or colleagues.

In terms of the effects on the school culture, over-dedication can lead to comparison and competition as to who is the most dedicated and to a lack of time for bonding or supporting each other's work.

You Will Embody Responsibility and Be "On," Always . . .

Most people value the ability to be responsible. Having responsible staff members is necessary for schools to operate and is completely understandable in the context of the safety

Box 1.3   In Their Own Words

Teachers Speak of the Pressures to Be Responsible at All Costs

- "Serve on numerous committees"
- "Have *all* students at grade level by the end of the year"
- "Cover *all* of the numerous state standards"
- "Have neat, well-organized classrooms"
- "Always keep in contact with all parents"
- "Have their students score high on standardized tests"
- "Teach math and language arts only: no art or 'frills'"
- "Provide homework that is clearly explained to kids (for the ease of parents) to 'keep kids busy at home' and be responsible for its completion'

and education of large numbers of children. Being a responsible teacher usually implies being reliable, organized, and well prepared. These skills contribute to the survival of teachers, given the extreme and varied tasks that need to be accomplished. Teachers who are organized and responsible are often admired, consulted, and perceived as competent. Often, however, these teachers take on a lion's share of the work, and this can also have negative effects. Again, it is the excessive form of this pressure that causes problems, not its appropriate and necessary form. In our research, 82% of teachers reported feeling the pressure to be organized and well prepared (beyond their preference) most of the time. In other words, while most teachers clearly value these ways of being and choose to function in a responsible and organized way, there are frequent instances where they feel compelled to engage in behaviors that they personally don't value but that seem necessary to avoid stigmatization from the community. We would like you, the reader, to reflect for a brief moment on your own ways of being responsible and organized.

- What does being responsible mean to you?
- Are you responsible and organized to your satisfaction?
- Do others perceive you being as responsible and organized as you think you are?
- What if your ideas of responsibility don't fit those of your school colleagues and administrators?
- What if you want to be responsible in a different way?

Consider this story:

I consider myself a good teacher and one who takes her responsibility seriously. I worked in this school district for nearly 10 years and was only absent in extreme cases. I had to be really ill to call in sick. I felt irresponsible being away from my class. I knew I had a problem when a family member decided to host a family reunion out of my town, and it happened to be during the middle of the school year. Attending the reunion would mean that I would be absent from teaching my class for almost a week. My family is quite important to me and knowing this event would only come around every 10 years made me quite interested to go. I wanted to be with my family and, yet, the stress of missing school was eating me up. My plan was to be honest with my district, explain the importance of this family time, ensure that I found myself an experienced, reliable substitute teacher, and leave a detailed education plan for him or her. I thought this was quite responsible. After talking to some colleagues, I was confused because each one warned me against being honest with our administration. I decided to see what the teachers' union president would say. The advice I received was to call in sick, plain and simple. Don't tell anyone where you are going and hope that you don't run into anyone at the airport. Now I was in a bind. I had planned to be honest. I was now burdened with worries and angry that I was being compelled to lie. What if someone commented on my tan? What if I found something educational from my travels that I wanted to share with my class? What if I ran into someone at the airport? What if someone from school phoned my home and I wasn't there lying sick on the couch?

—Second Grade Teacher

If you were this teacher, what would you have done?

This story illustrates well how pressures in the school system narrow possibilities and force teachers to act against their own integrity and will. In this story, everyone lost because of narrow ideas about being responsible.[4]

The school would have been more able to responsibly find an appropriate substitute who would have benefited from the detailed education plan prepared by the teacher, which would have been more relevant and appropriate for the students, who could also have shared the excitement of their teacher's trip. When criteria for responsibility are too narrow and inflexible, problems arise. When teachers are expected to model predictability and reliability as workers beyond the normal variations of life circumstances, more problematic, rigid ways of being become promoted.

You Will Never Smile Until Christmas

"Education 101" stipulates that control of your class, especially early in the school year, is critical to establish the foundation of a successful, effective instructional year. Most teachers fear that not following this pressure would either promote some sort of chaos or would be judged severely by their peers. This was evident in our research, as 68% of teachers (when asked directly) reported the need to control their students *beyond their personal preference* at least half the time. Above all of the fears associated with student behaviors was the concern that an observer would visit and evaluate, negatively, the state of the class.

Box 1.4   In Their Own Words

**Teachers Speak of the Pressures
to Be in Control**

- "Be strict and teach discipline"
- "Be in tight control of the class"
- "Keep classes silent when working, so you have a quiet 'you-could-hear-a-pin-drop' classroom"
- "Always be responsible for behavior of students"
- "Stay on top of them, don't let them get out of hand for a second"

- What is your personal definition of being in control of your class?
- What percentage of the time do you control your class to your satisfaction?
- Would your principal and colleagues agree with that number, or would they have a different estimate?

Although a certain amount of control can definitely be useful and necessary in some instances, an excessive focus on this issue can actually be costly to teachers and have the opposite effect. For example, the expectation of control can get teachers to spend a large amount of energy worrying and plotting new ways to use classroom management ideas. It can also influence them to be strict and impatient—not their preferred self. It can create an unrealistic context where one person (granted, an adult) is expected to be responsible for the behavior of thirty others. In its extreme form, this pressure, more than any other, can drain teachers' energy and enthusiasm. Some teachers even report feeling trapped between either connecting with their colleagues and being distant with students or connected with students but being distant from their colleagues. The following two stories illustrate these experiences, the first one being from a rather petite teacher who chose to be connected with her students while the second story illustrates a teacher's painful dilemma in attempting to stay connected with a colleague.

In the early 70s, I was teaching big classes and had found that the students worked best in small groups. These classes fairly bubbled with energy, and it sometimes happened that the door of the classroom was suddenly thrown open by the principal or vice-principal, who would stand with hands on hips and roar, "When your teacher is not in the classroom, I don't want to hear a sound out of you!" At such times I could never decide if it was worse to stand up and reveal that I was in fact present, or just to wait until he finished glaring and left! Whenever I tried later to explain my methods and reasons to the administration, there was no respect for such innovation, only respect for silence in the classroom. Years later I met one of my former students by accident, and she was very happy to see me again. She thanked me for these classes, as she had never forgotten the unique humanness of that environment in the midst of the rigidity of the school's style of education.

—Second Grade Teacher

Many years ago, I decided to share a classroom because I needed time to take care of educational demands and family needs. I was paired with a teacher who was thoughtful and passionate about teaching. We had things in common, so we assumed our management styles would be similar. As it turned out, she was more structured and controlling than I, and also more outspoken about her management program. I agreed to try to use it since I knew we should be consistent. My awkwardness grew as time went on because I knew I didn't want to control kids so much; I was used to a more democratic approach. The thing I most noticed was that my relationship with the kids was distant, like never before in my years of teaching. I attributed it to my not being there full time, yet later when I thought about it more, I realized it was because I was uncomfortable laying down thick laws, a strict point system, and not resolving conflicts in a way I was used to.

—Third Grade Teacher

Ironically, teachers themselves do not even meet those expectations. . . . Think back to those staff meetings. Consider those staff members who whisper their opinions to their neighbors, giggle in the back of the room, correct papers while the meeting is going on, allow their cell phones to interrupt, and make unmannerly comments during discussions.

When control is the overriding theme, the school culture also suffers. The pressure to control in some schools is so high that the level of excitement for learning barely exists. Such pressure creates a stressful environment for both teachers and students, who may experience disconnection and disengagement.

You Will Be 100% Pure

There clearly is a professional pressure that requires teachers to be good role models. Most of the time, this pressure matches with teachers' intentions, since they willingly want to help children understand the socially agreed-upon "acceptable" behaviors. Schools were created to assist children in becoming "good citizens." Problems arise from the limited ways in which a good role model or good citizen is defined— what it includes and what it excludes. In other words, the issue lies in the narrow criteria dictated by the pressure and its invasiveness in all areas of life.

Half of all teachers responding to the open-ended survey reported experiencing the pressure to be a good role model, and, when asked directly, 90% of teachers reported feeling the good-role-model pressure most of the time.

Being a good role model often means replicating and modeling the political beliefs and values of the dominant

Box 1.5   In Their Own Words

**Teachers Speak of the Pressure
to be a Good Role Model**

- "Reflect present political views, and be conservative"
- "Always smile; be happy, patient and agreeable"
- "Never get mad"
- "Be nurturing"
- "Always be professional and prompt"
- "Radiate confidence and remain positive"
- "Get along with everyone"
- "Behave with a higher standard of behavior outside of the classroom than other people (even higher than parents)"
- "Do not drink alcohol or smoke"
- "Always be well rested ('you work only nine months a year and only from 8:30 to 3')"
- "Have an impeccable memory (know 'Johnny's' name 10 years later)"
- "Of course, have perfect kids yourself"

culture—meaning white, middle class, heterosexual, and conservative. In our surveys, many teachers even reported the pressure to dress a certain way:

- "Dress in demure, modest, and conservative clothing"
- "Do not dye your hair, have body piercings or tattoos"
- "I can never run with my dog wearing old sweats"

The pressure around being a good role model requires that teachers walk, talk, and breathe according to society's standards of "acceptable" behavior. Many teachers have commented on the fact that they can never act totally free outside of their homes (unless the home is at a great distance from school). This pressure requires not only that teachers represent the dominant culture politically, but also that their actions are based in high moral standards. This means being a perfectly moral individual at all times, not only while at work. Even when the children are gone, anyone can walk into a teacher's classroom and make a judgment upon the appropriateness of her dress, her body language, her activities, and the cleanliness of her classroom, among other factors. When she leaves the school, a teacher is often conscious of the possible judgment or interpretation any bystander could make about everything. Within minutes, she could be judged on the vehicle she drives, the appearance of the car, any bumper stickers she has displayed, which type of music is coming from the car, where she is going, and if she is speeding.

This is even true when a teacher is enjoying a weekend or a holiday, as illustrated by the following story:

> *Once I was at the park on a weekend, enjoying a beer with lunch. I had on shorts and a bikini top because it was hot. As I played Frisbee, I heard, "Hi, Ms. M!" It was a student and his family. I felt completely awkward, as if I had been caught working at a strip club or something.*
>
> —Fourth Grade Teacher

As a result of this pressure, most teachers report hiding at least one aspect of themselves. In our surveys, 30% to 40% of teachers reported withholding personal information on a variety of items from their school colleagues. Aspects that were most commonly not disclosed fell in the categories of "experimentation during teen and college years" and "alcohol and drug use." Sexual orientation was the third most taboo subject, with close to 25% of teachers reporting that it was unsafe to share. These data are much higher than the proportion of gay, lesbian, and bisexual people in the general population, which is estimated at 10%. Overall, this shows that teachers are most likely to refrain from disclosing any personal information, especially if there is any risk of it being considered outside of dominant norms.

Question for Educators: What would *you* feel uncomfortable disclosing at your school site?

Why? _____

_____

For some of you, the discomfort would be so great that you may not even risk writing the information down in this book. For others, what you may or may not wish to disclose is not apparent to you, because you are used to functioning in such a way. Yet again, a few of you may have the good fortune of being at a school site where you have great trust and connection with your colleagues.

What are the effects of this pressure and the scrutiny associated with it? Teachers have to be aware that somewhere, somehow, someone could see them engage in socially questionable behaviors. The costs of having to follow this pressure, which may not fit for them, and also of being the subject of social scrutiny, can be great. Common effects of this situation include:

• *Isolation:* Especially if you have to hide an important part of yourself or your life. Examples of this include teachers from a different ethnicity, religion, or class or those struggling with an illness, a divorce, an out-of-wedlock pregnancy, political views, or simply hobbies that may stand outside of the norm. This isolation can disconnect these teachers from the rest of the staff and from their students, as they cannot fully relate. In other words, their whole sense of self cannot be involved genuinely in relationship.

• *Self-alienation:* Feeling like a fraud, like someone you are pretending to be

• *Wasted energy:* Spending energy engaging in practices that you don't necessarily believe in and filtering out your natural inclinations

• *Resentment and frustration:* Being sour about having to participate in this situation

In some ways, this pressure leads to expectations of teachers being icons of virtue in society. Given that teachers can never be a perfect role model, it may at times contribute to disrespect from the community. Parents may judge a teacher as being too strict or not strict enough, too nurturing or too cold, too academically focused or not focused enough . . . who can fit the narrow mold of the perfect role model?!

In some ways, teachers are "on" all the time. Regardless of location or time, they are seen as teachers. Whether the student-teacher relationship is current or not, the teacher will always be seen as a teacher. In other words, once a teacher, always a teacher. What are the effects of this good role model pressure on teachers' relationship with students? When a teacher develops contrived ways of dealing with students, potentially useful options of relating are left out along with the teacher's unique and creative talents. In addition, the narrow way of relating may not fit with all students' needs and leave some alienated, not to mention that all kids miss out on the possibilities of being exposed to the richness of each teacher's multiple ways of being.

In sum, the extreme pressure to be a perfect role model can have several negative effects on children by:

- Modeling limited ways of being
- Exposing children to only the dominant culture and leaving them less able to appreciate the value of diversity
- Depriving students who may not fit in the dominant culture of a valuable role model
- Confirming the necessity of pretending to be someone you are not, or of attempting to belong to the majority instead of accepting and honoring your differences

The expectation of high morality is more prevalent from adults than students, who in general connect more readily to a teacher's authentic self.

What are the effects of this pressure on the school culture? In extreme situations, the pressure on teachers to be perfect role models can create a false environment where everyone is pretending to be an icon of social perfection. In most situations, unfortunately, the staff know very little about each other as people, and, as a result, their conversation focuses on problem-saturated accounts of students or superficial conversations about work.

CONCLUSION

Which one of these pressures do you think would be amusing for people to read a century from now?

Although pressures can provide a sense of direction, their rigidity does not take into account the dynamics and complexity of relationships and context. As a result, these pressures can limit a teacher's access to possible solutions when faced with a challenging circumstance. These pressures

Figure 1.2   A teacher's mind and best judgment can become cluttered and impeded with confusing and opposing thoughts

can leave a teacher constantly doubting herself and her choices, which in the end can be very draining of energy and can actually contribute further to problems. This also contributes to the enormous teacher drop-out rate of 30% in the first five years (Merrow, 2001). In the end, a teacher's mind and best judgment can become cluttered and impeded with confusing and opposing thoughts. See Figure 1.2.

Despite all of these challenges, numerous individuals remain in education because of their love for children and the meaningful rewards of teaching (see the playful descriptions in the box below). In many ways this shows that these

---

Box 1.6   In Their Own Words

Teachers' Descriptions of Their Work Experience

- "Teaching is like a wild and crazy rafting adventure in mega challenging terrain . . . exhilarating, exciting, strenuous, exhausting, rewarding, and unpredictable, very up and down. One minute you are laughing and smiling, the next crying. But it's a rafting adventure for the huge cause of making a difference in the lives of others."
- "To be a teacher, you need to be able to have your eyes open, ears open, arms open, mind open, and heart open all the time."
- "Teaching is like being a Swiss Army knife, because you have to be ready each day and open to what tool is needed."
- "Teaching is quite a job! You are in charge of your own good time!"
- "Teaching children is like building a beautiful house . . . many tools are used, materials are needed, time is invested, and it is a labor of love."
- "Teaching is like holding the future in my hands."

(Continued)

> **Box 1.6** (Continued)
>
> - "As a teacher, I have to be a symphony conductor. Sometimes the brass is too brash and the percussion is too loud. I sense the tempo and mood and alter it, if necessary."
> - "Teaching can be a mini-adventure, almost every day."
> - "Teaching is a box of chocolates. Each day is a surprise. You never know what you are going to get."

pressures can be minimized to a point where many people can have a satisfying work life and function at their best. An awareness of teachers' experiences of the context can foster not only greater compassion in the face of problems but also allow a more realistic and effective approach to the prevention and solving of complex problems.

NOTES

1. The concepts of personalities, strengths and weaknesses are introduced here as a reflection of the everyday conversations in schools. They are however incongruent with the post-structuralist philosophy presented in this book where individuals are not assumed to have a core personality with a set reservoir of assets/deficits but rather are constituted by multiple selves shaped by a variety of relationships and contexts. This will be explained further in a later section of this chapter.

2. Please note that by "principals" we mean both principals and assistant principals. We have chosen to use only one title simply to reduce the complexity of the text. We are also aware that not all principals will experience contextual pressures in the particular ways in which they are discussed. The experience of these pressures will vary depending on race, socioeconomic status, class, etc.

3. Our survey methods involved using two overlapping questionnaires. These questionnaires were completed during staff gatherings, and the participants were given the option of remaining anonymous. The first contained mostly open-ended questions, where

teachers were asked, for instance, about the general pressures experienced. In answering the survey, most teachers did not have the time to detail an exhaustive list of all the pressures they experienced. It is likely that they mostly reflected on that which was salient in their experience that particular day or week. As researchers, it is a choice that we made to first ask open-ended questions to our participants in order to gather a broader range of ideas. The second questionnaire was a multiple-choice version that covered similar content area. It was interesting to contrast the response generated through free writing with the response from a more structured question.

4. Unfortunately, antagonistic relationships between the union and administrators add to these problems as tasks and responsibilities become so rigidly and narrowly defined that the possibility of being flexible and adapt to the changing realities of life becomes eliminated.

CHAPTER TWO

Creating an Environment for Change

Obviously you cannot change the broader cultural context and general expectations for educators. To a certain extent you can have a *local* effect in the subculture of your school, and we will discuss that in a subsequent section on school culture (Chapter 6). However, if you truly understand that specific contexts and cultures can pressure everyone into nonpreferred ways of being, it then becomes completely logical to talk about staff problems in an externalized way. In other words, if the context prevents people from functioning in a preferred and helpful way, then the problem can be talked about as coming from outside the person.

Externalization of problems is a fundamental concept in the Narrative Approach. This practice, developed by Michael White (White & Epston, 1990), is based on the idea that problems, just like unwanted habits, may develop because of a series of life circumstances. Externalizing a problem implies that it is perceived as distinct from the person's identity. As such, an individual will not be talked about as an "angry person" but rather as someone struggling with anger or disrespect. In many ways, this practice resembles the medical model of helping a well-intentioned person manage allergies or anxiety. People often experience problems as being out of their control even if it may not seem so to an observer. By externalizing problems, we recognize that problems are not indicative of who others want to be, but are reactions they can learn to escape from and control.

Talking about problems in externalized ways has several major impacts:

- It shifts people's perspectives in profound ways. Instead of hating themselves, they suddenly start hating the problem. Externalizing promotes *hope and agency.* In this process, a *space* is created where people are less weighed down, less paralyzed, and more able to take action against the "habit" of, for example, bullying and disrespect. (Although the word *habit* is incongruent with the cultural and post-structuralist conceptualization of the narrative approach, it can be useful in actual conversations with young people as long as we remain connected with the more accurate guiding concepts.)

- When a problem is externalized, it becomes a tangible entity that is nameable, contained, and clear. This new perspective allows people to *take a stand against "it"* and *take responsibility* for their behaviors of disrespect and bullying (often for the first time). People learn to control "it" as opposed to "it" controlling them. In other words, externalization makes the effects of the problem more visible, enhances the necessity of taking action, and renders people more capable of making different choices to change their lives.

- As the community starts seeing the problem as a separate entity, everyone starts noticing people's special talents, values, and intentions. The focus shifts from blaming people to working as a *team* and noticing people's efforts against problems.

The externalization of problems is often difficult to grasp at first. A good way to understand this concept is to apply it to your own life and consider, for example, your personal relationship to impatience. Many of you may recall having done or said something at school under the influence of impatience that did not quite fit with how you prefer to be. Later on, you may even have regretted your actions, felt guilty, and promised yourself not to do that again. Imagine, however, someone talking about you as an impatient person, and this becoming part of your reputation. This might trigger more frustration and a sense of being misunderstood or misrepresented. This *frustration in itself* would increase the likelihood that you'd engage in "impatient" behaviors again even if you did not want to. In other words, the way the problem is talked about will in itself create a context of resentment in which the problem is more likely to happen again.

Now imagine having externalized impatience. You would create a thorough list of effects that impatience might have on multiple aspects of your life; you would notice when it takes over and when it does not, and what it gets you to do, think, or feel that is against your preference. You might eventually be frustrated *at* the problematic aspects of impatience and make a decision that, given its effects, you do not want to let it rule you in those particular ways anymore. Through supportive externalizing conversation, you might identify the first signs that may lead up to an impatience problem and explore ways of going in a preferred direction. In a simplified way, this process of articulating, noticing, and making choices about the effects of the problem and simultaneously about the way you prefer to act will ultimately allow you to take responsibility, be clearer about personally relevant options, and have preferred experiences of yourself in difficult interactions.

Exercise: Externalization

Chose a problem that has affected you at school. It can be anything, such as an emotion (anger, anxiety, impatience, depression, frustration, self-hate, boredom, distrust, fear, shyness, discouragement, etc.), a thought (self-criticism or critical voice, blaming, perfectionism, comparison, self-doubt, evaluation, ambition, etc.), or a habit or behavioral pattern (sarcasm, interrupting, dominating, rushing, irresponsibility, disrespect, etc.). Explore how this problem has affected you in the past and how you've seen it affect other people by answering these questions.

1. How does _____ affect you?

    _____

    _____

2. What does _____ make you do, say, think, and feel?

    Do: _____

    Say: _____

    Think: _____

    Feel: _____

3. When and how did you first notice _____?

    _____

    _____

4. How does _____ affect your relationships?

    _____

    _____

5. How does _____ make you feel about yourself?

_____

_____

6. When are you *most likely* to resist _____?

_____

_____

7. Can you remember an example this past week where you could have given into _____ but didn't? What did you do to avoid _____? What were you thinking and doing as the situation evolved?

_____

_____

Externalization is not a technique that you use on people. A technique is a method, a procedure that you use to manipulate people into certain positions. For an externalization to be helpful, it has to be embedded in conversations that reflect its fundamental implications. The goal in externalizing conversations is to clearly support others in the face of their struggle; express the philosophy that people are constrained by contexts, patterns of interactions, and habitual reactions; and communicate that we know there is more to any individual than the problem. If one uses an externalization but maintains a blaming and personalizing attitude, the outcome of the conversation will not be any different. Given the importance of attitude, we will now distinguish deficit-focused assumptions in problem-solving conversation and the externalizing stance we are promoting in this book.

By "deficit-focused" we mean the process of:

1. Observing and Gathering Data on the Problem

Principals and educators are often trained to pay particular attention to the details that fit in certain diagnostic categories of pathology. This follows the deficit model of analysis where professionals are supposed to correct deficits instead of building on existing competence. This can be overwhelming and discouraging to educators. For example: A principal might wonder if a teacher has good control over students and scrutinize that teacher often in a way that is likely to cause unease to the teacher and support the assumption.

2. Comparing Your Perception of the Problem to Your Criteria of Normality

Principals and educators are often trained to observe and document thoughts, feelings, and behavior (in a vacuum) of staff and students to compare them to predetermined criteria of "normality." The goal then becomes to use various strategies to bring people closer to this "normality," which is often biased by the dominant culture and disregards the contextual constraints of the lives of staff and students. For example: A principal may be concerned about a teacher's mannerism and interprets it negatively without regard for the teacher's cultural background.

3. Making Assumptions

People's minds will often naturally fill in the blanks, and this becomes very dangerous if people are in positions of power, such as principals, and do not verify assumptions. This mind-filling can lead to principals ascribing meaning to the lives of staff and students as opposed to being respectful and empowering them to articulate their own preferred versus nonpreferred meanings. For example: A teacher may leave the staff meeting early because of family obligations and may be perceived as lazy and uncommitted to her career, while in reality she is very invested in both career and family life.

4. Fixing the Problem

Pressure is placed on principals to "fix" teachers and students. This inadvertently creates a hierarchy where principals can overanalyze problems and become disconnected from people as people. For example: A principal may decide to micromanage staff when perceiving that teachers are behind schedule.

Externalizing is not congruent with this stance as it implies the following:

1. There is more to people than their problems. Believing in the richness of people's ways of being allows for more *compassion*. For example: The principal assumes that a teacher has good intentions and is competent when faced with an issue.

2. Criteria of normality omit the many nuances of background, cultural diversity, and *contexts* of lives. For example: Staff can be invited to discuss how their social class backgrounds affect their interactions with children and parents and whether their policies are realistic given the culture of the school population.

3. An important goal of externalizing is assisting people to articulate their preferred way of being as different from their problem. This implies a certain *curiosity* about the invisible yet preferred aspects of others. For example: A principal could be intrigued by a teacher's ideas about discipline, his intentions, goals, and instances when he handled a situation in a way that was helpful to students.

4. Externalization places the responsibility of addressing the problem on the protagonist, as individuals are the best judges of their own lives. The principal is clearly there to support the process, *collaborate*, and participate as a team member, but does not dominate the process. For example: A principal can reduce hierarchy by giving teachers the opportunity to lead various staff meetings and make important decisions.

COMPARING DEFICIT-FOCUSED VERSUS CONTEXTUALIZED UNDERSTANDING

Summary of the 4 "C's" of Helpful Conversation

Comparative Table of Deficit-Focused Attitude Versus a Contextualized Understanding

Selective Attention to Problem	*Compassion: Acknowledge the Richness of People*
Educators are often trained to pay particular attention to the details that fit in certain diagnostic categories of problems or pathology. This follows the deficit model of analysis where professionals are supposed to correct deficits instead of building on existing competence. This can be overwhelming and discouraging to all.	Believing that people are really oppressed by these pressures and problems, and that there is another more preferred version of that same individual which is caring and successful and with whom it is possible to connect.
Comparing Your Perception of the Problem to Your Criteria of Normality	*Contextualized Perspective*
Educators are often trained to observe and document people's thoughts, feelings and behavior (in a vacuum) to compare them to predetermined criteria of "normality." The goal then becomes to use various strategies to bring people closer to this "normality," which is often biased by the dominant culture and disregards the contextual constraints of people's lives.	• Keeping in mind the broader context • Thinking at a meta level of the larger sociocultural perspective (gender, class, etc.) • Deconstructing or examining influences on individuals' responses to a situation and challenging beliefs in our own minds, communities, and dominant culture that simplify human behavior.

Making Assumptions	Curiosity About the Invisible Complexity of Others' Lives
People's minds will often naturally fill the blanks; this becomes very dangerous if people are in positions of power, such as principals, and do not verify assumptions. This mind-filling leads to educators ascribing meaning to people's lives as opposed to being respectful and empowering them to articulate their own preferred vs. nonpreferred meanings.	Adults and children are considered experts in their own experiences. Professionals' expertise lies in the ability to ask *helpful questions* and explore new possibilities by taking a genuine "not knowing" stance and being intrigued by a person's thoughts, values, hopes, and dreams. Focus is much broader than the problem in an attempt to identify the ingredients of preferred experiences.

Expert: Fix the Problem	Collaboration and Empowerment
Pressure is placed on principals to "fix" problems and people. This inadvertently creates a hierarchy where the principal can overanalyze problems and become disconnected from people as people. It can also leave the protagonist less actively involved in taking responsibilities for change.	Principals seek to minimize power imbalance between them as professionals and teachers. Given that most people have struggled with some form of disqualification in their lives, it is important that the process provide a forum for conversations that do not replicate contributing factors to problems.

Application: An Externalized Conversation Between a Principal and Teacher[1]

Principal Suzanne Hughes is concerned about the behavior of tenured teacher Alice Stevens during meetings. Alice has been making sarcastic comments, sighing dramatically, and using body language to show her disapproval or scorn for comments or suggestions from colleagues. Suzanne has noticed the effects, such as teachers' reluctance to speak up and meetings being less generative of creative ideas. As principal, Suzanne feels this is the most difficult aspect of her job: dealing with a staff member who acts in a negative and demoralizing way. She has asked Alice to meet with her after school. These two have worked together in the same school for a number of years. She prepares herself mentally for the conversation and takes a deep breath.

Example of an Externalized Principal-Teacher Dialogue

Alice: (knock, knock)

Suzanne: Hi Alice, please come in. I appreciate you agreeing to meet with me.	Starting the meeting with an acknowledgment of the effort.
Alice: It's OK, Suzanne. I have a lot to do, but I have some time.	
Suzanne: I have been wanting to talk to you because I am concerned about the atmosphere at the staff meetings. I am wondering . . . how are the staff meetings for you?	Suzanne is transparent about her concerns and puts the focus on the context of the problem: the staff meeting. She also approaches the issue with a stance of respectful curiosity rather than blame. She conveys that she is interested in the actual experience of her teacher, which in some ways implies that she knows Alice can be a different person.
Alice: Well, they are productive, but a little long . . . and boring.	
Suzanne: I really try to make them as short as possible. Can you help me understand what makes them boring?	Keeping the focus or blame on the context (staff meeting) and inviting Alice into a description of its effect on her.

Alice: I've got so much to do, and to have to sit and listen to naive questions and people discussing subjects like photocopying or playground rules for 30 minutes really takes it out of me.

Suzanne: What effect do these conversations have on you? (pause) When they happen you end up, what, . . . frustrated? Resentful? . . .

Having established a collaborative, compassionate, nonblaming-defensive pattern of conversation, Suzanne gently moves to externalizing a problem that develops for Alice in the context of staff meetings.

Alice: Well, frankly, it makes me angry and resentful that my time is being used up.

Suzanne: So some Anger and Resentment creeps in and it makes you feel like you're wasting precious time?

Suzanne externalizes the problems described by Alice, being careful to use Alice's names for her experience (anger and resentment); she also restates what Alice just said to make sure she understood correctly and to let Alice know that she is following her experience.

Alice: Yeah . . .

Suzanne: Have Anger and Resentment been creeping in more and more for you in the recent staff meetings than those at the beginning of the year? It seems like it to me . . .

Suzanne makes clear to Alice that she knows Alice is not at her best lately by conveying to her that she has noticed her on other, more constructive occasions. In other words, she reassures Alice that she sees more than just the problem and that she is aware that it is probably not Alice's preferred way of being.

(Continued)

(Continued)

Alice: Definitely.

Suzanne: I've noticed that in district meetings that Resentment and Impatience get me to act in ways I don't like, like raising my voice. Do you have an idea of what Resentment gets you to focus on during staff meetings?

Suzanne *genuinely* states that she has been affected by similar problems as well, which has the effects of: (1) Fostering collaboration and minimizing any hierarchy or unfavorable comparison/evaluation that could distance them in this moment of sharing; (2) Acknowledging that problems such as Resentment push everyone away from their preferred ways of being; this furthers the externalization, demarginalizes the teacher, and opens space to talk about more unwanted behaviors. Note that Suzanne in her personal sharing does not move away from the focus of the conversation; she shares the minimum necessary to create a sense of companionship in the experience without asking for support from Alice.

Alice: It gets me to watch the clock to see how many minutes are wasted, and it gets me to say something to help people move onto the next subject so that we can get done faster.

Suzanne: OK, so it gets you to want to move faster? (Alice nods) Yes, your comments do make people quieter and ready to move on, in my

Suzanne invites Alice into a noticing of the effects of Resentment on many areas of her life: effects on the meeting, relationship, and reputation.

observation. But do you have a guess on how this Resentment affects others, your relationship with them, and how they might perceive you?

Alice: I have friends here who know who I really am, but there are probably people who misunderstand me.

Suzanne: Where is this Resentment going to take your relationship with your colleagues?

Suzanne continues to map the effects of the problem in areas that are relevant to the situation. These questions are regrouped and condensed here, but would usually be spread in time and space to progressively and gently include effects on self, thoughts, feelings, school culture, and so forth.

Alice: I hadn't thought about that. I assume it will pass, that we'll get along.

Suzanne: Well, how does Resentment affect how you feel about yourself as a colleague? Does this align with the hopes you had for this year?

Alice: I'd have to think about it.

Suzanne: OK, but just think of how this Resentment affects the quality of the decisions made in our meetings.

(Continued)

(Continued)

Alice: They are made faster.

Suzanne: That's partially true; I wonder in the long run, if our decisions are rushed, we might end up with more meetings to go over the repercussions of decisions. Or we may have to take more time to revisit the issues later. For example, I have felt like I ought to bring back the computer lab issue because not everyone contributed an opinion.

Still exploring the effects of Resentment and Anger. Often, exploring the effects of a problem will make visible the fact that it has the opposite effect of that which was intended.

Alice: I hadn't thought about that . . . so the Resentment might actually bring more of what I try to avoid . . .

Suzanne: It's been my impression that it does. . . .

Suzanne: I know you work really hard and are committed to our community; I really appreciate that. It makes me wonder if there are other things going on that you feel comfortable sharing with me or that I can help with?

Suzanne conveys her awareness and appreciation for the "other side" of Alice, or, in narrative terms, her preferred self. She then proceeds to inquire about other potential contextual factors that may contribute to Alice not being her preferred self. Although she is aware that Alice may not share personal matters with her as an employer, it will at least give Alice an experience of being supported and understood.

Alice: My family life is kinda hectic right now. It's giving me a short fuse.

Suzanne: That must be hard. Is that something you want to talk about, or is there something I can do to help?

Suzanne expresses genuine compassion, knowing from her own experience how difficult it is to balance school and family issues. As for Alice, receiving compassion can in itself contribute to lowering the problem of Resentment. In making her feel more connected with her principal, the resulting context of the staff meeting is slightly shifted to one where she's not simply dealing with Anger and Resentment alone in her little corner.

Alice: No. Thanks, but that's fine.

Suzanne: Last year, I remember that you shared some struggles as well and yet I experienced you as participating more in staff meetings discussions. What is it that kept you going then?

Suzanne recalls times that were challenging and when Resentment and Anger could have taken over but didn't. She assists Alice in articulating what it was that might have helped her avoid Resentment then. In other words, she helps Alice articulate her very own strategies and the ingredients of her previous successes in avoiding the problem. By doing this Suzanne avoids the pitfall of giving advice, which is almost always ineffective in the lives of others.

Alice: Hmm . . . that's an interesting question. I had forgotten about that. I think maybe serving as a mentor teacher helped me understand their struggles and kept me connected with their needs for these discussions.

(Continued)

(Continued)

Suzanne: So Resentment and Anger are disconnecting you from that understanding?

Alice: I guess . . . I really don't want that to happen . . . (sigh) I'll try to keep Resentment to myself . . .

Suzanne: Is there something I can do in staff meetings to actually help you push away Resentment or even shrink it?

Suzanne again wants to offer her support and see if the context can be changed in a way that invites less Resentment.

Alice: I'm not sure; you could keep people on the subject . . .

Suzanne; I've got an idea . . . would you like to help me out in staff meetings by being a timekeeper for our agenda, or you could help me co-facilitate a meeting? I would really value your help.

Suzanne recruits the assistance of Alice. She is hoping to create a context that will bring forth Alice's preferred ways of being and special talents. When a voice is loud in staff meetings, it is often helpful to recruit the person's assistance in making other voices heard or in co-facilitating a more constructive process. Suzanne also genuinely values the involvement of her staff.

In this conversation, Suzanne holds onto the notion that there is a problem affecting Alice and pushing her away from her preferred self. In other words, Suzanne is connected at all times to the fact that people are affected in ways they don't like by problems and contexts, and consequently have multiple selves.

A Question From Educators: What do you mean by "multiple selves"? How do you know who someone really is?

Who Is the Real Person? How Can We Tell?

From a narrative point of view, people have many selves. One self is no more *real* than another. . . . This statement is contradictory to many popular psychology handbooks and traditional Western philosophies that assume a core personality.

People's experiences of themselves are constructed in relationships and evolve over time (Gergen, 1985, 1991; Hoffman, 1990). Relationships, particularly if they are with people having a significant influence over one's life, provide the canvas for the meaning making of experience. In other words, we could argue that a person who lived in a vacuum would have a very limited sense of self, if any, as no one would be affected by his or her presence, and no one would be available to reflect back their experience of that person. This individual would have no basis for experiencing him- or herself as clever or funny, for example, without an interaction with another being allowing the individual to ascribe that interpretation to those particular ways of being.

If the self is constructed in relationships, then each individual has multiple selves that reflect different experiences of self-in-relationships. These different selves exist in the past, present, and future, and particular versions of them are brought to the forefront of experience by the context and the presence of certain people in a certain space. Among the many possible selves, some are preferred to others in terms of their effects on relationships and their congruency with one's intentions (and others are less preferred). For instance, many people experience themselves as shy in certain relationships and very outgoing in others.

Similarly, teachers can be experienced as very kind and patient in certain relationships and very impatient in others. In fact, many educators come across students who give radically different stories about who a teacher is. It is quite common to have a person engage in behaviors that may appear contradictory in terms of the person's intentions. In reality, these are simply different versions of selves that are brought forth by the context. The only influence others can have is to engage people in a reflection and assist them in understanding, articulating, and eventually choosing which self is more in line with who they prefer to be. The concept of multiple selves is complex and confusing to many, especially those more familiar with popular psychology. Let us further explore this concept and its implications in the stories of your own life with an exercise.

EXERCISE: PROBLEM-SATURATED VERSUS PREFERRED STORY OF EDUCATORS' LIVES

1. Most people have faced challenges at work. In the following space, write four sentences about things you have done at school that you may not be proud of or that could be judged negatively by your colleagues:

_____

_____

_____

_____

2. In the following space, please write four sentences about a reputation or story that could have started circulating about

you at school if someone were to link the events listed in No. 1 and ascribe a negative meaning:

_____

_____

_____

_____

3. Now write four sentences about actions you took at school that you are most proud of and that reflect your true values and intentions:

_____

_____

_____

_____

4. Write four sentences describing the reputation or story that has or could have followed from someone noticing these actions and ascribing a positive meaning to them:

_____

_____

_____

_____

Notice that you have just written two different stories about yourself, one that is saturated with a negative focus and one that is more in line with how you truly prefer to be as an educator. Which is the real you? This question becomes pointless because these may be just different facets of you in different contexts. The actions you took in No. 1 may have taken place at times when you felt pressured to be a good role model, to be overly dedicated or appear in complete control, or you were simply overwhelmed, stressed, and tired. The actions you took in No. 3 may have happened when you were more connected with your intentions and/or when the context was one of confidence, appreciation, and self-reflection (such contexts are discussed in more depth in Chapter 6).

When applied to ourselves, this process makes visible the fact that most people experience their intentions and positive ways of being as being their true self. Our culture tends to support the concept that others' "true selves" are negative ones. This is especially the case when we are in a position of power and are evaluating others. There is often incongruence in how we determine who one's very own true self is versus who another's true self is (note that when people experience self-doubt, problems get them to think of their true self as the negative one). We would like to take these ideas a step farther and propose that even the concept of a true self is not accurate in that in reality people have many selves. What then becomes important is which self is preferred and what context is likely to bring this self forward.

In other words, every person can be seen as a reservoir of multiple ways of being. Context will often influence or determine which way of being becomes expressed, and this sometimes fosters the development of problems. This is particularly true if people attempt to be a way that doesn't fit for them or the context. Through helpful conversations, individuals can be invited to articulate what their preferred way of being is, how to access it more often, and how to shelter themselves from the context.

5. Summary: Write one line about a problem-saturated story and another about your preferred story:

Problem-saturated story:

_____

Preferred story:

_____

As you can imagine, you can write a story that presents all the people you know in quite a negative light or bring forth a perspective about their intentions, values, or effort that makes them knights in shining armor. Those multiple facets of people are always there. Sometimes people get trapped in the contexts of their lives and engage mostly in unhelpful actions, as in problem stories. Our goal in this book is to help you believe that the other version of this same person exists, find ways to support your compassion enough to create a context where this preferred educator may come forth, be his or her best, and contribute to your staff.

In general, it can be said that *perspective is the antidote to most problems*. Problems tend to narrow our views.[2] Understanding and gaining perspective makes visible many options that were initially in the shadow.

SUMMARY OF THE PRACTICE OF EXTERNALIZING AND RESTORYING

Summary of Basic Considerations in the Externalization of a Problem

Externalizing	Comments
A problem that is experienced as a feeling, behavior, or thought can be talked about as an external entity:	Make sure that you use people's words for describing their own experiences.

(Continued)

(Continued)

- Feelings: What did this "Anger" want you to do?
- Behavior: When "Blaming" happened, how did you feel inside?
- Thought: Is "Self-doubt" most likely to sneak into your mind at recess or in class?

If people focus on external events (e.g., another teacher), first thoroughly acknowledge the difficulties of the experience; then, when people are sufficiently heard, bring gently into the conversation the effect that this event might have had on them and what they might end up doing that they would rather not do.

Map the effects of the chosen externalization on all areas of life (feelings; thoughts; behaviors; identity; relationships with parents, teachers, and friends; hopes; dreams; activities; performances; sleeping; eating, etc.).

Make sure that you are in touch with people's experience and are not simply bombarding them with a redundant formulated effect question.

Statement of position: Invite individuals to reflect upon the effects and decide if they want to change the situation.

Leave yourself open to curiosity if, after reflection, people say they do not want to take a stand against the problem. Explore the costs and benefits (if any) of the problem and whether there are other ways to get the same benefits with less cost.

Unique outcomes: Notice and discuss the events and intentions that lay outside of the problem story, such as moments of success at functioning without the problem.

Preferred story: Link several moments of success together and explore the meaning of their increasing occurrence.

This simply becomes another map of effects, except that this time it is about the effects of the successes.

A Question From Educators: Will externalizing a problem remove a person's responsibility to deal with it?

Externalizing increases people's responsibility to deal with issues. Externalizing simply conveys to people that we see problems as not representative of who they can and may prefer to be. Externalizing sends a message of hope and support that allows people to articulate the effects of problems, develop an understanding of why they personally would want to change their connection to this problem, and notice their own capacity to be successfully different.

NOTES

1. The timing, sequencing, and appropriateness of these questions can be very variable depending on context (!!) and relationship. This conversation is reconstructed and abbreviated and is not meant to be taken as a recipe for difficult conversation but rather as one of many examples of helpful conversation.

2. For example, frustration often gets people to dwell on an upsetting event and be oblivious to the rest of the day and the bigger picture of the situation.

CHAPTER THREE

Typical School Culture Problems and Their Effects

I n this section we will explore the issues that contribute to common school culture problems. These problems are believed to result mostly from the context in which people and schools are embedded. For this reason, as elsewhere in the book, these problems will generally be externalized.

The most frequently mentioned problems[1] in school staff cultures, as well as their contributors and effects on school culture, will be covered. When staff cohesiveness is negatively impacted, nothing can really function at its best and everyone suffers, adults and children. This is clearly articulated by the following principal:

> *When teachers are not happy, then they don't work well together, the morale goes down, they're grumpy, and it shows in everything everybody does. The kids are affected. When teachers are not happy, they are rather dull and boring in front of a classroom.*

> —Elementary School Principal

Solutions and practices that can be used to avoid or solve these problems will be presented in Chapter 6.

GOSSIP

The Gossip habit recruits people into repeating information or rumors about someone, usually in a covert manner. It may provide a sense of power due to the telling and receiving of a secret, which can generate an experience of complicity and belonging. Remember the last time gossip reached your ears. How did it make you feel? Many people report that gossip gives them a sense of status and honor to be trusted and included in the exchange. This can be particularly appealing when people experience discontent and powerlessness in their general work situation. Gossip can be present to various degrees with different levels of effects. A contained gossip habit that is only occasional and has very little effect on the community is almost unavoidable in very large schools and districts. However, if it is constant and negatively impacts staff cohesiveness and trust, it can become dangerous.

Gossip About Teachers

Gossip is more likely to strike teachers when they have limited opportunities to bond and share openly meaningful aspects of their private life. It can also occur when distrust and criticism dominate a staff climate. If meaningful aspects of teachers' lives are not shared openly, the Gossip habit will make sure they are shared secretly. When the gossiping and judging habits occur, they ironically reduce the likelihood that people will share openly in the future. A vicious cycle of distrust, judgment, and secrecy is established between different subgroups of teachers. One educator commented,

I really hate it when I hear a teacher talk about people's personal lives in a way that makes you wonder what they say about you when you aren't there.

Gossip may also occasionally get a principal to repeat confidential information to trusted teachers. This is more likely to occur when principals feel isolated and have few out-of-school confidants with whom to process their concerns. Ironically, however, this gossip habit just fuels more isolation for the principals, as the staff, even the confidants, can become distrustful and ambivalent about sharing personal information, as revealed by the following teacher:

> *I love our principal—she has many, many strengths and is very respected by our staff and community. However, the one complaint I've had about her is that she can be loose-lipped and prone to gossip. I don't have a horror story, fortunately. I just feel that she often relays too much personal information to other confidants and me about fellow staff members and district people.*

Gossip can be the result of problem stories or can evolve into a powerful problem story so alienating that a teacher may feel that she has no option other than leaving.

> *I was in a situation that led to very horrible results. We had a principal for five years that was undermining staff members and causing people not to trust each other. She would pit one teacher against another. Even after she left, the results lingered. There was one teacher who was so mean to me and stayed that way, even after the climate changed under a new principal. I did try going to her to solve it, but, finally, I decided I couldn't take it anymore. I asked for a transfer to another school.*
>
> —First Grade Teacher

Gossip About Principals

Gossip gets teachers to spread stories about principals when a genuine relationship does not exist between the principal and the staff. From our research, it seems that this problem is more likely to occur when people are upset about or misunderstand an administrative decision, when differences of opinion dominate a situation, or when an "us-them" relationship with the administration has been established. For some people, a certain amount of gossip is understandable and acceptable because of the power differential of the principal and the limited personal contact between teachers and principal. As mentioned earlier, a small Gossip habit is often expected about isolated events or an occasional unpopular decision. Dangerous problems can grow, however, if Gossip contributes to the spreading of an elaborate problem story about the principal as a person. When a problem story like this develops, it can seriously interfere with the principal's credibility and the staff's cohesiveness. It also reduces the staff's willingness to follow the principal as a leader, explore novel educational experiences, and trust any invitations for change. The school community can become divided by this problem, polarized between those who believe in the problem identity and those who perceive their principal's actions in a different light (see Chapter 4 for the solving of such situations). The principal may also develop a problem story about the staff and may resort to gestures of power that may increase the distrust, as opposed to solving the misrepresentations. As discussed earlier, problem stories take on a life of their own when people notice only events that can justify or fit into a particular problem story.

In our research, a principal shared with us an unfortunate situation in which a staff member afflicted with a Gossip habit interpreted the principal's joy as being related to the resignation of a teacher, when in reality it was because of completely separate good news. This teacher then proceeded to spread the rumor that the principal was celebrating the departure of a fellow staff person. Fortunately, in this situation, the principal was able to pull the teacher out of class, explain the situation, and demand that the building gossip be clarified immediately.

At its worst, this problem can get staff to spend a lot of energy undermining principals. Meanwhile, principals spend a lot of energy defending and trying to prove themselves and, under pressure, may resort to decisions that may fuel the problem story. Sometimes attempts at solving the problem, whether by the use of power or by self-revelation, only further thicken the problem story.

When a Gossip habit is seriously spreading in a school, its general effects are to

- Reduce the likelihood of collaboration
- Increase isolation
- Create a judgmental and distrustful environment
- Generate misrepresentations and resentments

PROBLEM-SATURATED CONVERSATION

It really saddens me when I see fellow teachers treat students with disrespect. They yell and embarrass them in public and say negative comments. They usually just complain without trying to change the situation.

—Elementary School Teacher

It really gets to me when a teacher makes a judgment, has a negative attitude, and makes assumptions about my students before knowing ALL the facts.

—Elementary School Teacher

I only hear the complaints. For example, I had a teacher who stayed at school from 5–7 P.M. the night before Valentine's Day. This was so parents could come leave special valentines, which their child would receive in the morning. No parent came to acknowledge what a beautiful, over-the-top gesture this was! I only heard about it from the librarian.

—Elementary School Principal

Conversations between teacher and teacher, principal and teacher, parent and teacher, principal and parent, and parent and parent are predominantly based around problems. On school campuses, people discuss everything from budget problems to running out of paper to gossiping to discussing students' and parents' perceived problems. In the morning, a well-discussed session about how to deal with the outdated computer lab may occur. At recess, two teachers may touch base on the behavioral issues of a student. Often this is done in the public staff room with other teachers listening. A lunchtime discussion about union issues may involve many teachers. After school a teacher may have to call several parents about problems in the classroom, meet with the principal regarding a negative evaluation, and then journey back to the classroom to answer numerous e-mails and phone messages about student issues.

My first teaching job in Massachusetts was dominated by negative chatter. I felt I had to be enthusiastic and creative in secret. Eventually it wore me down to such a degree I (like it does the majority of them) even took up smoking cigarettes! Ugh!

—Elementary School Teacher

Even though the problem focus is present in many kinds of exchanges, it seems to particularly dominate in conversations about students. In that sense, Problem Talk about students has truly evolved into a school habit that leaves adults so comfortable talking about children in a negative way that it is done openly, with or without the student present. This habit may lure adults into a belief that they are connecting with each other on common ground (since everyone is familiar with that style of conversation).

Problem-saturated conversations particularly thrive in the staff room when teachers accumulate frustrations or become exhausted because of all the responsibilities and demands on their time. Teachers generally give a lot of thought and energy to their students and do not necessarily receive much appreciation from the community. Furthermore, there can be a sense that nothing is ever good enough, as you can always learn more, improve, or take care of someone's needs. Frustration can easily grow in that context and, coupled with the scarcity of time, create a perfect setting for Problem Talk.

Problem-saturated communications can become serious problems in schools. First, teachers suffer from a negative drain of energy. Not only is precious time spent receiving/giving negativity, but in the meantime teachers are not receiving refreshing positive energy. In addition, you never have a break from work if you talk about work during breaks. This focus on negativity can breed more negativity, as there is always something to be dissatisfied about. The whole atmosphere can become one of focusing on the glass being half empty. In such a context, only superficial connections can develop among teachers. If teachers spend much of their time dwelling on negative aspects of their work, there is no time left to discover each other's talents and uniqueness and to enrich their sense of community.

Second, Problem Talk may recruit teachers into speculating with each other about the cause of students' issues. This typically feeds the common problem story of parents or internal deficiencies as the "cause" of student problems and can seriously inhibit the precious collaboration between all the important parties in a student's life, which unfortunately thwarts a team effort to promote a child's well-being. We do not deny that family struggles have an effect on students, but rather we simply question the often quick assessment of parents as being "dysfunctional." It often seems a ready-made problem-saturated explanation for most problems.

Third, problem-saturated communication locks students into problem reputations or stories. Problem reputations limit student changes because people usually notice only problem events. Teachers also become locked into a static problem story that may blind them to student growth.

Unlike the Gossip habit, where individuals are fully conscious of engaging in a frowned-upon disrespectful exchange, problem-saturated conversations about kids are often unrestricted by social conventions. Why would bad-mouthing an adult be offensive and covert, while bad-mouthing students be commonplace and public? People may sometimes justify this type of conversation by assuming that it will help them deal better with the student later. The distinction between problem-saturated conversation and helpful consultations with colleagues, however, lies in the effects they generate. A professional consultation with a colleague is usually done privately, may include more objective, factual information about the situation, a description of the student as a whole person, and the teacher's inadvertent contributions to the problem. Such focused and honest conversations can be very valuable in generating ideas, especially if they remain respectful of the student. Problem-saturated conversations, however, are often one sided and focus mainly on the student, who is perceived as "the problem." While the teacher may feel some immediate relief through the mere sharing and talking about the problem, in the long run it often simply increases the problem reputation of the child (especially when it is done openly, in front of everyone). The increasingly negative focus on the child recruits more people into noticing and interpreting the child's behavior in a problem way and consequently punishing small incidents that would otherwise have been unnoticed or discounted. A problem story or perception of the child that is biased by the struggle and that makes preferred moments invisible generally increases students' unhappiness and frustration, which in turn contributes to more problem behavior.

CLIQUES

Cliques essentially develop in a context of differences. The staff may be too heterogeneous to understand each other, may not have enough time to process their differences, may carry unresolved conflicts, or may simply lack the opportunities to bridge and discover the values of differences in a safe way. Cliques can develop based on similarities, such as years of teaching experience, strict adherence to a specification, career goals, family orientation, religious affiliation, ethnic identity, race, educational philosophies, and more. Cliques offer a sense of familiarity, belonging, and exclusivity.

When I first joined my last district I felt like Goldilocks in The Three Bears. *The first group I sat with for lunch was "too hard." They were cynical, negative, and (though very friendly to me, at the time I perceived them as) quite cliquish. The second group was "too soft"—I thought each person was so uneducated I couldn't imagine how they managed to get a teaching degree. The third group was "just right" for me! We laughed, we gossiped, we complained, we shared ideas, personal stories, discussed politics, etcetera. I loved this group. I thought each person was smart, interesting, thoughtful, funny, and a good teacher. Sometimes we needed to "vent." We supported each other when any one of numerous aspects of teaching public school got us down. It lifted our spirits to spend lunchtime together, as I believe each teacher group lifted its members' spirits. Sometimes you need to feel you're not alone with your frustrations.*

—Elementary School Teacher

Everyone needs the support of close colleagues to share intimate aspects of life and lift their spirits. Cliques both overlap with and are distinct from friendships. The difference between close friendships and cliques is that membership in a clique often implies *disconnection* from the community. Specifically, Cliques may require that their members eat together (sometimes in a secluded place like a classroom), exclude nonmembers from socializing activities, and repeat unhelpful gossip about other members of the community. Cliques are often toxic to a school environment, as they prevent collaboration and the sharing of ideas.

Cliques thwart the richness of diversity, stifle creativity, and make it particularly hard for new teachers to feel welcome and to become contributing members of the team.

When I was new on a school campus, people didn't know who I was nor did they try to find out. I would look around at lunch for someone to eat with, but everyone was eating in their classrooms, either working alone during lunch or eating and chatting in small, impenetrable groups. By November, I was eating alone and contemplating moving to a new school!

—Fourth Grade Teacher

THE US-THEM ATTITUDE

Historically, unions were created to protect the rights of the worker. By the 21st century, the conditions of employees in most areas had greatly improved, due in part to the existence of unions. In fields such as education, where employees are typically overworked and underpaid, the presence of a union makes a lot of sense.

In certain districts, union representatives collaborate respectfully with administrators and simply do their work of protecting teachers' rights.

> *My experience is that the union is extremely helpful. They serve as an advocate for teachers on numerous levels. They defend teachers' rights to have a fair wage, good working conditions, and fair evaluations. I personally have never had experience with "a union going too far." I do know of a case where they offered support and advocated on behalf of a very ineffectual teacher who was on the brink of being fired. She had taught in the district for over 40 years. At one time she had been a wonderful teacher. Though I thought she was a bad teacher, I was glad the union was making sure she was being treated respectfully and fairly.*

—Retired Elementary School Teacher

Unfortunately, since negotiations have frequently been of an antagonistic nature, some union representatives have diverged from the position of protecting to one of fighting everything. In other words, what would normally be a side effect of negotiation (conflicting relationships with an employer) becomes a habit in and of itself, promoting an us-them attitude. This position erroneously promotes the idea that administrators are "enemies" who intend to take advantage of their staff. Moreover, the habit of fighting may represent the feelings of only a small group of teachers, leaving many others in the uncomfortable position of not agreeing with those supposedly there to represent them!

Union services are structured differently in different districts. In some districts, union leaders are simply teachers who chose to engage in this additional function. This may offer the advantage of the union representative knowing more about teachers on each school site. However, we can question the objectivity of representatives who are simultaneously part of a teaching staff. In many professions this corresponds to a dual-role relationship[2] and is considered unethical. In other districts, union leaders maintain their objectivity by not being attached to a particular school.

In our union, we have objective people who do not work on any school site, so they can help facilitate resolution. If two educators can't stand each other or don't see what the other sees, we have a conversation between all parties, list all options, and then take actions based on these actions. We have to get at the following: Is there trust? Is there belief in each other's moral and ethical compass? Are our beliefs set in the same core values? If the answers are yes, they can return to a productive working situation knowing that our decision was principled. If it's principled, we know that we can move on. If it's not principled, we may not be able to recover.

—Elementary School Educator

In some districts, adversarial union representation has created a philosophy of disconnection between principal and staff: an "Us-Them" Attitude. People in individualistic cultures tend to blame an individual for problems rather than exploring the broader context in which these problems occur. As a result, the Us-Them Attitude can often target principals and promote a belief that they are ultimately responsible for the dissatisfaction and frustration. Although this is occasionally the case when principals are experienced as micromanaging or as making too many decisions on their own, in reality most principals are also paralyzed in the very same oppressive system. Principals are overworked, isolated, have a limited support system, and rarely any job protection. Yet that is often invisible to staff members.

Sadly, in these situations, everyone loses. Many principals want to collaborate with their staff to minimize workloads. At its worst, the Us-Them attitude divides educators between those who focus on education and children's well-being and those who spend a lot of energy criticizing principals and programs. It polarizes the staff between those who are Pro-principal and Anti-principal, which leads to a very distorted view of who the principal actually is as a person. This process can once again create a vicious cycle where the staff distrusts principals, who are constantly walking on eggshells and defending themselves.

> I've developed collaboration with my staff, but, given what's going on in the district, I feel I'm constantly walking on eggs. So far, I am proud to say that I am grievance free, and I really hope it can stay that way.
>
> —Middle School Principal

Sadly, the Us-Them Attitude recruits educators into investing time and energy in conflicts and suspicions instead of focusing on exciting educational practices and professional growth. Ironically, this can require more work, time, and energy than simply compromising on the original issue.

> It would be so easy if people could be a little more rational. If we could look at it and say, "This is where you are and this is where they are. There's no way you are going to settle, so why don't you just meet in the middle, instead of sitting there and throw-ing ugly words at each other for the next three months?"
>
> —First Grade Teacher and Union Representative

RESENTMENT AND NEGATIVITY

We have visited several schools where some educators struggled with Resentment and Negativity. Often, these educators had once given much of their time and energy to their profession and had become unhappy with the constant pressures to do too much and the large number of responsibilities. As a result, Resentment now pushed these teachers away from their preferred selves and would typically get them, for example, to make sarcastic remarks, roll their eyes, or comment negatively in response to others' suggestions. Occasionally, a new teacher struggled with Resentment and Negativity, but most of the time this unhappiness afflicted veteran teachers who had experienced burnout in the profession.

> *I'm very discouraged now. When I was younger, I didn't understand what the older teachers were complaining about! I had a million other things I wanted to do. I thought [abiding by the contract] was stupid. It seemed fine to me. I can say in hindsight that gradually teachers are doing more and more and more and more for free. They are not valued, not respected, not paid. I think you need to build that awareness in the teachers themselves. The truth is, when you get older you get responsibilities, and then you come to realize how your rights had been eroded.*
>
> —Third Grade Teacher

Let us insist on the fact that not all veteran teachers struggle with Resentment and Negativity and, again, that when they are, it is usually as a result of the broader and subcultural pressures they've experienced over many years. Resentment and Negativity clearly don't fit with anyone's preferred self. In fact, the presence of veteran teachers in many schools had a variety of constructive implications. In the new era of increased workload, veterans often become spokespersons for protecting the rights of teachers. They have historical experience with which they can compare current work demands to expectations of five, 10, or 20 years ago. They have lived and witnessed the horrendous increase in the curriculum and responsibility of the teacher. A teacher shared with us that 30 years ago he used to have dinner with students' families and spend more time being involved in arts and afterschool activities with his students. In the past 30 years he has seen the curriculum for fifth grade doubled with no material being removed from it. He speaks:

> There is a lot more filling out of forms, more red tape than ever. You have to track the students all year with assessments. We didn't have all of this documentation when I first started. Each season something is being added on and nothing is being taken away. The curriculum is getting bigger and bigger and nothing is being taken away. It does take away from the joy of teaching.

Teachers with such extensive experience can often speak out for the rest of the staff. They know the new demands are unreasonable, and their voices are often heard and respected. In fact, younger teachers who may disagree with or resent some of the administration's demands may not feel that they have the power to speak up and will often count on veterans to do so.

Of course, not all veterans speak out or do so in a public manner. Some veterans may be rather quiet and may prefer one-on-one private communications. Others may be more involved in the mentoring of new teachers rather than being political participants.

> Glen Kamoto was a powerful force on campus. He led by example. The legacy of the number of people he's made better will live forever. He would spend hours giving you things, explaining and doing anything for you, but, maybe because of his [heritage], he wouldn't speak up in staff meetings or tell you what to do. He was a role model by his generosity and who he was. I feel honored to have known him.

—Middle School Principal

The distinction between the strong voice that protects and represents teachers' rights versus the one that is experienced as Negative and Resentful lies in the effect it has on others. Resentment and Negativity became a problem in certain schools when their main effects were to undermine others. In those situations, the majority of teachers felt oppressed by the Resentment in the following two ways:

The first problem occurred when Negativity was expressed directly to others as criticism and judgments of their opinions. In those situations staff gatherings became unsafe and less productive. Many teachers in those schools shared how they refrained from contributing creative ideas or expressing their opinions for fear of receiving a sarcastic comment. As one teacher explained, "I wish some teachers thought before they spoke at staff meeting. Everyone should feel safe to share an idea without getting 'shot down' abruptly." This also created a culture of disconnection and distrust. An impoverishment of staff discussions ensued, with a narrowing down of ideas and possible solutions.

The second problem surfaced when the Negativity led to protests against any new or creative attempts to improve or modify traditional practices. A teacher in just such a school shared this with us:

We have a couple of teachers who talk about what they do, without a give-and-take attitude, and who always imply that their way is the only way. It really upsets me and undercuts my own ideas.

In those schools, a significant majority of the staff as well as the principals had become resentful because of the limitations imposed by the Negativity-afflicted teachers, but no actions could be taken because of political seniority and threats of union involvement.

In the schools with those two particular problems, the staff had become completely divided by Negativity and Cliques. In one school, Negativity and Cliques were so powerful that they had some teachers believing that the right to speak came only with experience, and, according to our surveys, new teachers were given surprisingly harsh advice:

Do You Have Advice for New Teachers?

- "Keep your mouth shut and listen to the old-timers"
- "No one wants to hear from a person right out of college who thinks they know it all"
- "Get to know the old-timers and discover why they believe the way they do"
- "Listen and respect experienced teachers—even if they 'know it all'"
- "Don't come off as having all the ideas and don't be too forward"
- "Remember the teachers have been here a while and are used to the way things are"

On average, 32% gave that advice directly. This school had a very small but powerful handful of experienced teachers afflicted with vocal Negativity. It was saddening to see the impression a few people had made on the whole staff. We were left pondering several questions: What is it that keeps certain experienced teachers enthusiastic about their work despite the pressure of specifications and the oppression of the system? How can veterans be honored and appreciated for their experience without putting down the excitement of new teachers? How can schools prevent new teachers' enthusiasm and creativity from being transformed into Negativity after surviving the challenges of the system and its unrealistic pressures? Once Negativity is present, how can a community regroup and reclaim a sense of cohesiveness and excitement for their schools? (See Chapters 4, 5, and 6 for the prevention and resolution of issues similar to these problems.)

COMMUNITY DISRESPECT

Many educators we have spoken to feel quite bitter about the disrespect they have experienced from the community and found it difficult to understand, given the amount of work and care they give in general. A broader analysis of the situation may reveal several factors that can contribute to Community Disrespect. First, when problems arise in schools, the media are very quick to blame and scrutinize teachers. Teachers are visible as workers and stand at the front of the line. Their lower status in the structure of schools and their vulnerability make them easy to blame. Teachers lack the authority that was historically granted by the church and is contemporarily granted by income. Unfortunately, the less authority to validate your voice, the less respect is granted.

Second, in our current time, causality of problems is often simplified and linked to the actions of single individuals. In the fast pace of our lives, it is often tempting to forget that multiple factors contribute to problems and that it is easy to blame whoever is present at the time of the problem.

This simplified perspective can often blame bystanders or people who experienced limited power over a situation.

Third, given that most people have spent a great deal of time in schools, everyone has experiences and ideas about how schools should and shouldn't be. Based on their school attendance as young people, some parents (or reporters) with little knowledge of the actual context may nevertheless feel entitled to make judgments about school programs and personnel. This may lead to educators feeling disrespected because this makes their intentions, efforts, and the complexity of the situation invisible.

Finally, given the unrealistically high expectations and demands placed on teachers, they can only fail, at least in one area. Teachers would have to be superhuman to address all the students' needs, the curriculum, the committee meetings, and balance their own personal lives. Given that teachers cannot succeed with all the pressures placed on them, they are always vulnerable to disrespect, especially from an observer who is unaware of the bigger picture of a teacher's life.

In sum, then, Community Disrespect can be understood as arising from society's general dissatisfaction with the current public educational system and from a problem story of teachers. When teachers feel misrepresented by the media and put down by certain parents (under the influence of this problem story), they become resentful and frustrated toward their profession and sometimes try even harder to fulfill the impossible pressures discuss in Chapter 1. Community Disrespect can unfortunately get teachers to do more to prove their expertise, become more drained from over giving, and, in some situations, develop antagonistic attitudes toward parents.

Interestingly, this problem is less common in many underprivileged and multiethnic communities where families are often grateful for educators' assistance and are less influenced by a problem story.

I am happy to say that I have always felt extremely respected from my school's community. We (my husband and I) teach in a very ethnically diverse community that includes many immigrant families and many lower-income families. We have found them to be extremely supportive—I have gotten no complaints or negativity from my students' families, and they have always demonstrated being extremely grateful for the work I do. The disrespect that I have really been feeling is the lack of respect from the government and the public at large.

—First Grade Teacher

One reason for this can be that in many countries of the world, teachers are regarded with respect as the wise and educated ones in the community. This seems particularly true of cultures less dominated by capitalism (where financial gain in general and "scoring" in the workplace determine your status).

THE RUSHED FEELING AND SCARCITY OF TIME

John Merrow discusses in his book *Choosing Excellence* that teachers are feeling "rushed, crunched and isolated." Educators report that they are constantly running on borrowed time. The Rushed Feeling is a problem that pushes people to act based on speed as opposed to based on their values or better judgment.

A teacher who knew our interest in this subject once volunteered to give us a list of all of the activities she completed in one school day, in addition to the time spent teaching. She was amazed, herself, at the number of things she had to accomplish in a day, not to mention what she accomplished in a 20-minute slot of time (recess) that was supposed to be a "break." Most teachers, despite being well aware of how hard they do work, may be amazed to see a list of all the things they accomplish before school, during breaks, and after school. Statistics have shown that the actual completion of all the school standards would require thousands of additional hours.

Although it would require approximately 15,000 hours to cover the standards and benchmarks currently set forth, there are only 9,000 hours of instruction time available from kindergarten through grade 12. (Marzano & Kendall, 1998)

Many factors contribute to the Rushed Feeling:

- Unrealistic curriculum
- Large number of students
- Little support
- Great needs of families
- Diversity of the job with a great variety of requirements
- High expectations from administration and community
- Excessive amount of responsibility placed on one person

As discussed in Chapter 1 of this book, the messages are "Do more, more, more," "Do little extras constantly," and "It's never enough."

One morning I had a maintenance worker having a heart attack in the parking lot, fire trucks here, and a middle school was visiting with a presentation for the fifth graders. I ended the school day with the afterschool care group giving me a gun that one of the kids had passed to another kid on campus. I then had to deal with a police report, and, finally, the district office wanted me to come to a planning meeting for next year . . .

—Elementary School Principal

The Rushed Feeling is not without costs. It gets teachers and principals to sacrifice their own needs; experience guilt, frustration, and resentment; and be drained of energy to the point of facing professional burnout. As discussed earlier, this kind of stress contributes to a high teacher dropout rate of 30% during the first five years of teaching (Merrow, 2001).

The Rushed Feeling also can reduce the quality of education students are receiving. Learning is reduced to its measured outcome, such as standardized test scores. In the process, many important lessons of life are overlooked and relationships remain superficial, as illustrated in the following story.

> *I was on yard duty. I observed a child leaving her food wrapper on the ground as she left the bench to play. I stopped her and asked her to pick it up and then to pick up ten more pieces of litter because of her negligence. This interaction took less than two minutes and took no real compassion on my part. Later in the day, as I thought about how she walked away sadly, I realized my problem: I am at such a loss for time as a teacher, I feel like I have no time to discuss whether the child would prefer a clean yard over a messy one.*
>
> —Fourth Grade Teacher

This story also illustrates an effect on school culture: Educators under the influence of the Rushed Feeling are using time-efficient ways to solve problems. They attempt to control problems quickly, even if they would prefer facilitating a discussion with children and solving problems more democratically. What often seems to be a quick response to a problem may backfire. In a context where issues cannot be processed and discussed, the common adult decision of punishing, removing an object, or banning a game does not solve a problem, it creates another one. Ultimately, children will not learn to reflect on their actions or how to relate differently and will continue to engage in the behavior in other areas. What is thought to be the most efficient is in the long run less efficient and can contribute further to the Rushed Feeling and teachers having to deal repetitively with similar issues.

Finally, the Rushed Feeling may also get teachers to fall into a survival mode where they are just trying to get things done and keep their heads above water. It can decrease the likelihood of teachers being excited and interested in others' educational successes.

HIERARCHY

Schools are typically organized in a hierarchical fashion, where one person, the principal, governs a group of staff. In turn, teachers are expected to have control over students. Of course, this particular hierarchy is embedded in a much larger one, where the principal reports to the district office, which, in turn, reports to the county and state.

One of the reasons for maintaining this hierarchy is that it is assumed to be more efficient. From a capitalistic perspective, work is more efficient when each worker has a specialized role and the decision-making process is in the hands of only a few. It is certainly faster for one person to make a decision and impose it on others than to take the time to gather input from a group and come to a consensus. Yet we can wonder about the quality and relevance of the decisions made by distant authority figures, as well as people's actual commitment to follow these decisions.

Superintendents have the power to set the tone of staff relationships throughout the district. In our interviews, they reported working hard to develop a context of trust, respect, and democratic exchanges. Despite most superintendents' best intentions, we have come across principals in certain districts who felt the principal's voice would not be heard at the district level.

When principals lead mainly in a hierarchical way, they risk becoming disconnected from the realities of their teachers, making unreasonable decisions, and losing the cooperation, trust, and respect of their staff.

The principal in our school made a big mistake: he asked nonchalantly about everyone's opinion about something, then proceeded to do whatever he wanted without regard for what was expressed. People never forgave him . . . it's ugly sometimes.

—Middle School Teacher

Finally, hierarchy can also lead to responsibilities being shared unequally and ineffectively. In hierarchical situations, people can easily fall into the trap of always expecting the leader to solve problems as opposed to themselves (as mentioned in Chapter 1). A good example of this problem is in teachers' referral of students to the office when a problem arises in the classroom or on the playground. Unfortunately, principals are often removed from situations and may have less information, tools, time, and flexibility of options to solve these problems in the best manner. Teachers develop the habit of simply referring students to a higher level of authority rather than working out the situation, which leads to principals becoming stuck in an endless disciplinary role and teachers losing the respect of students (solutions to this example will be discussed in Chapter 5).

Of course, at times administrators need to make decisions and be accountable for them. It is a difficult balance to maintain, and people in power should never lose sight of the following questions:

If you have power and authority, does that mean you should use it? How do *you* think administrators should draw the line between decisions made in a unilateral way and decisions made in a democratic way? Can you think of decisions made in your school where it was helpful or unhelpful to involve the staff? What was the difference between the two situations? How can administrators ensure that everyone's voice is heard and valued?

COMPETITION

Competition in and of itself is not a bad stance. Its extreme presence in all aspects of education, however, is questionable, as well as the ways in which it is promoted and what is left out. Competition is a cornerstone of capitalism. The assumption is that Competition will increase motivation and performance and will generate the best possible outcome. Although Competition may sometimes have these results, it is not without cost. Competition honors one "winner" and makes the large number of "losers" invisible. From this perspective, then, the number of negative effects can significantly outweigh the positive effects on one "winner." Competition can get teachers to experience resentment, jealousy, discouragement, a sense of inadequacy, and working in isolation with their own ideas as opposed to collaborating. Competition certainly stifles the creativity and sharing that comes with genuine collaboration. When competition dominates a community, it can easily become a problem. This is particularly true in three situations:

- If Competition gets individuals to greatly desire winning or obtaining recognition—in other words, if the prize is highly desirable and the end justifies the mean;
- If Competition is the only or most obvious process by which one can receive appreciation or recognition;
- If individuals are vulnerable to Competition either because of evaluation, self-doubt, overgiving, under-receiving, or a dissatisfying situation.

The following are three of many situations that promote Competition among teachers.

First is the "Teacher of the Year" award, where one teacher gains public appreciation and may get a free dinner. Some teachers greatly appreciate that opportunity and thoroughly understand why one of their colleagues was chosen. Many others, however, wonder how this happened (most teachers work so devotedly). Given that one person wins and countless others don't, we can argue that this process doesn't have the intended effect of promoting appreciation or motivation. In many ways, we can question the validity of the process, its relevance and meaning. In our research, it became clear that most teachers do not begin the school year by stating, "I will work hard this year to get the Teacher of the Year award." Most teachers work hard for other reasons. Near the end of the year, they are asked to evaluate each other's performance and make recommendations for this honor without necessarily being aware of the scope of their colleagues' efforts, achievements, and even how appreciated they are by the students.

> *Teaching occurs behind closed doors. Some teachers are heroes, others are dangerous. The disparity in skill between teachers within the same district, school, department (etc.) is staggering. I was a very good teacher. Not great, but very good. I also had moments where I was a bad teacher. It is hard to be a fantastic teacher day after day. Some of my colleagues were phenomenal teachers—mentors to me and heroes to the students. I rejoiced when they received public recognition. During my six years of teaching, all teachers who received public recognition for their talent deserved it (and more). My district didn't use the term "teacher of the year." In fact we had no internal competition. Great teachers became "mentor teachers." No one could deny that these individuals were extremely talented. Awards for amazing skill in teaching came from outside the district; I imagine this helped in terms of potential jealousy. Personally, if teachers stand out as particularly skillful and talented I am delighted to celebrate with them in their public recognition. However, "teacher of the year" is a bad term because it is competitive and exclusive.*

> —Elementary School Teacher

"Bar Raising" is another example of a problem that is subtly invading teachers' relationships with each other. It occurs when teachers who feel dedicated and committed to teaching have decided that they are willing to take on extra responsibilities for the benefit of the school. Other teachers are not willing to do this for personal reasons or because of investment in other areas. The process of Bar Raising inadvertently indicates to the administration that extra work can be completed without compensation. Unless used with caution, these added activities could soon become part of the norm at the school or district level. Bar Raising can also occur with the hiring of new teachers who may be unaware of the historical work expectations at a school site. They may either be influenced by the administration to do more or may find themselves matching the level of performance of Bar-Raising teachers.

I'm pretty new to this school, and, to be honest, worried about myself and my career. There's a bunch of teachers here who work so many extra hours overtime on committees and such without compensation. They are definitely on the career track. I work hard too and love my job, but I have outside commitments that fulfill me, like my dance classes, my volunteer positions, and trying to start a family. I am worried that, compared to them, my commitment level and reputation is going to pale in comparison.

—Second Grade Teacher

The third example pertains to standardized testing. In certain schools, Competition pits teachers against each other, even if it goes against their preferences and personal values.

The thing I think that is not good [about standardized testing] is that I really found myself wanting to know how all the other teachers at my grade level did compared to me. I start to get into "I did this and that, they did this and that." We knew how we did as a grade level and I knew how my class did, but I found myself wanting to know, "Did I do better than (Sandy)? Did (Mary) do better than I?" How awful! I think that's unhealthy to be competitive like that.

—Fifth Grade Teacher

These three situations are simply examples and do not constitute an exhaustive list of the ways in which Competition insidiously affects teachers' relationships. Competition can also recruit teachers to compete for principal attention, parental respect, career gains, student appreciation, status, and popularity, among other things. Competition can get a whole staff to compete with other schools for district approval, grants, status, popularity, and student enrollment. Competition renders visible only that which is the focus of the competition. In that process many other important issues can become overlooked. For example, at a glance, Competition can give a bad impression of the lowest performing or lowest socioeconomic school in the area. The school can even be perceived as the black sheep of the district. Yet, who is to say that the work of educators assisting poverty-stricken, malnourished students to achieve C's is less worthy of recognition than the work of educators who help privileged students to maintain A's? When broader contextual perspectives are taken into account, comparison of and competition between performances often become nonsense.

How can these problems be addressed?

In the next chapters we will explore how to solve these issues once they are undermining a staff, how to invite staff to change these habits in constructive ways, and how to create contexts that will prevent the development of these problems.

NOTES

1. Problems are named and described based on the experiences of the educators in the research and not necessarily based on the best possible externalization.

2. A dual-role relationship refers to a situation where a person's roles may have conflicting demands. For example we have witnessed situations where teachers' union representatives had conflicts with the principal of their schools. Their personal relationship with their principal, as teachers, prevented an objective and neutral role of negotiator with their colleagues' dilemmas.

CHAPTER FOUR

When Serious Problems Divide the Staff

School culture issues involving a dominant problem story about principals are always serious since no one then has the leadership or respect of others to facilitate a problem-solving process. Changing such a school environment is certainly not an easy or simple task. Following the narrative approach, one must first gather the participation of all the staff, or, at the minimum, a great majority of the staff. People may not agree on many specific issues and may have developed serious antagonistic relationships, but everyone may agree that the climate is painful and that something has to be done.

If the group can be moved away from its focus on specific individuals to focusing on a joint problem, then a lot can be accomplished. In many schools this requires the involvement of a neutral third party who can act as a professional mediator, gather the trust and respect of everyone, and explore possible territories of resolution. If the budget allows enough time for this mediator, individual meetings with each staff member can be very useful; otherwise a carefully crafted questionnaire may provide the minimum information necessary.

Problems cannot be swept under a carpet and expected to disappear. An anonymous educator shared with us that her principal was not a "touchy, feely kind of a person" and had consequently avoided needed processing sessions with the staff. Over the years, this resulted in an ever-increasing disintegration of the staff and the departure of committed teachers. Any unaddressed issue will undermine the whole culture of the school, teachers' job satisfaction, educational improvement, and, in the end, will result in the most enthusiastic staff leaving.

For this reason we will explore in more depth the development of severely divisive staff problems and ideas to address them.

THE SCENARIO

Elaine Schaffer is the new principal at Jefferson Elementary School. She is taking the place of a much-appreciated colleague who is retiring after a 15-year principalship at Jefferson. Elaine is enthusiastic, committed, and thoughtful. She has been generally well received by the staff, which is mostly pleased with her efforts to get to know them and the families that Jefferson serves. Elaine is quite busy but feels proud of doing things well. She has built connections, promoted academic growth, and observed the running of the school to better understand how Jefferson Elementary ticks. She is known for being everything to everyone at all times. Elaine's first year is celebrated as a success by the district office and the community. She has developed confidence in her abilities to lead the school community, and the district notices that she has done everything by the book.

The second year, Elaine returns with her big heart and her usual enthusiasm. Because of her commitment to education, she has spent the summer reading and attending conferences. She has been exposed to the value of community-building curriculum, mixed-age classes, and cross-age activities. She is considering moving the school in the direction of this philosophy and would like the opinion of the staff. At the first staff development day, everyone arrives filled with the excitement of a new school year. Teachers are filled with the buzz of starting fresh, getting their rooms ready, and being reunited with colleagues. Elaine hands out material to read about multiage classes, student-led conferences, and community meetings. She announces her interest in improving the school's educational stance and her desire for the school to catch up with the latest developments in education. She understands that the staff are quite busy so she requests that they review the material and be ready to discuss it at the staff meeting in two weeks.

After placing a gentle reminder to review the materials in each staff member's mailbox, Elaine is visited by Terry, the most outspoken teacher on the staff. Elaine welcomes her and is surprised by Terry's objections to both the reading assignment and the consideration of a major philosophical change on campus. Terry states, "Why fix something that isn't broken? We are all happy with how things are here." Elaine's response is, "It seems to me that everyone in this school wants to provide the best possible education for our students. I hear your concern, but let's just wait and give the staff a chance to discuss it."

As soon as the meeting is over, Terry walks to Room 15, where she knows many of her grade-level team are congregated. She grumbles to her colleagues about her meeting with Elaine, whom she feels doesn't understand, and how she is mad that Elaine is asking so much in the beginning of the year. Some teachers respond, agreeing that it does sound like a lot for a principal to ask, to read pages of information while they are busy beginning the year, assessing new students, and planning their year. Two other teachers quietly state that they are somewhat intrigued by the changes that could be possible with this new philosophy and while it is a lot of work, they are willing to give it a try.

A week later, Elaine gathers the staff to discuss the reading. She soon discovers a group that is interested in implementing change, a smaller group that is vocally against it with loud Negative voices, and a group that remains silent. After some discussion, Elaine makes an announcement: "Since the majority of those who have voiced an opinion are interested in these ideas and since this is heavily supported by research, let's go forward and give it a try."

In the subsequent weeks, gossip and cliques slowly develop. The staff becomes divided. The union representative schedules a lunchtime meeting to discuss the contract as it applies to the planned changes. As Elaine is becoming increasingly aware that some staff members are rejecting her leadership, she receives a phone call from the superintendent, who is concerned about developments he has overheard about her school.

In response to this situation, Elaine becomes visibly worried. As a result, she becomes more rigid, controlling, and edgy with both teachers and students. Several months later, as things are getting worse and worse, she realizes that she needs assistance and she calls you. How would you go about helping Elaine revitalize her school culture?

APPLYING A NARRATIVE METAPHOR

There could be many ways of addressing the problems faced by the staff at Jefferson School. However, if you intended using the narrative metaphor presented in this book, you would:

1. Find ways of understanding the experience of everyone involved

2. Externalize the problems that accurately represent the experience of each party and map their effects

3. Conceptualize a problematic pattern of interaction

4. Restory and bring forth preferred ways of being for everyone

Understand the Experience of Everyone Involved

Individual staff members need to feel heard, understood, and that their opinion is important. As discussed earlier, individuals' experiences could be gathered either by hiring a neutral third party to briefly interview each person, or, given that cost is often an issue, by giving out a carefully crafted survey.

In this particular context, examples of useful narrative questions are:

- How would you characterize your current school culture? Would you call it a climate of Tension, Distrust, Antagonism, or _____?
- How have you personally been affected by this climate? What does it get you to do, think, and feel that is different from your usual self?
- What have you personally tried to change this problem?
- What do you end up doing to shelter yourself from this problem?
- How has it affected your relationship with your administrator(s)? With your colleagues?
- What are the losses that you currently experience and foresee for the future if this is not addressed?
- Would you be willing to contribute to a movement of improvement? What is the most important reason (for you personally) to change this climate?
- If you were to put aside the laws of budget and reality, would you have any ideas about what could be done?
- What does change mean to you as an educator?

A more thorough and specific survey of the unique situation of the consulting school should be carefully created. All involved should provide information, including administrators and counselors, in an anonymous and confidential way. Once the results are compiled, the staff can be invited into a series of discussions of the results and their implications, with brief handouts being provided as integrated summaries to foster reflection.

Externalize the Problems

Computing the percentages of people experiencing similar negative effects can offer several benefits. First, it moves staff members from a place of alienation and isolation to one of a *shared* experience of discontent. If everyone is unhappy about

Criticism, for example, then everyone can be mobilized to take a stance against It (as opposed to against each other). As slight as this might seem, this shared experience provides a common ground for mobilizing change. Second, an increased awareness of the problem and its effects as well as a clearly articulated conceptualization of the externalized problem can often move the group to another level of processing. If the problem becomes externalized, then participants shift from a position of attacking, defending, or avoiding to one of greater reflexivity and openness to exploration. Third, the new, externalized definition of the problem creates a much larger space for solutions. When people are divided against each other, the focus often becomes which party will succeed at defeating or marginalizing the other. The new perspective offers a much greater number of options for coexistence. In the end, two people may still dislike each other but will perhaps be able to function better and, at the very least, have less of a negative impact on the whole staff.

In our scenario at Jefferson, a survey of the staff revealed that the biggest common problem discussed by most of the staff was the negative and divisive climate dominating their staff. By the time assistance was sought, the issue of change versus no change had almost become secondary. The division rendered everyone distrustful in general. A meeting was scheduled to talk specifically and openly about Distrust (externalization) and its effects on everyone. Given the nature of the problem and its silencing effect, the early phases of this process had to be facilitated with patience and compassion. Several staff members courageously began to share their grief and longing for lightheartedness and more collaboration. The staff was asked what Distrust had taken away from their school. Many commented on the absence of spirit and enthusiasm, the dwindling of collaboration and mentorship, fewer social gatherings, and less commitment. One teacher commented shyly that the most obvious indicator of the staff's mood was the absence of chocolates and other treats in the staff room. She reminded others of the former state of the staff room where people talked, laughed, shared, and ate sweets together. When asked where Distrust was leading the school, many thought they were heading for burnout and frankly were looking for other job opportunities. They were also worried about the reputation of their school. In the end, most candidly acknowledged that Distrust had the following important effects:

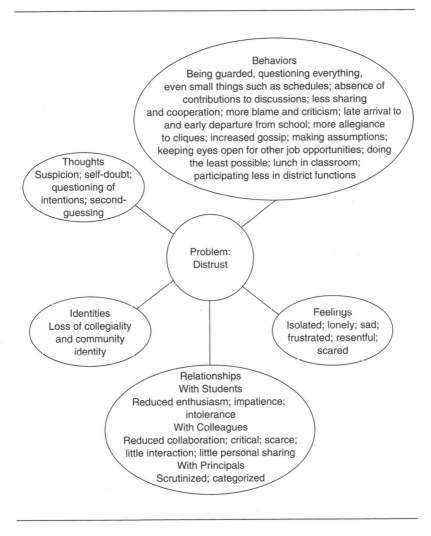

Conceptualize a Pattern of Interaction

You may be wondering . . . how did Elaine respond to these developments? While Distrust had all the effects discussed above on the staff, it also had effects on the principal. In response to the problem situation, Elaine became increasingly defensive. She had always dreamed of being a leader who earned respect rather than demanded it, and she grieved the loss of that identity. She found herself being less collaborative and more secretive about decisions than she preferred, but felt she had no choice. She was losing sleep and gaining weight. She found herself dressing in more conventional suits to assert her professional status and disprove the reputation of her being an unrealistic idealist. She felt trapped and isolated in her role. In an attempt to reduce her isolation she developed closer relationships with certain staff members, which also gave her a reputation of playing favorites.

In the end, Defensiveness pushed Elaine away from her preferred self and into the following ways of being:

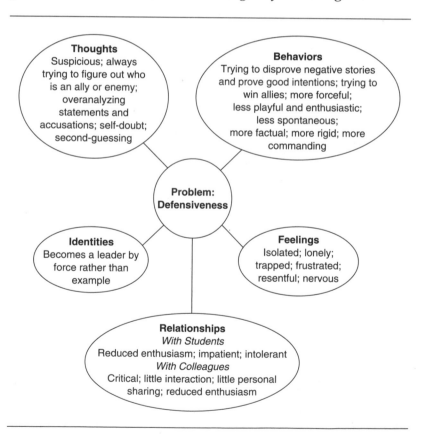

The more Elaine was under the influence of Defensiveness, the more the staff became distrustful, disconnected, and unresponsive. Elaine started perceiving the staff as unwilling, negative, and uncooperative, while the staff developed a story of Elaine as being forceful and smug. In this process, everyone started noticing little behaviors that confirmed each of their problem-saturated stories.

The only way vicious cycles of interactions can be broken is when both parties become keenly aware of their contributions to the pattern and very articulate about how the externalized problem pushes them into acting against their better judgment (their preferred versions of themselves). Everyone was invited to notice for themselves times when Distrust or Defensiveness might infiltrate their brain and influence their decision to engage or not to engage in a certain way of being.

As everyone became more articulate and increasingly aware of each moment in the day when they were making decisions based on Distrust or Defensiveness rather than on their preferred self, they began to gain a little more power over their own contribution to the climate. The facilitator eventually engaged the staff in the sharing and discussion of the times when they could have chosen to operate under the influence of Distrust or the problem stories, but instead consciously chose not to. While this exercise was challenging early on, people progressively noticed that they had actually sheltered some interactions from Distrust or problem interactions. In other words, Distrust or Defensiveness was not necessarily there 100% of the time. Even though it was there a lot of the time, some small instances of collaboration and connection were still cherished. One teacher, Juliet, shared her happiness at still being able to meet with two colleagues for planning meetings that she said were lighthearted, friendly, and completely cooperative. The facilitator became intrigued by Juliet's experiences and attempted to articulate and bring forth the ingredients of those preferred interactions. Juliet pondered for a moment and then shared how they had formed a friendship based on sharing and connecting ever since bonding on a long bus ride home after a field trip. She continued that she knew for a fact that these colleagues had very similar educational philosophies and shared common goals.

Although it is commonly useful to invite a staff to explore their joint philosophy as a group, it is always preferable to have the usefulness of this activity presented by the staff themselves, rather than having it forced upon them by a facilitator or a leader, especially given the history of the problem.

The staff was then asked what effect it would have on Distrust if their goals and philosophies were made visible. As most people recognized that knowledge about others would probably assist in reducing Distrust, another meeting was scheduled to try to explore each other's vision as educators. In our experience, staff that have had the opportunity to discuss, explore, and articulate a common vision that is truly inclusive of everyone's ideas is the best starting place in any transition. In the end, most educators will agree that they want what is best for kids even if the ways in which this is done can include some nuances (see the last section of this chapter for more).

This meeting proved to be very fruitful as it became visible that despite Cliques, Distrust, and Negativity, most valued their relationship with students, quality education, school as a community, and personal growth. However, they were clear that they didn't want growth to be forced, as they already felt overextended and needed time to read and think about newly presented ideas. Distrust had created a context in which they feared being forced toward change. They hadn't taken the time to explore whether or not they would welcome change. In other words, when anticipating force, most people automatically prepare to counter that force. The process always takes precedence over consideration of the nature of change.

Making Visible Intentions, Values, and Preferred Identities

The discussion of the staff's vision was followed by an invitation to make visible the principal's vision and leadership dreams. This can be done effectively by interviewing the principal in front of the whole staff. For this to be meaningful, principals have to trust their interviewers and feel confident that the conversation will make visible their preferred ways of being. The interview can assist both the principal and the staff to realize that the intentions were originally compassionate and well meaning, even though the method and effects may have been overly negative.

With that in mind, Elaine was interviewed and asked the following questions:

- What were your hopes and dreams when you decided to become an educator?
- Was there an educator who was particularly inspiring to you? What was it about this person that you admired?
- What was it like for you as a teacher? What is your fondest memory? What was your biggest struggle?
- What was your vision when you decided to be an administrator?
- What are you proud of having accomplished with your staff at your previous school?
- What did you most appreciate about this staff at Jefferson when you first arrived?
- Is there a particular moment that you remember experiencing with this staff that made you think highly of them?
- I know from our personal conversations that you are committed to respecting your staff and leading in a democratic way. Even though it may not always have worked that way, what were your intentions in balancing your role as an administrator with the desires of your staff? Do you recall an instance where you were able to put thought into making it happen?
- The staff have discussed that Change means a lot of work for them. What does Change mean to you?
- The staff have commented that Distrust has taken away their sense of community and enthusiasm. What has the Distrust cycle taken away from you?

- You and your staff have been through quite a bit of suffering. What is it that keeps you coming back each day? How is it that you haven't given up on this school?
- Is there anything that I haven't asked you that you would like to make visible at this point? (See Resource B for a more thorough interview.)

After such conversation, everyone is usually more open and receptive to new perceptions (stories) of each other. In this situation, for example, Elaine restoried her perception of the staff from unwilling to interested but hesitant. The staff also restoried their perception of Elaine from forceful and idealistic to seeing her more as a compassionate person. Their view of her included the fact that she was a dedicated leader who became blindsided by her enthusiasm. It became visible to the staff that Elaine's intentions were not to force them into change but rather to invite them into a process. Her enthusiasm and exploration of these ideas, however, had taken place in isolation during a summer vacation, and, without her realizing it, she had moved too quickly beyond the staff's experience.

With Distrust and Defensiveness shrinking and preferred stories of people becoming more visible, the school moved to a phase of teambuilding where connections were fostered beyond superficial characteristics, age, years of experience, and hobbies (Beaudoin & Walden, 1997; Heatherington, 1995).

Eventually a committee was formed to explore the educational advancement of the school. They selected a few educational bestsellers that were made available to interested staff, but otherwise summarized and presented. The staff then freely discussed their interest in pursuing some of these ideas. A few particularly interested teachers volunteered to try some of these ideas, and Elaine supported people's personal pace when experimenting with new concepts in their classrooms. The pioneers were then invited to report back to the staff as to the effects they had noticed on the students and on themselves as educators, as well as the direct feedback they received from the students and their families. As a result, more and more teachers became interested in exploring and experimenting with these concepts, finding ways to make them their own. Elaine, in the end, became the principal she had always wanted to be: supporting her teachers in their own quest for educational enlightenment. The staff ultimately became strengthened by this journey, and they developed a greater empathy for each other, including Elaine, who became included as one of them.

If you ever visit Jefferson Elementary School, you will notice that chocolate and other treats now abound in the staff room!

Can principals bring change in their school's philosophy or practices without going through all these problems?

CHAPTER FIVE

Changing Staff Habits Without Conflict

PROCESS OF CHANGE

Readers must be cautioned against the temptation to implement radical change too quickly in their school environment. It is part of this philosophy to institute change through dialogue and discussions, in a process, rather than imposing it. Change can really only happen if all involved have had a chance to reflect on the process, articulate their personal position on the issues, experiment with the process, and eventually become committed to the idea that it serves their best interests. This process in itself can take anywhere from a few months to a few years, depending on the number of people involved and their level of alignment with it. Adjustments will have to be made along the way. Regardless of the time spent in conversation, the process is more important than the outcome. It is in the process that the values of cooperation, respect, and appreciation are truly expressed. In the end, the lived experience of these ideas will serve as the foundation for building an improved school culture.

If the staff have developed a particularly negative story about a principal, it may be almost impossible for this principal to facilitate conversations that chip away at the problem story. Remember, if a problem story is very elaborate, people will pay attention only to information that confirms the negative perspective.

Implementing a New
Idea or Changing the Status Quo

Novelty is always frightening to some and exciting to others. You can be assured that you will have both extremes represented in a staff. For many, the mere thought of changing a practice that has been relied on for 10 or 20 years can trigger significant amounts of insecurity, doubt, concern over the time required, and reluctance to do what may appear to be extra work. For others, the prospect of experimenting with new ideas and staying up to date with new educational ideas is paramount and a vital source of enthusiasm. Regardless of your personal position, you have to be willing to understand and patiently collaborate with those who hold another position. Remember that people always have a reason to be a certain way; your own willingness to take risk may have developed from a life of safety and/or successful experimentation, while others might have suffered greatly from harsh transitions and instabilities.

Any significant change of philosophy has to occur both from the bottom up and from the top down. The principal can expose the staff to ideas, distribute reading material, invite speakers on the subject, organize visits to other schools that have successfully implemented the idea, and support individual teacher excitement over trying new practices. As discussed in previous chapters, principals have little power, in reality, and cannot require a change without risking sabotage or resentment from reluctant staff. Moreover, if people do not want to engage in a new practice or are not committed to it, it will almost certainly fail, thereby "proving" its inadequacy. As in most situations, collaboration and allowing each person his or her own unique pace of slow or rapid change will, in the end, change the school in a much more efficient way.

Principals commented on this process:

You can't change overnight. I work with those teachers who want to [change] and you build a successful program slowly.

I look for ways to support people that are taking little tiny steps. I work with the people who are in favor of [an innovative new idea] and let their success speak for itself. I would say, "Go ahead. You really believe in this, go ahead!"

—Elementary School Principal

We used to have a student of the month award but it didn't work because I had to constantly press the teachers for the students' names, waste my time going over and over again to the staff when they hadn't thought about it, and often ended up facilitating the event on my own in front of parents and students with the awarding teachers not showing up. We stopped it. If the teachers aren't backing the idea, it just won't work.

—Middle School Principal

Resolving Minor Problems

Problems are minor when they involve a smaller number of individuals, are not related to the principal's perceived integrity, have a limited impact on everyone, happen only occasionally, are of limited intensity, or are recently developed. Problems such as gossip, problem-saturated communication, competition, and the like, can usually be addressed by honest group discussions. The principal or facilitator can engage the staff in a discussion of the effects of this problem or invite grade-level teams to review the matter in smaller, private groups. Ultimately each individual has to come to an understanding of the personal efforts and benefits that would ensue from changes. Another option is to invite speakers with an expertise in the area or representatives from another school who might have successfully implemented the new idea.

STEP-BY-STEP EXAMPLE OF THE THINKING BEHIND A CONSTRUCTIVE PROCESS OF CHANGE

Many principals nowadays want their staff to stop sending students to the office for discipline. They are clear that they didn't join the profession to punish lines of students after recess and feel that it is highly ineffective in developing student-teacher problem solving. Many principals will be tempted to simply tell their staff to stop the referral process. This sometimes works; however, it often doesn't. Consider the following:

If You Can Use Power, Does That Mean That You Should?

Principals certainly have the power to determine new procedures and rules in their school . . . in theory. In our example, imposing this new procedure is likely to anger the staff, particularly those who send students to the office all the time! If some of the staff are angry, there will simply be a switch in problems for principals: Instead of dealing with upset students, they will have to deal with resentful staff. In some case, principals have to deal with a bigger problem because upset teachers generally deal with students in negative ways, especially if the teachers feel powerless.

Do Not Pull the Rug Out From Under People Before They Have Something Else to Stand On

Teachers who constantly send students to the office are also sending the administration a message: They do not know how to handle these situations in an effective manner. Telling them to stop sending students to the principal's office will not necessarily empower them to solve things in a more effective manner. In reality, such a rule may create an experience of powerlessness, fear, and being overwhelmed and, further, bring out the worst in teachers who have no other means of handling the situation. This may at times simply escalate conflicts to such a level that there really is no choice other than sending the student to the office. These teachers, more than anyone else, need time to think and articulate why change is useful in order for them to explore alternative options willingly. Pulling the carpet out from under their feet will focus their attention on resentment against the principal instead of on the development of new problem-solving strategies.

The Farther Away One Is From Better Practices, the Less an Intellectual Presentation Is Likely to Work

Teachers, just like everyone else, will respond to an intellectual presentation[1] on class management or attitude only if it is close to their experience. In other words, teachers who will benefit from these types of workshops are usually those who are already committed to learning such practices or who feel that the presentation adds interesting nuances to their current ideologies. For individuals who most need it, the presentation will slide over their heads like water slides off a duck's back. For many, the presentation and its implications, even though amusing and interesting, may be long forgotten when the busyness of the school year starts.

Questions Are Cost-Effective

Although it may seem more effective time wise to simply tell or present to people what to do, in reality that is likely to end up being much more time-consuming and less effective.[2]

In our example (reducing office referrals), people will not fully grasp why and how they are supposed to deal with this situation, which will leave the administrator not only having to deal with upset staff as discussed above but also having to give advice, which seldom works. In a narrative approach, the savvy administrator will assist the staff in articulating their own concerns about the process of referring students to the office. The starting point is the same as it was initially for the principal, which is that of simply wondering what the effects are of sending students to the office. A principal can either gently invite the staff in a conversation or ask their counselor, a neutral third party, to facilitate the process (especially if the principal is very invested in the outcome). As discussed in Chapter 2, the staff can be engaged in a discussion externalizing "Referrals" and systematically mapping its effects on multiple areas. For example:

- What are the general effects of Referring students to the office?
- Has anyone noticed how this affects your relationship with them? Is your long-term relationship with students improved, unaffected, or worsened by Referrals?
- When Referring is frequent, how do students talk, feel, and think about their teachers? Do students have more respect or less for teachers who refer?
- What does Referring tell students about you as a teacher? Might it inadvertently convey a certain message about your authority or ability to handle situations?
- When students come back to your classroom after being Referred, how do they perform? Are they the same as before, more likely to participate, succeed, and be on task, or to be frustrated and withdrawn?
- How does it affect your day and your teaching to have these conflicts/referrals with students?
- Would you all be willing to experiment with fewer Referrals for the next two weeks and discuss your experience in our next meeting?

Listen to All Voices

Clearly some staff members will be in favor of the status quo and will want to voice their appreciation of existing systems such as Referrals. The process of exploring the effects of school practices, such as Referrals, can certainly include a list of advantages. Ideally, two columns can be drawn on a board with the facilitator writing down the staff's reflections on positive and negative effects. It is important to listen to it all and to leave space for teachers to reflect freely without feeling pressured in any particular direction. Pressure will usually result in counterpressure, leaving little space to ponder and reflect in any meaningful way. Being open to hearing advantages and disadvantages will create a nonjudgmental context that will foster flexibility and trust. This same attitude is crucial to hold when connecting to students.

Principals are becoming increasingly interested in students' voices and are exploring various ways to invite them into the educational system. In doing that, however, some fall in the trap of privileging the newer voices at the expense of the older voices. Silencing teachers and siding with students will typically not solve the problems, but rather shift them elsewhere. Teachers who do not feel heard and respected by their administrators are less likely to respect students. This can create a scenario where students (and their families) complain to the administration, which then tries to manage teachers, who become increasingly resentful at students. A triangle of interaction is never optimal in any situation. If the goal is to provide a respectful environment, then the method must be thoughtfully respectful of all. Decisions are also generally enriched by including the contributions of multiple voices and perspectives.

Listening Is Communicating That You Understand

Whether you are a principal or an educator, listening is probably one of the most important practices you can develop if you truly believe in a community. Listening is a much harder "activity" than everyone thinks for two main reasons:

1. People speak about 125 words per minute in our culture, while our brains can actually process about 800 words per minute (Communication Research Associates, 1995). This means that most people can listen to the content of a speech and, at the same time, in the back of their mind, take mini mental vacations elsewhere, or make negative judgments or large numbers of assumptions. Have you ever experienced the frustration of not feeling listened to by someone and yet, when challenged, the person can actually retell the content of the conversation? The retelling of the content usually doesn't alleviate

the experience of feeling not heard because you know the listening was not of high quality. Quality listening is about using the remaining capacity of your brain to do the following:

- Imagine what it's like to live the particular experienced talked about
- Relate to its implications
- Spend energy understanding how it makes total sense for this person (given their context)
- Put yourself in their shoes
- Ask relevant, empathetic *questions*

Listening is an active process. It is different from hearing, even on the physiological level; you actually spend more calories and have a faster pulse when actively receiving information.

2. Listening is also about letting the other person know that you understand. Again, people will not feel listened to unless you communicate to them that they are heard. This usually requires a stance of compassion, collaboration, curiosity, and genuine interest in the person's experience (as discussed in Chapter 2). For staff members to feel heard, the facilitator or principal must often repeat the statements that were made, or, more specifically, restate what *you* understood, with a genuine attempt to understand and not judge.

Think of Long-Term and Solid Instead of Quick and Upsetting

Although the first two weeks after such discussions may lead to a few more referrals than if a new rule had been established, they will likely be less than the usual routine. Staff may try different ways of managing issues in their classrooms, which at times will be successful and at others quite exhausting. In the process, however, they are thinking and exploring, which is laying a very solid foundation for long-term, successful change.

Change Is a Process, Not an Event

When the staff reconvenes, teachers can be invited to discuss the times they could have Referred but didn't and how they successfully handled those situations. A list of each staff member's unique resolution of the situation can be made on the board. Often people are tentative initially and have not even articulated for themselves how they actually handled the situation differently. It is useful that the facilitator, whether the principal or another, is comfortable asking for the details of what they tried, the effects on students, what it meant to student, how they felt as educators afterwards, and so on. In the meantime, others who may have been less invested in the change are listening and learning lived, meaningful strategies from each other. The process of sharing strategies that have been experienced and successful for a colleague is much more powerful than having a didactic training on management. One is connected with experience, the other with intellectual learning. One will be remembered for the richness and relevance of the story, the other will be forgotten like a chemistry formula. The sharing and exploring creates a powerful process of change to which everyone can become profoundly committed.

Contrast Intentions and Effects (Using Another Example)

I was consulting at a new school. I spent several very pleasant lunches chatting with a few interested teachers about my work. One male teacher in particular was very much in agreement with some of my beliefs around education. He shared how he loved his work as a teacher and believed in creating a safe and exciting context for learning. For that to happen, he said, "You have to let go of unnecessary disciplining and really build a caring connection with your students. Students learn best when they have nothing to worry about except discovery of new material." As the bell rang and everyone went back to their classrooms, I was left alone, pondering on how lucky these children were to have such a kind and devoted teacher.

As I walked back to the office to touch base with the principal, I was suddenly pulled out of my thoughts by screaming sounds. I was getting closer to a classroom where a teacher was yelling at a student: "This is MY classroom, and I can do whatever I want here! You don't deserve to be in MY room! Get OUT NOW and sit outside! I will teach you to be respectful!" A young boy burst out of the class, became embarrassed when he saw me, and collapsed by the door, in tears. As I approached the student, I could see through the window that the teacher was the gentleman I had just left.

Were this teacher's intentions the most accurate representation of who he was? Or was it his behavior? Who would you say is the real person?

Several months later, as complaints and concerns arose about this teacher, the principal asked me if I would get involved in that class. After I respectfully approached the teacher, asked him his understanding of the problem, and connected with him, he became interested in exploring some ideas with me.[3]

From a narrative perspective, this gentleman was gently invited into a conversation about his intentions and the effects that his behaviors actually had. His increased awareness of the incongruence between intentions and effects assisted him in making a decision about who he preferred to be.

At a later time, I gently interviewed him in front of his students about his values and life experiences around respect. The process assisted him further in publicly articulating his goals and preferences, and allowed students to better understand what was personally important for him in terms of respect and why. I was later told by several students and the principal that this teacher had developed a very good connection with his class. The principal was relieved to have fewer complaints about an educator she knew was very committed to his work.

Think Meaning, Not Facts

Facts never stand alone. They are always interpreted and ascribed meaning. People usually interpret and ascribe meaning based on their own personal experience with, inadvertently, very little consideration for the actual context of others' lives. When witnessing or speaking to someone who has engaged in a negative practice, make sure to consider the bigger canvas of this incident, how the person thinks of him- or herself as a person (story), and how he or she believes others interpret the action. Noticed events always carry meaning, and addressing that meaning is of the utmost importance in bringing about any significant change. The gentleman discussed above was eventually engaged in a conversation about the meaning of being respectful to students and what it said about him as an educator.

NOTES

1. An intellectual presentation is one in which the facilitator presents expert concepts and ideas before a mostly passive-listening audience. This can be useful at times but will not lead to any significant climate change in itself. This process is in contrast to the material presented in this book about engaging educators in a discussion, where the facilitator mostly asks questions and invites everyone to reflect and articulate the changes they would like to make and which strategies best suit their unique styles. Another example of this active process is inviting teachers into experiential exercises to increase their awareness of their own behaviors and communication styles. People in general are more likely to learn and change through observing their own limitations in action rather than being told to do something differently. An interactive process empowers them to be committed to change. Examples of such activities can be found in Resource B of this book.

2. This same limitation applies to students. Principals, who often have limited school budgets, may hire volunteers or people with no clinical training to do the counseling work. Although these people may be invaluable in connecting with students and have compassionate intentions, they may end up simply engaging in giving advice, which will assist only the few students with minor issues. A more successful approach is to keep these generous

volunteers as student mentors and hire a trained professional for a few hours per week for the more complex sufferings and problems.

3. I would never impose myself in a classroom or to a teacher at the request of the principal. Teachers must be approached respectfully and involved in choosing whether or not they are interested in exploring the climate in their classroom.

CHAPTER SIX

Preventing Problems and Creating a Climate of Support

In this chapter we will cover aspects of what we have come to consider as the ingredients of a climate of respect, appreciation, and collaboration. Aside from instances when problems have to be solved, it is important to establish a general climate of belonging that will prevent these problems from developing and minimize conflicts in difficult times.

In our survey regarding job satisfaction, we found that the four strongest predictors of teachers' job satisfaction, in order of importance, were: (1) sharing of materials (collaboration), (2) relationship with principal (personal connection, trust, and approachability), (3) appreciation by colleagues, and (4) general connection with staff (see Figure 6.1). We also found a negative correlation between the experience of disrespect from students and job satisfaction. In other words, the equation that could predict teachers' job satisfaction would read as follows:

Job Satisfaction = Connection + Collaboration + Appreciation + Trusting Relationship With Principal – Disrespect

Figure 6.1   The four strongest predictors of teachers' job
satisfaction

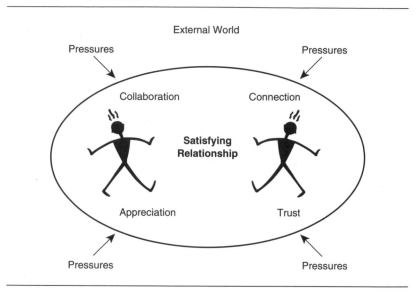

We will present these powerful components as well as
others that, although not formally included in our surveys,
became obvious in interviews and in our full research.

CONNECTION

Schools are often presented as the ultimate cradle of socializa-
tion for children, and teaching is often considered one of the
most social professions for adults. Interestingly, however, conversations with adults and children often reveal a profound
sense of alienation, isolation, and disconnection that is further
intensified by the innumerable possibilities for relationships.
In other words, there is nothing worse than feeling alone in a
crowd, and that is true for both students and adults.

By connection we mean a process of being open and accepting of the other as a whole person, with his or her multiple
versions of self. It is a process of valuing diversity at all levels,
including ethnicity, religion, age, generation, interest, experience,
and more. In this compassionate process of honoring each other,

we find the best is brought out in each individual. Connection is about *being* together, as well as *doing* joint activities.

Connections among staff create a shield against problems and foster a nurturing environment where solutions are easily generated.

For connections to develop in a group, people need to agree that connection is part of the climate they want to create and promote for each other. Principals can certainly set the tone for such a philosophy, as some have done. Ultimately, however, the principal can do only so much. The staff need to be recruited into a joint agreement on the importance that *they* want to ascribe to connections in their school culture.

As discussed in the process of change section in Chapter 5, the staff can be invited to make a list of what it means to have connections. Common, agreed-upon ingredients for meaningful connection include trust, safety, time, attentive presence, nonjudgmental listening, honesty, compassion, perspective, and humor, among others. When you, the reader, think about your current school culture, what is the number of people with whom you experience these characteristics? (See Table 6.1.)

Table 6.1   When you, the reader, think about your current school culture, what is the number of people with whom you experience these characteristics?

Ingredients	Ingredients of Connection That I Value	Number of Colleagues With Whom I Experience This Ingredient
Trust		
Safety		
Time		
Attentive presence		
Nonjudgmental listening		
Honesty		
Compassion		
Perspective		
Humor		
Other		

Developing and maintaining rich connections, as discussed here, might seem to take a lot of time, but it doesn't have to.

Several principals report having staff meetings every other week, mostly to process issues and connect with each other. Dry information can be distributed in staff memos or informally by a small group of elected grade-level representatives instead of being discussed in depth in meetings to make room for more meaningful connections. One of the most basic ways of creating a more harmonious staff climate is to have a discussion on teachers' educational values and philosophies. A certain sense of unity in educational mission and goal can go a long way. This is particularly true about educational philosophies, where educators, committed to a cocreated set of values or a mission statement, may connect on a deeper level.

Connections can be further developed when staff have opportunities to share a wide range of information about themselves. There is a point where people know so much about each other that similarities are easily found, even on school sites where educational philosophies are wide ranging. Sometimes it is simply about making the person behind the role more visible. An example of this would be to publish teachers' biographies along with their values, hobbies, and special interests. Once made available to the community, a teacher's biography would make the multiple aspects of the person behind the role more visible, more human and interesting.

We have facilitated workshops where we engaged participants in a merging stories exercise: Participants co-construct a single story of their lives as if they were one person (see Resource B). Through this process they notice how rich and diverse each person's experience has been, and they deepen their intimacy through the sharing of historically important events in their lives. A version of a similar process was experienced by an elementary school principal:

In a round table "big wig" meeting, the head of the meeting asked everyone to tell their story. He started with his story, which set parameters for the people that followed. This made it safe, so by the time the guts of the meeting started, everyone was equal.

Regardless of title, experience and backgrounds, the playing field was leveled. I will facilitate that exercise in my new school in September.

Connections are invaluable in contributing to teachers' job satisfaction, sense of belonging to their school, and, in the end, to their performance. Deeper connections would solve or at least reduce problems such as gossip, cliques, problem-saturated conversations, and competition. The specific method of connecting is not as important as it happening in a meaningful way. For some it may be a phone conversation, for others it may entail putting paperwork aside and spending time in another's classroom. For still others it may simply be using time already available, such as lunches and recesses, to talk about more energizing and connecting subjects (as opposed to problem-saturated gossip).

You have got to be connected to survive. [My principal] and I talk on the cell phone each evening when we are driving home to process how things are going.

—Middle School Assistant Principal

In our research, it seemed that women principals actively promoted connection in their staff more often than men. Although this could simply be a sampling bias, there is a possibility that women may be more comfortable in promoting social relationships because they benefit from a thorough socializing process of caring and expressing feelings that is not consistently offered to boys (Ashton-Jones, Olson, & Perry, 2000; Kimmel & Messner, 1998; Pollack, 1999; Tannen, 1990). This woman principal, for example, shared a list of examples of practices, while several male principals would mostly refer to parties as the main process to develop relationships:

At each meeting, I try to include some sort of opportunity for sharing personal issues. Sometimes we talk about where we are. I also have these "angel cards," so we each will pull a card and discuss what it means. Other times we draw a face about what we each are feeling right now, and we'll have conversation about that.

Finally, fun times are always an opportunity for people to see each other in a different light and develop deeper connections. Some schools organize nonwork-related, fun, social gatherings. Other schools will reserve a piece of their budget to organize team-building retreats where people play games, engage in personal reflections, and spend time together. Finally others, even from underprivileged schools, reserve funds to send any interested teachers to special and interesting conferences as a group, as illustrated in this example:

If you manage the budget right, you can have resources for conferences. We try to send as many people as we can to this conference. Sometimes up to twenty go. We'll book airfare and hotels for them. They all fly down together and stay together and have a wonderful experience doing that. I have really committed myself to providing them with something special.

—Middle School Principal

On a daily or weekly basis, school staffs could determine ways to structure recesses and lunches so that teachers can spend time connecting with each other instead of having yard duty. When the staff is really committed to connection and develops even the habit of sitting at one big table, these few minutes of time together can be really significant:

Our staff sits together around one big table. Once we had to split our tables for a California State Distinguished School visit, and the staff was so uncomfortable! At the end of that day we shoved the tables together and everyone felt better.

COLLABORATION

In most schools that we visited and/or surveyed, teachers' most frequent comment about each other and the staff was the presence or absence of collaboration. This was also the strongest predictor of job satisfaction on another independent survey. In general, teachers were extraordinarily grateful to their colleagues for sharing ideas, materials, advice, and the workload (see Box 6.1).

Box 6.1

In our research, we found that teachers experienced being a team member, collaborating, and sharing as the top three most helpful aspects of their staff relationships. The following are examples of teachers' comments on what they valued in staff relationships:

1. Being a Team Member

- Sharing ideas, information, strategies, and materials
- Interacting and sharing information about successes they are having
- Planning lessons together as a team
- Offering help; for example, running copies for each other
- Working together on special events

2. Connecting in Friendship and Camaraderie

- Talking with you and being willing to really listen
- Smiling, finding humor in daily situations, laughing together, being cheerful
- Extending themselves with a friendly, inviting attitude
- Being supportive daily, but especially during a crisis
- Showing appreciation

(Continued)

Box 6.1 (Continued)

3. Sharing Professional Encouragement

- Offering encouraging words and emotional support
- Giving reassurance and support in and out of the classroom
- Offering suggestions and giving advice

Significant collaboration can happen only when people are connected. In other words, collaboration occurs within the shadow of connection. Collaboration also occurs at different levels. The extent of the collaboration depends on the school's and the teachers' philosophies. Many schools have a minimum level of collaboration, such as sharing materials within grade levels. Schools that are most collaborative coteach, team-teach, discuss philosophies, exchange classes, and peer-coach, among other practices. In addition to the extent (quantity) of collaboration, there seem to be two main types (quality) of collaboration: horizontal and vertical.

Horizontal collaboration is the close working relationship between colleagues at the same grade level. This is common and very necessary. Practices include grade-level meetings, swapping classes for coverage of different subject matter, and co-teaching.

Vertical collaboration occurs across grade levels and across hierarchies. Its occurrence is infrequent yet equally valuable. It involves teachers working with all ages of students, or teachers of one grade level working with another, or principals switching places with teachers as illustrated in the following stories.

This year I am teaching a sixth grade class and swapping places with a teacher. This teacher is interested in an administrative career and appreciates the opportunity to work in the office, while I enjoy the opportunity to work with the students and build a relationship that will last during their stay at this school. I love teaching this class. It's something really special in my day, and we do all sorts of cool and meaningful projects.

—Middle School Principal

I have lately wondered why we don't collaborate across grades. For example, when I taught about water in second grade, I realized the kids were also studying water at fifth grade. Why didn't we get together and do cross-age projects based on students working together, teaching each other and collaborating?

—Elementary School Teacher

Collaboration offers many advantages. It:

- Reenergizes
- Fosters an open mind and creativity
- Generates a greater number of ideas when faced with a problem
- Fuels enthusiasm and fun
- Provides rewarding experiences of shared success
- Can increase performance (which is not the reason to promote collaboration, but it is a profitable side effect)

I have a colleague who will always share with me. She's not stingy with her ideas at all. I truly feel like she wants me to be successful, and I feel like it was her that made me successful here last year. I was able to get a good name in one year, and that's real hard to do. She introduced the intrinsic rewards, you know, how to look for a little more out of teaching. She said I'm going to take you through it this year, and she really held my hand. You have to have those people.

—Elementary School Teacher

THE MANY FACES OF APPRECIATION

Gratitude is the best medicine for the illnesses of our community life.

—P. Johnson Fenner, 1995

Appreciation, as we define it, is expressing acknowledgment. The intention is to be transparent about our personal experience of gratitude or admiration. Sharing appreciation is a process of the genuine expression of gratefulness without the intention to alter the recipient's behavior in any way. As discussed throughout this book, educators work so hard, give so much of their time, money, and devotedness, that in the end they can be very hungry for appreciation. Yet appreciation is scarce. Everyone recognizes its value and craves it, yet people lack the context and means to express it in meaningful ways. Invisible obstacles can limit the ease with which it is expressed. In a 15-minute break, problem-saturated communication may be perceived as more important than the expression of appreciation; hierarchical relationships may create a unidirectional pattern for the expression of feedback, including appreciation; feeling rushed may get teachers to be task-oriented and therefore forget their preferred value of acknowledgment. In some situations, this absorption into roles may disconnect educators from their own human experiences around connection. People become task oriented, and appreciation becomes a tool rather than an experience.

In most of the schools we have visited, however, it was often astonishing to interview principals who would systematically elaborate on all the ways they attempted to promote appreciation and then to find in our surveys the extent to which the staff actually felt unappreciated. Upon further reflection, the explanation became obvious: One person can have the experience of giving a large amount of appreciation, yet when divided among 30 staff members and a large number of children, the amount each recipient experiences may be minute.

It became clear to us that for a context of appreciation to exist, the distribution of acknowledgment should be circulated by a larger number of people. This means a less hierarchical system needs to exist where appreciation offered by people in lesser positions of power also become meaningful. In other words, appreciation offered by a principal then carries more or less equal weight as appreciation offered by a peer. A good example of this is when teachers pass on a small symbol of appreciation from one to another each month.

Ideal systems allow appreciation for everyone and by everyone. The student population is an enormous pool of appreciation untapped by most schools. Once again, this may be due to the lower status ascribed to students in a hierarchical system. It is particularly surprising given that ultimately most educators went into education for their love of young people and their desire to contribute to their lives. In our research we have encountered only a handful of schools that took the time to gather significant student feedback on their teachers' style, classroom leadership, and general climate issues of the school.

The staff at a certain middle school facilitates a beautiful example of this practice. Twice a year students who wish to are given the opportunity to write a letter of appreciation to any school staff member who may have made a difference in their lives.

We have a tradition here on campus where students are asked to select people that have really made a difference for them and write a letter. It happens a couple times a year. Students are encouraged to sit down and write letters to different people in the school. It may be the secretary, the custodian, teachers, etc. . . . The student can send it to whomever they want, and if a student doesn't want to do it, they don't have to.

I'll receive letters from kids who I don't really know who they are. They'll indicate to me, "You stopped and you said something to me that really meant a lot." For me, it was just an action; for them, it was something they hadn't experienced.

Teachers look forward to these letters. The teachers save the letters; they keep them to read. Often they will receive a letter from someone that will totally surprise them. I seldom hear of anyone who doesn't receive one. Everyone is receiving one.

—Middle School Principal

The beauty of this practice is that it also creates an opportunity to acknowledge everyone contributing to the school, such as the yard duty volunteer, custodians, cafeteria workers, therapists, tutors, bus drivers, and instructional assistants, who often feel invisible in the system and very rarely benefit from any inclusion.

Another principal shared a very creative practice of sending singing telegrams on Valentine's Day. Those telegrams are sung by groups of students in appreciation of teachers' and principals' efforts. The telegrams can be ordered by anyone on the school campus and present a very kind gesture of appreciation:

On Valentine's Day, kids are able to send singing telegrams to other people on campus. Student volunteers (singers) are coordinated by a teacher. They'll receive a request to sing and go to that class. We'll have four or five teams of kids singing in different places. We have kids who are sending singing telegrams to their teachers. One day I was stopped in the office by these three girls, who gave me a card from someone and started singing to me a cappella. It was wonderful, beautiful, and uplifting.

Although appreciation can certainly be spontaneous rather than structured, we believe a more formatted system can generate a climate where people develop the habit of showing acknowledgment. Some other ways for educators to gather positive feedback and appreciation from students and parents are to:

- Conduct a survey on positive aspects of classroom/ school procedures and projects.
- Facilitate class discussions on appreciated aspects of teacher/class relationships, whether facilitated by principal, teacher, or parent.
- Create a playful yet sincere report card for teachers and/or principals.
- Have a response form on notes sent home where parents could ask questions and share gratitude.
- Have a class box where kids could leave notes for the principal to share with teachers at staff meetings or put into their mailboxes.

These broader practices of acknowledgment can offer the advantage of creating a sense of community for everyone.

Appreciation Specifically for Teachers

Often principals and sometimes superintendents make great efforts to appreciate teachers.

One superintendent and his district staff were even able to give gift certificates to a local restaurant to each employee as a token of appreciation. Others prefer to offer small tokens of appreciation informally, as described in the following principals' examples:

We look for ways to celebrate everyone's success. Our school has an Apple Award. It is presented from one teacher to another teacher. Each month it would be passed on, and the teacher passing it tells the staff why before presenting it. Reasons for receiving the award might be for asking for support because someone had a tough week, for sharing information and/or curriculum, among other things. People worked really hard to not let cliques influence the award. It wasn't coming from me, so that there wasn't any competition or evaluation.

I've just started this new practice where at every staff meeting I randomly pick two names, and everyone in the staff has to write a note of appreciation or a comment to those two people. I've noticed that the chosen teachers, so far, have walked out of the meeting really uplifted.

This year I'm really paying attention to the celebration of our successes. I want to start a Thank You Board in the staff room. I am hoping that as people pass by, they might get into the habit of spontaneously writing down something they are grateful for, a thank you to the custodian or to someone they've received help from.

We have a basket that we pass around at staff meetings where people can write an anonymous note and throughout the meeting we randomly share them.

This last practice is particularly meaningful, as it creates a context of appreciation that is truly genuine. No one is obligated to force himself or herself to write something about someone they barely know. The voluntary choice of writing in itself guarantees that what will be written will be very real and received in a powerful way.

Self-Appreciation

In the end, the most important form of acknowledgment is self-appreciation. Self-appreciation develops naturally in environments that are supportive and provide various forms of approval.

When staff set personal goals for themselves that are not academic, they give themselves permission to focus on personal growth as well as the curriculum. This can even be done in small teams of four teachers, for example, where they could assist each other in noticing events that fit each teacher's goal of developing his or her preferred self. This process could be particularly important for experienced teachers who may enjoy new challenges to keep alive their enthusiasm for their profession. Succeeding at one's own established goals certainly promotes self-appreciation and a sense of accomplishment.

Appreciation for
Other Members of the School Community

Secondary staff should also be included in a process of recognition. It can be painful for them to be (unintentionally) excluded from yearbooks, T-shirt distribution, and parties.

The more appreciated and welcome they feel in the school community, the more committed they will be.

Although often invisible, these staff members can contribute in significant ways to children's lives and the school community.

I had a cafeteria manager who had to go in for surgery. I sent her flowers and was glad I did, because I soon noticed how smoothly it runs when she's here!

Appreciation of Principals

Last, but certainly not least, principals should also be the recipients of appreciation and engaged in the experience of appreciation. Principals and authority figures tend to receive less appreciation in general. People can feel intimidated when approaching them, perhaps because of a problem story about the principal not needing feedback or that it would be insulting to comment on a superior's performance.

One principal speaks of her transition from teacher to principal:

That's been the hardest thing. When you leave the classroom where kids will hug and love you and parents are constantly telling you how good a job you are doing, you come into this job and nobody tells you. It's very rare that I get a compliment, so it's very special when it happens.

Boss's Day is one of the rare, structured days when people are reminded of the possibility of expressing appreciation to their principals. Otherwise, principals who have an open-door policy and maintain trusting, honest relationships with the community may receive little droplets of appreciation here and there. Ultimately, principals have to find their own ways of experiencing or detecting appreciation, whether from a child's smile or a staff's trust or a parent's respectful communication style.

When we shared the positive results of our survey with principals, which included reverence for them from their staff, some of them were tearful. Some principals commented on how they do so much and can only guess at how it is appreciated. Our kind words and summaries were very meaningful to them. Although many principals are hesitant to ask for feedback, it can become part of the end-of-the-school-year ritual for principals to pass out a slip and anonymously ask teachers' suggestions or what they most appreciated about the leadership of the school. This builds in a bidirectional communication model based on appreciation.

SELF-REFLECTION

No one does their best thinking on fast forward . . . speed kills great ideas. The faster we speed up, the less time we have to think, to incubate, to ponder, to dream . . . in schools the answer has always been more important than the thought process.

—Reiman, 2000

The current educational system does not allow for reflection time for either teachers or students. As discussed by Peter Senge (O'Neil, 1995), many educators are advocating cooperative learning for students but seeing teaching as individualistic work and are not taking the same stance for themselves. He believes that creating a safe environment in which teachers can reflect on what they are doing, rediscover what they really care about, and learn more about what it takes to work as teams is crucial for teachers to succeed in their profession.

Principals may have only sporadic opportunities to reflect, given that they begin the school year earlier than everyone else and are able to leave the campus occasionally for some "alone time."

Everyone needs time to reflect. Time for reflection is important, as it allows for refueling, connecting with a purpose, reviewing accomplishments, processing mistakes, examining congruency with one's values, and ultimately self-improvement.

The main advantages of self-reflection include:

- Time to explore ways of being that fit who you truly want to be
- Becoming grounded in one's values
- Clarifying goals and intentions
- Learning from mistakes and planning different responses to challenges
- Slowing down to a relaxed place of more peace
- Becoming more able to be attentive and relate to others
- Integrating the lessons of life

Self-reflection can be encouraged in numerous ways and integrated in schools' practices, for teachers and students, without it becoming overly time-consuming.

Self-reflection is a great antidote to many of the negative specifications mentioned in Chapter 1. It allows space for people to decompress from control, dedication, responsibility, and the pressure of being an expert or good role model. The space provides for reenergizing, nurturing, and maintaining a relaxing connection with oneself. All the specifications require that educators be overly outwardly focused. Self-reflection allows for inner concentration. It can be a time to make peace or a time to make plans. Self-reflection can "reboot one's system"; it can reconnect educators with broader visions of themselves. Greater perspective can be obtained, and the challenges of the day can be reevaluated as relatively small in the grand scheme of things.

There are numerous ways to incorporate self-reflection in the school lives of educators. This can be done at transitory moments during a school year, such as the beginning, the end of a quarter or a semester, or at the end of the year.

Teachers should be paid from August to June so that they can talk and review. You can't reflect when you are on the treadmill running through the school year. You can't become a better hitter during the baseball game. It's when you practice and experiment ahead of time that you'll improve.

—Middle School Assistant Principal

Another example might be for educators to make very concrete personal goals at the start of the school year, such as: "I want to attach myself to a student who is struggling or whom I could easily dislike"; "I will reach out to two colleagues I don't know well and connect with them as persons"; or "I will be more patient with students who struggle with reading." These are goals that are very congruent with personal values and promote self-growth as a human and as an educator.

Some schools find ways of including a weekly period of reflection for both their teachers and their students.

The teachers here have been requesting yoga classes for some time. We finally requested it as part of a grant and got it! We all need stress reduction, we have so many things on our plates and try to serve so many people, we really need time to reflect on ourselves. Children also need to learn to reduce stress. They have to know how to help themselves relax and get under control, whether it's on the playground or for class presentations. It's a way of giving them more ownership of their lives, too.

—Elementary School Principal

A variety of means can also be used to incorporate self-reflection in daily lives of teacher. It does not have to be time-consuming, as long as people make a commitment to focus inwardly on their state of being.

We have often offered stress reduction workshops for teachers where they could become engaged in a meditation, a body scan, or a relaxing visualization. This was sometimes scheduled at lunch, but most frequently was facilitated during staff meetings so that no additional demands were placed on staff time. Often we would generate a list of stress-reduction strategies and reconnect teachers with their own coping methods and preferred selves. These occasional workshops were always appreciated and successful.

Self-reflection is also useful for teachers to connect with their own past experiences as students, to remember what it was like to be young and keep that in mind while encouraging current students in academic endeavors.

DEALING WITH THE SYSTEM:
TESTING AND UNIONS

The current educational system in the United States is obviously fraught with many problems, many of which, unfortunately, are unlikely to change in the near future. Educators therefore need to learn to function in the best possible ways within that structure, creating space for different experiences. Principals and teachers must find ways to honor and respect their preferences and values while still satisfying the state requirements.

Testing

Certain schools have had the liberty to decide whether they would subject themselves to the pressures of assessment and scores. Although remarkable and certainly advantageous for teachers and students, this is not a luxury that all schools can afford. Educators trapped in a district that values scores might still retain the liberty to choose the extent to which they will let the pressure affect them and their students. Principals can also have an influence on the extent to which these pressures will affect their staff, as described by the following principal:

> I see myself as a big filter between the district and my teachers. For example, the district may give us assessment priorities. I will absorb it all, reflect on it, and then present it in a way that's manageable and workable for my staff.

Our colleagues Richard Prinz and Cindy Gowen now work at a school where extensive games and silly activities are organized at breaks and lunch during testing week to help everyone relax. It really changes the climate of that week for students and teachers alike.

At one extreme there are educators who suffer the most and feel that their job depends on the score, while at the other are educators who subject themselves and their students to the score without making a big deal of it, as illustrated in this principal's statement:

> If we did a picture that is a puzzle of you and your body, only one small puzzle piece is your standardized test score.

Principals can at least choose not to emphasize the importance of scores. In that way, they avoid the vast majority of the negative effects. This, of course, has to be made public and explained to parents, as well as which other priorities the school decides to embrace.

Unions

Schools are also structured with certain policies and subgroups. Although these may be unavoidable, the ways in which they are exerted can vary greatly. As discussed in the previous chapter, union groups in certain districts are collaborative, useful, and constructive members of school communities. In other districts, however, they are experienced as a waste of finances for teachers (dues) and as heartache for principals. The best that principals can do in these districts is to develop strong connections with the union and have a process of honest collaboration with each other. In addition to that, the staff can decide as a group to hire an external ombudsperson to be available once in a while if conflicts arise between any members of the school community. It is interesting that the service of an ombudsperson is offered in most universities and many companies, yet the only recourse many teachers have in the educational system is often a bureaucratic or antagonistic involvement by the union. The ombudsperson, who does not have a political agenda, offers the advantage of being neutral, objective, simple, cost-effective, and having no other goal than resolving conflicts in the best possible way for both parties.

LEADERSHIP

The only power the principal really has is that of creating a context where everybody, students and adults, can be at their best.

What makes good leaders is not so much what they accomplish, but how they make people feel. In order for administrators to promote such a context, they must be connected to their staff and be in touch with each person's true experience. This idea is in line with newer research on leadership, which has shown that traditional leadership (taking command with a strong voice in front of the group) may not be as effective as once thought. The recent increase in diversity in leaders has rendered visible a variety of approaches to leadership. In particular, networking in more subtle and personalized ways with each individual may in fact be more effective and successful. Such a personalized approach offers the advantage of people feeling heard and seen as a human being *as well as* a worthy and valued member of the community. As stated by Reiman (2000), "Acknowledge people, not their jobs." The success of this leadership style came across very clearly in some schools we visited:

> *The new principal at our school has done a wonderful job with the staff. She makes sure to touch base with each person in a very genuine way. People can tell she is really interested in them as people and really cares how they are feeling.*

The most successful principals in our research were also those who were able to engage their staff in shared meaning and goals. By shared goals, we mean a vision that every member believes in and is committed to contribute to for the good of the community.

Leading teachers to agree on shared goals is certainly a challenging undertaking given the diverse personalities on many staffs and the focus on classroom goals over community. Yet research has shown that people can come together despite their differences to work on a common, meaningful goal or against a common threat. In schools, time must be created for teachers to come together as a community so that each can contribute to a decision regarding a theme for the year, such as diversity, deepening staff relationships and mentoring. A facilitator must be acutely aware of and sensitive to the level of involvement of each individual. For example, when 80% of staff members are interested in a subject but 20% are uninvolved, the outcome could be severely affected.

Aside from these general descriptions of successful leaders, our research showed that in schools, principals were most appreciated when they fulfilled the five criteria below. These five criteria were extracted from our survey's open-ended question regarding principals' actions that contribute to a positive, supportive environment.

Communicate Constructively. Give positive feedback. Encourage frequently, listen, understand, and also acknowledge misunderstandings.
  Examples of quotes from surveys include:

- "Gives constructive criticism"
- "Has good communication skills"
- "Shares personal stories"
- "Says positive things (personal and professional)"
- "Gives encouragement, appreciation, and acknowledges efforts"
- "Shares positive growth seen in students"
- "Apologizes when necessary"
- "Maintains good rapport with parents"

Be a Proactive Ally. Provide guidance. Support teachers regarding parent and district office issues, and maintain order at school.
  Examples of quotes from surveys include:

- "Supports a teacher when confronted by a parent (right or wrong, the teacher's intentions and efforts should be supported)"
- "Always tries to help if there's a problem in my class"
- "Backs my decisions"
- "Handles serious behavior problems"
- "Comes to parent meetings and supports me in parent discussions"
- "Treats me with respect and stands up for teachers"
- "Presents a strong, visible force on campus, maintaining order and discipline"

Be a Supportive Administrator. Provide needed materials. Encourage professional growth, show interest in teachers and students as humans, be flexible on how to achieve goals, take necessary action to support staff, value teacher and student input, and handle changes cautiously.

Examples of quotes from surveys include:

- "Provides funding for continuing education opportunities"
- "Buys us lunch/treats/water at staff meetings"
- "Covers a class in case of emergency"
- "Supports my teaching style and decisions"
- "Is open minded about change and is flexible on how to achieve goals"
- "Works with us as peers rather than making changes from above and gives us advance warning about upcoming changes"
- "Has a good understanding and promotes schoolwide learning goals"
- "Promotes a team environment"
- "Respects the amount of work you already have and does not add any more to your plate"
- "Often leaves brief notes of appreciation and support after visiting my classroom"

Be Available and Visible. This means the principal is interested in students, interacts with teachers and students, and is there when needed for advice.

Examples of quotes from surveys include:

- "Is always approachable and welcoming"
- "Comes to meetings and parent conferences when invited"
- "Gets kids involved in recess activities"
- "Really knows the children"
- "Takes your class so you can go observe someone else's class"
- "Offers suggestions and support concerning curriculum"

- "Visits my classroom to deliver good news or 'just stopping by'"
- "Answers my questions in a genuine way"
- "Keeps an open door to her office"

Lead With Integrity. Leaders should be persons of their word, returning calls promptly, following through with agreements, being accountable, and taking necessary actions.

Examples of quotes from surveys include:

- "Asks if I need any help or resources and follows through on it"
- "Is a good listener then acts on it"
- "Is really honest with us and can acknowledge mistakes"
- "Has trust in our abilities"
- "Follows through when I ask for assistance"

One of the dangers of power and authority in many professions is a sense of entitlement to disregard others' opinions and a feeling of being above the rules. It is useful for all leaders to ask themselves what method they will use to keep themselves in check. How are they being accountable to others? Are they using power in an appropriate way?

When there is an imbalance of power, there is always a misuse of power, somewhere, somehow (inadvertent or not).

How do you limit the occurrence of misuse of authority?

An example of such effort came from a superintendent we interviewed who told us about a decision that his administration made to be more respectful of principals' time. Although the district office has the power to simply mandate meetings, they have decided to do this different:

One year our assistant superintendent of instruction was trying to visit a particular classroom and found she was too busy. We decided that if she was the lead of instruction and was too busy, that must shed some light on how busy principals are. The next year we canceled principal meetings at the district office, and we visited each principal once a month on their school site for a structured conversation. These conversations included whatever they needed to talk about. "Rather than you meet with us, we'll meet with you." We tried to model a different kind of access and communication. It sent an amazing message about the values here.

With these ingredients, a school culture can resonate with substance and vitality.

In the end, it is not our techniques, our talents, or our knowledge that matter, it is our being.

—W. Bennis (in Bolman & Deal, 2001)

All of these ingredients of a supportive school culture are summarized in Resource C. Although these practices can go very far in eliminating several problems, some of the experiences of pressure and having too much responsibility can remain. For this reason, we will now briefly share specific strategies and words of wisdom from principals who are happily surviving the system!

CHAPTER SEVEN

Practices That Support a Caring School Culture

I n this chapter we will summarize words of wisdom shared by several experienced principals who had developed the following survival strategies in the face of contextual pressures:

1. *Connect, connect, connect.* Do not let the pressures of power, efficiency, and availability push you into isolation. With all the pressures to answer demands from district, parents, and teachers, it is easy to isolate oneself with work. Many principals have attempted that lifestyle in their first year and barely survived. In the end, those who maintained some enthusiasm for their profession were those who networked in meaningful ways with their teachers and connected with students. Ultimately, knowing the names of students and their hobbies, having personal conversations with staff, and using some of the precious and scarce time to network was not only enriching for principals but yielded a greater unity and collaboration in the whole school. This networking was also critical *among* principals, where those who consulted actively with their vice-principal, another principal, a mentor, or a buddy regarding in-school problems felt much more confident, made better decisions, and were less isolated.

I have a core group of principals to go to and I am lucky to have my vice-principal, otherwise I'd be in total isolation.

—Middle School Principal

You can't be afraid to go to bocce ball with your staff or go in the staff room and talk and joke with them. You've got to be seen as a human, as a person. Then they find out . . . He doesn't have all the answers. He's not God sitting up there in his office!

—Middle School Principal

2. *Name the pressure.* Talk about your experience to trusted colleagues. Pressures are most oppressive when they are invisible and unquestioned. The easiest way to tackle them is, once again, to externalize the problematic pressure and map its effects, as explained in Chapter 2 of this book. Once aware of and clear about the situation, you can make a choice as to other ways of being and can explore your comfort zone.

In some cases you can even invite the whole staff to explore the effects of a certain pressure and list strategies used by everyone to minimize its harmful effects. We have visited schools where everyone secretly resented what was assumed to be a group expectation. Yet when asked in confidence or surveyed anonymously, most of the staff were against that expectation! When made visible, certain pressures can be redefined and/or softened greatly.

3. *Consciously limit the impact of pressures by remembering that you do have multiple identities.* You are a principal, a person, a friend, maybe an intimate partner and a parent.

I live 45 minutes away [from school] and that is by choice. It does feel more comfortable to me knowing I can not shave a day or put on my gardening shorts and go to the store without worrying about parents and kids seeing me.

—Middle School Principal

Make a choice as to when you can let go of pressures and when you have to fulfill them. Be clear with yourself and even with employees that, as a principal, it is your responsibility to take specific actions, even if, as a person, you really dislike an action (e.g., asking a teacher to leave). Some of our principals would even specify as they spoke that they were putting on a principal hat or that they were taking it off. When a principal makes it visible that he or she is taking off the principal hat (e.g., the hat of evaluation), the principal becomes more accessible, real, and human. Principals may intend to "take off the hat," but if they do not articulate it verbally, people may not notice the change because of the differential of power. If you let people know "I'm going to take off this hat," it creates a different kind of communication.

4. *Resist the temptation associated with the pressure of power to have "your fingers" on everything.* If the district makes controversial decisions or the staff is divided by educational differences, engage a mediator or facilitate the discussion in a neutral way so that each perspective can feel heard. Ultimately, if you favor an educational practice but no one else does, you have to be ready to be patient or to let it go. The staff has to be willing to engage in a practice on their own for the practice to be successful.

> *You can't change overnight. I work with those teachers who want to [change] and you build a successful program slowly. I look for ways to support people that are taking little tiny steps. I work with the people who are in favor of [an innovative new idea] and let their success speak for itself. I would say, "Go ahead. You really believe in this, go ahead!"*
>
> —Elementary School Principal

This principal told us how she was intrigued with the idea of teachers looping with their classes. This means a teacher keeps the same class of students two years in a row and teaches each year's curriculum. The staff read articles about the process and did other research to determine if it would be beneficial to them. One teacher chose to loop from kindergarten to first grade, and she could not stop talking about how wonderful it was. The principal reported that, all of the sudden, there were many people willing to try it.

Another principal speaks of the difficulty of letting go of situations and issues on campus. This could be anything from what is happening in the cafeteria to seeing a child with whom he had really connected in trouble with the assistant principal:

> We want to have our finger on the pulse of what's going on at school. You have to delegate and let go of some of that control to other people. It's hard for us to do as principals because we're supposed to have that power and control over things. You have to keep your good faith in other people and even if they [make mistakes] along the way, it's part of learning.

> —Middle School Principal

5. *Simply accept that you will never fulfill the pressure of doing it all.* Find your own personal standards for what counts as "having accomplished something" at the end of your day. It is most likely that, of all the items you planned to accomplish at the beginning of the day, many will remain incomplete. Know, however, that unfinished paperwork will remain just that, while an unattended relationship will swell with resentment.

> I have to be proud of what I did accomplish. Whatever paper you miss will always come back to you. However, if you leave [the district/education] tomorrow, you still need to have your relationships, your friends, your spouse, and your kids. Fifty years down the road when you end your career or [are] on your deathbed that's who will be with you. I try never to lose sight of that.

> —Elementary School Principal

> I often set myself three little goals for the day and make sure I accomplish them before I leave, which I've decided is 5 P.M. I make the choice to spend time with my wife every day

and sacrifice a half a day on the weekend to have a quiet paperwork period.

—Middle School Principal

You can always say, "Gee, I'll get back to you. Thank you for your opinion." Unless it's blood and guts you don't have to solve it immediately. The thing you learn as a new principal is that the only thing you really have to get to right away is blood and guts. Then you call 911. (laughs)

—Elementary School Principal

6. *Realize that the pressures tend to make you ultimately responsible for everything, while in reality you can delegate.* So many responsibilities can be trusted to the hands of others. Staff or parents, when appropriate, may appreciate the opportunity to be in charge of a specific assignment or to be an administrator for an hour while the principal attends to other necessities.

I've realized that I can delegate many items. For example, I asked the librarian to be in charge of the surveys reviewing our services. It's her department, she's excited to do it, and it frees my time for other issues.

—Elementary School Principal

7. *Remember to keep some perspective on the pressure of power and the misleading stories it promotes.* Redefine the power differential as a difference of roles.

Really we are all on the same team but just have different roles.

—Middle School Principal

The kids here have a realistic view of me. They get to know me inside and outside of the classroom and on the playground. They call me by my first name, which helps.

—Elementary School Principal

Power is how you react.

—Elementary School Principal

8. *Although the pressure of efficiency pushes you to accomplish more and more as quickly as possible, give yourself permission to think and be in touch with the school community and your role as a leader.*

If you really want to be collaborative in your decisions, then it does take longer, and in general there really are decisions you can postpone. Other times, if I have to make a decision, I'll leave campus to get a sandwich and it gives me time to think.

—Elementary School Principal

You could sit, listen to voice mail, and answer e-mail all day. You could sit and react to things all day. Or you could decide you are going to get out there for two hours a day and be a leader. Hopefully it's your collective vision and you will stay with that vision.

—Elementary School Principal

9. *Use your sense of humor to keep some perspective on those unrealistic pressures.* There are times where it is important to laugh at the impossibility of doing it all.

We have a serious job to do, but humor is a big part of my life and if I can't laugh at myself, I'll be in trouble.

—Elementary School Principal

10. *Finally, hold on to your values and preferred visions of yourself.* Why were you attracted to the field of education in the first place? What were your hopes and dreams? What is energizing for you in your role? The following are additional educators' survival tricks in the face of pressures:

Keep breathing and stay present.

Take a quiet walk every morning before coming to school.

Notice positive encounters with students.

Ask questions of your colleagues to see where they are really at.

Remember, everyone has a story of feeling out of place. You are not alone.

CHAPTER EIGHT

Working With Parents and Volunteers

I n this final chapter we will generalize the ideas presented throughout this book to address issues with other adults working in schools. We will first discuss the presence of parents and their relationships, at times problematic, with teachers. We will then end with the transcript of a workshop facilitated with yard duty volunteers at the request of a concerned principal.

PROBLEM STORIES OF PARENTS AND BATS

News Flash: Seemingly overnight the Austin City Council was faced with a dilemma . . . their new and architecturally innovative bridge was invaded by bats. The humans considered possibilities. They could keep them out, control their comings and goings or . . . welcome their presence. The people soon discovered that welcoming bats into their environment could be quite an asset, despite initial fears and mythical stories. In the end, the presence of bats enriched the community in terms of education, activities, and financial gains.

Some of you may not appreciate bats because of the numerous negative stories you may have been exposed to as a youngster. As an adult, you may reluctantly concede the fact that bats are actually an important part of many habitats, reduce certain problems in many ecosystems, and deserve respect.

This is only one of many examples of a community welcoming another group of beings and being enriched by their presence. Could the same parallel be drawn with the historical exclusion of parents?

There has been a growing trend for schools to involve parents instead of exclude them.

> *It used to be that the principal's job was to keep the parents out; now you need to bring them in, embrace them, and not try to avoid it. It's the only salvation for the public school system.*
>
> —School District Superintendent

Parents are typically excluded from the classroom because of a problem story based on a series of fears and misconceptions (see Figure 8.1). This problem story may get teachers to

- Fear that parents will not be responsive, reliable, responsible, and suited for work with children
- Be concerned about parents' evaluations, misperceptions, and gossip about their work
- Fear that extra time will be needed to manage these additional people in the classroom, the context where teachers are already overwhelmed by limited time and large numbers of students waiting for directions

These fears become intricately organized into a problem story, which exaggerates the likelihood and frequency of problem events and makes invisible any alternative stories about parents, which may include rich experiences of collaboration and helpfulness. These stories have the general effect of reducing collaboration between many teachers and parents in schools.

Figure 8.1   Teachers have a problem story of parents. They mostly see potential problems and are suspicious of the good intentions

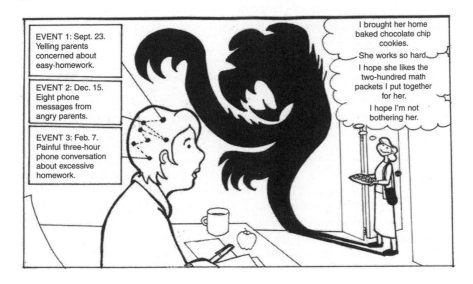

For years, I really struggled with parent help. I had some parents who wanted to work in my class, but I didn't know them well and kept hearing from other teachers how parents frequently gossip and how they flake out when you are counting on them. A colleague next door to me always had parents in her room and she was always running around like a maniac, trying to keep them busy. I kept a little stack of papers in the back of the room for parents to correct in the library or some masters to copy at the office. This way I was addressing their need to work in the class, but I didn't really have to have them underfoot. I felt awful about it. It really wasn't how I wanted it, but honestly, they made me nervous.

—Third Grade Teacher

The existence of a problem story about parents is made evident by comparing results from our surveys. In our research, teachers' problem stories of parents in traditional versus parent-participation schools led to strikingly different comments.

Teachers from parent-participation schools usually expressed appreciative comments that were varied and rich about building a collaborative relationship with parents, whereas remarks from more traditional schools were narrow, scripted, and dealt mostly with communication skills. See Box 8.1.

Box 8.1

Advice From a More Traditional School	*Advice From a Parent-Participation School*
• Use good communication (newsletters, phone calls, notes home, and e-mail as much as possible) • Get to know their name RIGHT away and use it • Have a firm handshake and look them in the eye when meeting • Start with the positive first • Be proactive • Be careful what you say; it will be repeated • They can be your best partner or your worst rival • Remember you are in charge; know where to draw the line • Get parents involved as volunteers but don't expect miracles • Respond in a professional manner • You can't win them all!	• Feel free to talk about your family and your background so they know you are a person • Tell them about yourself—open up • One of the most important jobs is to be sure parents have input. A teacher needs to hear what parents have to say and be open-minded • Let them know they are valuable and important! Let them know that their participation in their child's education is important! • Respect their experience as parents • Be inviting and inclusive • Don't lose your backbone and pretend you know what you are doing even if you don't • Try to remain open and positive even when parents are not; find common ground and listen

Parents may also have their own problem stories. Parents, especially those who are minorities or from underprivileged backgrounds, may have a story about teachers being unapproachable. Parents fundamentally want the best for their child and may be ambivalent about stepping in because of fear of retaliation or judgment. Parents may also possess a problem story about feeling unwelcome in schools. These stories contribute to a lower volunteer rate than what would truly serve schools.

The following are two examples; the first from an elementary school principal and the second from a parent:

I remember when I was a volunteer in my child's class. Recess came and I had to go sit outside on the bench, then I'd go back in the classroom when the bell rang. I was not invited into the staff room. Teachers had coffee and relaxed in the staff room and talked with their friends in the staff room, which was totally off limits to us. I think that is one of the bad things that continue in this day and age. Teachers think that they deserve to have a break from parents, but with that mentality, how can you ever work in partnership to educate? Particularly if you have people there that are giving up their time.

I was told at school that they didn't allow parents in the classroom and that they only wanted help from parents with fundraising. This felt like a major discount of what I could bring into the equation and asked for a set of skills I neither have nor care to develop. Also, I wondered what were they hiding that they didn't allow parents in the classrooms?

PARENT INVOLVEMENT: FROM PROBLEM STORY TO COLLABORATION

The most obvious and beneficial way to increase a sense of community and reduce problem stories is to involve parents.

Schools have a variety of policies regarding parental involvement. Some schools require a minimum number of hours of parent involvement, others welcome parent volunteers as helpers, some schools prefer that parents do not remain in the classroom, and still others are begging for help.

As discussed earlier, there are problem stories that exist around relationships with parents. For most public schools, the first step to increasing parent involvement is to process with teachers their beliefs about parent involvement and to support a gradual exploration of parent involvement.

When I have a teacher who is not so comfortable with parents being in the classroom, I have the teacher wean them in, an hour a week or so. I have them work in the copy room helping the teacher copy papers, then slowly as the teacher becomes more comfortable with the parent, I suggest the parent come in and run a reading group or something in the class.

—Elementary School Principal

Involving parents is a "ground-up" change in a school. Teachers need to understand that this is not something that is happening to them; they are a part of the change. Without their active involvement and support, it will not be successful. Teachers become so autonomous, so you have to lead them by giving lots of examples of successful programs, reading books about parent participation, and having discussions about why it works. You also need a parent group ready to go.

—Parent Participation Elementary School Principal

Teachers need to understand that when parents want to be involved that does not mean that we want to take over their job or critique their teaching. Well, most of us anyway. We want to support them as teachers; we want to show our kids that school is important, enough for us to spend time there. We want to provide extra adult assistance for the students.

—Parent of an Elementary School Student

Many individuals who have had the opportunity to deconstruct and examine these fears have come to the following conclusion: "For every one parent who causes trouble, there are 29 others who help in many ways."

The second step is to establish a helpful parental infrastructure not only to welcome parents, especially if they are from an underprivileged minority group, but also to coordinate their activities in a way that is helpful to the school and meaningful to the parent.

Work and issues of embarrassment keep parents from schools. Parents may not have been comfortable in schools as children and still feel that. It's good to make them comfortable and slowly build the relationship. People will come on campus if their kids bring them. So we try to bring people together for important things, like family reading night. This gets them to be more comfortable here. We'll go from there.

—Elementary School Principal

We worked with two BAFTTA (Bay Area Family Therapy Training Associates) interns who hosted parties for their students' families at a community day school. Many of these families felt disconnected from school, so they were all invited together to socialize and have fun. It was made very clear that there would be no problem talk and no mention of any recent trouble with any student. The student's "ticket" to get into the party and the "movie room" was to bring his or her parent(s). It was an overwhelming success, with requests from all the families to do it again.

Parent involvement in schools is determined by the parents' interests and requires a lot of work on the part of the administration and educators.

It takes a lot of work and a conscious effort to match parents with their strengths, to match their schedules, and to give them really meaningful tasks in the classroom. Teachers must be willing to be flexible and adjust to parents being in the classroom, knowing in the long run it will make their program that much more meaningful. A lot of teachers are not comfortable with being observed and it does change the dynamics when visitors come; yet a teacher does have to be comfortable teaching in a fishbowl. In my opinion, it's a professional duty because you should be teaching that way anyway.

—Elementary School Principal

What I am trying to do is set a culture that welcomes parents and supports them. Those really involved parents are invited in. We are now coordinating them. I want them to be doing more than stapling papers and running dittos. Schools need to open up activities that are meaningful to parents, such as working with kids, teaching, helping with reading intervention, and assisting with school plays. They can be working with kids, and we should train them on how to do that, including what is confidential.

—Middle School Principal

There is growing evidence that school communities greatly benefit from parent involvement. There are advantages for all groups of people involved: teachers, students, and parents.

Advantages for Teachers

When educators are able to shrink the problem, they are able to see parents as teammates in the education of children, and a variety of interactions become possible. Teachers are less isolated and gain valuable support on multiple levels.

On a relational level, teachers and parents can have adult conversations, share enjoyable moments, support each other in difficult situations, and witness the complexity and beauty of classroom interactions.

On a functional level, teachers can delegate some of the work, assign subgroups of children to another adult, teach a more child-centered curriculum, have more possibilities of addressing specific needs, share the organizing and supervising of celebrations and field trips, be more able to launch exciting and special projects, and benefit from a variety of adults' special talents and expertise, such as computer expertise.

One parent shared the extensive jobs she had taken on at her children's school:

I have worked with small groups of children, mostly on math, but also on reading, discussion and language. I have lead groups on science investigation and have created and run cooking workshops with the help of two other parents. I have driven and chaperoned on field trips. I have also helped with special art projects and been a literacy tutor for struggling readers, under the guidance of a curriculum specialist who trained me.

An added benefit is that parent volunteers see what is going on in the class and become stronger advocates for the school.

Advantages for Students

Children benefit greatly from the presence of their own and other parents in the classroom. They feel supported in their academic challenges, safer in the face of peer conflicts, and engaged in creative projects. In addition, children have reported appreciating simply having the presence of their parents in schools. Parent participation can increase students' exposure to adults from minority groups and convey a context where students learn to value diversity.

It's no secret that kids that have involved parents do well at school.

—School District Superintendent

Advantages for Parents

Parents who are involved in their child's classroom become more connected to their child, as their relationship is enriched by the shared experience of an important journey. They can gain a better understanding of their child's experience of school, peer and teacher interactions, and the curriculum.

When parents are involved, they not only develop a realistic perspective of the challenges of education but also can take action on problems they witness. When schools exclude parents, one of the ways parents might express their dissatisfaction can be to criticize teachers and principals. If you invest time and energy in an institution, you feel a sense of belonging to it, and it becomes uncomfortable to slander that to which you belong. Parents whose children may struggle with a trouble habit may also gain important insights into their child's challenges instead of oscillating between wanting to protect their child and trusting the adult in charge. This can be particularly true for minority families, who may wonder whether their child's constant discipline is a result of racism or the consequence of actual misbehaviors.

Parents who may have less confidence in their parenting abilities because of social status or other life experiences can experience a school's welcoming of their contributions as uplifting, validating their parenting abilities and strengthening their preferred stories of being caring, worthy, and knowledgeable parents.

> We had a couple of meetings where we brought in parents for schoolwide meetings. We explained this whole life skills program which tied in with this social awareness curriculum. We explained the class rules and showed these words (responsibility, motivation, respect, etc.) and we said to them, "What do these words mean to you?" They met together and talked and shared what the words meant to their family. It was an amazing conversation. It was amazing because most of the parents had never been asked to participate in a dialogue with teachers like this. They were excited to be having a conversation but also it made them realize they had a lot to offer their kids. A lot of these parents would tend to discount what they have to offer compared with what the school has to offer. It also was to show that we have similar values. There are certain universal ones we can agree on.
>
> —Fifth Grade Teacher

WHEN CONFLICTS ARISE

When an educator is in an authentic relationship with parents, conflicts may be solved more easily. The following ideas have been helpful to the participants in our research when interacting with parents:

1. See parents as knowledgeable allies.

   Parents are their child's best advocates 99% of the time. Listen to what they know and understand, what they see as the complexity of the situation, and what kind of educational environment their child should be in. If you understand all of these things and try to be proactive, not reactive, if you value their input, and work with them, they are your best allies.

   —School District Superintendent

2. Be open to cultural differences.

   It is really an ongoing exercise to see if teachers can overcome their biases. I once had a teacher who came to my office quite upset because she had a conference with a father who promised he would read with his son each day, but found out the family was not reading together. She didn't understand why he wouldn't do it. Later my friend visited, who worked with this particular father. She said he was in tears each morning because he couldn't read with his child. I went back to the teacher to discuss this matter. The teacher said, "He told me he could do it!" I responded, "Do you think he wants to sit with an educator and admit that he can't read with his son? To admit that he may be literate in his own country but not here? Of course not! Do you know how embarrassing that is?"

   —Elementary School Principal

3. Be realistic and take notes. Document meetings with parents for future reference.

   I keep a detailed account of dialogues or problem-focused conversations that have occurred with parents. It gives me some protection when conflicts arise and also refreshes my memory of previous agreements.

   —Elementary School Principal

4. Accept the unpredictability of parents, and be aware of your needs *and* theirs.

   Interaction with parents is a very complex part of teaching. I have to meet a large number of parents' needs and talk to them from where they are. That's a complex and difficult thing. I know what I'm doing in the classroom. I never really know what I'm doing with an adult. Every interaction is like, "What's going on next? How am I going to react to that? What are my emotions? What are their emotions?" With adults, you never know what you are going to see. There's just an endless variety of person. That makes it quite an interesting job.

   —First Grade Teacher

5. Put yourself in their shoes and remember that they passionately want the best for their child(ren).

   I know these parents are young and anxious. The parents here are particularly overanxious and striving. I remember when my kids were little, I was anxious, so I really understand that sentiment where you want the best for your child and that this teacher will be the one to prevent your child from going to Stanford. Once I had kids of my own, it was more humbling. I realized what these parents are going through. That doesn't mean the way I approach it is any different, but I am more understanding of where they are coming from.

   —Second Grade Teacher

   I had an opportunity to work in high S.E.S. [socioeconomic-status] schools and poverty-stricken schools. What I got out of that is, that parents, no matter what their S.E.S. level is, no matter what their level of education or the parent language, all parents want their children to have something better than what they had when they were kids.

   —Elementary School Principal

I always try to remember to relate to parents as parents, and remember they are talking as a mother or a father who is intensely preoccupied with their child's well-being.

—Elementary School Principal

6. Remember the humanity of people and hold on to kindness.

I don't have any trouble, normally, with parents. I don't have any trouble with any parent, because I do exactly what I do with the children. I love them, you know, in another way. I'm kind to them. I encourage them. I care about them. I listen. It's the same to me. They are just big kids.

—First Grade Teacher

7. Schedule a home visit, especially if the family is culturally different from you. Home visits, although time-consuming, have been found to be useful in fostering connection and understanding and in preventing problems.

If you meet someone in [their] own home you have a different sense of who they are. To have that trusting relationship is worth it to all these teachers. They get paid for making these home visits, but they said even if they didn't get paid, based on what they know now, they would do those home visits as much as possible. It cements the support they get from families better than anything else they have ever done. We had a child who was having severe troubles; he was soiling himself, he always had a runny nose, and he had struggles in class. We were really concerned. The teacher made a home visit and found out the kid was living in a cardboard shack. So his inability to focus and his sickness were understood in a different light. The teacher's understanding of who that child was when he was struggling was different than this child is lazy and unclean.

—Elementary School Principal

There are things I say to children that I feel very foolish about afterward, once I see their home and the things they have and don't have. I relate to them differently when I know what their bedroom looks like.

—First Grade Teacher

MORE IDEAS FOR YOUR SCHOOL COMMUNITY

- Unravel the problem stories about parents in an honest staff dialogue
- Articulate advantages and disadvantages of parent presence
- Accept that parents will be present in some way or another, so find a context for them to be there constructively
- Have a parent-volunteer coordinator
- Create arrangements to receive feedback from families and be genuinely interested in listening to families about school experiences
- Have a person from within the community's subculture act as a parent liaison and assist in communication when families speak a different language than the educator's
- Offer workshops for parents (regarding language, parenting, educational issues, etc.)
- Give meaningful tasks to parents
- Make parents feel good about themselves
- Have social events so that families feel connected to the school

WORLD WIDE WEB RESOURCES

http://www.rci.rutgers.edu/~cfis/

The Center for Family Involvement in Schools provides professional development programs and resources that strengthen family-school-community partnerships. The Center is a part of the Rutgers Center for Mathematics, Science, and Computer Education (CMSCE). The Web site provides links to other parental involvement sites and includes information about afterschool programs, family math and science involvement, and professional development workshops.

http://www.gse.harvard.edu/

Harvard Family Research Project (HFRP) promotes child development, student achievement, healthy family functioning, and community development by researching and publishing findings on such topics such as early childhood care, family involvement in education, and community partnerships. The Web site includes information about The Family Involvement Network of Educators (FINE), which is a national network of more than 2,000 people who are interested in promoting strong partnerships between educators and community members.

http://www.ncpie.org/

NCPIE is a coalition of major education, community, public service, and advocacy organizations working to create meaningful family-school partnerships in every school in the United States. The Web site includes a database with hundreds of resources for educators and families.

http://www.csos.jhu.edu/

The National Network of Partnership Schools, established by researchers at Johns Hopkins University, brings together schools, districts, and states that are committed to developing and maintaining comprehensive programs of school-family-community partnerships. The Web site includes partnership program components, a 12-month guide for the work of action groups, and Frequently Asked Questions (FAQ) about school-family-community connections.

YARD DUTY VOLUNTEERS

Yard duty volunteers are another group of people for which we are often consulted. Principals' and teachers' concerns are usually about the appropriateness or helpfulness of yard duty volunteers' interventions. Teachers do not have the time to deal with a student who comes back from recess over and over again angered by an interaction with a yard duty volunteer. Yard duty volunteers in those situations may have good justifications for their actions or helpful intentions, but the result can impede the system instead of helping. For this reason we have on several occasions been invited to speak with those generous volunteers. The two one-hour meetings usually simply have the tone of exploring and sharing their experiences with each other while we ask questions that promote reflection. The following is a summary of the process (which is generally distributed to them after the two meetings).

What Are the Goals of a Yard Duty Volunteer?

- Safety
- Refereeing—teaching kids other ways of resolving conflicts
- Contributing to a context where kids can be happy
- Helping kids solve problems on their own
- Helping kids to stop and think
- Empowering kids to work it out
- Teaching respect

What Does Respect Mean
When You Are in This Role?

- Be physically at their level
- Listen to their stories
- Explain why x, y, or z has to be done
- Be willing to apologize
- Have same expectations of ourselves as we have for them in terms of talking (yelling, tone of voice, words chosen, etc.)

What Are the Values and the Preferred
Ways of Being You Bring to This Job?

- Letting young people know you care
- Remembering that young people are thoughtful, loving, good inside, learning, and that they are CHILDREN!

- Realizing they may not have developed tools
- Realizing there may be problems in their lives
- Realizing there is probably a reason why they do x, y, or z
- Recognizing that ESL students sometimes may feel lonely and lost
- Creating a space for young people to think
- Validating their stories, listening to them
- Letting them know you'll come back to them in a few minutes
- Having them sit
- Being curious
- Using metaphors/examples
- Keeping a sense of humor
- Going for walks

When Do Yard Duty Volunteers Inadvertently Contribute to Problems?

Adults get pulled into doing unhelpful things when frustration gets them into

- Making quick decisions
- Shutting off, not wanting to hear something
- Taking things away over and over again
- Forcing young people to apologize (it's disrespectful and doesn't mean anything)
- Yelling at young people—telling them to "shut up"
- Being impatient
- Repeating rules over and over (there could be something preventing a child from understanding or following the rule)
- Giving advice (which we know generally doesn't work) and being upset when the child doesn't follow it
- Overfocusing on an upsetting event
- Taking a "This is the way it is" attitude

Have You Noticed the Effects of Adults' Frustration on Kids?

- Young people tune out
- They feel misunderstood
- They disconnect
- They give up talking to you
- They walk away
- They don't listen to you anymore
- They become sad, discouraged
- They feel bad about themselves
- They go into a shell
- They lose confidence in themselves
- They get more frustrated, shake their heads, and raise their voices

Adults' frustration/disrespect can escalate the problem and feed a vicious cycle:

Figure 8.2   The vicious cycle of disrespect between adults and students

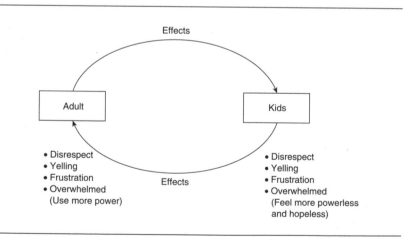

STRATEGIES FOR CHALLENGING SITUATIONS

- Readjust your expectations instead of blowing the whistle day after day

- Have a *conversation* before a conflict arises or when there is less frustration
- Give them a choice: "What would be more helpful now—to sit for a few minutes? Or to talk about it?"
- When appropriate, remove the threat of punishment—it will allow for a more constructive and honest conversation
- Allow each child to explain his or her story while the other listens—and let them know you won't take sides or punish, you just want them to understand each other
- Give them a chance—it will give them some power and the feeling that you care

How Can Adults Hold Onto Their Values / Preferred Ways in Challenging Situations?

- Remember that the more a child struggles with problems, the more he or she needs a recess to play, run, have fun, and let it out. It is the most important time of the day for many unhappy young people. Don't take it away unnecessarily.

- Remember that young people who struggle with problems have many, many adults on their backs, yelling at them and punishing them.

- Remember the teacher who made such a difference in your own life by being kind to you, despite your struggles as a child (e.g., would your favorite teacher ask a lot of questions, listen, raise her voice, ask you what you wanted, be loving, giving, patient? Did this teacher take the time to count to ten under her breath?).

- Have confidence in young people's abilities. Acknowledge them and allow the time necessary.

- Remembering helpful people can perhaps help each one of us to stop the cycle of frustration and to remove ourselves mentally from the situation, reflect/think, and then go back to dealing with it in a fair, caring way.

- Parents, teachers, yard duty volunteers, and children often do the best they can, given the circumstances of their lives.

Conclusion

Questions and Answers

I've tried everything to build a greater cohesiveness with this staff. I've tried conversations, organizing parties, special events, . . . nothing has worked. What more can I do?

Some situations have become so ugly that they seem unsolvable. If some school members become entrenched in destructive patterns of relating and have defeated a variety of problem-resolution efforts, the only option may be to move them. This can happen, however, only after other more constructive attempts, extensive documentation on the issue, and with serious backup from the superintendent. Staff can also be surveyed as to their general ideas on how to solve the current disagreements in their school. Although anonymous, this survey could provide the administration with alternative ideas or at least a sense of support from the rest of the staff. Conversations with the staff then need to take place to explore the effects of this decision and to address any distrust that may grow out of the incident.

Will having a school mission statement help us come together as a group of educators or will it be just another exercise that will be forgotten in the busyness of the year? I have a stable staff of teachers who come back each year. Do we really need to review it?

When everybody contributes to a mission statement and a vision in a meaningful way, they are more likely to be

167

committed to it. Schools whose teachers are vested in very different methods can be invited to discuss when a particular method is useful and when it is not. What are students' reactions to it? Who benefits and who is marginalized? In the end, articulating these ideas will allow for more flexibility and overlap in teachers' approach.

Ultimately a school staff can also be invited into a discussion about diversity and how they determine which differences are contributing to diversity on the staff and which are differences in philosophical ideology that make collaboration too difficult.

I am a principal with teachers on staff who have radically different philosophies. I can't start fresh with a whole new staff of teachers who agree on their philosophy. How do I deal with the vast differences?

A school community needs to learn to process and embrace differences, as opposed to seeking to eliminate them to become a homogeneous culture. Teachers will be exposed to heterogeneity in their students; how can they possibly be respectful of the differences between their students if they struggle with dealing with the differences in their staff?

I am uncomfortable with the decisions made by the district and do not feel that I can speak up much more without endangering my job. I feel very stuck and unhappy.

Ultimately, if a district's philosophy becomes too distant from your own on many levels and for an extended period of time, you have to face a serious decision: stay or leave? Being honest with yourself and exploring the effects of this problem on your life (thoughts, feelings, behaviors; who you are becoming; relationships with staff, friends, or family; your dreams, goals, values) must be done in-depth. When a context is systematically bringing out the worst in you, it may be easier and more gratifying to move on than to continue fighting a losing battle that will destroy you. It is important to talk to someone about these thoughts and perhaps give yourself a deadline for reevaluation of the improvements achieved, if any. You might remember an intimate relationship where you were miserable for a long time, then left, discovered life again, and ended up wondering why you did not leave earlier. Sometimes the miserable but familiar seems more comfortable than the novel unknown, especially as we grow older. Yet the self you once were that was willing to take risks and explore the world is still in you, somewhere; buried perhaps, but still retrievable if you reconnect with its memory.

There is a teacher in our school who seems a bit burned out by the profession. She used to participate in meetings, mentor younger teachers, and really care about her students. Now she seems grumpy and negative. Last year I gave her a bad evaluation, hoping to motivate her, but it just made her more resentful. What should I do?

Devoted teachers can burn out very quickly in public schools nowadays. Those who survive long years have either developed intricate ways of reenergizing themselves or have become burned out, disconnected, and tired. Principals, who are often at a loss as to how to motivate some of these teachers, may resort to the only power they seem to have: evaluation. Unfortunately this usually alienates the teachers and causes further resentment. Even if these teachers would like to change and have the best of intentions, they will feel misunderstood, unfairly judged, and further discouraged in their work. In this situation, the best possible scenario is one where a compassionate conversation can be held with the teacher, gently making visible her decreased enthusiasm for her work. If the conversation is supportive and collaborative, the teacher may be able to articulate what blocks or constraints actually stifle her performance. Once those blocks are named, a plan of action can be created that, hopefully, will remove or at least reduce those blocks. Ultimately most people, younger and older, need support rather than punishment when they engage in troublesome behavior.

I have a teacher who is harassing students, yet no parents have complained. My hands are tied because I can't document the problem. How is it that students and parents are not complaining about this offensive issue?

Parents and students are often fearful of retaliation if they speak of a problem that involves hierarchy. A teacher can be seen as the powerful one in a classroom, with no other adults as witnesses or protectors. Parents and young people may be worried that the teacher's mistreatment may simply worsen if they speak up and that students will suffer from an even greater experience of disrespect and unfairness.

It is always important to talk with the teacher who is scrutinized and explore his or her intentions or understanding of the situation. Sometimes the problem story results from a misunderstanding or a mistake. If this is the case, it can hopefully be resolved through conversation. If the problem is actually occurring and is harmful, this will at least inform the teacher that the problem is now named and will be under investigation. Sometimes that is all that is needed to reduce the frequency of the harmful behavior.

In a school where the context is one of respect, students will feel more empowered to make their voices heard and will express their concerns to trusted adults. Teachers who are in this situation will already be thinking and practicing in non-hierarchical ways and be inspired to make changes in their philosophy of interacting with young people. When parents are involved in a school, they also witness classroom interactions and may be in a better position to demand accountability, or at least to feel less intimidated about speaking up. Principals who cannot rely on these resources must resort to evaluation and documentation of the concerns and hopefully involve their superintendent in exploring remediation or transfer possibilities.

What happened to Karen, John, and Chris, who struggled with issues in the very first chapter?

Perhaps you would like to try to solve these dilemmas yourself. How would you apply the ideas in this book to those problematic situations?

Here are our solutions: You might remember that Karen yelled at her students and struggled with feeling like a fraud. A discussion was facilitated with the whole staff around such questions as: "How many of you have done something against your better judgment as a teacher?" "How many of you end up yelling even though you would really rather not?" In this process it became visible for Karen, as well as for many others, that they all struggled with Impatience at times and that Impatience could make them act against their preferred values. Impatience was then externalized, and its effects were mapped on thoughts, feelings, behaviors, relationships with students, experiences, and identities. Contexts that were more likely to invite Impatience were discussed, and strategies everyone had developed to remain connected with their preferred selves were shared. The staff ended the meeting with a determination to observe their own successes and strategies for avoiding Impatience for the following two weeks. When they gathered again, almost everyone shared new ways they had used to remain connected with their values. Several of the staff also acknowledged that sometimes Impatience had crept in despite their best intentions. In the end everyone agreed that they would keep trying but that it was impossible to completely eradicate Impatience in certain contexts. The question became more one of how to keep Impatience and its negative effects to a minimum and what an acceptable margin of mistakes was for each of them. The discussion enriched all the staff with several new strategies and knowledges about themselves. Most important, they acknowledged that they would feel comfortable talking to each other about It when they needed support.

Why did John run away, despite the pleas of his staff?

John felt overwhelmed by the endless responsibilities. He also resented having to be everything for everyone all the time, especially when he didn't feel he had much power in the end. He really needed "alone time." He grew up as one of nine children and, as a young person, vowed he would take time whenever he needed it. These lunchtimes provided him with energy and self-reflection, something he really wanted to provide for his staff. He didn't realize the effect on his staff until a veteran teacher kindly mentioned it. Once he realized the implications and the problem stories that were circulating about him, he became quite concerned and even considered resigning. John was invited to try a few things before resorting to resignation. He was first invited to listen quietly while his staff was asked to gently map out the effects of "principal absence" on their feelings, thoughts, behaviors, relationships with students, and sense of community. Efforts had to be made initially to keep the tone respectful and constructive, but everyone eventually found a constructive style of sharing. At another meeting, John was interviewed gently in front of his staff as to his experiences as a principal, examples of a typical day, his intentions, values, and attempts to make the best possible decisions. He genuinely apologized, acknowledging that he hadn't realized how important this was for all of them. Ways to minimize the staff's excessive demands on him were explored. Some ideas around reducing student referrals to the office were collectively discussed, determining, first, a short but specific time when teachers would attempt to minimize their visits to him so that he could concentrate on paperwork and, second, the delegating of certain responsibilities that did not need to be accomplished specifically by him. Staff members were shocked when they realized the degree to which he had been burning out, and they were all willing to explore different ways of being together as a community so they could all perform to their own satisfaction.

Why was Chris so distant with this woman, when
he was so good with colleagues and children?

The yard duty volunteer lived quite near Chris and knew of his "secret" life. Chris had not revealed his homosexuality to the staff and was concerned about public opinion, especially in the wake of the very positive attention he currently received from the staff. Chris had quite a bit of anxiety about this situation, as he feared being misunderstood and judged by some families and staff members. Worry that the yard duty volunteer would spill the beans, as he knew that she knew, made him avoid her at every possible turn.

The situation was eventually solved indirectly by facilitating a staff discussion externalizing the Pressure to be a good conservative role model and its implications. As part of this process, the staff and principal grew interested in furthering their awareness of diversity issues. A series of workshops on cultural awareness and tolerance was facilitated, and it became visible to all that this staff's intentions were to be open-minded and accepting of a variety of differences. After a few conversations on diversity and the effects of the pressure, people became more trustful of their community, and it became more comfortable for several of them to share a variety of experiences. Over time Chris worked on his own personal discomfort and was eventually able to share about his lifestyle with some staff, which eliminated the problematic secrecy.

Resource A

Glossary

Audience A group of people that witness a protagonist in a certain way. Since we see ourselves through others' eyes, audiences can be very important in supporting our preferred view of ourselves. In other words, if people see us as clever, it will be easier to experience ourselves as clever. For example: Groups of people such as families, classrooms, and communities who witness our different ways of being.

Contextual blocks Invisible pressures that limit people's sense of possible ways of being. Originally connected to a culture's set of discourses and specifications, these pressures intersect in complex and unique ways for each individual. Contextual blocks prevent individuals from conceiving of certain options. For example: Pressures such as overdoing, overcontrolling, or being responsible at all costs.

Discourse A pervasive and insidious cultural system of beliefs and customs that shapes people's lives at all levels (i.e., language, thoughts, feelings, behaviors, dreams, values, expectations, roles, relationships, understandings, lifestyle, politics, etc.). Discourses provide guidelines and assumptions that direct the manner in which people experience their lives. Discourses structure so much of individuals' lives that it is rare to question them and impossible to completely escape them. One can only learn to become aware of their effects and make choices as to which prescriptions may be more congruent with preferred ways of being. For example: individualism, capitalism, and so forth.

Externalization   The process of acknowledging that people's identities are separate from unwanted problems. Problems are treated as entities external to one's sense of self because they are believed to develop as a result of complex and unique experiences of contextual blocks (originating from discourses). For example: I wonder if overworking gets in the way of having friends.

Problem   An unhelpful way of being that can be named, explored, circumvented, and clearly distinguished from an individual's preferred identity. Problems usually develop when people are unable to successfully fulfill the pressures in the contexts of their lives (specifications of a particular discourse); or if they attempt to fulfill the pressures but feel unhappy with the results. For example: "Yelling habits," "Self-doubt," "Worries," to name some.

Preferred story   A series of experiences that becomes articulated as representing one's preferred way of being. For a story to become salient in one's life, it must be connected to relationships, witnessed by an audience, and explored across time. For example: People now think of me as a Helpful person.

Problem story   A problematic way of being that has come to be taken as a representation of an individual's identity. Problem stories can often take over people's lives in such a way that their actual values, special talents, and successes in avoiding the problem become discounted or unnoticed. For example: "Everyone thinks I'm strict, and I really hate that reputation."

Specification   A cultural pressure that prescribes very specific ways of being and that originates from cultural discourses. It is usually identifiable by its implication that an individual "should" or "shouldn't" engage in a certain behavior. For example: Principals should not be too sensitive.

Unique outcome   An action or event that illustrates a person's preferred identity and that could not have been predicted given a problem story. For example: Seeing a teacher with a problem reputation for being mean engaging in devoted tutoring for a struggling student.

Resource B

Staff Development Activities

Merging Stories Exercise

Participants co-construct a single story of their lives as if they were one person. Through this process, they notice how rich and diverse each person's experience has been, how their stories do not encompass all of their lived experience, how we naturally narrate our lives as stories, and how stories are co-constructed in relationships and interactions.

Goals

- To notice to what extent people's lives are shaped differently by their sociocultural environments
- To makes visible the process of experiencing our lives as stories
- To notice how being in a relationship involves coauthoring a joint story—to deepen intimacy and connectedness by allowing participants to share historically salient events in their lives

Group Size

Unlimited

Time

30–45 minutes

SOURCE: From *Working With Groups to Enhance Relations*, by Marie-Nathalie Beaudoin and Sue Walden. Copyright 1998 by Whole Person Associates. Reprinted with permission of Whole Person Associates.

Materials

None

Process

1. Ask participants to pair with a partner with whom they feel comfortable sharing aspects of their life experience.

2. Provide the following introduction:

   • We all typically have a story of our lives based on certain salient events or experience that are tied together in a linear sequence. Our lived experience is much richer than this story we tell. How do we determine which events we include in our story and which ones we don't? Events that we remember and include in our narrative are typically the ones that have involved interaction with others and a certain meaning. In that sense we can say that our stories of ourselves are co-constructed.

   • In this exercise, you will be invited to co-construct a story by merging aspects of each of your lives into one single story.

   • Through this process, I would also like to invite you to notice how differently you have been shaped by your social environment. If it feels comfortable and it occurs to you, feel free to include a statement about the social discourses or the contextual constraints that affected that particular experience.

   • Concretely, this means that one person will start by making a *short one- or two-sentence* statement about his or her birth, then the other person will make one or two statements about an event in his or her first year of life, then the first person will continue with a statement about his or her second year, and so on. This alternating process would give a listener the impression that it is one person telling the story.

3. It is often helpful to give an example with your cofacilitator.

For example:

- *Participant 1:* When I was born my mother was so shamed by her religious community that she had to place me for adoption;
- *Participant 2:* When I was one year old my parents moved to San Francisco because my father's job was relocated;
- *Participant 1:* When I was two years old I fell on the floor, broke my leg, and we couldn't afford the surgery I needed to fully recover.

4. Remind participants to make only one or two statements as the game is already quite long, and people typically enjoy it so much that they easily elaborate on each event.

5. When half of the group is done, instruct the others to wrap up within the next five minutes, and ask the ones who are done to discuss their experience of the exchange.

6. Conclude with a discussion of their experience and of the following questions:
   - What was it like to coauthor a single story?
   - What did you notice about your own storying process?
   - Where you surprised by the level of differences and similarities in your lives?
   - Did you become aware of any privileges you may have had that your partner didn't have?
   - How are your behaviors, emotions, and thoughts affected by the stories you tell of yourself?
   - How can that knowledge of your mutual stories affect your relationships?
   - (With couples) Are you now understanding aspects of your partner's life that were confusing to you before?

Post-it Puzzle

This activity offers a powerful way to experientially discover each person's strategies to communicate in an effective and efficient way.

Goal

- To invite participants to notice their ideas and strategies on how to send clear messages
- To increase participants' awareness of the effect of their way of communicating

Group Size

Unlimited number of pairs

Time

30–45 minutes

Materials

Rectangular paper (6" × 9") with the picture of an arrangement of eight to ten Post-its (any arrangement of Post-its can work; readers wishing an example can consult Beaudoin & Walden, 1997), and cardboard (6" × 9") with movable shaped Post-its. One of each of the pairs needs the picture, and the partner needs the cardboard.

Process

1. Invite participants to sit back-to-back with their partners along a straight line with about three feet between them and other pairs on either side of them (if space allows).

2. Introduce the activity by telling the participants:
   - This game involves communicating a set of instructions in a limited amount of time

- Participants will use only verbal communication to complete the task and are not to look over each other's shoulders

3. Show the partners who will have the picture an example of the cardboard and movable Post-its; then show the partner who will have the cardboard an example (not the real one, of course) of a picture that their partner will be working with.

4. Hand out the picture of the arrangement of triangles to all the partners facing one way and the cardboard with the Post-it triangles to their partners sitting behind them.

5. Participants with the picture must communicate clear instructions to their partners on how to reproduce what they see by arranging the Post-it triangles. Both participants need to clarify and verify their understanding of the information both sent and received.

6. Signal to start, allowing three to five minutes to complete the task.

7. After calling time, allow a few minutes for the partners to compare the original picture and the Post-it picture and discuss their process.

8. Roles are changed and new pictures are supplied.

9. Conclude the exercise by asking participants to discuss some of the following questions:
   - What worked and what didn't work in achieving this task?
   - What strategies did you discover to facilitate the process?
   - What caused miscommunication?
   - Did certain words have different meanings for each of you? Can you share examples?
   - How is this exercise similar to and/or different from your day-to-day communications?

Resource C

Summary of School Culture Problems and the Practices That Prevent Them

Externalized Problems (from Chapter 3)	Remedies (from Chapter 6)	Examples of Positive Practices
Gossip	Connection Appreciation Leadership	• Provide more visibility of educators' private lives • Embrace a genuine philosophy of valuing differences • Create a context for communication and a space where problem solving occurs (forums, e-mails, meetings, honest conversations) • Share appreciation for others • Redefine leadership as a difference of role • Share a democratic process for change and make intentions and constraints visible for unpopular decisions • Have a commitment to team building • Host a community discussion on the effects of the gossip habit
Problem-saturated communication	Appreciation Self-reflection	• Remember the effects and implications of problem-saturated communication • Have a general agreement not to speak negatively in the staff room

Externalized Problems (from Chapter 3)	Remedies (from Chapter 6)	Examples of Positive Practices
		• Structure events that make appreciation visible between educators, students, and parents (e.g., singing telegrams, letter day) • Use self-reflection as a way to unwind
Cliques	Appreciation Collaboration	• Start staff meetings with appreciations • Facilitate retreats where each person's educational values are visible • Host workshops on valuing diversity, strengthening the importance of belonging to a community • Hold fun staff events • Promote vertical and horizontal collaboration • Keep your staff seating arrangement in mind
The Us-Them attitude	Connection Collaboration Leadership	• Connect with your staff • Create a spirit of collaboration • Minimize hierarchy and embrace reciprocal leadership • Develop relationships with union representatives • Make your intentions visible • Hire an ombudsperson to facilitate meetings
Resentment and negativity	Appreciation Connection Self-reflection	• Host an individual compassionate meeting with an educator struggling with a critical problem story • Review the pressures of the specifications • Study the feasibility of meeting the demands made on staff members • Share appreciation; this is essential in rendering the profession more rewarding and satisfying

Externalized Problems (from Chapter 3)	Remedies (from Chapter 6)	Examples of Positive Practices
		• Keep staff engaged in staff development, creating a context that inspires curious learners of all ages (examples include: invite speakers, read books, attend professional development courses, reflect upon goals/values)
Community disrespect	Connection Collaboration	• Involve parents and grandparents in many roles on campus • Create a space for teachers to be seen as people with unique talents (not just as "teacher") • Make teachers' work visible (newsletter acknowledging each teacher's biography/ programs) • Contact the media about positive events (if reporters have relationships with the schools, they are less likely to bash) • Work on community service projects • Involve local businesses by their adopting a school and sending in volunteers • Reevaluate your vision of self as an educator as well as the nature of relationships you want to have with staff, students, and community
Rushed feeling/Scarcity of time	Self-Reflection Collaboration Appreciation	• Discuss how the pressures to perform affect the unique community and the staff • Facilitate staff conversation to clarify their priorities as a group • Make time for self-reflection, articulating and holding onto what energizes you as an educator

Externalized Problems (from Chapter 3)	Remedies (from Chapter 6)	Examples of Positive Practices
		• Involve community members to assist with demands • Collaborate on planning, chores, etc.
Hierarchy	Collaboration Leadership Connection	• Introduce cross-age buddies who meet weekly, between teachers (a teacher can befriend a kid from another class and age group) • Facilitate groups of administrators, teachers, parents, and students to meet, study, and debate issues • Promote vertical collaboration between grade-level teams • Create a context where everyone can be at their best • Connect with people as people; be accessible, visible, open, and inclusive • Encourage a more democratic environment
Competition	Collaboration Appreciation Connection	• Collaborate on many levels • Share appreciation for self and others • Facilitate a staff conversation about the sneaky habit of competition • Find alternative ways to promote enthusiasm • Have individuals set their own goals for performance and be self-reflective on their own progress • Reward all for efforts (e.g., gift certificates for educators or joint celebration for classes) • Create a context where everyone can be at their best

Resource D

Job Satisfaction Survey

A s discussed elsewhere in this book, we have interviewed and/or surveyed well over 200 educators from a wide range of elementary and middle public schools, mostly in North California. The populations in these schools varied in terms of socioeconomic status, race, and ethnicity. Schools were visited in rural and suburban areas as well as in the city. Four schools involved parent participation; the remaining were general public schools. Here are some of the survey and interview questions that we have used. As we progressed in the research, some questions were eliminated, some improved, and some were added or modified to suit the particular school staff we were visiting. These are provided here as examples of possible surveys that can be helpful to use in your own school.

BRIEF JOB SATISFACTION SURVEY

Please answer ALL questions.
Thank you for your time!

Gender: M   F

Years of teaching experience: _____

Please circle your choice.

How would you rate your overall job satisfaction?

1. Lacking   2. Tolerable   3. Acceptable   4. Good   5. Excellent

What are the three most important contributors to your job satisfaction?

_____

_____

_____

How would you generally characterize your relationship with your teaching colleagues?

1. Lacking   2. Tolerable   3. Acceptable   4. Good   5. Excellent

Would you like to be more connected with your colleagues?

Yes   No   Okay as is

How: _____

Is your educational philosophy similar to that of the majority of the staff?

Yes   No

Specifically, _____

Do you feel that overall the staff is homogeneous in terms of educational philosophy?

Yes   No

At school, how many teachers would you trust with personal information? _____

Are the teachers at your school willing to share material and collaborate with you?

1. Never   2. Occasionally   3. Sometimes   4. Most of the time   5. Always

Do you feel appreciated by the rest of the staff?

1. Never   2. Occasionally   3. Sometimes   4. Most of the time   5. Always

How would you generally characterize your relationship with your principal?

1. Lacking   2. Tolerable   3. Acceptable   4. Good   5. Excellent

Would you like to be more connected with your principal?

Yes   No   Okay as is

How: _____

How much do you appreciate the leadership style of your principal?

1. Not at all   2. Sometimes   3. Generally   4. Mostly   5. Very much

Any suggestions: _____

Please circle only what characterizes the leadership style of your principal and its extent (1. A little   2. Sometimes 3. Very much)

Trusting	*Appreciative*	*Democratic in Most Decisions*	*Approachable*
1 2 3	1 2 3	1 2 3	1 2 3

Micro-Manages	*Evaluates*	*Unilateral Decision Making*	*Distant*
1 2 3	1 2 3	1 2 3	1 2 3

How connected do you feel to most of your students?

1. Not at all   2. Somewhat   3. Generally   4. Mostly   5. Very

What percentage of the time do you experience disrespect from students? _____

Do you like to have parents assist you in the classroom?

1. Not at all   2. Maybe   3. Not sure   4. Probably   5. Very much

Do you currently benefit from parent assistance in the classroom?

1. Not at all   2. Somewhat   3. Generally   4. Most of the time   5. Very much

If you were to write a creative or powerful statement/metaphor about what it is like to be a teacher, what would it be?

_____

_____

_____

Resource E

Teacher Survey

We are writing a book on bullying and other school culture issues. We really appreciate your input. These surveys are confidential, and you may choose to remain anonymous.

Years of experience (including this year): _____

Gender: M   F

How often do you experience the following? Please circle a number.

The pressure to be a good role model

1. Never 2. Rarely 3. Sometimes 4. Half of   5. Most of   6. Always
                                    the time   the time

Please define what you personally mean by "good role model."

The need to be a dedicated teacher

1. Never   2. Rarely   3. Sometimes   4. Half of   5. Most of   6. Always
                                      the time   the time

Having to sacrifice personal time to get the job done

1. Never   2. Rarely   3. Sometimes   4. Half of   5. Most of   6. Always
                                         the time   the time

The pressure to be organized and well prepared (beyond your personal standards)

1. Never   2. Rarely   3. Sometimes   4. Half of   5. Most of   6. Always
                                         the time   the time

The pressure to know all the answers all the time with:

Your colleagues

1. Never   2. Rarely   3. Sometimes   4. Half of   5. Most of   6. Always
                                         the time   the time

Your students

1. Never   2. Rarely   3. Sometimes   4. Half of   5. Most of   6. Always
                                         the time   the time

Your students' parents

1. Never   2. Rarely   3. Sometimes   4. Half of   5. Most of   6. Always
                                         the time   the time

The need to be in control of your students (beyond your personal preference)

1. Never   2. Rarely   3. Sometimes   4. Half of   5. Most of   6. Always
                                         the time   the time

How do you define being in control?

Does standardized testing fit in your educational philosophy? Please explain.

How does the pressure for good test scores affect you as a teacher?

How does the pressure for good test scores affect your relationship with your students?

What percentage of the time do you enjoy your job as a teacher? _____. Please give an example.

Things principals in general may do that are positive, helpful, and supportive:

Things principals in general may do that are negative, upsetting, or instill self-doubt:

Things other teachers do that are positive, helpful, and supportive:

Things other teachers may do that are negative, upsetting, or instill self-doubt:

Resource F

Principal Interview Protocol

REWARDS

What are your biggest rewards?

What do your students see in you that they appreciate?

What do you think is the most important thing a kid gets out of a relationship with the principal?

What do you think is the most important thing a kid gets out of time at your school?

Remember a student who made a profound impact on you.

What do your staff members see in you that they appreciate?

Is there a teacher you worked with that had a profound affect on you? What was it?

Is there a parent from whom you really learned something?

CHALLENGES

What is your biggest struggle?

Was there a child you felt that your school couldn't help?

How does competition affect you and your staff (between teachers, between schools, for test scores, etc.)?

How do you handle the pressures from the district office and the state?

What philosophy do you have when dealing with parents who have a conflict with a teacher?

How do you deal with union issues?

What is the effect of the union on your job?

How do you deal with having to choose a teacher—without favoritism—for a position (master teacher, committee member, curriculum specialist, vice-principal) if teachers from your staff are vying for the same position?

How do you deal with a teacher who doesn't want to do anything new and wants to stick closely to the contract?

How do you deal with a teacher who has a negative attitude?

How do you deal with a staff that is in an "us-them" relationship with you and the district administration?

What do you keep in mind when you are trying to communicate with a staff member?

IDEAL SCHOOL

How do you promote bonding with your staff?

How do you promote collaboration among teachers and between teachers and yourself?

How do you express appreciation for individual staff members without creating favoritism?

How do you reduce the effects of isolation?

How do you reduce the effects of evaluation on you and your staff (from parents, the district administration, and the public)?

SPECIFICATION STORIES

Do you feel that principals are expected to know everything about everything? Why do you think this is? What are the effects of this?

Some principals have told us that they felt like they needed to serve everyone's needs at all times. Do you feel that this is true? Is there an example that comes to your mind?

Other principals have told us that they feel pressure to be in control of their teachers. This pressure seems to come from society and parents. Is that a part of your experience as well?

Principals have also expressed that they feel responsible for being political and being the school visionary. Do you feel pressure to create the vision for your school and inspire the community? What does this look like when you are doing this?

A PRINCIPAL'S LIFE

What would you like parents to know?

What do you wish teachers understood about your work?

If you were to come up with a metaphor about being a principal, what would it be?

What is the difference between your dreams and expectations of your job and the realities of the job?

What would you change if you could?

Do you have a dream for yourself professionally? Personally?

References

Ashton-Jones, E., Olson G. A., & Perry, M. G. (2000). *The gender reader.* Needham Heights, MA: A. Pearson Education Company.

Beaudoin, M.-N., & Taylor, M. (2004). *Breaking the culture of bullying and disrespect, grades K-8.* Thousand Oaks, CA: Corwin Press.

Beaudoin, M.-N., & Walden, S. (1997). *Working with groups to enhance relationships.* Duluth, MN: Whole Person Associates.

Bird, J. (2000). *The heart's narrative.* Auckland, New Zealand: Edge Press.

Bolman, L. G., & Deal, T. E. (2001). *Leading with soul: An uncommon journey of spirit* (rev. ed.). Indianapolis, IN: Jossey-Bass.

Communication Research Associates. (1995). *Communicate: A workbook for interpersonal communication* (5th ed.). Dubuque, IA: Kendall/Hunt.

Education Writers Association. (2002). *Special report on principals.* Available online at www.ewa.org

Freeman, J., & Combs, G. (1996). *Narrative therapy.* New York: Norton.

Freeman, J., Epston, D., & Lobovits, D. (1997). *Playful approaches to serious problems.* New York: Norton.

Gergen, K. (1985). The social constructionist movement in modern psychology. *American Psychologist, 40,* 266–275.

Gergen, K. (1991). *The saturated self: Dilemmas of identity in contemporary life.* New York: Basic Books.

Heatherington, C. (1995). *Celebrating diversity: Working with groups in the workplace.* Duluth, MN: Whole Person Associates.

Hoffman, L. (1990). Constructing realities: An art of lenses. *Family Process, 29,* 1–12.

Johnson Fenner, P. (1995). *Waldorf Education: A family guide.* Amesbury, MA: Michaelmas Press.

Kimmel, M. S., & Messner, M. A. (1998). *Men's lives.* Needham Heights, MA: Allyn & Bacon.

Madsen, W. C. (1999). *Collaborative therapy with multi-stressed families.* New York: Guilford.

Marzano, R. J., & Kendall, J. S. (1998). *Awash in a sea of standards.* Aurora, CO: Mid-continent Research for Education and Learning. (Available online at www.McREL.org)

Merrow, J. (2001). *Choosing excellence.* Lanham, MD: Scarecrow Press.

O'Neil, J. (1995). On schools as learning organizations: A conversation with Peter Senge. *Education Leadership, 52*(7), 20–23.

Pollack, W. (1999). *Real boys.* New York: Henry Holt.

Reiman, J. (2000). *Thinking for a living.* Marietta, GA: Longstreet Press.

Tannen, D. (1990). *You just don't understand.* New York: Ballantine.

White, M., & Epston, D. (1990). *Narrative means to therapeutic ends.* New York: Norton.

Winslade, J., & Monk, G. (1999). *Narrative counseling in schools.* Thousands Oaks, CA: Corwin Press.

Winslade, J., & Monk, G. (2000). *Narrative mediation.* San Francisco: Jossey-Bass.

Zimmerman, J., & Dickerson, V. (1996). *If problems talked.* New York: Guilford.

Index